ESSAYS IN HISTORY
and
INTERNATIONAL RELATIONS

George H. Blakeslee

Essays in History
and
International Relations

In Honor of
GEORGE HUBBARD BLAKESLEE

Edited by
DWIGHT E. LEE
and
GEORGE E. MCREYNOLDS

KENNIKAT PRESS/PORT WASHINGTON, N. Y.

ESSAYS IN HISTORY AND INTERNATIONAL RELATIONS

Copyright 1949 by The Trustees of Clark University
Reissued in 1969 by Kennikat Press by arrangement with
The Clark University Press
Library of Congress Catalog Card No: 72-86036
SBN 8046-0568-8

Manufactured by Taylor Publishing Company   Dallas, Texas

ESSAY AND GENERAL LITERATURE INDEX REPRINT SERIES

To
GEORGE HUBBARD BLAKESLEE
Teacher and Counselor
These Essays Are Dedicated by His
Former Students

Preface

The contributions which George Hubbard Blakeslee has made as a scholar and an administrator are well known. The wide significance and influence which his work as a special consultant with the State Department and as a lecturer merit can be estimated by one familiar with his life.

The present volume is a tribute to the inspiration which Professor Blakeslee, as a teacher and friend, has given to Clark men and women for the past forty-five years. Any attempt on the part of the editors to develop a central theme in the selection of material had to be abandoned because of the variety of subjects suggested by his former students. This variety in itself is indicative of the catholicity of interest which was so stimulating in his seminars. The selection which has been made, however, emphasizes Professor Blakeslee's paramount interest in international relations and especially in the role of the United States in world affairs. Only one significant area of his work has been omitted, that of Latin America. Another, public opinion and its relation to the formulation of foreign policy, which he was among the first to study, has been slighted in comparison with the proportion of his students whom he guided into this subject. Since every student who worked with him or sought his counsel in any field obtained a better understanding of the hard, painstaking nature of historical research and of its rewards, no single volume could indicate by its inclusion or omission of articles the wide influence Professor Blakeslee's scholarship and friendship have had.

It is a happy coincidence that in 1949 Clark University begins the celebration of the 60th anniversary of its opening, and that in the same year this book of essays is published to honor a Professor who has served the University for so many years of its existence.

The editors pay tribute to the late Professor Hartley W. Cross of Connecticut College who died in April, 1948, shortly after plans which owe much to his advice were made for this volume. They sincerely appreciate the loyal spirit of the Alumni who have co-operated in this project, both those whose articles are here printed and those who submitted manuscripts for consideration. The editors also acknowledge their debt to their colleagues at the University of Connecticut and at Clark University to whom they have turned for advice and assistance.

Publication has been made possible financially by the generous support of the President and Trustees of Clark University and of alumni and colleagues who wanted to honor a great teacher in the field of history and international relations.

George E. McReynolds
University of Connecticut

Dwight E. Lee
Clark University

January, 1949

Table of Contents

The Shifting Strategy of American Defense and Diplomacy

By SAMUEL FLAGG BEMIS*

Nothing is more misleading than the widely prevailing belief that, unlike other nations, the United States does not have a consistent foreign policy. Such a misconception is due more than anything else to the failure to distinguish between foreign policy on the one hand and diplomacy on the other. The effort of this essay is to show that we do have a foreign policy, to recall its primaeval principles, to trace its historical shape, and to point out its present-day design. At the outset, one should bear in mind the distinction between general principles and objectives defining foreign policy on the one hand, and on the other hand the changing circumstances and situations and specific test cases which those principles and objectives continually encounter in the historically shifting strategy of American defense and diplomacy, particularly in relation to the balance of power.

The fundamental bases of the foreign policy of any state are security for the state and what the state stands for in the world. Every state seeks security first; if it cannot have security, if it cannot be its own sovereign master, it cannot stand for much in this world. In the lack of collective security, its foreign policy must then be subordinated to that of another state. At least so it has been until now in history. After security, the foreign policies of states differ according to what they stand for in the world: divine-right monarchy, republicanism, free trade, mercantilism, democ-

*Samuel Flagg Bemis is Sterling Professor of Diplomatic History at Yale University. The essay here published is a revision of an article under the same title which first appeared in the *Virginia Quarterly Review*, XXIV (Summer 1948), 321–35. Permission to republish it is gratefully acknowledged.

racy, the rights of man, communism, authoritarianism, imperialism (old-fashioned or new-fashioned), freedom of trade, autarchy, international peace, et cetera.

In terms of security, American foreign policy first meant the winning and preservation of our independence as an Atlantic-Coast republic in a world of rival colonial empires; afterwards, security to expand through the empty continent of North America and to found a transcontinental republic fronting on the two great oceans; then, security for our established domain and for our republican and democratic institutions in a world of legitimate divine-right monarchy; next, in a new order of world politics and power ushered in by the twentieth century, security for the whole republican New World against the menace of imperialistic colossi arising and joining in the Old World; finally, security for all free peoples against the new imperialism of today.

The foundations of American foreign policy, in terms first of security, and then of principles which we stood for, had been laid in classic form by the year 1823. They were:

(1) Sovereign independence, in order to preserve the rights of English freemen.

(2) Continental expansion.

(3) Abstention from the ordinary vicissitudes and ordinary combinations and collisions of European politics: first implemented in Washington's neutrality proclamation of 1793, then definitely expressed as a Great Rule of foreign policy in the Farewell Address of 1796, and again in the Monroe Doctrine of 1823. Washington used the qualifying word *ordinary* twice in his Address.

(4) Non-colonization principle—no further European colonization on the American continents.

(5) No-transfer principle: i.e., opposition to the transfer of colonial dominions in North America from one European sovereign to another; after the revolution of Latin America this was extended to the entire New World, including former colonies now independent. They should not be transferred back to any European sovereignty.

(6) Freedom of international trade without discrimination between nationals and foreigners, including freedom of trade with colonial dominions.

(7) Self-determination of peoples—as evidenced by our recognition of the revolted republics of Latin America. We hoped and expected that, despite temporary imperial regimes in Mexico and Brazil, these new states would all be republics, based on the rights of man, modeled on the United States.

(8) Freedom of the seas for neutral ships in time of war, according to certain dicta of neutral rights, and freedom of navigation of international rivers.

(9) The right of expatriation and the wrong of impressment.

(10) Non-intervention—as testified first in the Monroe Doctrine, opposing the intervention of European nations to control the destiny of the free nations of Latin America.

(11) Implicitly, in all this, never quite articulate, was a feeling of anti-imperialism. If one defines imperialism as dominion over alien people, the United States can scarcely be said to have been an imperialistic nation during the nineteenth century. At the cost of a great Civil War it resisted that temptation. The old Manifest Destiny was not imperialism. The new Manifest Destiny and the imperialism of 1898 that went with it have, as we shall see, been liquidated.

Nothing is clearer than that these were the main tenets and objectives of American foreign policy during the eighteenth and nineteenth centuries. No historian disputes their existence, or even their validity. They have remained fairly constant throughout our history despite the shifting strategy of our defense and diplomacy.

We did not immediately consummate all these principles and objectives, but on the whole we were remarkably successful in making most of them prevail as respected ourselves during the nineteenth century, despite the hazard of a paralyzing Civil War— as successful as any other great nation during that period of history, even more successful, it might be argued.

Before the twentieth century our principles did not reach much beyond the New World in the application of our foreign policy. Today they reach out to all the globe in tests of strength.

II

Our early diplomatic success was due to taking advantage, for the most part unwittingly, of the wars, rivalries, and distresses of the powers of Europe; to the detached and distant position of the United States; and to the fact that the principles and objectives of its foreign policy, just enumerated, were perfectly compatible with the genius and interests of its people. One other significant factor, the most vital of all, must be emphasized, *the favorable balance of power* behind the British balance in Europe and Asia.

From 1815 during the remainder of the nineteenth century the rival powers of Europe and of Asia were balanced fairly evenly behind the supremacy of British sea power. None of them was able to undertake an adventure in the New World without the assistance of the British navy, or at least the acquiescence of Great Britain. Thus no non-American power could hurt the United States or even gainsay its will in North America, except Great Britain. During all that century the two seacoasts of the United States, not to mention the entire New World, lay at the mercy of the British navy. Britain did not choose to collide uncompromisingly with American policy, whether over Florida, Cuba, Texas, Oregon, Mexico, the Isthmus of Central America, or Alaska, if only because of the long, undefended, exposed flank of Empire, presented by Canada.

In a war between the United States and Great Britain, a contingency happily growing more and more unthinkable decade by decade after 1815, Canada must have taken one of three possible positions: (1) loyal participation in the war against the United States—this would have meant the conquest of Canada; (2) neutrality—this would have been tantamount to secession from the British Empire; (3) war against Great Britain. Obviously, none of these choices was agreeable either to Great Britain or to Canada. Thus Canada served, historically, as a hostage for the good conduct of the British navy toward the United States as we expanded from coast to coast to become a great power. To prevent the growth of such a great power in North America adjacent to Canada, British policy relied on diplomacy rather than force. Great Britain encouraged the independence of Texas and California and tried to prevent their annexation to the United States. The British government, at least, hoped for the success of the Southern Confederacy during the Civil War. If successful, British diplomacy would have South Americanized North America. Texas would have been the Uruguay, California the Chile, the Confederate States the Brazil, the remaining United States the Argentina of North America, none of these nations strong enough to disturb the balance of power behind the British navy in this continent as elsewhere all over the world. Needless to say, British policy in balancing North America into a constellation of independent states like South America was unsuccessful. The victory of the North during the Civil War put an end to any such policy—fortunately for the fate of Great Britain; for had Britain balanced North America into a congeries of small nations, whence finally would have come the power from the West to redress the balance in the Old World during the First and Second World Wars of the twentieth century? Is it not a curious commentary on British foreign policy, the policy of the balance of states in all the continents behind an all-powerful British navy, that British diplomacy strove to prevent the growth of a transcontinental republic in North America while it did nothing to prevent the rise of the German Empire on the continent of Europe?

One should not leave this interesting phase of Anglo-American relations during the nineteenth century without stressing two things. One is the value to mankind of the British Century, 1815–1914, when world peace rested on a balance of power in Europe, Asia, and South America, behind the navy. It was the happiest century that modern history has known, with self-government burgeoning out all over the five continents to enthrone the rights of man. As a people, as a nation, the United States was content with the British Century. During it our foreign policy, so clearly defined, was successful.

The other point I wish to make is that the historian could not have regarded Canada in the hands of any other strong imperialistic power as a hostage. In that case there would have been no undefended frontier. Canada in the possession of France, or of Germany after 1815, or of Russia, would have been regarded as a vestibule of invasion of the United States. The increasing affinity and benevolence of Anglo-American relationships in all their broad walks of liberty has to be constantly kept in mind when we think of Canada the hostage, the magnetic field of American foreign policy during the nineteenth century.

III

The isolated position of the United States, secure, if only because of Canada, behind the balance of power held by the British navy, was a happy one in which we grew up uncudgeled to be a transcontinental republic—call it the continental republic with due respect for the continental dominion—in the choicest region on the surface of the globe, with an optimum climate for human welfare and energy, and a national estate fronting on the two great oceans. That position, however, began to disintegrate toward the end of the nineteenth century, when an unprecedented phenomenon suddenly took place in the almost simultaneous appearance of three new world powers: the United States, Germany, and Japan.

The advent of one new world power in the international firmament is in itself a spectacle of tremendous significance. It is certain to cause major perturbations in the orbits of the older powers. A triple birth of world powers—that was unknown in history. It unbalanced power in Europe and in Asia.

Two of the new powers confronted the third, the United States, one across either ocean.   Each had a formidable army.   Each was building a strong navy.   Either would soon be in a position to threaten one of our populous seacoasts, if we did not reconstruct the strategy of our defense.   Neither had a hostage like Canada alongside the United States to guarantee its benevolence.   North America was no longer a safe, isolated landmass.   It was becoming an island-continent menaced by new potentials of power.   By the same tokens the British Empire was becoming a world-archipelago threatened by hostile continents.   The new picture of power and politics caused the United States and Great Britain to look more and more to each other for the security of their own futures.   Great Britain was first to feel the significance of the new order of power and began to look for allies.   As the old balance began to tremble under these phenomenal impulses, the American outlook on the world began to change, too.

Ever since the completion of the continental republic, American opinion had focused increasingly upon the project of an Isthmian canal.   The new frame of power and politics of the twentieth century made such a waterway indispensable for national security.   Without a canal two new navies would be necessary, one on each ocean.   With a canal one navy might suffice, to be passed back and forth through the Isthmus to protect either coast as circumstances might require.   Nobody seems to have dreamed, in the early decades of the present century, that the United States might have to fight simultaneously a two-ocean war.   It was Germany who loomed up as the principal disturber of the old balance.

Such was the situation when the United States went to war with Spain over the Cuban Question.   Behind the Cuban Question lay the Isthmian Question.

The United States emerged from the Spanish-American War a full-fledged world power, protector of Cuba, mistress of the Caribbean, ready to build, control, and fortify a canal across the Isthmus of Central America.   The necessary arrangements, diplomatic and engineering, were quickly completed.   Great Britain, eager for firm friendship with the United States against the rising menace of Germany, recognized our paramount interest in the future canal and in Central America and the Caribbean. From 1898 until the Second World War, Panama, not Canada, became the pole of American diplomacy toward which the compass needle came back in every major question despite violent fluctuations east and west.

The diplomatic history of the United States should have taught us by 1914 that there was one danger which ought to disturb the sleep of every American diplomatist—the vision of an undivided Europe agglomerated under one power which could be turned against the United States after overpowering or neutralizing Great Britain; more dreadful still the nightmare of a similar great mass of force united in the Far East which could be allied with Europe against the United States and the New World. As we look back on the First World War it would seem that the real motive for our entrance into that conflict should have been a clearly discerned *raison d'état:* to prevent Germany and her allies from overturning the balance of power against us. It should have been perfectly evident that if the Allies won the war, the United States had nothing to lose by their victory, as proved by the previous British Century and, we can add today looking back, as proved also by the actual event of Allied victory in 1918. It should have been obvious, on the other hand, that the United States had much to fear, much to lose, if Germany should win. Our statesmen did not see this as clearly then as we can see it now.

Woodrow Wilson did not shift the strategy of American diplomacy from Panama to Europe expressly to meet the danger that had now threatened our historic security. He did his best up to the very last moment to keep his country out of the holocaust. We would like to believe that he finally brought the United States into the war on the Allied side in order to prevent Germany from upsetting the balance of power against us. There is no satisfactory evidence that he did. It was rather his *choice* of alternatives of neutral policy between the opposing retaliatory systems of the maritime belligerents, rather than his choice of peace or war, which led this peace-loving President into the First World War against his will. Fortunately he took his country into the conflict on the right side, if belatedly, and thus saved the balance of power for the United States and its associates. Had the United States stayed neutral a few months more until after the Russian collapse, Germany would have won the war, would have become the dominant sea power, and would have been in a position to ally herself with Japan to crush the United States and Canada, to possess herself of Latin America and the Atlantic while Japan took over Asia and the Pacific and perhaps Alaska. Our victory in the First World War saved us from that disaster.

Once in the war Wilson shifted the strategy of American diplomacy in a wholly new and untried direction—world peace through collective security in the form of a League of Nations rather than through the "forever discredited" system of the balance of power. But after the military victory, after restoration of a safe balance in Europe, and the establishment of a new balance in the Pacific and Far East, in short, when everything seemed perfectly secure again in North America and in the New World, the United States turned its back on Woodrow Wilson's League of Nations and his plan of collective security.

After the election of 1920 neither the Republican nor the Democratic party dared to stand on a League of Nations platform, not till the closing months of the Second World War.

We may appropriately designate as the "Washington Period" the fifteen years of apparently perfect continental security which followed the Washington Conference of 1922. Never did the Western Hemisphere seem safer, a paradise of peace. Perhaps it would be more accurate to call that period the Fool's Paradise of American history.

During the Washington Period, American foreign policy degenerated into five postulates: isolation, anti-imperialism, disarmament, neutrality, pacifism.

Under the shadow of a new European war, Congress, pressed

on by a powerful historiography of revision and disillusion, com-
pletely repudiated the policy of Woodrow Wilson during the First
World War. One by one the new neutrality laws of 1935–1937
outlawed the issues of neutral rights which had brought the United
States into that conflict. They all but renounced the ancient
American "birthright" of Freedom of the Seas.

All these legislative precautions, all this new retrograde strategy
of American diplomacy, designed to keep the United States out
of the next war, only served the purpose of keeping it out of the
previous war, so to speak, a war which had already been fought
and won. The neutrality legislation said in effect to Germany
and to Japan and to the would-be world power, Italy, that the
United States would not go to war to preserve the balance of power
in the Old World, that it would not even allow the democratic
allies of Western Europe to replenish their depleted forces from
the potential arsenal of American supplies. Such was American
world power on the eve of Munich, when Hitler overthrew the
balance in Europe and we looked on still satisfied at peace in
our time.

IV

When Germany overran Western Europe, and made the Tripartite Pact with Japan and Italy, it was apparent that the anti-
imperialistic, pacifistic United States now faced the greatest peril
of its history, the nightmare of its diplomatists, the prospect of a
two-ocean war with a one-ocean navy. Only England stood
between us and destruction, until Hitler made the mistake of
attacking Russia. If Germany defeated Great Britain and seized
the British fleet, the new Alexander could then organize the sea
power, air power, and man power of Europe for an irresistible
attack on the New World and the United States from the Atlantic,
while Japan attacked from the Pacific.

The strategy of American defense and diplomacy shifted again
with the change in the balance of power, from Panama as a life-line
of hemisphere security to England as a base for a war of defense

to be waged in Europe instead of America to restore the balance. American neutrality, already shaken by the initial impact of the war, broke down completely in 1941, notwithstanding the pledges of both major parties and their candidates, in the national election of 1940, to keep the United States out of the war.

It will be Franklin D. Roosevelt's claim to statesmanship as compared with that of Woodrow Wilson, that, whatever his initial vacillations and his campaign deceptions, he came to see the American *raison d'état*, the vital relation of the United States to the balance of power at the advent of the Second World War. He protected that relation at the risk and fact of a double war, rather than permit Japan to destroy the British Empire in the Pacific while the United States was striving to preserve it for our defense in the Atlantic. Despite Pearl Harbor, the greatest humiliation of American history, for which Roosevelt seems as much responsible as any one, he was right in taking on the double war: with the help of the British Commonwealth we licked Japan left-handed while our right arm was busy together with so many other arms in Europe.

Roosevelt's understanding of the vital interests of the United States in the new shift of the balance of power after the defeat of Germany and Japan was, I suggest, more questionable.

Now, after the Second World War, the geographical basis of American defense and foreign policy is shifting again with the balance of power, shifting back to the north.

Three unexpected political phenomena of victory are: (1) the rise of a new colossus, in the potential supremacy of Russia in the world; (2) the disintegration of the British Empire; (3) the demoralization, at least temporary, of the United States in the Great Let-Down of 1945–1947.

These three phenomena have perturbed international politics and the prospect of world peace almost as profoundly as the sudden birth of three new world powers at the advent of the twentieth century. None of them offsets the others: on the contrary they all supplement each other in favor of Russia. What does that bode for the balance of power and the traditional principles of American foreign policy?

There is increasing reason to believe that the leaders of Russia for reasons of domestic policy fear the *friendship* of the Western world, particularly of the United States, much more than they do its enmity. In fact, given the phenomena of victory just mentioned, and the perfect security of Russian frontiers brought about by the complete defeat of Germany and Japan, they do not fear our *enmity* at all. It is we who fear *their* enmity and want their friendship.

We have extended an eager hand of friendship to Russia to grasp, for the rights of man, for the principles of non-intervention, democracy, self-determination, and freedom; freedom of speech, freedom of religion, freedom from fear (including the fear of atomic warfare); freedom (hopefully) from want, freedom from the crushing burden of armaments, freedom of trade, freedom of the international rivers and straits; in short, the things we have traditionally stood for in the world and still stand for. We had hoped that Russia would grasp that hand, for on such a sincere handclasp is the only hope for world peace. But these are not the things that Russia stands for in the world. What she wants rather is the extension of her opposite principles, by revolution if necessary, to the rest of the world: a W.U.S.S.R., that kind of a United Nations.

V

What is the strategy of American security and defense now that collective security has failed and the balance of power has turned against us?

It consists in three lines of defense: a first line, in Europe; a second line, in the New World, south; a third line in the New World, north; along the Arctic Circle, perhaps south of it. That third line may become, at any moment, the first line, in a new Pearl Harbor.

In respect to Europe, the foreign policy of the United States, since Pearl Harbor, would seem to have undergone nothing less than a diplomatic revolution, but, on second historical thought, it is still the problem of maintaining a safe balance of power. Before the Second World War it was the policy of Great Britain first, and of the British Commonwealth of Nations and the United States behind Great Britain, to rest upon a balanced Europe and a balanced Asia. Now that that balance has been lost, by defeat in victory, at Yalta, at Potsdam, and at home in London, Ottawa, and Washington, in the will and morale of our people, we have had to reform our ideas of the balance. We are making a desperate effort short of war itself to encourage not the division but the union of Western Europe in a new balance before the present precarious situation leads to war. We have sluiced money and munitions, to say the least, into Turkey and Greece to hold back the weight of totalitarian power pressing down upon the Dardanelles. If the plug is pulled, so to speak, at the Dardanelles, Soviet power will pour unobstructed through the Near East into Africa, as Japanese power did through the straits of Singapore in 1942, into Micronesia and Australasia, only more devastatingly: on the one hand into Persia and India, on the other hand flowing into Africa to occupy a springboard for a jump across to sedulously prepared ground in South America.

In addition to sustaining Greece and Turkey, the people of the United States have expended eleven billions of dollars worth of economic aid and loans for the peaceful rehabilitation of an exhausted Western Europe, and are preparing to expend twice as much more in a mammoth program, the Marshall Plan, put together by the free governments in consultation, to rehabilitate the economy of those countries 25 per cent above their prewar level as a means of firming them to resist the threat of revolution from within and aggression from without.

If I were a member of Congress, I would have voted for these aids, but with misgivings. I would vote for them because the American people, still not fully recovered from their postwar demoralization and disillusion, are not yet willing to take other measures more resolute in nature. I would have misgivings because such devices are essentially mercenary in character. If history teaches any lesson, it is that no great people has ever been able safely to rely on mercenaries, on foreign legions, on subsidies, to maintain its liberties. They may help but they cannot be a substitute for valor. The hope of the Marshall Plan is that it may transfuse enough health into Western Europe to enable those peoples to regain a consciousness of liberty, and health to defend it. But it cannot be a substitute for our own right arm and resolution. If it does not work, we shall have to fall back on our second line of defense—in South America; and, perhaps simultaneously, on our third and last line of defense in North America. Here I venture to think the line will eventually be drawn; and we had better use what little time there may be gained by the Marshall Plan, resolutely to prepare for the worst, in order that the best may be saved.

These successive lines of defense are also the lines of defense of those other countries which lie behind them, first, second, and third. People may grieve to find their countries a possible battleground between two great potentials of power; they may wish, they may strive, they doubtless will strive to be neutral. But as they do so, they cannot but realize that the battleground, if such it becomes, is one of liberty against slavery in a struggle for the rights of English freemen, for those fundamental freedoms which flowered in the recent British Century. To be neutral in any final Armageddon means surrender of those priceless human rights, of all the long constitutional log of freedom from Magna Carta to the Statute of Westminster and the Charter of the United Nations. It is inconceivable to me that Britons, Canadians, and Americans, nay before them that Swiss, Frenchmen, Belgians, or Dutchmen, should lie down without a struggle and accept the yoke of Moscow in a W.U.S.S.R. Suppose then that these three lines of defense left for Anglo-Saxon liberty did not remain? Suppose that back of the last there were left no final power for the defense of freedom? Where could free men look for life? The Iron Curtain would be an Iron Cover closed down over all the globe, and no man could tell, no man would be permitted to tell, how many centuries must pass before it could be lifted.

The United States—Paramount Power of the Pacific

By Russell H. Fifield*

The rise of the United States as the paramount power of the Pacific is not an expression of Manifest Destiny but rather the consequence of a shift in the distribution of world power. Through defeat and default other great powers have been removed for the present from a decisive role in the affairs of the Pacific basin. The fall of the New Order in Greater East Asia under the aegis of Japan, the rise of nationalism in the British, French, and Dutch possessions of the Pacific Far East, the tragic civil war in China, and the emphasis up to the present of the Soviet Union on European politics have created a power vacuum in the Pacific. At the same time, the decisive role of the United States in the defeat of Japan, the changing of the Pacific into a veritable American lake from the viewpoint of sea power and air power, and the influential voice of Washington in Japan, southern Korea, Nationalist China, the Republic of the Philippines, and even to a certain extent in Southeast Asia reflect the paramount position now held by the United States.

Unless a resurgent Japan regains its prewar position or a unified China emerges as a great power, only the Soviet Union may be able to approach the influence and power of the United States in the Far East within the next one or two decades. As the outstanding land power of Eurasia, occupying an increasingly industrialized continental base, the Soviet Union will be able to exert more and more influence in the Pacific Far East, especially in those areas adjacent to Soviet territory. Abraham Lincoln's Secretary

*Russell H. Fifield is Assistant Professor of Political Science, University of Michigan.

of State, William H. Seward, foresaw the eventual meeting of Russian and American power in the Far East when he significantly said in 1861: "Russia and the United States may remain good friends until, each having made a circuit of half the globe in opposite directions, they shall meet and greet each other in regions where civilization first began, and where, after so many ages, it has become now lethargic and helpless."[1]

The interests of the United States in the Pacific basin and Far East have territorial, economic, and political foundations, all of varying importance at different times in American history and all affecting the problems of American security in a changing world. The territorial interests have never been predominant while the economic have usually outweighed the political. The beginning of the present century saw a growing American political interest in the Far East which culminated in the defeat of the Japanese Empire and the present paramount position of the United States.

II

American territorial interests in the Pacific and Far East represent a definite pattern. Alaska, Hawaii, and the Panama Canal Zone form the American Pacific triangle of defense. One line of power extends westward through Midway, Wake, Guam, and the new Territory of the Pacific Islands to the American bases in the Republic of the Philippines, while another power line extends southwest through a number of steppingstones to American Samoa. Political changes in the American empire in the Pacific do not fundamentally mean a relinquishment of American territorial interests. The changes in the various dependencies are probably binding these areas more closely to the United States. Through independence, but retained bases, in the Philippines, by the means of probable statehood in Hawaii and Alaska, and through anticipated organic acts in Guam and Samoa, the pattern of change is revealed.

[1] Frederic Bancroft, *The Life of William H. Seward* (New York, Harper and Brothers, 1900), II, 472.

Plans are now well advanced to admit the Territory of Hawaii, at the crossroads of the Pacific, into the Union as the forty-ninth state.[2] Although Pearl Harbor on Oahu in the Hawaiians is 2,400 statute miles from San Francisco, it is a noted strategic outpost of the United States. Annexed in 1898 and made an incorporated territory in 1900, the Hawaiian Islands have rapidly approached the threshold of statehood. The majority of the people of the islands—519,423 in 1948—do not want independence in the family of nations or the continued status of an incorporated territory, but prefer statehood. In a plebiscite held in 1940, 67 per cent of the voters favored entrance into the Union.[3] A bill to provide a constitutional convention for Hawaiian statehood passed the House of Representatives of the United States on June 30, 1947, by a vote of 196 to 133, but failed to receive the approval of the Senate. Although the Hawaiians were disappointed, the setback is only temporary. Statehood for Hawaii will tighten the bonds between the people of the islands and the mainland, and consummate a logical development in American territorial evolution.

Alaska, the northern point of the Pacific triangle, is located about 2,300 miles from Pearl Harbor and about 1,400 miles from Seattle. Purchased from Russia through the influence of William H. Seward for $7,200,000 in 1867 and created an incorporated territory in 1912, Alaska is important in the defense of the northwestern approaches to continental United States. In an age when great circle routes across the Arctic are feasible for military aircraft, the strategic value of this base of 586,400 square miles is obvious. The late General "Billy" Mitchell believed that Alaska was the most central place in the world for aircraft and that whoever held Alaska dominated the world. The general may have unduly emphasized the strategic value of the territory, but the growing rivalry between the United States and the Soviet Union places "Seward's Folly" in the limelight.

[2] Report of the Subcommittee of the Committee on Territories, the United States House of Representatives, on Statehood for Hawaii, U. S., *Congressional Record* (79th Cong., 2d Sess., January 24, 1946, Appendix), 92, Part IX, 209–12.

[3] Joseph R. Farrington, "Hawaii's Fight for Statehood," *The American Foreign Service Journal*, XXV (June, 1948), 13.

Although the population of Alaska is now only between 80,000 and 90,000, hardly more than half of which is white with the rest native, the territory is seeking admission into the Union.[4] In a plebiscite held in 1946, 60 per cent of the voters favored statehood.[5] In 1948, President Harry Truman even sent a special message to Congress urging it to act favorably on the admission of Alaska into the Union. However, the necessary legislation in Washington is delayed, at least for a while, because of the alleged lack of political maturity in the territory.

As the final link in the Pacific triangle of defense, the Republic of Panama in 1903 granted in perpetuity to the United States the Panama Canal Zone, an area some ten miles wide extending from the Pacific to the Atlantic.[6] The Canal is over 5,400 miles from Hawaii and 3,525 miles from San Francisco. The Canal Zone is a military reservation administered by a governor who reports to the Secretary of the Army in Washington. The opposition of the Republic of Panama in 1947 to American bases in its territory, the danger in an atomic war of a canal utilizing locks, the inadequacy of the Panama Canal for capital ships of present-day size, and the possibility of an alternative route across Nicaragua are factors weighing in the future decision of Congress about the Panama Canal.

The Pacific defense of an isthmian canal is not so easy as the Atlantic because of the almost general absence of islands in the eastern part of the Pacific Ocean. The Galápagos, about 1,010 miles from Ecuador, are dependencies of that country but important in the defense of the Canal. The United States in the past has expressed interest in the acquisition of the islands. In the recent war, Ecuador allowed the United States to station forces on the Galápagos. On June 30, 1946, American forces were removed, although the interests of Washington in the islands

[4] H.R. 206 is entitled "A bill to provide for the admission of Alaska, the forty-ninth state," U. S., *Congressional Record* (80th Cong., 1st Sess., January 3, 1947), 92, Part I, 45.

[5] "The Alaskan Story," *The Congressional Digest*, XXVI (November, 1947), 274.

[6] *Papers Relating to the Foreign Relations of the United States, 1904* (Washington, 1905), 543-51.

will remain in an unstable world. Attention on occasion has also been directed to the French island of Clipperton and the Cocos Islands of Costa Rica in the eastern Pacific.

Extending westward from Hawaii are the steppingstones of Midway and Kure, annexed in 1867, Wake acquired in 1899, and Guam annexed in the same year. Midway is 1,320 miles from Pearl Harbor; Wake 1,198 miles from Midway; Guam 1,535 miles from Wake; and Manila in the Philippines 1,595 miles from Guam. All of these islands are under the administration of the Navy Department although an organic act, giving the people of Guam the status of citizens and more self-government, is under consideration.

The only territorial "addition" of the United States in the Second World War is the old Japanese mandate of the Carolines, Marshalls, and Marianas, now christened the Territory of the Pacific Islands. Stretching between the Philippines and Hawaii for about 2,700 miles from east to west and for about 1,300 miles from north to south, the islands have an area of only 846 square miles and a native population of about 48,000. The economic significance of the Territory of the Pacific Islands is little, but the strategic importance is great. As long as the United States maintains bases in the Philippines, American control over the Carolines, Marshalls, and Marianas is essential. The danger of a hostile foreign power in control of the islands was well demonstrated in the Second World War. On April 2, 1947, the Security Council of the United Nations granted the United States a strategic trusteeship over the area.[7] From a practical viewpoint in a world of power politics, a strategic trusteeship constitutes a polite form of annexation.

The disposal of the Volcanoes with Iwo Jima, Bonins, Marcus, and the Ryukyus with Okinawa, all integral territory of the old Japanese Empire, remains to be settled. All these island areas are presently occupied by the United States. To a certain degree the ambitions of Commodore Matthew Perry of the nineteenth

[7] Text of Trusteeship, *Department of State Bulletin*, XVI (May 4, 1947), 791–92, 794.

century are being fulfilled in the twentieth. He advocated American occupation of the Bonins, Ryukyus, and Formosa. In fact, Commodore John Kelly in 1853 took formal possession of some of the Bonin Islands, and the United States did not disclaim all rights to them until 1862.[8]

Although independence was formally granted the Republic of the Philippines on July 4, 1946, the United States is largely responsible for the defense of the islands, less than 700 miles from China.[9] In an agreement signed on March 14, 1947, the Republic of the Philippines granted the United States a ninety-nine-year lease on eleven army bases and four naval "operating areas" in the islands. The economic relations between the two countries are certain to be close, at least until the end of twenty-eight years when the Philippine Trade Act of 1946 expires. This Trade Act provides for free trade between the two countries for eight years followed by the gradual imposition of tariffs over a twenty-year period until the full duty is collected by 1974. The historic and intangible ties uniting the Philippines and the United States really place the islands on a dominion relationship with the latter.

Southwest of Hawaii, a number of American islands dot the route to Samoa and the British dominions of Australia and New Zealand. Johnston, Palmyra, and Kingman Reef were a part of Hawaiian territory when it was annexed to the United States in 1898. Jarvis, Baker, and Howland are old guano islands of the United States, the first two annexed in 1857 and the last in 1858. Canton and Enderbury are in dispute between the United States and Great Britain, but the two powers agreed in 1939 to exercise joint control over the islands for fifty years, when the claims would be reconsidered. Canton and Enderbury represent the only present condominia of the United States. The goal of these steppingstones in terms of American territory is Pago Pago on the island of Tutuila in American Samoa, located 2,620 miles

---

[8] Tyler Dennett, in *Americans in Eastern Asia* (New York, Macmillan Company, 1922), 270–77, has an interesting section on Perry's ambitions in the western Pacific.

[9] Text of Proclamation of the President on the Independence of the Philippines, *Department of State Bulletin*, XV (July 14, 1946), 66.

from Pearl Harbor. In 1878 the United States acquired the right to have a naval station at Pago Pago. Rivalry among Germany, Great Britain, and the United States was ended in 1899 when Western Samoa went to the Reich and Eastern Samoa to the United States.[10] American Samoa has been governed by the Navy Department, much to the resentment of some of the 12,908 inhabitants. However, an anticipated organic act will provide for citizenship and more self-government.

The general interest of Congress and the American Navy in the Pacific basin was reflected in the report of the Subcommittee on Pacific Bases of the Committee on Naval Affairs of the House of Representatives on August 6, 1945. The subcommittee frankly stated that "with the maintenance of peace in the Pacific being primarily the responsibility of the United States, we must have the necessary authority for such responsibility."[11] The report asserted that

with respect to Manus, Noumea, Espiritu Santo, Guadalcanal, and other sites of American bases on islands mandated to, or claimed by, other nations, full title to those bases should be given to the United States because:

(a) These other nations are not capable of defending such islands; they do not possess the man power and materials that the United States does for the holding and maintaining of these bases; and

(b) As these bases are links in our chain of security, and no chain is stronger than its weakest link, we cannot permit any link to be in the hands of those who will not or cannot defend it.[12]

The report of the Navy on the subject in September, 1945, was more moderate, calling for bases in "regular operation" at Kodiak, Adak, Hawaii, Balboa, Guam-Saipan, Bonins-Volcano Group, Ryukyus, Manus, Tutu-Tawitawi, Subic, Leyte-Samar, and Puerto Princesa (Palawan); in "reduced" operation at Attu,

[10] *Papers Relating to the Foreign Relations of the United States, 1899* (Washington, 1901), 665–69.

[11] U. S., *House Reports* (79th Cong., 1st Sess.): *Study of Pacific Bases* (Report by the Subcommittee on Pacific Bases of the Committee on Naval Affairs, August 6, 1945. Washington, 1945), 1014.

[12] *Ibid.*, 1010–11.

Galápagos, Johnston Island, Midway, Wake, Samoa, Eniwetok, Kwajalein, Truk, and Palau; and in "caretaker-emergency" status at Dutch Harbor, Canton Island, Palmyra, Majuro, and Ulithi.[13]

On February 14, 1946, Vice-Admiral Forrest P. Sherman, Deputy Chief of Naval Operations, told the Senate Committee on Naval Affairs that Pearl Harbor would be operated as "the main overseas naval base in the Pacific"; that "the next most important base" would be the islands of Guam and Saipan "which together make our major operating base in the western Pacific"; and that secondary operating bases, anchorage facilities or air staging points would be maintained in such places as the Ryukyus, Philippines, Eniwetok, Kwajalein, Palau, Marcus, Wake, Majuro, Johnston Island, Palmyra, Canton, Kodiak, Adak, Dutch Harbor, and Attu. The Navy also desired "to retain the right to use the facilities that exist" on Manus in the Admiralties, at that time under Australian mandate.[14]

III

Turning from the territorial and strategic factors to economic considerations, a new frame of reference emerges. Between the depression and the outbreak of World War II, the United States annually sent only 15 per cent of its total exports to eastern Asia but bought 24 per cent of its total imports from that region.[15] Many of these imports from the Far East consisted of strategic materials like rubber, tin, quinine, manila hemp, tungsten, and silk. American trade with China has been much smaller than with Japan. In 1931–35 American exports to China aver-

[13] U. S., *House Reports* (79th Cong., 1st Sess., Report No. 1107): *Composition of the Postwar Navy* (Washington, 1945), 10.

[14] U. S., Senate (79th Cong., 2d Sess.): *Authorizing Permanent Officer and Enlisted Strength of the United States Navy and the United States Marine Corps* (Hearings before the Committee on Naval Affairs, on H.R. 4421, February 14, 1946. Washington, 1946), Part II, 92–93.

[15] An excellent study of prewar trade between the United States and the Far East is Ethel B. Dietrich's *Far Eastern Trade of the United States* (New York: Institute of Pacific Relations, 1940). Professor Dietrich includes India and Ceylon in her study, countries not included in this discussion.

aged $62,570,000 yearly and American imports $48,175,000 while exports to Japan averaged $169,560,000 and imports $148,186,000. In trade with the Philippine Islands during the same period, the United States sold $47,680,000 as an annual average and bought $89,173,000. This trade, however, depended upon preferential commercial relations. All the other areas of eastern Asia bought less than 1 per cent of total American exports but furnished 7 per cent of American imports. The latter figure is due to the importance of tin and rubber in Southeast Asia and the East Indies.

Prewar American investments in the Far East amounted to only about 5 per cent of the fourteen billion dollars representing total American investments overseas. Half of the American investments were located in Japan ($375,000,000), and the rest largely in the Philippines ($150,000,000), China ($132,000,000), and Southeast Asia and the East Indies ($80,000,000).[16] These figures indicate that the American financial stake in the Far East is not very extensive.

The future of American trade and investments in eastern Asia depends upon political stabilization and economic stability in key areas like Japan, China, the Philippines, Malaya, and the East Indies. Under favorable conditions the Far East offers a great potential market for American goods as well as a source of important materials. It is doubtful, however, if eastern Asia can achieve for some time the degree of stability prevailing before the war.

The political interests of the United States in the Far East now undoubtedly outweigh the economic in the formulation of American foreign policy. A comparison of the statement of Secretary of State Cordell Hull in a letter to Vice-President John Garner on January 8, 1938, with that of John Carter Vincent, Director of the Office of Far Eastern Affairs, Department of State, in the fall of 1946 reveals a basic similarity despite the events of the Pacific

[16] Professor Carl F. Remer's *Foreign Investments in China* (New York: Macmillan Company, 1933) is a thorough prewar study of this problem.

War that separated the two statements.   Cordell Hull had written six months and one day after the Marco Polo Bridge Incident starting the Sino-Japanese War:

The interest and concern of the United States in the Far Eastern situation, in the European situation, and in situations on this continent are not measured by the number of American citizens residing in a particular country at a particular moment, nor by the amount of investment of American citizens there nor by the volume of trade.   There is a broader and much more fundamental interest—which is that orderly processes in international relationships be maintained.   Referring expressly to the situation in the Far East, an area which contains approximately half the population of the world, the United States is deeply interested in supporting by peaceful means influences contributory to preservation and encouragement of orderly processes.   This interest far transcends in importance the value of American trade with China or American investments in China; it transcends even the question of safeguarding the immediate welfare of American citizens in China.[17]

John Carter Vincent, delivering a lecture in the Mayling Soong Foundation at Wellesley College, stated a little over a year after the end of the war that the over-all objectives of American foreign policy were

(1) To provide for the security of the United States and the maintenance of international peace, and (2) to bring about in the relations between ourselves and other states mutually beneficial commercial and cultural exchanges which will promote international welfare and understanding.[18]

He added:

If my estimate is correct, our aim in Japan and Korea is to neutralize these areas so that they will not constitute a threat to us, or, for that matter, to any other nation.   We hope that China, through a settlement of her internal difficulties, will become a stabilizing rather than a disturbing influence in the Far East which would adversely affect peaceful international relations.[19]

[17] Department of State, *Press Releases*, No. 431–56 (January 1—June 25, 1938), 104.

[18] John Carter Vincent, "Our Far Eastern Policies in Relation to Our Overall National Objectives," *America's Future in the Pacific* (New Brunswick: Rutgers University Press, 1947), 3–4.

[19] *Ibid.*, 5–6.

IV

For a consideration of the present American role, the Pacific Far East may be conveniently divided into three great areas: first the northwest embracing Russia, Japan, and Korea; second, the great Republic of China; and third, the southwest including Southeast Asia and the Southwest Pacific. In the northwest area the two outstanding developments are the appearance of a power vacuum created by the collapse of Japan and the emergence of the rivalry between the United States and the Soviet Union to fill this vacuum. On the other hand, in the southwest area, the most significant developments are the rise of nationalism, the growth of Communist influence in Southeast Asia, and the noted Anglo-Saxon co-operation in the Southwest Pacific. The Republic of China represents the transition between the northwest and southwest areas through its sovereignty over Manchuria in the north, its civil war with American and Russian ideologies supporting opposite sides, and the significant role of its citizens in Southeast Asia.

Japan is still the potential pivot of the northwest sector of the Pacific. In terms of territorial possessions, Japan has been stripped of her empire and restricted to her main islands. The territorial settlement of the Pacific was not so difficult a problem to solve as the issue of the future economic and political structure of Japan. As previously stated, the only territories once under the Japanese flag, the disposition of which has not been settled, are the Ryukyus with Okinawa, the Volcanoes with Iwo Jima, the Bonins, and Marcus. China has regained Manchuria, Formosa, and the Pescadores in accordance with the Cairo Declaration;[20] Russia has acquired southern Sakhalin and the Kuriles as agreed at Yalta;[21] Japan has been deprived of Korea; and the islands of the old Japanese mandate have been granted to the United States as a strategic trusteeship. The peace conference of the Pacific

[20] Text of Cairo Declaration, *Department of State Bulletin,* IX (December 4, 1943), 393.

[21] Text, *Department of State Bulletin,* XIV (February 24, 1946), 282.

will put the final mark of approval on the territorial distribution of the old Japanese empire.

The broad outline of the new Japan is slowly beginning to emerge.[22] The disarmament and demilitarization of the country, the constitution of 1947,[23] the efforts to make the emperor a human being, the abolition of state Shintoism, the acquisition of basic civil rights, reforms in education, the right of collective bargaining, the attempted destruction of the power of the Zaibatsu, and the postwar agrarian reforms highlight the program of the occupation under General Douglas MacArthur. At the same time the future course of Japan will be greatly affected by world politics, the length of the occupation, the amount of reparations, the level of industry, the extent of foreign trade, the loss of the empire, and the crowding of more than 78,000,000 Japanese into an area about as large as Montana, only one-fifth to one-sixth of which is arable.

An evaluation of the success of the occupation of Japan is difficult to make because of the lack of impartial data. The first objective, namely, the disarmament and demilitarization of Japan, has undoubtedly been attained. Under present conditions, Japan is no longer a military threat to her neighbors or to the world. As long as the country is restricted to the main islands and the import of war supplies prevented, Japan cannot regain her prewar status. Chapter 2, Article 9 of the new constitution contains a renunciation of war although it is doubtful if the Japanese are taking the renunciation seriously. It is more likely that the Japanese are more aroused at losing the Greater East Asia War than they are at the use of war as a national policy.

The second broad objective of the occupation is to convert the people of Japan to the democratic way of life. General Douglas MacArthur appears convinced that the defeat and occupation of the country have converted the Japanese to democracy and peace. Mr. W. Macmahon Ball, British and dominion repre-

[22] Department of State (Publication 2671, Far Eastern Series 17), *Occupation of Japan: Policy and Progress* (Washington, 1946).

[23] Department of State (Publication 2836, Far Eastern Series 22), *The Constitution of Japan* (Washington, 1947).

sentative on the Allied Council in Tokyo from March, 1946, to September, 1947, has unofficially but publicly questioned this conviction of the Supreme Commander.[24] Mr. Ball asserts that the former ruling class is still in control with no "real desire to resist and overthrow the social, bureaucratic, and economic hierarchy." He believes that "no considerable body of Japanese opinion takes the new Constitution seriously" and that the purge has created "a united and embittered group of able men from whom you have stripped privilege but not power." The securities of the holding companies of the Zaibatsu have been taken over by a Liquidation Commission but "solid little" men with ample capital to buy them have not been located. Land reform has been more successful but it has not yet been completely accomplished. Mr. Ball asserts that the "real political power" of the emperor is "even stronger than before the war."

The future role of Japan in the Pacific will depend to a great extent upon the development of relations between the United States and the Soviet Union. Apprehension is already rising in China, the Philippines, and in Australia that the United States may be pursuing a policy that will encourage the rise of Japan as a military power to serve as a possible ally against the Soviet Union. The Japanese Foreign Office is reported in early 1947 to have "informally sounded out Allied representatives on the prospects of being allowed a standing army of 100,000 men and a small air force."[25] The Japanese knowledge of Western techniques has been increased by observation of the occupation. Japanese patriotism is still probably influenced by the militarist spirit. In general trade within the vast area of the Far East Japan would be able to assume a highly significant role. The emergence of a resurgent Japan in the Pacific is a possibility although not yet a probability. It would be a bold American statesman who would create a resurgent Japan in the hope that it would always carry out the suggestions of its creator.

[24] W. Macmahon Ball, "Reflections on Japan," *Pacific Affairs*, XXI (March, 1948), 3–19.
[25] *Ibid.*, 4.

In Korea the forces of the United States and of the Soviet Union meet face to face at the thirty-eighth parallel.[26]   Although this parallel was only an initial "military expedient," it has now become an iron wall separating more than nine million Koreans in the Soviet zone of occupation from more than nineteen million in the American.   A rigid trade barrier is maintained and no integrated Korean economy is possible.   The Soviets and the Americans cannot agree on the type of government that should emerge in the strategic peninsula that the Japanese once considered a dagger pointed at their heart.   On November 14, 1947, the General Assembly of the United Nations, following an American plan, set up a United Nations Temporary Commission on Korea to supervise elections in the peninsula leading to the establishment of a Korean government.   Although the Soviet Union refused to let the Commission enter the Russian zone of occupation, elections were held on May 10, 1948, in the American zone.   The peninsula of Korea is now split with the northern zone under a constitution and government fashioned along Soviet lines and the southern zone under a constitution and government patterned along Western lines.   The proclamation of the Korean Republic on August 15, 1948, and its subsequent recognition by the United States emphasized the complete divergence of Soviet and American policy.

In many respects Korea is the Achilles heel of the United States in the Far East.   Nowhere else on the mainland of Asia are American occupation forces stationed.   American naval and air power can defend the Japanese and Philippine islands under present conditions, but United States occupation forces in southern Korea would soon be overwhelmed by superior Russian land power. The withdrawal of American forces from southern Korea would probably mean that the well-trained, well-indoctrinated, and well-organized Communist Koreans of the Russian zone would quickly

[26] Department of State, Office of Public Affairs, *Foreign Affairs Background Summary: Korea* (August, 1947); Department of State, Office of Public Affairs, *Korea's Independence: Current Developments* (March, 1948).

overrun all the peninsula which would then presumably look to Moscow for leadership. The "Land of the Morning Calm" reflects the plight of a small nation in a world of power politics. The old rivalry of China and Japan, of Japan and Russia, and now of the Soviet Union and the United States over Korea highlights this plight. Only co-operation between Washington and Moscow can produce a united Korea.

In Manchuria the policies of the United States and the Soviet Union also clash. After the war, the Soviet forces withdrew from Manchuria, removing valuable industrial equipment and allowing important Japanese military supplies to fall into the hands of the Chinese Communists. Manchuria is vital to the industrial development of China because of its deposits of iron and coal. The Chinese Communists, aided at least ideologically by Moscow, have acquired most of the vital areas of Manchuria. Although the United States has opposed Soviet policy in Manchuria, the American position was weakened by the Yalta Agreement of Roosevelt, Stalin, and Churchill. In this agreement the United States undertook to urge Chiang Kai-shek to accept a Russian lease on Port Arthur as a naval base and on Dairen as a free port with joint ownership by China and the Soviet Union of the Chinese Eastern and South Manchurian Railways which were to be consolidated into the Chinese Changchun Railway. By the treaty and related agreements between the Soviet Union and China, signed on August 14, 1945, Russia regained with American blessing much of the stake in Manchuria that she had lost in the Russo-Japanese War of 1904–5.[27]

V

After the recent war, the basic hopes of the United States in the Far East rested on the emergence of a united, strong, friendly, and democratic China, serving as a bastion of peace in eastern Asia. Toward this end the United States sent General George C. Marshall

[27] Text, *Department of State Bulletin*, XIV (February 10, 1946), 201–8.

to China in an effort to mediate the civil war and to establish a coalition government in Nanking. The Marshall Mission did not succeed as neither the Communists nor the Nationalists were prepared to accept any substantial compromise. The continued civil war, the growing weakness of the Nanking regime, the ineffectiveness of the 1947 constitution,[28] the great inflation of the currency, and the increasing economic chaos contribute toward a dark picture for the country. In Greater China, Formosa has been in revolt; Manchuria is largely in the hands of the Communists; Outer Mongolia has won formal independence; Sinkiang is moving into the Soviet orbit; and Tibet is practically independent of Nanking.

American foreign policy toward China since the turn of the century has been based on the concepts of the Open Door and the territorial integrity of the country. The concept of the Open Door presented by Secretary of State John Hay in 1899 fundamentally called for the equality of commercial opportunity for all powers in China. The concept of the territorial integrity of China enunciated on July 3, 1900, during the Boxer Rebellion embodied the preservation and not the division of the "Chinese melon." The circular note of the United States to the powers in 1900 is well worth recalling: ". . . the policy of the Government of the United States is to seek a solution which may bring about permanent safety and peace to China, preserve Chinese territorial and administrative entity, protect all rights guaranteed to friendly powers by treaty and international loans, and safeguard for the world the principle of equal and impartial trade with all parts of the Chinese Empire."[29] The violation of the Open Door and the territorial integrity of China by the Empire of Japan was one of the reasons for the outbreak of war between the United States and Japan. Secretary of State Cordell Hull in his famous note to Japan on November 26, 1941, called for agreement on "the principle of

[28] *The Constitution of the Republic of China* (New York: Chinese News Service, 1947), 25.

[29] *Papers Relating to the Foreign Relations of the United States, 1900* (Washington, 1902), 299.

inviolability of territorial integrity and sovereignty of each and all nations" and on "the principle of equality, including equality of commercial opportunity and treatment." [30]

The growing tension between the Soviet Union and the United States coupled with the civil war between the Kuomintang and the Communists has created a serious problem over the course of American foreign policy toward China. If China were still the Middle Kingdom isolated from the rest of the world, undoubtedly the best policy would be to let the Chinese settle their own civil war. But China is an important part of the world and the ideologies and struggles of the great powers have direct repercussions among the Chinese. The Great Wall is no longer a barrier in the politics of Asia.

Many Americans now believe that the failure of the United States to grant economic or military aid to China will mean a victory of the Communists throughout the country. Even if the Chiang Kai-shek regime collapses, it is not necessarily true that the Communists will be able to create a strong central government. It is quite possible that the country will experience a revival of the tuchuns who were so influential from 1916 to 1926. And even if the Communists were able to create a strong central government, it is quite possible that the leaders would be Chinese first and Communists second and that the Titos of China would be very influential.

The real basis for present American aid to China lies in the conviction that the Chiang Kai-shek government is more friendly to the United States than a Communist regime would be and that in the event of war between the United States and the Soviet Union, Nationalist China would be an asset to the West. In an effort to insure the security of the United States, an ally is needed in the Far East. If China does not play the role, Japan may be the chosen instrument. On the other hand, unlimited economic and military aid to China without any attached conditions re-

---

[30] Department of State, *Peace and War, United States Foreign Policy, 1931–1941* (Washington, 1943), 810.

sembles a blank check which the Chinese can use for any purpose. In so far as possible, American aid should be honestly used for the strengthening of a China friendly to the United States.

Since China has only recently been freed from the "unequal treaties," any effort of a foreign power to place conditions upon its aid will be met with strong opposition from an increasingly nationalistic people. American officials who represent the United States in China must display both firmness and tact: firmness in order to insure that American aid is honestly used and tact in order to accord due recognition to a country with a great cultural heritage and a prominent position in the United Nations. Across the years, China will be increasingly important to the United States in the Far East. The prophecy of President Theodore Roosevelt in 1905 may yet be realized: "Our future history will be more determined by our position on the Pacific facing China, than by our position on the Atlantic facing Europe." [31]

VI

Southeast Asia represents an area which may become a power vacuum if the forces of nationalism succeed in overthrowing foreign rule but not in establishing strong native governments. In this eventuality rivalry between the United States and the Soviet Union could easily result. Developments in Southeast Asia, indicating that the Communists are utilizing the nationalist movements for their own ends, have given concern to Washington. Independence was achieved by the Union of Burma on January 4, 1948, but the government of Premier Thakin Nu has led Burma more and more to the left. The Hukbalahaps, a leftist group in central Luzon, have been in open rebellion against the government of the Philippine Republic. Fighting has been under way between the Annamese in the Republic of Viet Nam in Indo-China and the French and between the Indonesians in the Republic of Indonesia and the Dutch. The outstanding leader of the Annamese

[31] Tyler Dennett, *Roosevelt and the Russo-Japanese War* (New York, 1925), 3.

is Ho Chi Minh who was trained in Moscow and some of the leaders of the Indonesians are sympathetic to communism. A terrorist campaign in British Malaya under the leadership of Communists has been directed at disrupting normal trade in strategic materials and in overthrowing British rule. Communist influence in Siam is not so strong as in Burma, Viet Nam, and Malaya, and the Siamese government is determined to prevent the establishment of the headquarters of any possible Southeast Asia Cominform in Bangkok.

The United States must face the possibility of Soviet penetration into Southeast Asia under the guise of promoting nationalistic movements through the native Communists. At the same time the United States has welcomed the new states of Southeast Asia into the family of nations and has urged the colonial peoples of Indo-China and of Indonesia as well as the governments of France and the Netherlands to work out a peaceful settlements of their quarrels. The future of Southeast Asia is closely related to the politics of the great powers.

Finally in the Southwest Pacific the American role is also influential. The United States has close relations with the British dominions of Australia and New Zealand and is an active member of the South Pacific Commission. In 1940, diplomatic relations were established between Washington and Canberra and in 1942 between Washington and Wellington. The United States has taken an active role in the discussions leading to the change of Western Samoa from a mandate to a trusteeship under New Zealand in 1946;[32] of the Territory of New Guinea from a mandate to a trusteeship under Australia in the same year;[33] and of Nauru from a mandate to a trusteeship under Australia, New Zealand, and Great Britain in 1947.[34] In July and August, 1947, the United

[32] Great Britain, *Parliamentary Papers*, Cmd. 7197 (Foreign Office, "Treaty Series," No. 65): *Western Samoa. Text of Trusteeship Agreement . . . December 13, 1946* (London, 1947).

[33] Great Britain, *Parliamentary Papers*, Cmd. 7200 (Foreign Office, "Treaty Series," No. 68): *New Guinea. Text . . . December 13, 1946* (London, 1947).

[34] Great Britain, *Parliamentary Papers*, Cmd. 7290 (Foreign Office, "Treaty Series," No. 89): *Nauru. Text . . . November 1, 1947* (London, 1947).

States participated in a special mission of the Trusteeship Council of the United Nations that investigated the complaints of the people of Western Samoa regarding the government of the area.

Significant is a report in July, 1947, of the Senate Committee on Foreign Relations agreeing with a House report that "because of the demonstrated strategic importance of the area [South Pacific] in that war [World War II] and its possible future strategic importance, this Government has taken an interest in the development of the area parallel to that taken in the Caribbean, though on a smaller scale."[35] The importance of the South Pacific with its island steppingstones was well demonstrated in the recent war. It is significant that the first offensive blow of the United States against Japan came in Guadalcanal in the southern Solomons.

On February 6, 1947, the United States, the United Kingdom, Australia, New Zealand, France, and the Netherlands signed an agreement at Canberra, Australia, leading to the establishment of the South Pacific Commission. The purpose of the Commission is "to provide the means by which Governments which administer nonself-governing territories in the South Pacific may co-operate with one another to promote economic and social advancement of the peoples, numbering about 2,000,000, of the fifteen non-self-governing territories in the region."[36] The area includes all the nonself-governing territories of the Pacific under the flags of the powers mentioned, located wholly or in part south of the equator and east of and including Dutch New Guinea. The organs of the South Pacific Commission are the Commission proper, composed of twelve members, a Research Council, a Conference of representatives of the dependencies, held at least once every three years, and a Secretariat. The co-operation among the powers in the South Pacific should serve as a beacon light to the rest of the world.

[35] U. S., *Senate Reports* (80th Cong., 1st Sess., Report No. 685): *Providing for Membership and Participation by the United States in the South Pacific Commission and Authorizing an Appropriation Therefor* (July 22, 1947), 2.

[36] *Ibid.*

The paramount position that the United States now holds in the Pacific places a great responsibility upon the American people. First they must be a public properly informed on an area long removed from general attention. Second they must demand leadership that is capable of understanding the complex problems of the Pacific and of guiding American policy along channels that promote respect and trust for the United States. Finally they must accept the price of power affecting millions of people in the dawning age of the Pacific.

The United States and Greece

The Truman Doctrine in Historical Perspective

By LEFTEN S. STAVRIANOS*

During the past decade Greece has assumed a constantly increasing importance in the calculations of the Western powers. In the war years Greece won recognition and acclaim as the first nation to check and repulse Fascist aggression. In the postwar years Greece won uncomfortable attention as a key position in the developing struggle between East and West. When the battle lines were drawn, Greece became the West's beleaguered outpost in Southeastern Europe. By March, 1947, President Truman deemed it necessary to inform Congress and the world, that this outpost was in jeopardy and that its preservation was essential for the security of the United States. Thus America's strategic frontiers were extended to Epirus, Macedonia and Thrace.

This concern of the West in the fate of Greece is in sharp contrast to the utter lack of interest in earlier periods. During the four centuries of Turkish domination Greece was forgotten by the West as completely as though the country had sunk to the bottom of the Mediterranean. This is well illustrated by the experience of Adamantios Koraes, the eighteenth century Greek scholar who spent many years in France. During the French Revolution he applied for a *carte de sécurité* in Paris and identified himself as a Greek. Immediately, he relates, "the eyes of everyone present were fixed upon me; some approached me as if to convince themselves that a Greek was the same as any other human."[1]

This situation changed drastically in the course of the eighteenth

---

*Leften S. Stavrianos is Associate Professor of History, Northwestern University.
[1] *Lettres inédites de Coray à Chardon de la Rochette, 1790–1796* (Paris, 1877), 122.

century. Trade between Greece and the West developed to appreciable proportions.[2] More significant was the contemporary sentimental admiration and idealization of Greek antiquity that led hundreds of Westerners to flock to Greece to view the ruins of classical civilization. Many of these travellers wrote books about their experiences. Gradually Greece ceased to be the *terra incognita* of Europe.[3]

The young American republic scarcely shared this interest in Greece. Some Yankee skippers made their way to the Eastern Mediterranean but most of them sailed directly to the great port of Smyrna. Very few considered it worth while to stop at any of the Aegean islands or ports on the Greek mainland.[4] Likewise there was no American counterpart to the stream of British, French and German travellers that visited Greece during these years. An outstanding exception was the case of young Nicholas Biddle of Philadelphia. Biddle was graduated from Princeton in 1801 and journeyed to Greece in 1806. A significant feature of his visit is that at the outset he was concerned only with the ruins of antiquity, but before he left he became interested in the position of the Greek people under Turkish rule. "The people," he noted in his diary, "hate their masters with the most rooted enmity, and wound up as their feelings are, the slightest spark of either foreign assistance or a favorable moment is all that is wanted to enflame the whole nation into rebellion."[5]

[2] F. Beaujour, *A View of the Commerce of Greece* (London, 1800).

[3] See Nicolae Iorga, "Une vingtaine de voyageurs dans l'Orient européen," *Revue historique du sud-est européen*, V (October–December, 1928), 288–354; Panos Morphopoulos, *L'image de la Grèce dans les voyageurs français du seizième siècle au début du dix-huitième* (Baltimore, 1940); and B. H. Stern, *The Rise of Romantic Hellenism in English Literature, 1732–1786* (Menasha, Wisconsin, 1940).

[4] Samuel E. Morison, *Maritime History of Massachusetts 1783–1860* (Boston, 1921), chap. xviii.

[5] William Nickerson Bates, "Nicholas Biddle's Journey to Greece in 1806," *Proceedings of the Numismatics and Antiquarian Society of Philadelphia*, XXVIII (December, 1917), 178. For the interesting story of the short-lived "Greek Colony" of New Smyrna, Florida, founded in 1768 by a Scottish physician, Dr. Andrew Turnbull, see Carita Doggett, *Dr. Andrew Turnbull and the New Smyrna Colony of Florida* (Jacksonville, Florida, 1919).

The rebellion that Biddle foresaw came in 1821 and it stimulated the first significant contact between the American republic and the Greek nation. The war of independence excited the imagination and aroused the sympathy of the American people. Not only was it a crusade of the descendants of the ancient Greeks against the Moslem infidel,[6] but it was also a revolutionary cause—a struggle for freedom from tyranny, similar to the American revolution only a few decades earlier. Accordingly philhellenic sentiment swept the country, and funds and relief supplies were contributed on a large scale to aid the Greek revolutionaries. This popular interest was reflected in Congress, where Daniel Webster and Henry Clay strongly championed the Greek cause and urged the appointment of a commission of inquiry to ascertain whether the situation warranted American recognition of Greece as an independent nation. Due to the insistence of Secretary of State, John Quincy Adams, who was opposed to any intervention in European affairs, the commission was not appointed and the American Government refused to take any official action. Nevertheless the activities of the philhellenes definitely had made the American people aware of Greece and the Greek people. This constitutes the opening chapter in the history of American-Greek relations.[7]

Following this flurry in the eighteen-twenties, Greece was forgotten by an America engrossed in the opening up and exploitation of the Western lands. When the Greeks on the island of Crete revolted against their Turkish overlords in 1866 and fought three years for union with the motherland, the response in the United States was relatively feeble. A few veteran philhellenes organized a Cretan relief committee, but with the exception of Boston and New York, the support was negligible. Despite appeals

---

[6] See Virginia Penn, "Philhellenism in England," *Slavonic Review*, XIV (January, 1936), 363–71; XIV (April, 1936), 647–60; "Philhellenism in Europe, 1821–28," *Slavonic Review*, XVI (April, 1938), 638–53; and David P. Whitehill, *The Philhellenic Movement in France, 1821–1830* (Unpublished Harvard University Ph.D. Thesis, 1939).

[7] See Myrtle A. Cline, *American Attitude toward the Greek War of Independence* (Atlanta, 1930); H. J. Booras, *Hellenic Independence and American's Contribution to the Cause* (Rutland, Vermont, 1934); and the works therein cited.

for American recognition of Cretan independence, the administration followed John Quincy Adams' policy of non-interference in Turkish minority controversies.[8]

II

The most significant developments in the relations between the two countries during the decades following the War of Independence were the activities of American Protestant missionaries in Greece and the emigration of Greek peasants to the United States. The missionaries began their work about the time of the Greek revolution. Within a few years the various American Protestant denominations established several "stations" in Athens and the provinces. The results were disappointing. In comparison to the Armenians, the Greeks were quite unresponsive to Protestantism. One reason was the sectarianism of the missionaries, who quarrelled amongst themselves over questions of tenets and religious forms. Much more important was the tendency of the Greeks to identify religion with nationality, so that attempts at proselytism met with popular opposition and occasional interference by the government. It was not until the end of the nineteenth century, when the missionaries turned from proselytism to general education and health work, that they met with a response commensurate with their labors.[9]

Immigration from Greece to the United States was very limited until the last decade of the nineteenth century. Between 1821 and 1890 only 2,706 immigrants arrived, in contrast to 476,980 in the four decades between 1891 and 1930. With the passage of the Immigration Act of 1924 Greek immigration virtually ended, the quota being set at 307 persons a year. The great majority of the immigrants were peasants who left their villages

---

[8] Details in Arthur J. May, "Crete and the United States, 1866–1869," *Journal of Modern History*, XVI (December, 1944), 286–93.

[9] For a critical analysis of missionary enterprise by the first American minister to Greece, see Charles K. Tuckerman, *The Greeks of To-Day* (New York, 1872), 211–30; and for the missionary viewpoint, see Julius Richter, *A History of Protestant Missions in the Near East* (New York, 1910).

for economic reasons. Accordingly they arrived in the United States with the intention of earning as much as possible in a few years and then returning to the mother country. Many did return, but the majority remained and, as a rule, engaged in various lines of business.[10]

More significant than its influence on the United States was the impact of this immigration on Greece itself. It meant in the first place an enormous boost for the precarious economy of the mother country. Greek-Americans subscribed heavily to Greek Government loans and contributed generously for the relief of earthquake victims at Corinth, for the establishment of Athens College, and for general relief following the two World Wars. In addition the thrifty Greek immigrants regularly sent money to their relatives back home, principally for buying real estate or for lifting mortgages. During the decade between 1919 and 1928, their remittances averaged no less than $52,600,000 per year, the high point being $121,000,000 in 1920.[11]

As significant as this economic influence, though less tangible, has been the leavening effect of the immigrant who returned to his native village with American ideas as well as American dollars. As Arnold J. Toynbee has put it:

It is a strange experience to spend a night in some remote mountain-village of Greece, and see Americanism and Hellenism face to face. Hellenism is represented by the village schoolmaster. He wears a black coat, talks a little French, and can probably read Homer; but his longest journey has been to the normal school at Athens, and it has not altered his belief that the icon in the neighboring monastery was made by St. Luke and the Bulgar beyond the mountains by the Devil. On the other side of you sits the returned immigrant, chatting irrepressibly in his queer version of the "American language," and showing you the news-

[10] Henry Pratt Fairchild, *Greek Immigration to the United States* (New Haven, 1911); Francis J. Brown and Joseph S. Roucek, *One America; the History, Contributions and Present Problems of Our Racial and National Minorities* (New York, 1946), 242–56.

[11] In the thirties the remittances fell off sharply, the chief reasons being the depression in the United States and the weakening of family ties with the cessation of large-scale immigration. See Eliot G. Mears, "The Unique Position in Greek Trade of Emigrant Remittances," *Quarterly Journal of Economics*, XXXVII (May, 1923), 535–40, and "Financial Aspects of American Immigration," *Economic Journal*, XXXIII (September, 1923), 332–42.

papers which are mailed to him every fortnight from the States . . . .
his greatest gift to his country will be his American point of view.[12]

It is not too much to say that this immigration constituted the
most important single development in the relations between the
two countries during the century prior to 1914.

III

With the conclusion of World War I the United States was
involved in the negotiations for a near eastern settlement, including the question of the adjustment of the Greek frontiers. Greece
laid claim to southern Albania, western and eastern Thrace, and
Smyrna with its hinterland. Britain and France generally supported these demands, but Italy opposed them consistently and
strenuously because they conflicted with her own aspirations in
the Near East. The United States also opposed most of the Greek
claims but for different reasons—the claim to Smyrna because
the port was the natural outlet for Asia Minor; the claim to Thrace
because Bulgaria needed access to the Aegean; and the claim to
southern Albania because the population was predominantly
Albanian.[13]

As a result of this disagreement it proved impossible to conclude
a treaty with Turkey before the last American delegate left Paris
in December, 1919. The United States therefore did not participate in the negotiation of the Sèvres Treaty (August 10, 1920) by
which Greece received Thrace and Smyrna. The United States
also was not involved in the Greco-Turkish War that followed, or

[12] N. Forbes, A. J. Toynbee, D. Mitrany, and D. G. Hogarth, *The Balkans; a History
of Bulgaria, Serbia, Greece, Rumania, Turkey* (London, 1915), 249.

[13] The United States favored a slight extension of the Greek frontier at the expense
of Albania and Bulgaria, but Venizelos, with British and French support, claimed
much more territory. It should be noted also that Wilson agreed in May, 1919 to
the landing of Greek forces in Smyrna in order to forestall a similar move by Italy.
See A. A. Pallis, *Greece's Anatolian Venture—and After; a Survey of the Diplomatic and
Political Aspects of the Greek Expedition to Asia Minor, 1915–1922* (London, 1937), 140–48;
Harry N. Howard, *The Partition of Turkey; a Diplomatic History, 1913–1923* (Norman,
Oklahoma, 1931), *passim;* and the references therein cited.

in the negotiation of the Lausanne Treaty (July 24, 1923) which deprived Greece of all her gains excepting western Thrace.[14]

Thus the United States played a minor role in Greek affairs during World War I and immediately thereafter. By contrast, the period between the two World Wars marked a high point in American influence in Greece. The United States took a leading part in providing relief for the 1,200,000 refugees who poured into Greece following the Asia Minor disaster. For a time the most important foreign agency operating in Greece was the American Red Cross which, through its extensive distribution of food, clothing and medicine, kept alive half a million refugees. In addition the Near East Relief, although concerned primarily with war orphans, gave freely to all classes of refugees. Not only did it distribute foodstuffs and clothing, but it sent doctors, nurses and medical supplies to needy centers.[15]

American organizations also increased tremendously their educational activities. With the exodus of the Greek and American populations from Turkey at the end of the war, a number of American mission schools there found themselves without students and accordingly moved to Greece, where they were hospitably received. The outstanding American school is the excellent Athens College, founded in 1925, and comparable to the other American colleges in Constantinople, Beirut, Smyrna, and Sofia. Note

[14] An American delegation attended the Lausanne Conference but stated that while it would not take part in negotiations or assume engagements, it would be present at all discussions and would expect to be treated on a footing of perfect equality with all other delegations. The main concern of the American delegation apparently was to safeguard the Open Door in the Near East in behalf of American oil companies. Howard, *Partition of Turkey*, 299; Edward H. Bierstadt, *The Great Betrayal; a Survey of the Near East Problem* (New York, 1924), chaps. vii and x.

[15] Various British organizations also participated in the relief work, and on September 29, 1923, the Council of the League of Nations established the Refugee Settlement Commission to secure productive employment for refugees. Harold B. Allen, *Come Over into Macedonia; the Story of a Ten-Year Adventure in Uplifting a War-Torn People* (New Brunswick, 1943); Laird Archer, *Balkan Journal; an Unofficial Observer in Greece* (New York, 1944); James L. Barton, *A Story of Near East Relief (1915–1930); an Interpretation* (New York, 1930); Henry Morgenthau, *I Was Sent to Athens* (New York, 1929); and F. A. Ross, C. L. Fry and E. Sibley, *The Near East and American Philanthropy; a Survey Conducted under the Guidance of the General Committee of the Near East Survey* (New York, 1929).

should also be made of the American School of Classical Studies which was founded in 1881 and which has conducted excavations in various parts of the country, including Corinth, Olynthus, and the Agora in Athens.[16]

In addition to these cultural activities, the commercial relations between the two countries increased markedly during the postwar years. Prior to 1914 Greece traded mostly with the great powers of Europe: Britain, Germany, Austria-Hungary, France, and Russia. After World War I trade with America increased so rapidly that by the mid-twenties the United States had risen to first place as the source of Greek imports and to second place as a market for Greek products. This situation prevailed until the depression, when Germany quickly outstripped all other countries in both the export and import trade.[17]

Such is the history of American-Greek relations prior to World War II. There is little doubt that during these years American influence in Greece increased more rapidly than that of any other great power. Yet the fact remains that Greece, both politically and economically, was inconsequential in American calculations. The trade between the two countries was basic for Greece but insignificant for the United States. And as for strategic considerations, Greece was far beyond the range of American interests. It was very natural, therefore, that the United States, even after being involved in World War II, should follow a hands-off policy with respect to Greece, and consider that country as lying within the British sphere of primacy.

IV

The first agreement in accordance with this policy was reached at the Quebec Conference (August, 1943) where the delicate

[16] Louis E. Lord, *A History of the American School of Classical Studies at Athens* (Cambridge, Mass., 1947). For a list of all the American organizations now functioning in Greece, see the letter of George E. Edman, First Secretary of the American Embassy in Athens, to the *New York Times*, June 7, 1948.

[17] An excellent analysis of Greek economy is to be found in Eliot G. Mears, *Greece Today; the Aftermath of the Refugee Impact* (Stanford, 1929). For the post-depression period see *South-Eastern Europe; a Political and Economic Survey Prepared by the Information Department of the Royal Institute of International Affairs* (London, 1939), 157.

problem of Greek domestic politics was discussed. The reason
was the precarious position of King George II, who had fled from
Greece with the 1941 German invasion and had established a
government in exile. Due to the growing strength of the EAM
leftist resistance forces[18] and to the popular association of the
King with the prewar Metaxas dictatorship, much sentiment
had developed against the continuation of the monarchy after
the war.

The position of Britain on this issue was made clear on June 23,
1943, when the British ambassador in Cairo advised Emmanuel
Tsouderos, premier of the Greek exile government, that ". . . it
is now time that His Majesty should state publicly over the radio
that the political question will be settled after the war by the free
election of a Constituent Convention."[19] In accordance with this
advice the King declared over the Cairo Radio on July 4 that
". . . free and general elections will be held for a Constituent
Convention and . . . these elections will be held within six
months after liberation. . . ."[20] The situation was now complicated by the arrival from Greece (August 4) of representatives
of all the guerrilla organizations and of the political parties. These
representatives submitted on August 17 a memorandum to Premier
Tsouderos in which they expressed the view that, for the sake of
national unity, the King should not return to Greece until after
a plebiscite had been held. The Tsouderos cabinet agreed with
this view, passed a resolution to that effect, and presented it to
the King.[21]

Faced with this united front of the guerrilla organizations, the
political parties and his own cabinet, the King addressed a message

[18] The principal resistance organizations in occupied Greece were the leftist EAM
(National Liberation Front), the comparatively conservative EDES (Greek Democratic National League), and EKKA (National and Social Liberation). The EAM
was by all odds the strongest. For bibliographical references to the developments
within Greece, see L. S. Stavrianos and E. P. Panagopoulos, "Present-Day Greece,"
Journal of Modern History, XX (June, 1948), 149–58.

[19] E. Tsouderos, Ἑλληνικές Ἀνωμαλίες στή Μέση Ἀνατολή [*Greek Anomalies in
the Middle East*] (Athens, 1945), 59.

[20] Full text of speech in *ibid.*, 60–61.

[21] Texts of memorandum and resolution in *ibid.*, 64–65.

to Roosevelt and Churchill asking for advice.[22] The message was discussed at the Quebec Conference where, according to Secretary of State Hull, the following decision was reached:

> Roosevelt and Churchill agreed that the British Foreign Office should reply to the King, supporting his contention that he was prepared to return to Greece as soon as possible, and that he would then submit the question of the royal house to a plebiscite. The President said this Government would not take any different position.[23]

The significance of this incident is that it illustrates that British policy was the determining factor in Greek affairs at this time, and that the United States recognized and accepted British leadership. This had already been foreshadowed at the Casablanca Conference (January, 1943) where Roosevelt agreed that Britain should be in complete charge of Allied military operations and corollary diplomatic policy in the Middle East.[24] When the Greek armed forces in the Middle East mutinied in April, 1944, it was the British again who took the lead in suppressing the mutiny and in establishing a new exile government under Premier George Papandreou.[25] Likewise the great majority of Allied agents in occupied Greece were British, and the few American officers who reached Greece in September, 1943 were dependent upon the British mission.[26]

This British primacy in Greece was strengthened further by

---

[22] Text in *ibid.*, 66–67.

[23] *Memoirs of Cordell Hull* (New York, 1948), II, 1240. Both Roosevelt and Churchill sent letters to King George supporting his position that he should return to Greece before a plebiscite. Texts of letters in Tsouderos, *op. cit.*, 67–68. In December 1944, when Churchill intervened with armed force in the Greek civil war, Ernest Bevin, then a member of the Churchill cabinet, defended the intervention on the basis of the Quebec Conference agreement. He declared that his government's plans for Greece were taken to Quebec, where they were approved and initialed by Roosevelt. "Highly authoritative official circles" in Washington at once replied that "The 'proposals' concerning Greece referred to by Mr. Bevin as having been initialled at the Quebec Conference, concerned Greece as a military theatre for the British. . . . " *New York Times*, December 14, 1944. This suggests that a military agreement was reached at Quebec, in addition to the decision described by Hull concerning the King's return.

[24] *New York Times*, December 17, 1944.

[25] Tsouderos, *op. cit.*, 130–85.

[26] Stephanos Saraphis, 'Ο ΕΛΑΣ [*ELAS*] (Athens, 1946), 169–71, 184, 185.

Roosevelt's decision in the summer of 1944 to accept an Anglo-Russian division of the Balkans.[27]   The initiative in this matter was taken by the British.   On May 30, 1944 Ambassador Halifax handed a written communication to Secretary Hull inquiring whether the United States had any objections to an agreement between Britain and Russia, whereby Rumanian affairs would be the concern of the Soviet Government and Greek affairs the concern of the British Government.   It was explained that this was intended to serve only as a temporary wartime arrangement and that it would not affect the rights and responsibilities of the three great powers at the peace settlement.

Hull replied that he would give this proposal serious consideration, but added that he was opposed to spheres of influence in the Balkans which he feared would sow the seeds of future conflict and weaken the postwar international security organization.   On the following day, May 31, Churchill sent a telegram to Roosevelt urging strongly the acceptance of the proposed agreement and explaining once more that it would apply only for the war period and did not involve spheres of influence.   Churchill also revealed in this telegram that the British Government had first suggested this agreement to Russian Ambassador Gusev in London and that Moscow had replied on May 18 that it was agreeable but had inquired whether Washington had been consulted and had approved.   On June 8 Churchill sent another message in which he repudiated again the idea of spheres of influence and added that it seemed reasonable to him that Russia should deal with Rumania and Bulgaria, and Britain with Yugoslavia and Greece.

This casual inclusion of Bulgaria and Yugoslavia in the negotiations meant that the proposed agreement would cover the whole Balkan peninsula.   Secretary Hull was convinced more than ever that the plan should be opposed.   Accordingly Roosevelt on June 10 sent a negative reply to Churchill, expressing the opinion that even though the agreement were limited to military affairs, it would lead to spheres of influence and engender future trouble

[27] The following account is based on the *Memoirs of Cordell Hull*, II, 1451–59.

between Britain and Russia. The President concluded that he favored consultative machinery for the Balkans to resolve misunderstandings and to prevent the development of exclusive zones of influence.

Churchill replied the following day in "a long and forceful telegram" to the President, stating that a tripartite committee would be too cumbersome and that in any case it would be overridden in emergencies by direct interchanges amongst the leaders of the Big Three. He urged, therefore, that the proposed Anglo-Russian agreement be given a three months' trial, following which it would be renewed or ended as seemed desirable. Roosevelt now decided to accede to Churchill's request. Without consulting his Secretary of State, Roosevelt replied the next day (June 12), accepting the three months' proposal and adding that care should be exercised to avoid the establishment of postwar spheres of influence.

So far as is known, the provision for a review after three months never was acted upon. On the contrary, the division of the Balkans was extended when Churchill and Eden visited Moscow in October, 1944. According to reports from the American embassies in Moscow and Ankara, it was agreed at the Moscow meeting that Russia would have a 75/25 or 80/20 predominance in Bulgaria, Hungary, and Rumania, while Britain and Russia would exercise equal influence in Yugoslavia.[28]

The significance of these agreements for the future is apparent. Theoretically they were limited to the war period, but the dividing line between war and peace scarcely could be sharply drawn. During the vital and formative transition period between liberation and the peace settlement, Russia obviously would expect a free hand in the northern Balkans and Britain a similar freedom in Greece.

It is equally apparent from these negotiations that the American position differed fundamentally from the British and Russian.

[28] Greece is not mentioned in Hull's account of this agreement, but obviously British influence in that country was to be predominant, if not exclusive.

The basic reason was that Roosevelt's whole program assumed a postwar system of joint tripartite action for political and economic reconstruction. Exclusive spheres of influence obviously were incompatible with such a concept. Hence the reluctance of Roosevelt and Hull to accept the British plan, and their insistence that it should not lead to exclusive zones. These conditions may have been unrealistic and utopian, but there is little doubt that they were taken seriously by the President.

Churchill discovered this to be the case when he intervened in Greek affairs in December, 1944. The occasion was the dispute that developed when the Papandreou government, that had returned to Greece in October, insisted that all guerrilla forces be disbanded. The EAM leaders agreed to this, but on the condition that the government also dissolve certain regular army units that were known to be strongly royalist. Papandreou first accepted this condition but later rejected it at the insistence of the British ambassador in Athens, Reginald Leeper. When a deadlock developed, General Ronald Scobie, in his capacity as Commander-in-Chief of the Land Forces in Greece, issued an order for the disbandment of all guerrilla bands by December 10. The EAM members of the cabinet resigned on December 1 in protest against what they considered foreign intervention in domestic Greek affairs. The climax came on December 3 when Greek police fired on an EAM demonstration in Athens, inflicting a considerable number of casualties.[29]

Two days later the new Secretary of State, Edward R. Stettinius, Jr., expressed the disapproval of the United States in sharp terms. Taking advantage of a political crisis in Italy, precipitated when Churchill vetoed the appointment of Count Sforza as foreign minister, Stettinius issued the following statement:

[29] For the British and Greek Governments' version of these negotiations, see Great Britain, *Parliamentary Papers*, Cmd. 6592, *Documents Regarding the Situation in Greece, January, 1945* (London, 1945); G. Papandreou, ʻΗ ἀπελενθέρωσις τῆς Ἑλλάδος [*The Liberation of Greece*] (Athens, 1945), 145–224. For the EAM version, see Saraphis, *op. cit.*, 433–51; and the *National Liberation Front (EAM) White Book* (New York, 1945), 13–47.

Since Italy is an area of combined responsibility, we have reaffirmed to both the British and Italian Governments that we expect the Italians to work out their problems of government along democratic lines without influence from outside.

And then Stettinius added, with an unmistakable reference to Greece,

This policy would apply to an even more pronounced degree with regard to Governments of the United Nations in their liberated territories.[30]

A year and a half later Churchill described the attitude of the State Department at this time as "sourly critical," and added that, "Even President Roosevelt, whom I kept constantly informed about our policy, remained silent under a series of personal protesting telegrams from me."[31] This indicates that the Stettinius statement expressed the views of the President as well as of the State Department. Roosevelt apparently regarded British actions in Greece as an unfortunate manifestation of the exclusive sphere of influence attitude, and refused to accept them as justifiable under the terms of the Anglo-Russian agreement as he interpreted it.[32] The President also had to take into account, however, the fact that the war still was in progress and that the grand alliance had to be preserved at all costs. Hence his refusal to intervene further in the Greek affair despite appeals by EAM spokesmen.[33] His views at this time are clearly expressed in his annual message to Congress on January 6, 1945.

[30] *New York Times*, December 6, 1944.

[31] Winston Churchill, "If I Were an American," *Life*, XXII (April 14, 1947), 112.

[32] The President is reported to have severely criticized in private Churchill's Greek policy. Elliott Roosevelt, *As He Saw It* (New York, 1946), 222–23. On January 23, 1945 the Foreign Office received from Washington a note defining the bases of American foreign policy and emphasizing the right of liberated peoples to governments of their own choice. *New York Times*, January 23, 1945.

[33] When the American ambassador in Athens was presented with a memorandum supporting the EAM case, he explained to the emissary that the United States was preoccupied on the Western front and in the Pacific, and had agreed to leave decisions in the Middle East to Britain. Accordingly he would transmit the memorandum to Washington but American intervention on behalf of one side or the other was out of the question. H. A. Thompson, "Athens during the Civil War: 1944," *University of Toronto Quarterly*, XV (January, 1946), 170–81.

. . . we shall not hesitate to use our influence—and to use it now—to secure, as far as is humanly possible, the fulfillment of the principles of the Atlantic Charter. We have not shrunk from the military responsibilities brought on by this war. We cannot and will not shrink from the political responsibilities which follow in the wake of battle.

At the same time he warned against dissension among the allies and emphasized the necessity for continued unity in war and peace:

The nearer we come to vanquishing our enemies the more we inevitably become conscious of differences among the victors.

We must not let those differences divide us and blind us to our more important common and continuing interests in winning the war and building the peace. . . .

I should not be frank if I did not admit concern about many situations —the Greek and Polish, for example. But those situations are not as easy or as simple to deal with as some spokesmen, whose sincerity I do not question, would have us believe. We have obligations, not necessarily legal, to the exiled governments, to the underground leaders, and to our major allies who came much nearer the shadows than we did.

This is reminiscent of Woodrow Wilson's readiness after World War I to accept distasteful compromises in the peace treaties in order to assure the establishment of the League of Nations. Likewise Roosevelt now admitted his concern about developments in Greece and Poland, but asserted his willingness to accept them in order to win the war and build the United Nations. "Perfectionism," he declared, "no less than isolationism or imperialism or power politics, may obstruct the paths to international peace."[34]

Roosevelt acted in accordance with this philosophy at the Yalta Conference the following month. Greece was not discussed at the conference because the British a few days earlier had rushed through the Varkiza agreement by which the EAM agreed to disarm in return for certain political guarantees.[35] As regards eastern Europe, Roosevelt obtained what he regarded as a reasonable compromise in the form of provisions for the broadening of the Warsaw and Belgrade regimes and for the holding of free elections as soon as possible. Roosevelt also secured the adoption

[34] *Congressional Record*, 79th Cong., 1st Sess., January 6, 1945, XCI, 69.
[35] Richard Capell, *Simiomata; a Greek Note Book 1944–1945* (London, 1946), 162.

of the Declaration on Liberated Europe providing that the Big Three would "jointly assist" the peoples of the liberated and former satellite states "to form interim governmental authorities broadly representative of all democratic elements in the population and pledged to the earliest possible establishment, through free elections of governments responsive to the will of the people." [36]

It was Roosevelt's hope that these Yalta agreements would check the trend towards exclusive spheres of influence and lay the foundation for effective postwar co-operation among the Big Three. [37] The events of the following few months shattered this hope. In Italy no effort was made to apply the Declaration on Liberated Europe. In Greece the political liberties guaranteed in the Varkiza pact were nullified to a very considerable degree by rampant reaction. Likewise in Rumania, Poland, Yugoslavia and Bulgaria, the governments were coming increasingly under communist and Russian control, and moving in precisely the opposite direction from that which Roosevelt had envisaged.

These developments inevitably strained the relations among the great powers. Russia rejected western interference in eastern Europe on the ground that the 1944 Anglo-Russian agreement accepted Soviet predominance in the northern Balkans in return for British predominance in Greece. Churchill recognized the strength of the Soviet position. In a letter to Roosevelt, dated March 8, 1945, Churchill, after deploring Russian actions in Rumania, commented as follows:

> We have been hampered in our protests against these developments by the fact that, in order to have the freedom to save Greece, Eden and I at Moscow in October recognized that Russia should have a largely preponderant voice in Rumania and Bulgaria while we took the lead

[36] Stalin is said to have regretted later this commitment to representative governments. See Philip E. Mosely, *Face to Face with Russia* (Foreign Policy Association, *Headline Series*, No. 70, New York, July–August, 1948), 23.

[37] On his return, Roosevelt declared before a joint session of Congress that: "I think the Crimean Conference was a successful effort by the three leading nations to find a common ground for peace. It spells—and it ought to spell—the end of the system of unilateral action, exclusive alliances, and spheres of influence, and balance of power, and all the other expedients which have been tried for centuries and have always failed." *Congressional Record*, 79th Cong., 1st Sess., March 1, 1945, XCI, 1622.

in Greece. Stalin adhered very strictly to this understanding during the thirty days' fighting against the Communists and ELAS in the city of Athens, in spite of the fact that all this was most disagreeable to him and those around him.[38]

When the Western powers persisted in making representations concerning developments in eastern Europe, the Soviets pointed an accusing finger at the conditions in Greece on the other side of the Iron Curtain. As James Byrnes put it, "Whenever the Soviets were faced with an issue that annoyed them or placed them on the defensive it was standard operating procedure for them to gather up a sheaf of British and American press reports from Greece and launch a counterattack."[39]

Thus the more the wartime unity of the Big Three disintegrated, the more Greece became the bone of contention between East and West. Inevitably this meant the increasing involvement of the United States in Greek affairs. It was not without significance that the year which began with Yalta ended with the visit of the *U.S.S. Providence* to Athens.

V

At the various international conferences that were held in 1945 and 1946, America's Greek policy shifted from a position of neutrality to one of strong support for Britain against Russian attacks. At the Potsdam Conference (July, 1945) Byrnes did not take sides when the Greek question was raised.[40] At the London Conference of Foreign Ministers (September, 1945) he directly challenged Molotov on Greece and maintained that the Greek Government was representative of the people in contrast to the Groza regime in Rumania.[41] In the same month the State Department announced, in the face of Soviet objections, that the United States would take equal part and "responsibility" in the Greek elec-

[38] *New York Times*, October 18, 1947.
[39] James Byrnes, *Speaking Frankly* (New York, 1947), 73–74.
[40] *Ibid.*, 73.
[41] *Ibid.*, 98–99.

tions.[42]   When the Greek premier and the leaders of several political parties of the center and left urged postponement of the
elections because of rightist excesses in the provinces, the American *chargé d'affaires* in Athens supported the Foreign Office by
stating that Washington was opposed to postponement.[43]   The
personnel of the American-British-French mission that observed
the elections (March 31, 1946) was predominantly American, and
its report, to the effect that the election results accurately reflected
the views of the population, was strongly defended in the United
States.[44]   Finally the American representative at the Paris Peace
Conference publicly pledged United States aid to Greece in case
of aggression.[45]   This obviously was intended as a sop for the
Greeks, whose territorial claims against Bulgaria and Albania
had not received American support.   The pledge also represented,
however, another indication of the gradual abandonment of the
Yalta policy of tripartite accord in favor of a policy of co-operation
with Britain to keep the Soviet Union out of the Mediterranean.

The center of interest now shifted to the United Nations Security
Council where the Greek question was raised three times within
a year.[46]   The first occasion was in February, 1946 when the Russians charged that British troops and general British policy in
Greece constituted a threat to world peace.   During the long
and bitter debates between Bevin and Vyshinsky, the American
representative, Edward R. Stettinius, Jr., gave effective though
unobtrusive support to the British position.   He did not introduce
a resolution specifically absolving Britain, which was what Bevin
demanded.   Instead he proposed that the Council "refrain from
intervention," and this was the decision finally taken by the Coun-

[42] *Department of State Bulletin*, XIII (September 26, 1945), 283; *New York Times*,
September 21, 1945.

[43] *New York Times*, March 30, 1946.

[44] Department of State (Publication 2522), *Report of the Allied Mission to Observe
the Greek Elections* (Washington, 1946).

[45] *New York Times*, October 12, 1946.

[46] An excellent analysis of American policy at these meetings of the Security Council
is available in John C. Campbell, *The United States in World Affairs, 1945–1947* (New
York, 1947), *passim*.

cil. But in proposing this, Stettinius declared that his government was satisfied, "after thorough consideration," that the presence of British troops in Greece did not endanger international peace. In addition he stated that the United States favored ". . . the rapid withdrawal of foreign troops from the territory of any member of the United Nations occupied during the war, if the Government of the Member State desires their departure."[47] This reference to the desire of the state concerned covered the presence of British troops in Greece, as well as of American troops in China, Brazil and elsewhere.

When the Ukrainian Government brought the Greek issue before the Security Council for the second time in September, 1946, the American representative, Herschel Johnson, was much more outspoken than Stettinius, and vigorously supported Britain and Greece. He stated that it was "entirely beyond the realm of credulity" that Greece should have aggressive designs against its neighbors, and he referred to the British troops in Greece as "a stabilizing factor." He added:

> In fact, I welcome the opportunity which has been presented to the Council to clear the British and Greek Governments of the serious accusations leveled against them. I hope and expect that the Council will reject this motion by a large majority.[48]

Johnson thus was asking for precisely what Bevin had demanded the first time the Greek question was brought before the Security Council—a vote of confidence for British policy in Greece. In addition Johnson stated that a vote of confidence would not settle the border troubles of Greece and he proposed, therefore, that a Council sub-committee investigate the situation on both sides of Greece's northern frontiers. His proposal was defeated by Russian veto and the Council dropped the Ukrainian charges from its agenda over Soviet and Polish objections.

Nothing had been settled, but America's new position on the

---

[47] United Nations, Security Council, *Official Records*, 1st year, 1st series, No. 1, p. 111.

[48] *Ibid.*, 1st year, 2nd series, No. 215, p. 366.

Greek question now was evident. In the February meeting of the Council Stettinius had spoken quietly and infrequently, almost as a bystander seeking compromise and conciliation. In the September meeting Johnson talked frequently and vigorously, backing Britain and Greece to the hilt. And while he did so, an American naval squadron was cruising off the Greek coast in what Secretary of the Navy Forrestal frankly described as a display of power to support United States interests in the Near East.[49] It is significant that when the *U.S.S. Missouri* visited Greece in April, British officers expressed disapproval of the presence of American warships in regions hitherto under British influence.[50] But by the autumn of the same year they welcomed an American squadron as a token of support for their increasingly precarious position in Greece. Thus it might be said that the United States now was not merely backing the hard-pressed British; she was rather in the process, consciously or unconsciously, of assuming their traditional primacy in Greece.[51]

VI

Since liberation in October, 1944 Britain had bolstered the various Athens governments with an army stationed in Greece and with financial aid totalling £134 million by March 31, 1947. This policy was successful in keeping "friendly" governments in office. Since these governments, however, failed to take root, they remained dependent on British support. Despite the financial aid, the Greek economy failed to show any appreciable improvement during the two years following liberation. Likewise the military aid did not prevent the development of an insurgent guerrilla force of 10,000 men by the end of 1946. This situation led to a growing demand within the ranks of the British Labor

[49] *New York Times*, August 27, October 1, 1946.

[50] *Ibid.*, April 11, 1946.

[51] The changing relationships of Britain and the United States in the Mediterranean area are analyzed in William Reitzel, *The Mediterranean; Its Role in America's Foreign Policy* (New York, 1948), *passim*.

Party for the adoption of a new policy in Greece. A British All-Party Parliamentary Mission that investigated the situation in August, 1946 was extremely critical of the existing state of affairs and recommended "That the opportunity given by the return of the King should be used to initiate an entirely new policy in and towards Greece."[52]

Thus by the close of 1946 a political vacuum had developed in Greece, a vacuum created by the weakness of the Athens regime and by the increasing doubt in Britain as to the wisdom of continuing a policy that had proven burdensome financially and unrewarding politically. Since the United States by this time was committed to the policy of keeping Russia out of the Mediterranean, it followed naturally that she should take measures to fill the vacuum. These measures included the sending of an economic mission to Greece, the sponsoring of a United Nations investigation of Greek border troubles, and finally, the enunciation of the Truman Doctrine.

In October, 1946 the Greek Premier, Constantine Tsaldaris, appealed to Secretary Byrnes for financial assistance[53] and for the appointment of an American mission to study the economic problems of Greece. Subsequently Paul Porter was appointed to head the mission which arrived in Greece in January, 1947, with instructions to estimate the extent of "foreign or international aid" necessary for the restoration of the Greek economy.[54]

In addition to requesting American economic aid, Premier Tsaldaris complained to the United Nations that Albania, Yugoslavia, and Bulgaria were supporting the Greek guerrillas and thereby undermining the territorial integrity of Greece. Accordingly the Security Council in December, 1946 considered the Greek question for the third time. After the usual accusations and counter-accusations, the American representative, Herschel

[52] *Report of the British Parliamentary Delegation to Greece, August, 1946* (London, His Majesty's Stationary Office), 15.

[53] For figures on American economic aid to Greece since liberation, see "Aid to Greece and Turkey," *Department of State Bulletin, Supplement*, XVI (May 4, 1947), 873.

[54] For summary of the mission's report, see *ibid.*, 898–909.

Johnson, proposed once more that a United Nations commission be appointed to investigate the alleged border violations. The Soviet delegate at first was opposed, but after a personal appeal by Byrnes to Molotov, the Council voted unanimously in favor of the proposed investigation. The commission, on which all members of the Security Council were represented, gathered in Athens at the end of January, 1947, later moving to Salonica and the border districts.[55]

While this United Nations mission and the Porter economic mission were still in Greece, and before they had made their recommendations, the Truman administration decided to take immediate and decisive unilateral action. Word had come from London on February 24, 1947 that Britain would be unable to give further economic aid to Greece and Turkey after March 31, and planned to withdraw the 16,000 remaining British troops in Greece shortly after that date.[56] Faced with this imminent British withdrawal, the President and his advisers concluded that American assumption of British responsibilities in Greece was necessary to prevent that country from becoming a Soviet outpost in the Mediterranean. Recourse to the United Nations was rejected as impractical, due to lack of time and financial resources, and hence the President's message to Congress on March 12 requested an appropriation for assistance to Greece and Turkey in the amounts of 300 million dollars and 100 million dollars respectively. Russia was not mentioned anywhere in the message. The emphasis rather was on the defense of free institutions against totalitarianism. Nevertheless the objectives behind the message were clear:

The gravity of the situation which confronts the world today necessitates my appearance before a joint session of the Congress.

The foreign policy and the national security of this country are involved. . . .

The very existence of the Greek state is today threatened by the terror-

[55] For the details of the negotiations see Byrnes, *op. cit.*, 302–3; United Nations, Security Council, *Official Records*, 1st year, 2nd series, No. 24–28, pp. 529–701.

[56] "Aid to Greece and Turkey," *loc. cit.*, 868 ff. The British decision to withdraw appears to have been sudden, as Byrnes received no intimation of it during his talks with Bevin in December, 1946 (Byrnes, *op. cit.*, 300).

istic activities of several thousand armed men, led by Communists. . . .

Greece must have assistance if it is to become a self-supporting and self-respecting democracy.

The United States must supply that assistance. . . .

There is no other country to which democratic Greece can turn. . . .

. . . the United Nations and its related organizations are not in a position to extend help of the kind that is required. . . .

. . . totalitarian regimes imposed upon free peoples, by direct or indirect aggression, undermine the foundations of international peace and hence the security of the United States. . . .

I believe that we must assist free peoples to work out their own destinies in their own way. . . .

Should we fail to aid Greece and Turkey in this fateful hour, the effect will be far-reaching to the West as well as to the East.

We must take immediate and resolute action.[57]

This "doctrine" was unique in its forcefulness and comprehensiveness, but it was the natural outcome of the historical background described above. In the nineteenth century American interest in Greece was humanitarian and sentimental in character, based upon sympathy for a people struggling for independence from foreign rule. Greek immigration to the United States at the turn of the century created strong ties between the two countries, though of a nonpolitical nature. In 1919 the United States was involved for a brief period in the negotiations concerning Greek frontiers, but was prevented by postwar isolationism from participation in the final near eastern settlements. The years between the two World Wars witnessed a great increase in American economic and cultural influence in Greece, but from the political and strategic viewpoint, Greece still remained far beyond the range of American interests.

With the outbreak of World War II, it was natural that the United States should recognize British leadership in Greece. President Roosevelt's acquiescence in the 1944 Anglo-Russian Balkan agreement further consolidated British predominance. Then with the deterioration of the postwar relations among the Big Three, the position of Greece on the international chessboard

---

[57] Text in "Aid to Greece and Turkey," *loc. cit.*, 829–32.

altered fundamentally. Britain challenged Russia in Iran and eastern Europe; Russia countered by opposing Britain in Greece; and the United States gradually decided in favor of co-operation with Britain to resist Soviet pressure. In this manner America's Greek policy shifted from neutrality to active involvement.

When the Greek question was raised at the various international conferences, the United States backed Britain increasingly as the conflict between East and West became more acute. By 1946 America had adopted the traditional British policy of preventing Russian penetration to the Mediterranean. Thus when the Foreign Office announced Britain's inability to maintain her position in Athens, Washington was ready to take the logical final step. With the enunciation of the Truman Doctrine in the spring of 1947 the United States assumed the century-old British primacy in Greece. A new chapter in the relations between Greece and the United States had begun.

Canada's Department of External Affairs

H. L. KEENLEYSIDE*

In the gradual transition of colonial areas from dependence to independence, the control of foreign policy is usually the final historical step. When this step has been taken, the self-government of the new state is an established and internationally recognized fact. In studying the evolution of the Department of External Affairs in the Canadian Government, which corresponds to the State Department in the United States, this change from a colonial to a self-governing status is clearly defined.

I. CANADA'S EMERGENCE AS A NATION

The first world war hastened the emergence of Canada as a self-governing nation. The great contribution made by the Canadian people to the successful prosecution of that grisly conflict, and the suffering that it entailed for them, made it inevitable that they should demand for their government an independent voice, free to speak on their behalf, in the ordering of the postwar world. Strengthened by opinion at home, Sir Robert Borden was able by insistence and persistence to gain at least partial recognition of Canada's new status at Versailles.[1] Still wider acknowledgment of Canadian autonomy in foreign affairs came with the organization of the League of Nations.[2] Recognition and practice then developed, *pari passu*, until, with Canada's independent declaration of war seven days after that of the United Kingdom in 1939, and

*H. L. Keenleyside is Deputy Minister of Mines and Resources and one time Assistant Under Secretary of State for External Affairs, Canada.

[1] Henry Borden, ed., *Robert Laird Borden: His Memoirs* (London, 1938), 891–95.

[2] Canada, a signatory of the Treaty of Peace, was one of the original members of the League of Nations. See *Covenant of the League of Nations: With Annex* (Geneva, December, 1928), 17–18.

the recognition of Canadian neutrality in the interim,[3] the last academic argument over this issue seems to have been formally ended.

As the first world war marked the beginning of the end of the argument over Canada's status in foreign affairs, so the second world war signalized the emergence of Canada as a major focus of military, industrial and financial strength. While not one of the great powers (a rapidly narrowing category), Canada by 1945 had demonstrated a strength that was surpassed by that of not more than half a dozen of the nations of the world. Among the United Nations the industrial production of Canada was exceeded only by that of the United States, the Union of Soviet Socialist Republics, and the United Kingdom. Before the end of the war, Canada had the third navy in the world, and had assumed a major part of the responsibility for all North Atlantic convoy work throughout the whole period of hostilities. Financially, only the United States is today in a better position to provide capital for foreign investment or the development of backward areas.

In addition to these things, Canada, through her resources in strategic materials, occupies a position of importance in the industrial and military world that is not always recognized even by Canadians themselves.

To these facts should be added a reference to the important part that Canada has played, and the very much more important part that her tremendously increased industrial capacity will require her to play in the future, in the development and maintenance of foreign trade.[4] Occupying fourth or fifth position among the trading nations before the war, Canada may move still higher in the list when the nations achieve a balance in their postwar commercial intercourse.

This brief outline of Canada's international significance is offered, not for the purpose of justifying a foolish boast of Canadian impor-

[3] Canada, *House of Commons Debates* (5th [Special War] Sess., 18th Parliament, 3 George VI, 1939), 51, 88, 89.
[4] "Canada's Industrial Expansion," *Monthly Review*, Bank of Nova Scotia, New Series, No. 25, June, 1948.

tance, but to emphasize the quality and extent of the new responsibilities that Canada must assume in the strange and incredibly dangerous world that is now in process of crystallization. *Whether Canadians like it or not, their country has to play a new and gravely broadened role in international affairs.*

II. CONDUCT OF FOREIGN RELATIONS AFTER 1867

The British North America Act of 1867, which established the new federation, was concerned chiefly with defining the relationship between the provinces and the central government of Canada. It made no specific provision for the exercise by the Government of Canada of increased authority in relation to foreign affairs, a matter which in British countries is constitutionally a part of the royal prerogative, and in which the King (or his representative) acts upon the advice of his cabinet.[5] The development of Canada's control over its foreign relations is, in the main, a gradual transfer, by the development of conventions and conventional understandings, from the British Government to the Canadian Government, of the right to advise the King in this field.

The only specific reference to foreign relations in the Act is found in Article 132, which reads as follows:

132. The Parliament and Government of Canada shall have all powers necessary or proper for performing the obligations of Canada or of any Province thereof, *as part of the British Empire*, towards Foreign Countries, *arising under Treaties between the Empire and such Foreign Countries.*

The wording of this article, it has been suggested, may indicate that, while the fathers of Confederation foresaw the difficulty which has since arisen in the enforcement of Canadian treaty obligations affecting matters within the control of the provincial governments, and sought to ensure to the central government the necessary power to bring such treaties into operation notwithstanding, they did not

[5] "Distribution of Legislative Powers," *British North America Act* (1867), VI, 91; Canada, *Report of the Secretary of State for External Affairs, 1947*, "Constitutional Developments," 20–21. It is worth noting that, according to the British North America Act (1867), the name of the united country was to be "Canada," not "the Dominion of Canada."

foresee the eventual transfer to the Canadian Government of control over foreign relations which has since taken place. They took it for granted that Canada would be involved in only such treaty obligations as were assumed by the British Empire as a whole or, strictly speaking, by His Majesty, on the advice of the United Kingdom cabinet only, but affecting Canada in common with other parts of his realm.

The new federation was given control over its foreign trade, for in Article 91 among the responsibilities of the Federal Government was included: "2. The regulation of Trade and Commerce."

After federation, as before, the actual conduct of Canada's negotiations on matters relating to trade, boundaries, or other problems in which it was necessary to deal with foreign governments was handled by the diplomatic and consular officials of the United Kingdom. Even in dealing with Washington, which was then, as now, the most important of the foreign capitals insofar as Canada was concerned, all negotiations were channelled officially through the British Embassy in that city. This is not to suggest, of course, that in practice Canadian officials did not meet and discuss matters of mutual interest with officers of the United States Government. But all formal contacts and exchanges of official correspondence were handled through the established diplomatic channels.

As British ambassadors, ministers, consuls, and other representatives generally were unfamiliar with Canadian needs and conditions, this method of handling the foreign affairs of the new country was obviously unsatisfactory. Thus, there gradually developed the custom of accrediting Canadian ministers or other senior officials as members of the British delegations when formal negotiations involving Canadian interests were in progress with foreign governments.[6]

In order to facilitate the conduct of business with the British Government itself, a Canadian High Commissioner was sent to

[6] The discussions held in 1891 relative to the extension and development of trade between the United States and Canada afford a case in point. See Canada, *Sessional Papers* (1st Sess., 7th Parliament, 1891), Vol. 17, Sessional Paper No. 38.

London in 1880 to act as a resident spokesman for Ottawa in its dealings with the British authorities.[7] In the special case of France the British diplomatic and consular agencies were supplemented in 1882 by the appointment of a Canadian Agent General who resided permanently in the French capital.[8] Neither the High Commissioner in London nor the Agent General in Paris had any diplomatic status.[9]

Throughout this period the complicated but official and invariable channel for the conduct of Canadian business with foreign countries was from the Government in Ottawa to the Governor General; from the Governor General to the Colonial Office, London; from the Colonial Office to the Foreign Office; from the Foreign Office to its embassy, legation, or consular office abroad; and thence to the government of the foreign country concerned. In dealings with the other parts of the British Empire the channel was the same, except that the Foreign Office and its diplomatic or consular agents were omitted and the communication went straight from the Colonial Office to the Governor General or Governor of the other part of the Empire involved.

Between the Canadian and the British Governments themselves the normal channel of communication was through the Governor General to the Colonial Office. The Canadian High Commissioner in London could urge his country's case at the Colonial Office, but all *official* communications followed the formal procedure. The extensive role played by the Governor General in international affairs is explained by the fact that in addition to being, as the King's representative, nominal head of the Government in Canada,

[7] Sir Alexander Galt was the first Canadian High Commissioner in the United Kingdom. See Joseph Pope, "The Federal Government," *Canada and Its Provinces* (Toronto, 1914), VI, 369–70.

[8] Hon. Hector Fabre was the first Agent General for Canada in France. *Ibid.*, 370–71.

[9] The High Commissioners of Commonwealth countries are still placed below the Ambassadors or Ministers of foreign countries in the official order of precedence in all Commonwealth capitals, although recent consideration has been given to the introduction of a more appropriate procedure. For examples of diplomatic listings see: Canada, Department of External Affairs, *Diplomatic Corps, British Commonwealth High Commissioners and Their Staffs and Consular Representatives in Ottawa* (Ottawa, 1948), 3–6.

he was the representative in Canada of the British Government. It was not until after the Imperial Conference of 1926 that the Governor General's status as the representative of His Majesty alone became finally recognized and established.[10]

In addition to the High Commissioner in London and the Agent General in Paris, Canada was represented abroad in the later years of the nineteenth century by trade commissioners and immigration officials. These, however, were the appointees of individual departments of the Canadian Government, did not act as representatives of the government as a whole, and did not enjoy diplomatic status.

In Ottawa itself the situation was complicated by local conditions and practice. Before the establishment of the Department of External Affairs any department of the government concerned in a matter which had external implications was free to approach the Governor General and to recommend that a communication be sent to a foreign government; and, unless the matter was of considerable importance, the Governor General would act upon this request as a matter of course. Contradictory or conflicting communications to other governments sometimes resulted.[11] Although the usual practice was to approach the Governor General through the Privy Council, this did not always prevent such difficulties. A matter fully considered from the standpoint of one department might be presented to the Cabinet and a decision might be taken by members who had not had an opportunity to check it with their own permanent officials. Unless the Governor General was paying very close attention to his papers and, in addition, was blessed with a phenomenal memory, difficulties were sure to arise. On more than one occasion gross inconsistencies were brought to the attention of the Canadian Government by a foreign power to which contradictory views had been communicated.[12]

[10] Great Britain, *Parliamentary Papers*, Cmd. 2768, Imperial Conference, 1926, "Summary of Proceedings" (London, 1926), 16. Hereafter cited as Cmd. 2768 (1926).

[11] Pope, "Federal Government," *loc. cit.*, VI, 322–24.

[12] *Ibid.*, VI, 323–24.

In connection with despatches addressed to the Governor General by the officials of other governments the need for more specialized machinery was also evident. Under the old practice these were referred by His Excellency's Secretary to the departments which he judged best fitted to supply answers or deal otherwise with their contents; or if the matters involved were considered of greater importance, or concerned more than one department, they were referred to the Privy Council office. But there was no provision for following up these despatches in order to ensure that they should be answered, and the Colonial Office, in particular, frequently complained of the failure of the Canadian Government to reply to important communications.[13]

III. Evolution of the Department

As Canada grew in size and importance, as her foreign trade expanded and her interest in problems of an international character increased, the inadequacy of the domestic arrangements for the formulation of Canadian foreign policy became increasingly apparent. The fact that it was possible for Canada, through no volition of her own, to become legally committed as a belligerent in a war in which Canadian interests were not at stake had caused a certain amount of heart-searching among the more thoughtful Canadians. The South African war was an illustration of this possibility. Moreover, the gathering clouds of a greater conflict in Europe were visible even from Canada, and some Canadians were beginning to question the propriety of a system under which their sons could be committed to battle without the Canadian Government participating in, or knowing very much about, the diplomatic activities which preceded the conflict.

The first step in any program designed to increase Canadian responsibility for the conduct of its own international relations

[13] Canada, *Sessional Papers* (4th Sess., 10th Parliament, 1907–1908, Vol. 15, Sessional Paper No. 29a): Royal Commission on the Civil Service, "Minutes of Evidence," I, 48–50; Pope, "Federal Government," *loc. cit.*, VI, 323–24.

obviously had to be taken at home. Responsibility had to be matched by recognizable capacity.

It was against this background that Mr. (later Sir) Joseph Pope prepared his memorandum of May 25, 1907, for the Royal Commission on the Civil Service. Mr. Pope was at that time Under Secretary of State of Canada and his official duties had made him more aware perhaps than any other member of the public service of the inadequacy and weaknesses of the existing methods of conducting Canadian business with other countries. He pointed out that "a more systematic mode" of handling what he termed "external affairs" was desirable, because with the growth of the Dominion it was no longer possible, as it had been in the early days, for the Prime Minister to keep in his own hands the questions arising in foreign relations. Mr. Pope wrote:

The practical result of the system in vogue is that there does not exist today in any department a complete record of any of the correspondence to which I have alluded. It has been so scattered, and passed through so many hands, that there is no approach to continuity in any of the departmental files. Such knowledge concerning them as is available is, for the most part, lodged in the memories of a few officials. . . .

My suggestion, is, that all despatches relating to external affairs should be referred by the Privy Council to one department, whose staff should contain men trained in the study of these questions, and in the conduct of diplomatic correspondence. These officials should be in close touch with the other departments, from which they could draw all necessary information, the raw material, as it were, of their work; but the digesting of this information and its presentation in diplomatic form should rest with them, through, of course, the same channels as at present; for in this suggestion there is no thought of change in that regard. . . . I wish most earnestly to impress upon all concerned that if this work is not soon systematically begun it will be too late. The few men throughout the service conversant with these questions are growing old, and must soon disappear. So far as I know, they will leave no successors. Much of the early history of these subjects, so far as Canadian records are concerned, will thus be lost.

I recommend that a small staff of young men, well educated and carefully selected, be attached to the department whose creation I have advocated, and that they be specially trained in the knowledge and treatment of these subjects. In this way we shall acquire an organized method of dealing with international questions which at present we wholly lack.[14]

[14] Canada, *Sessional Papers* (1907–1908, Vol. 15, No. 29a), I, 48–50.

From these quotations it will be seen that Mr. Pope proposed no very radical innovations. He made no effort to change the theory upon which current practice was based; he merely endeavoured to increase the efficiency with which the system could work. Indeed, in the article on the subject which he later contributed to *Canada and Its Provinces* he specifically emphasized the limitations of his proposed reform:

No constitutional change was intended by the measure, which merely aimed at improvement in departmental procedure, and that Canada's official communications extending beyond the bounds of the Dominion would continue to be made through His Excellency the Governor General as before.[15]

The Royal Commission to which Mr. Pope's memorandum was addressed took no action upon it. Indeed, according to the author, the Commission "failed completely to grasp the point" of his argument! Nevertheless, because the situation so obviously demanded attention, the matter was not allowed to drop and a bill providing for the establishment of a Department of External Affairs was introduced in the House of Commons on March 4, 1909. The urgent necessity for the proposed change precluded serious criticism and the bill passed the scrutiny of both the House of Commons and the Senate with very little objection from either side.[16]

In the bill as originally drafted, the Prime Minister was designated, *ex officio*, as head of the new Department, but after discussion in the Cabinet this was changed, and the duty was placed upon the Secretary of State. He was to be assisted by an Under Secretary of State for External Affairs, who would be appointed by the Governor in Council and would rank as the permanent deputy head of the Department. In the Act the duties of the new Department were described as "the conduct of all official communications between Canada and other countries in connection with the external affairs of Canada," and such other duties as might be assigned

[15] Pope, "Federal Government," *loc. cit.*, VI, 322–24.
[16] "An Act to Create a Department of External Affairs," *Statutes of Canada*, 8–9 Edward VII, 1909, C. 13.

by the Governor in Council relating to such affairs, or to "the conduct and management of international or intercolonial negotiations" appertaining to Canada.

A minor difficulty arose in connection with the phrasing of the Act. The Colonial Office and the Governor General both objected strenuously to the description of the Secretary of State as having "the conduct" of all official communications between the Government of Canada and the government of any other country. The "conduct" of such negotiations, according to Lord Grey, Lord Crewe, and Mr. Harcourt, was a function of the Governor General, and the use of the word in the Act could be looked upon as an "improper attempt to shelve the Governor General." The Colonial Office suggested that the word "care" be substituted for "conduct." The question was brought up again three years later, but the offending word was never altered. The original Act came into effect on June 1, 1909.[17]

The duties of the new Department were set forth in an Order-in-Council promulgated on the date when the Act came into force. As this document provided the effective basis upon which the work of the Department has ever since been conducted, it may be useful to quote its text here:

The Committee of the Privy Council, who have had under consideration the question of the constitution of the Department of External Affairs, are of opinion that it would further the purposes for which the Department was established, if all Despatches, at present communicated by Your Excellency to the Privy Council, or direct to individual Ministers, should be, in the first instance, referred to the Prime Minister, and also to the Secretary of State as head of the Department of External Affairs, which Department shall then distribute them among the several departments to which they relate, for the necessary consideration and action, and the Committee recommend accordingly.

The Committee further advise that in the case of such of the Despatches so referred as call for communication with the Secretary of State for the Colonies, or with His Majesty's representatives abroad, or with the Government of any British possession, in respect of any matter forming the subject of diplomatic negotiations in which Canada is interested; or any private claim on the part of any Canadian subject of His Majesty against

[17] *Ibid.;* also see *The Canada Gazette* XLII (Extra), Ottawa, June 1, 1909.

any Government, whether foreign or otherwise, external to the Dominion, the Department or Departments to which such Despatch was referred, shall furnish the Department of External Affairs with all available information bearing upon the matter to which it relates, and the Secretary of State, having informed himself by this means, shall thereupon make a report in the premises to the Governor in Council.[18]

In using the title "Department of External Affairs" instead of "Department of Foreign Affairs," the Canadian Government was following the precedent set by the Government of Australia in 1901, and was giving recognition to the fact that the one department was charged with the conduct of correspondence with other governments within the Empire as well as with the governments of foreign states. In the United Kingdom, where there are the three corresponding Departments—the Foreign Office, the Commonwealth Relations Office, and the Colonial Office—the appropriate and specific designations are used; in Canada, and in the other Dominions, where only one department exists, an omnibus title is essential.

Following the change of government in 1911, Mr. Pope's proposal that the Department should be placed directly under the Prime Minister was again considered, and after April 1, 1912, the Prime Minister held the additional portfolio of Secretary of State for External Affairs.[19] From time to time the appointment of a separate minister was suggested, but for many years both Liberal and Conservative administrations held to the conviction that the arguments against the proposal outweighed those in favour.

The heavy volume of business transacted by the department during the second world war, and the likelihood that the scope and extent of Canada's diplomatic services would be increased measurably in the postwar period, caused Mr. Mackenzie King to raise the question again in the House of Commons on July 12, 1943. With the House in committee, Mr. King said:

May I take advantage of this moment to explain why . . . I myself have retained the position of Minister of External Affairs while holding the office of Prime Minister at this time of war. . . . I would point out

[18] Order-in-Council, P. C. 1242, June 1, 1909.
[19] *Revised Statutes of Canada*, 1927, C. 65.

that in time of war nine-tenths of the Prime Minister's work is related to external affairs, and it would be making his task in some ways more difficult were he to try to assume the responsibilities of the office of Prime Minister without being responsible as well for external affairs, when practically every decision of vital importance at this time, which has to be made by the Prime Minister, is one that is related to external affairs or would have to come as a recommendation from the minister of External Affairs. I am perhaps stating this in an exaggerated way, but it is impossible to separate the two at this time, and the more so in Canada for the reason that they have never been separated. The Department of External Affairs originated under Sir Wilfrid Laurier's administration, Sir Joseph Pope being the first deputy minister, and from that time to the present the two offices have been actually working together as one, so much so that the Prime Minister gets no appropriation from parliament and what he receives in the way of salary comes to him from External Affairs.

I could enlarge upon what I have said, but I hope I have made it clear to the committee that at this time it would be practically impossible to separate the two offices. I think they should be separated, and I hope I may have something to do with seeing that they are; but so long as the war continues I am afraid that it will be necessary to keep them together.[20]

In order to make it legally possible to appoint a separate Secretary of State for External Affairs if desired, a bill was introduced into the House of Commons by the Prime Minister on March 18, 1946, to amend the Department of External Affairs Act by repealing the section which requires that: "The member of the King's Privy Council for Canada holding the recognized position of first minister shall be the Secretary of State for External Affairs."

The evolution of the Department as a separate entity in the Government of Canada was brought to its logical and timely conclusion September 4, 1946, when the Prime Minister relinquished the portfolio of Secretary of State for External Affairs and the Right Honourable Louis S. St. Laurent, then serving in the Federal Cabinet as Minister of Justice, assumed these duties in an acting capacity. Mr. St. Laurent subsequently relinquished the Justice portfolio and became the first full-time Secretary of State for External Affairs on December 10 of the same year.

[20] Canada, *House of Commons Debates*, 1943, Vol. 5, Cols. 4670–71. A year later, in answer to a question by the leader of the opposition, Mr. King again spoke in the same vein. See Canada, *House of Commons Debates*, 1944, Vol. 5, Cols. 4940–41.

Speaking in the House of Commons on April 29, 1948, Mr. St. Laurent discussed at length the position of Canada in the post-war world community of nations. In his estimate of the future responsibilities of the Department of External Affairs, the following words are significant:

The Canadian Department of External Affairs . . . represents a necessary and, I think, useful development in the progress of this country from colonial status to national maturity. This expansion—and it has not been allowed to grow carelessly and extravagantly—reflects the magnitude and complexity of the relations between nations in this interdependent age and the increasing importance of these relations for Canada.[21]

IV. Channel of Communications with Great Britain

In the *Summary of Proceedings* published following the Imperial Conference of 1926, the following sentences were included:

It seemed to us to follow that the practice whereby the Governor General of a Dominion is the formal official channel of communication between His Majesty's Government in Great Britain and his Governments in the Dominions might be regarded as no longer wholly in accordance with the constitutional position of the Governor General. It was thought that the recognized official channel of communication should be, in future, between Government and Government direct.[22]

In pursuance of the principles recognized in these words it was subsequently decided that from July 1, 1927, communications from the British Government would no longer be addressed to the Governor General, but would be addressed directly to the Secretary of State for External Affairs. The same rule applies to communications from foreign governments. All communications from a foreign or Commonwealth government, regardless of the subject matter or ultimate destination of their representations, now pass, in the first instance, through the Department. There is normally no direct official intercourse between any outside government and

[21] Canada, *House of Commons Debates*, 1948, Vol. 87, Col. 3438.
[22] Cmd. 2768 (1926), 16.

any Department of the Canadian Government or any provincial government.[23]

In correspondence with the Government of the United Kingdom, the Secretary of State for External Affairs most frequently communicates with the Secretary of State for Commonwealth Relations, although a practice of direct correspondence between Prime Minister and Prime Minister has also developed. The High Commissioner for the United Kingdom in Ottawa and the High Commissioner for Canada in London fulfil functions somewhat similar to those performed by the ambassadors or ministers plenipotentiary representing foreign states in the two capitals. There is, however, one difference. The Canadian Government can communicate with the Government of the United Kingdom either through the Canadian High Commissioner or by direct communication to the Commonwealth Relations Office, whereas such direct contact between governments is not customary where diplomatic representatives have been exchanged. The High Commissioner for the United Kingdom in Ottawa deals directly with the Secretary of State for External Affairs.

V. Expansion of the Department's Activities

As Canadian autonomy in international affairs gradually achieved recognition, the activities of the Department of External Affairs naturally expanded. When the Department was first organized there were, of course, no Canadian legations abroad, and even the office of the High Commissioner for Canada in London was not placed under the direct control of the Department until March, 1921. The growth of Canadian responsibilities abroad, however, made expansion inevitable. Moreover, Canadian interests, in some countries at least, no longer could be handled conveniently by the British diplomatic and consular authorities, whose primary duty was the promotion of the interests of the United Kingdom.

[23] Certain correspondence originated by the Post Office Department is an exception to this rule.

As the Canadian Government began to take a larger part in the direct administration of Canadian external relations, it developed in the new Department an agency to handle the task. In 1921 the Office of the High Commissioner in London was attached to the Department.[24] In 1923, Canada's right to negotiate and sign her own treaties without a British co-signatory was first exercised. In 1925 a Canadian Advisory Officer was stationed in Geneva to represent Canada at various conferences and to keep Ottawa informed as to the activities and programme of the League of Nations and of the International Labour Office. In 1927 Mr. Vincent Massey opened the first Canadian Legation in the capital of the United States of America. This was followed, in 1928, by the appointment of Mr. Philippe Roy as Canadian Minister to Paris, and of Mr. H. M. (later Sir Herbert) Marler to Tokyo in 1929.[25] Reciprocally, United States, French, and Japanese Legations were opened in Ottawa.

The expansion of the service was, of course, halted during the depression of the 1930's, although by 1938 it had become possible to open legations in Brussels and The Hague. With the outbreak of the second world war, however, it became imperative that Canada should have more intimate contacts with other members of the British Commonwealth, and with many foreign countries as well. In 1939 a Canadian High Commissioner was appointed to Australia, and in 1940 similar appointments were made in Ireland, New Zealand and South Africa. In 1941 Mr. C. J. Burchell, who had been the first High Commissioner in Australia, was appointed to Newfoundland, where he served until 1944. In 1947 Mr. J. D. Kearney was appointed High Commissioner in the newly formed Dominion of India.[26] An agreement has also been made with the Government of Pakistan for the eventual exchange of High Commissioners, and a Canadian Trade Commissioner's Office already

[24] Canada, Department of External Affairs (Information Division), "The Department of External Affairs," *Reference Paper No. 16* (revised January, 1948), 2.

[25] For these successive steps in expanding the foreign service, see Canada, *Report of the Secretary of State for External Affairs*, 1923; 1925; 1927; 1928; and 1929.

[26] See *ibid.*, 1939; 1940; 1941; and 1947.

has been established in Karachi. In September, 1948, following the referendum to determine the political future of Newfoundland, Mr. Burchell was appointed High Commissioner in the Old Colony for the second time, pending final arrangements for the union of that country with Canada.

The legations opened in 1938 in Brussels and The Hague were supplemented by the appointment of Ministers to the following countries in the years indicated: Brazil, 1941; Argentina, 1941; Chile, 1942; China, 1942; U.S.S.R., 1942; Cuba, 1945; Denmark, 1947; and Switzerland, 1948.[27]

During the war there was a general trend towards the gradual elimination of legations, except in special cases, and their replacement by embassies. Canada participated in this trend by raising most of its offices abroad to embassy rank and by giving certain new missions the rank of embassy from the beginning. Embassies were established in Mexico and Peru in 1944, and in Greece in 1945, while in 1944 the legations in Washington, Santiago, Rio de Janeiro, Chungking, Paris, Brussels and Moscow were raised to embassy status. Buenos Aires was added in 1945. An embassy was established in Ankara in 1947.[28]

Originally, and particularly in the days of effective royal power, there was a valid and real distinction to be drawn between an ambassador and a minister (head of a legation). The Ambassador alone was considered as representing the person of his sovereign before the head of another state. In recent years, however, this distinction has become unreal and illogical, and there is now, as noted, a general tendency among foreign governments towards uniformity of representation by ambassadors only. The failure of certain countries to keep up with the tendency resulted in curious situations in certain capitals, where the representative of a great power, being of ministerial rank only, was forced to grant precedence to the representative of a minor power who enjoyed ambassadorial status.

[27] *Ibid.*, 1941; 1942; 1945; and 1947.
[28] *Ibid.*, 1944; 1945; and 1947.

During the war Canada had a single Minister accredited to a number of the allied governments then functioning in London— Belgium, Czechoslovakia, Greece, Yugoslavia, the Netherlands, Norway and Poland—and received Ministers from each of them in Ottawa.[29] This, however, was only a temporary arrangement, and separate missions have since been appointed to the various capitals.[29a]

Canada, in contrast to many other countries, developed its diplomatic service before beginning to establish a consular corps. On financial grounds alone, in the experience of other nations, the development of a consular service often has justified itself; the income-producing activities of consular offices are frequently sufficient to cover the expense of the diplomatic establishments. In the case of the United States, for example, it is reported that in normal times the consular income not only covers all the costs of its own establishments and of the United States embassies and legations, but returns a sizeable profit annually to the national exchequer.

The first Canadian consulates were opened during the dark days of 1940 and 1941. Their sites clearly indicate the purpose of their establishment, for they were located in St. Pierre (of St. Pierre and Miquelon) and in Godthaab, the capital of Greenland.[30] Obviously the Canadian Government was anxious to keep in touch with developments in the critical sea approaches to the northern coasts of America. In addition, Canada was able to give material assistance to the people of the islands in the Gulf of St. Lawrence,

[29] Canada, Department of External Affairs, *Reference Paper No. 16*.

[29a] Sir Joseph Pope, the chief architect and first permanent head of the Department, had retired in 1925, and on April 1 of that year Dr. O. D. Skelton, sometime Dean of the Faculty of Arts and head of the Department of Political Science at Queen's University, who had entered the Department of External Affairs as a Counsellor in 1924, became Under Secretary of State for External Affairs. He held this post through the great period of expansion at home and abroad until his death in January, 1941. Following the death of Dr. Skelton, the post of Under Secretary was held by Mr. Norman A. Robertson, who entered the Department as a Third Secretary in 1929. In 1946 Mr. Robertson was appointed High Commissioner to the United Kingdom and Mr. L. B. Pearson, previously Ambassador to the United States, became Under Secretary.

[30] *Ibid.*

and more especially to the inhabitants of Greenland, through the contacts thus established. With the improvement in the war situation it was found possible to close the consulate at St. Pierre in 1943, but the consulate in Greenland was maintained until 1946.

In 1943 it was decided to open a consulate general in New York for the purpose of co-ordinating and supervising the ever increasing Canadian interests in that area of the United States. More recently, consulates general have been opened in Chicago and San Francisco, consulates in Detroit and Boston, and a vice-consulate is maintained in Portland, Maine. No doubt a further expansion of Canadian consular offices in the United States may be expected within the next few years, if for no other reason than to relieve the British consular officers of the many and various calls that are made on their time and activity by their present responsibilities for protecting Canadian interests.

The External Affairs service of Canada, now open to qualified women as well as men, is recruited on a career basis patterned after the British merit system. While heretofore it has been necessary to fill many of the highest posts by special appointment, it is the ultimate intention that these positions will normally be open to competent officials who have come up through the service. In a number of instances career officers have already been appointed to ambassadorial posts, and the late Under Secretary also entered the service by competitive examinations.[31]

In recent years efforts have been made to co-ordinate the policies and to provide for increased co-operation between the personnel of the Department of External Affairs and the Department of Trade and Commerce. Co-operation in recruitment and, to a limited degree, interchangeability of personnel have been accepted as basic principles in the promotion of Canadian interests in the fields

[31] Hon. Lester B. Pearson entered the Department of External Affairs by competitive examination in 1928 and was appointed Under Secretary in 1946, after a distinguished career in the service. In September, 1948, Mr. Pearson was appointed to the federal cabinet as Secretary of State for External Affairs, succeeding Rt. Hon. Louis S. St. Laurent, then Acting Prime Minister and newly elected leader of the Liberal Party. As a result of his appointment to this important seat in the Government, Mr. Pearson resigned his former position in the Civil Service to seek election to the House of Commons.

in which both departments operate. The liaison thus established has proved very helpful, especially in foreign posts where only one of these services has active representation.

The increase of Canadian offices abroad, however, has not yet been matched by the expansion in the permanent personnel of the service. In 1930 there were only eighteen Foreign Service officers in the Department or in the offices abroad. In 1935 this had increased by only three. In 1940 the number was thirty, and in 1947 the service had 175 Foreign Service officers employed at home and abroad. The personnel of the Department as a whole has grown from 163 in 1930 to 1,002 in 1947.[32] It is of interest to note that during the first eight months of 1948 twenty Foreign Service officers and 140 other personnel were recruited to augment the rapidly increasing ranks of the Department.

Another evidence of the growth of the Department is found in the annual estimates. In recent years these have expanded as follows:

Fiscal Years	Amounts (Approximate)		
1929–1930	$748,000		
1934–1935	824,000		
1939–1940	General—1,111,000 War — 185,000	}	$1,296,000
1944–1945	General—2,305,000 War — 328,000	}	2,633,000

The estimates for the fiscal year 1948–49 amount to approximately $15,809,000, but the amount spent on external affairs is only a minute fraction of the total annual expenditure of the Government of Canada.[33] In this connection, it should be noted that the Department is sometimes made responsible for the supervision of expenditures covering items which do not come within the normal sphere of its activities. For example, the annual estimates for the fiscal year 1947–48 amounted to approximately $33,383,000, of

[32] Canada, *Report of the Secretary of State for External Affairs*, 1947, 23.

[33] The total expenditure of the Government of Canada for the fiscal year ended March 31, 1947, was 2,634.2 millions of dollars. See *Public Accounts of the Dominion of Canada for the Fiscal Year Ended March 31, 1947*, "Introduction," C., Table IV, p. xix.

which $20,000,000 was allocated for post-UNRRA relief and charged to the vote of the Department of External Affairs.

It is of interest to note that in 1947 Canada opened ten new offices in foreign countries. During the same year, Canada became party to seventeen multilateral agreements, twenty-seven bilateral agreements with sixteen different countries, seven trade agreements, and air agreements with Ireland, Portugal, Sweden, and the United Kingdom territories in the West Atlantic and Caribbean areas and in Fiji and Canton Island. A previous air agreement with the United States was amended and fourteen other agreements on a variety of subjects were concluded with different countries. During the same twelve-month period Canada was represented at no less than eighty-six international conferences and meetings.[34] These figures will serve to emphasize the extent of the responsibilities which the Department of External Affairs must assume as a result of Canada's emergence from the second world war with many new international commitments.

VI. The Department in World War II and After

The opening of the second world war presented the Department of External Affairs with new responsibilities and new problems. The amount of work that had to be done increased immediately and tremendously. Unfortunately, as has been indicated, recruitment for the Department was slowed down during the depression years, and far from having a surplus of personnel to take on the new duties that accompanied the outbreak of war, the Department had barely enough trained or partly trained officials to attend to the most essential responsibilities. Evenings, Sundays, statutory holidays, and annual leave in many cases were given up for years to the imperative necessity of coping with the new demands made upon the department by the war.[35]

[34] Canada, *Report of the Secretary of State for External Affairs*, 1947.

[35] Dr. Skelton's death in 1941 was an inevitable result of the almost incredible way in which he was working. The same cause contributed to the death of Loring Christie, Canadian Minister to Washington, also in 1941.

Some additional recruits were brought in following examinations held early in 1940.[36] It was subsequently decided, however, that it would be unfair to the young men who were enlisting in the armed services to fill the posts in External Affairs which they otherwise might have sought, with candidates who either would not or could not serve in the Navy, Army, or Air Force. For this reason it was ruled that no more open examinations would be held and that posts in the external service would be filled on a temporary basis only, pending the return of those men who had sacrificed their civilian careers in order to serve their country on the sea, on the land, or in the air.

As it was imperative that additional personnel be obtained, however, appointments of a temporary character were made to posts in the Department and to the offices abroad. Some twenty older men were brought in from the universities, from the professions, and from business, and were given wartime assignments as "Special Assistants." In a further attempt to obtain skilled assistance, an examination was held for women candidates. Ten women received appointments which frequently involved duties similar to those usually assigned to newly appointed members of the diplomatic staff, though they did not receive the Third Secretary grading. Whatever the work to which they were assigned, these young women accepted and performed it with a general competence and an untiring devotion which were essential factors in enabling the Department to meet its wartime responsibilities.[37]

In order to meet the staff shortage it was also found necessary to refuse permission for enlistment in the armed forces to members of the diplomatic service.

[36] The staff arrangements which were temporarily in effect during the war years, subsequent to 1940, were suspended as a result of the general qualifying examination held in 1946. The recruitment policy of the Department was dealt with by the House of Commons Standing Committee on External Affairs (Session 1947–48), *Minutes of Proceedings and Evidence*, No. 4 (May 26, 1948), 89–92.

[37] Women were first admitted as candidates for permanent appointment in the Department of External Affairs at the competitive examinations held in July, 1947. Those employed in the Department during the war years were engaged under special arrangements designed to ease the staff problem caused by the national emergency. After the war all but a few, who qualified by examination for permanent appointments, returned to their peacetime vocations.

In the autumn of 1944, with the war drawing to its conclusion, and with many young men already returning from military hospitals to civil life, it was decided that an effort would be made to obtain for the External Affairs service new recruits from among those who had served or were serving in the forces overseas.[38] The Navy, Army, and Air Force were asked to circulate announcements drawing attention to the needs of the foreign service and to invite applications for appointment from among overseas personnel. A general form of examination then was devised and a committee was set up to examine applicants. From this source new recruits have been enlisted and others are being rapidly enrolled. Thus the government and the department ensured that those young men who had served their country in arms would be given an opportunity to compete among themselves for appointment to posts that had been kept open for them in this other branch of public service.

The Department of External Affairs is still small in numbers as compared with many of the other branches of government, and its annual budget, including all the overseas offices, contributions to international organizations, and other expenses, still represents a modest expenditure in view of the rapidly increasing responsibilities of Canada's diplomatic service. Yet, as has been indicated, the work that falls within the purview of the Secretary of State for External Affairs is likely to increase in extent and importance. Apart from such fundamental problems as war and peace, the relations of Canada with the other members of the British Commonwealth of Nations, and its connections with the various international organizations—all of which are being more actively and widely discussed in Canada today than ever before—there is no problem that so directly affects Canada as does the condition of world markets and the volume and direction of international trade. This fact is fully appreciated by the members of Canada's external service. If not the first, it certainly ranks near the top of their official preoccupations.

In this paper an attempt has been made to sketch the develop-

[38] Canada, *Report of the Secretary of State for External Affairs*, 1947.

ment of Canada's diplomatic service from the period of colonial administration, with all its restricting influences, to the present organization designed to deal with the problems and responsibilities that have devolved upon Canada as an independent and increasingly important member of the world community of nations. In this modern age, with its many threatening aspects and concurrent opportunities for good, the conduct of the nation's affairs, especially in its international relationships, is a vital factor in shaping the course of world events. This cannot be done without the aid of enlightened statesmanship, and this in turn must find its inspiration amongst citizens who are well informed on foreign affairs. The old barriers of isolation and self-sufficient nationalism are down for ever in a world fused together by such scientific developments as atomic energy and modern air transportation. The democratic peoples, who still have the opportunity to make their decisions freely in the light of all circumstances known to them, have a responsibility to ensure that the peace so hardly won, and not yet secure, is preserved. In this great task, Canada, in common with the other democratic peoples, will play its not insignificant part.

Canada, the United States, and Latin America

By Eugene H. Miller[*]

Seldom have two countries bound by ties of culture, economic interdependence, and geographical propinquity followed more divergent paths in international affairs than have the United States and Canada. The former looked to the south, and westward across the Pacific. In the Monroe Doctrine and Pan Americanism she expressed her confidence that her future lay in the New World. In the Far East, too, she played an active role. But toward Europe she remained, for the most part, consistently isolationist until recent years.

Canada's attention, on the other hand, was turned largely toward England and the British Empire. For many years, in fact, her foreign policy was directed from London. The extent of Downing Street's authority was sometimes painfully demonstrated, as in the Alaskan Boundary dispute in 1903, when the Mother Country resolved a clash of Canadian–United States interests in favor of the latter. This affair increased Ottawa's growing reluctance to follow London's lead—a reluctance clearly apparent in her refusal to furnish three dreadnoughts for the British Navy in 1912. Canada's signature of the Treaty of Versailles and membership in the League of Nations constituted formal recognition of her status as a fully sovereign state. From this point there was no doubt of Canada's firm determination to conduct her own external affairs. This was signalized by Meighen's insistence at the Imperial Conference of 1921 that the Anglo-Japanese Alliance be dropped,[1] by

*Eugene H. Miller is Professor of Political Science at Ursinus College.

[1] For a full account of this incident, see J. Bartlett Brebner, "Canada, the Anglo-Japanese Alliance and the Washington Conference," *Political Science Quarterly*, L (March, 1935), 46–54.

Canada's refusal to support Lloyd George in the Chanak affair, and by the appointment of a Canadian Minister to Washington in 1927.

However, Canada's heightened concern for foreign affairs after 1918 did not extend to Latin America. Her economic energies were concentrated in building her own west. She had developed no substantial interests in the countries south of the United States. Despite hints from the Latin American states that she would be welcomed into the Pan American Union she apparently preferred to confine her activities to the British Commonwealth and the League of Nations.

The United States for her part had remained aloof from both the Treaty of Versailles and the League. Nor did she evince a desire to draw Canada into the orbit of the Western Hemisphere. In 1928 the United States delegates to the Havana conference received these instructions:

> The Pan American Conferences are essentially conferences of governments and not of mere geographical groups or territorial units. Being conferences attended by the official representatives of Governments, they necessarily reflect the exigencies and policies of the Governments participating. If colonies, possessions or dominions, whose foreign relations are controlled by European States, were represented in these conferences, the influence and policies of European Powers would be injected into the discussion and disposition of questions affecting the political entities of this hemisphere. Whatever value such conferences would have it would not be that attaching to a conference distinctively American. Should Canada be proposed as a member of the Pan American Union, you will be guided by the oral instructions given by the Secretary of State to the Delegation . . . on December 28, 1927.[2]

Did this mean that the United States was opposed to Canadian membership? It generally has been so interpreted despite the fact that Canada's foreign relations were not in 1928 "controlled" by a European state. However, James B. Scott, a member of the United States delegation, later declared that the delegates were directed to second a motion favoring an invitation to Canada if such a mo-

[2] *Papers Relating to the Foreign Relations of the United States*, 1928 (Washington, 1942), I, 583.

tion were introduced by a Latin American country. No invitation was issued, said Mr. Scott, because a rebuff in the form of a negative answer was feared.[3] Actually, it is probable that neither Canada nor the United States desired to encourage Dominion membership at that time.

II

During the nineteen thirties the picture began to change and World War II served as a strong catalyst in crystallizing United States–Canadian relations toward each other and toward Latin America. While the United States, even before the outbreak of hostilities, set about strengthening the machinery of the Inter-American organization through the conferences at Buenos Aires in 1936, Lima in 1938, Panama in 1939, and at Havana in 1940, Canada, too, showed a quickening interest in Latin America. As anarchy increased in Europe the more isolationist segment of Canadian opinion turned increasingly to the Western Hemisphere as a possible bulwark against entanglements in the Old World. For the first time voices began to be raised in the press and in Parliament in favor of Canadian participation in the Pan American Union.

The outbreak of war in 1939, the fall of France, and the disappearance of continental markets emphasized Canada's interest in the Western Hemisphere by forcing the Dominion to look for new customers and additional dollar balances to offset her imports from the United States. James A. McKinnon, then Minister of Trade and Commerce, made a 15,000 mile trip around South America to negotiate trade agreements with Chile, Argentina, Brazil, Uruguay, and a commercial *modus vivendi* with Ecuador. Canadian embassies were opened in Argentina, Brazil, Chile, Peru and Mexico, and a legation in Cuba. The Canadian Information Service, the Canadian Broadcasting Company and the National Film Board increased their efforts to make Latin America Canada-conscious. Would the exigencies of war, then, fuse United States–

[3] Gordon H. Skilling, *Canadian Representation Abroad* (Toronto, 1945), 220.

Canadian policy into support for a strong regional organization for the Western Hemisphere? Was Canadian enthusiasm for Latin America a passing phase dictated by the circumstances of the moment, or was it a permanent factor to be considered in New World relations? The answer to these questions would depend, in the long run, on the Dominion's stake in trade and investment south of the Rio Grande, the problem of defense, and the path she might choose to follow in the general field of international politics.

Estimates of Canadian investments in Latin America vary from $200,000,000 to $250,000,000.[4] This sum represents only 3 to 3.5 per cent of the total Canadian overseas investment.[5] Some Canadian enterprises, however, do play an important role in individual Latin American countries. For example, International Petroleum Co., Ltd., a subsidiary of Imperial Oil Ltd., is the leading petroleum producer in Peru. Brazilian Traction is a holding company for nine subsidiaries that provide both Rio de Janeiro and São Paulo with public utility services. Three Canadian Banks— the Royal Bank of Canada, the Canadian Bank of Commerce, and the Bank of Nova Scotia—have extensive interests in Latin America. The first of these, in addition to operating numerous offices in the Antilles, has well established branches in Argentina, Brazil, Colombia, Peru, Uruguay, Venezuela, British Guiana and British Honduras.[6] Canadian insurance companies are also active in Latin America. The Sun Life Assurance Company of Canada has written a substantial number of policies since opening its first branch in Jamaica in 1881, and has sold insurance in all but four

[4] The $200,000,000 estimate is given in R. A. McKay and E. B. Rogers, *Canada Looks Abroad* (Toronto, 1938), 145. Paul Redwood states that the approximate amount of Canadian investments in Latin America both in 1939 and 1945 was $250,000,000. See his chapter on "Canada" in Arthur P. Whitaker, ed., *Inter-American Affairs, 1945* (New York, 1946), 37.

[5] The total of Canadian investments abroad for 1946 was $7,130,000,000, according to information given to the author by the Bureau of Statistics, Ottawa, December 5, 1948.

[6] The importance of the Royal Bank in the financial life of Argentina is indicated by the fact that it ranks third among the foreign banks operating in that country. See monthly report issued by the Argentine Government: *Estados de los Bancos al 31 de Diciembre de 1946*.

Latin American countries (Venezuela, Brazil, Paraguay, and Bolivia).[7]

In general, Canadian capital has tended to concentrate in these four fields—oil, utilities, banking and insurance. Dominion money is, however, invested in numerous other enterprises—Cuban sugar, Cinzano vermouth, mines and railways—to name but a few. A recent survey indicated that about fifty firms incorporated in Canada are operating in Latin America.[8] Important as this business is, it at best constitutes a minor Canadian interest, and an interest, furthermore, which is not likely to increase so long as political and economic conditions in Latin America tend to be unstable and nationalistic regimes incline to circumscribe opportunities for foreign investments.

Although Canadian trade with Latin America is likewise small it constitutes a more important interest than do investments. To the third trading nation of the world,[9] a country in which one out of every three jobs depends on foreign trade, exports of any amount are vital. In 1946 Canadian shipments to Latin America amounted to $90,000,000 or about 4 per cent of her total exports. These exports provided employment for many Canadian workingmen and also helped to bolster the Dominion's dwindling supply of dollars. The question naturally arises: Can Canada maintain this volume of trade, or is it a temporary war and postwar phenomenon? Some believe that when a foreign buyers' market returns Canada will be unable to compete with the United States. The growing shortage of dollars is also regarded as an unfavorable omen inasmuch as Canada will not be in a position to finance continued Latin American purchases through extensions of credit.[10]

Others more optimistically believe that the war has transformed

[7] On December 31, 1946 "assurances in force" in Latin America amounted to $145,211,554. Letter from Mr. R. T. Black, Superintendent of Agencies, to the author, May 1, 1947.

[8] Henri Beaupré, "Les premiers ambassadeurs canadiens en Amerique Latine," *Revue Dominicaine*, LII (December, 1946), 286.

[9] Canada, Department of External Affairs, Information Division (*Reference Paper*, No. 30, August 9, 1948), "Canada's Foreign Trade" (Ottawa, 1948), 4.

[10] Based on a confidential interview with a government official in Ottawa.

Canada into a mature industrial nation, an efficient producer able
to compete with the United States in the export market. They
also point to the continued demand for newsprint (which leads the
list of Canada's exports to South America), and express the belief
that offshore purchases for the Economic Co-operation Administration will tide Latin America over her dollar shortage. Thus far
sales to Latin America have continued to grow. In May 1948
they totaled $13,226,000 as against $10,170,000 in the same month
of 1947.[11]

The Canadian Government has given evidence that it considers
trade with Latin America a primary interest and that it will do
everything in its power to maintain the large postwar gains. Thus
MacKinnon followed his 1941 trade mission to South America
with a postwar tour of Mexico, Central America, and Colombia.[12]
Furthermore, commercial secretaries are now attached to the
Canadian diplomatic missions in Argentina, Brazil, Chile, Peru,
Mexico, and Cuba; consulates have been established in Caracas,
Venezuela, and São Paulo, Brazil; and trade commissioners are
stationed in Trinidad, Jamaica, Colombia, and Guatemala.[13]
Most-favored-nation trade agreements have been negotiated with
Argentina, Brazil, Chile, Colombia, Dominican Republic, Guate-
mala, Haiti, Mexico, Nicaragua, and Uruguay; and *modi vivendi*
with Ecuador and Venezuela. British trade treaties cover Canadian tariff relations with Bolivia, Costa Rica, and Panama.[14] The

---

[11] *Canadian Weekly Bulletin*, III (July 2, 1948), 2.

[12] See the address "New Markets for Canadian Trade" by Mr. MacKinnon before
the Canadian Inter-American Association, Montreal, March 21, 1946. Mimeographed
copy of speech is on file in the library of the Information Division, Department of
External Affairs, Ottawa.

[13] Countries in which commercial secretaries or trade commissioners are not located
are covered by those in neighboring states. Thus the commercial secretary in Argentina
is also responsible for Uruguay and Paraguay; the one in Chile for Bolivia; the officer
in Cuba for Haiti, the Dominican Republic, and Puerto Rico, and the one in Peru
for Ecuador. Some trade commissioners likewise have multiple jurisdiction. Trinidad
includes the Leeward and Windward Islands, the Guianas, and the French West
Indies; the trade commissioner in Jamaica covers the Bahamas and British Honduras;
and the one in Guatemala is responsible for all of Central America with the exception
of Panama and British Honduras.

[14] Canada, Department of Trade and Commerce, *Annual Report for the Fiscal Year
Ended March 31, 1946* (Ottawa, 1947), 51–54. The Nicaraguan agreement went into
effect December 19, 1946. See *Commercial Intelligence Journal*, LXXV (1947), 1056.

only Latin American countries with which Canada has established no formal commercial arrangement of any kind are Cuba, Honduras, and Peru.

III

World War II also focused Canadian attention on the problem of Western Hemisphere defense. It became increasingly apparent as the war progressed that a hostile move against the bulge of Brazil or the Panama Canal might be a grave blow against Dominion security. The Joint Defense Board set up in the Ogdensburg Agreement of 1940 provided a bi-lateral arrangement between Canada and the United States for the defense of the "north half of the Hemisphere."[15] The last phrase generally has been interpreted to include the Panama Canal and probably the territory as far south as the equator.[16] Beyond this Canada has been unwilling to go. Postwar suggestions that she become a signatory to the Rio Security Treaty of 1947 thus far have gone unheeded. Ottawa has preferred to base her defense on the Ogdensburg Agreement and not on a multilateral Western Hemisphere Pact.

Canada's attitude toward defense has reflected her traditional attitude toward world politics. She had, before World War II, consistently regarded herself as a Northern Hemisphere and not a Western Hemisphere state. This was due not only to her ties with Britain and her lack of real interests in the nations to the far south but also to her fear of being dragged at the wheels of United States foreign policy. As John P. Humphrey, Associate Professor of Law at McGill University, has said:

> Most Canadians believed that the Pan American Conferences were nothing more than a cloak for United States hegemony in Latin America. The Pan American Union looked suspiciously like a colonial office. It is not surprising that in the circumstances a country whose greatest fear was annexation should have preferred to leave the twenty-second chair severely alone.[17]

[15] A joint declaration in Ottawa and Washington, February 12, 1947, defined the peacetime role of the Permanent Joint Defense Board. See *Department of State Bulletin*, XVI (February 23, 1947), 361.

[16] John P. Humphrey, *The Inter-American System* (Toronto, 1942), 17.

[17] John P. Humphrey, "The Twenty-second Chair: Is It for Canada?" *Inter-American Quarterly*, III (October, 1941), 6.

Canada's foreign policy, then, was based on three fundamental points: (1) friendly relations with the United States; (2) co-operation with the British Commonwealth of Nations, and (3) support of the League of Nations. As western Europe went down to defeat Canada was forced to re-examine her position. Of the continued importance of co-operation with Washington there was no question, in fact such liaison was more vital than ever before. Likewise with England gravely threatened it was deemed impera-tive to give all out support to the British Commonwealth. But on the third issue, the nature of postwar international organization, the answer was not clear. From the standpoint of immediate defense the bilateral agreement of Ogdensburg was, perhaps, ade-quate. Was it sufficient to meet the long-range needs of a small power in an interdependent world? Should she not instead seek security through regional organization? With this in mind an increasing number of Canadians began to advocate adherence to the Pan American Union. The facts of geography, they argued, were inescapable. Canada was a Western Hemisphere nation and whether she liked it or not would be drawn into Latin American affairs. It would be far better for her to participate in than to ignore the councils that inevitably would affect her welfare. Such action would not be incompatible with her responsibilities toward other members of the British Commonwealth or toward a future world organization and would materially strengthen her position from the point of view of defense.[18]

To many Canadians, however, the Pan American Union did not constitute an answer to their problems. Not only did they believe that the Dominion's economic interest in Latin America was slight and likely to decrease when normal conditions returned, but they thought the only major accomplishments of the Union had been made in its technical conferences. These Canada was already

[18] Eugene H. Miller, "Canada and the Pan American Union," *International Journal*, III (Winter, 1947–1948), 26–28.

free to attend.[19]   Geographically, it was said Canada was closer to
Europe than to South America and such phrases as "continental
brotherhood" and "hemispheric solidarity" were but meaningless
phrases of rhetoric.   Moreover, if Canada joined the Union she
would be forced at conference meetings to "take sides" and thereby
might alienate the United States, on the one hand, or Latin American states on the other.   Since good relations with the United
States were a keystone of her foreign policy Canada had much to
lose and nothing to gain by such a step.   Finally, on the crucial
point, security, they maintained that in the One World of the
twentieth century national safety lay ultimately—and only—in
world organization, that regional organizations represented a form
of isolationism, and that Canada, already a member of one such
group, the British Commonwealth of Nations, should not join
another.   To do so would weaken the fabric of world organization
on which so much depended.[20]

How did the Canadian press react to these arguments?   Contrary
to their earlier indifference, and even hostility, a majority of the
influential newspapers in 1942 not only devoted considerable space

[19] Canada has been represented at the following special conferences: The First
Pan American Medical Congress (Washington, 1893), Second Pan American Medical
Congress (Mexico City, 1896), Pan American Road Congress (Oakland, Calif., 1915),
First Pan American Aeronautic Convention and Exposition (New York, 1917), First
International Congress of History of America (Rio de Janeiro, 1922), Pan American
Conference of Women (Baltimore, Md., 1922), Second Pan American Red Cross
Conference (Washington, 1926), Fourth Pan American Congress of Architects (Rio
de Janeiro, 1930), First Pan American Postal Congress (Madrid, 1931), Third Pan
American Red Cross Conference (Rio de Janeiro, 1935), Fourth Postal Congress of
the Americas and Spain (Panama, 1936), First Inter-American Travel Congress (San
Francisco, 1939), First American Conference of National Committees on Intellectual
Co-operation (Santiago, Chile, 1939), International Congress of Democracies of
America (Montevideo, 1939), Fourth Pan American Conference of National Directors
of Health (Washington, 1940), First Pan American Congress on Mining Engineering
and Geology (Santiago, Chile, 1942), Eleventh Pan American Sanitary Conference
(Rio de Janeiro, 1942), Inter-American Conference on Social Security (Santiago,
Chile, 1942), meetings of the Inter-American Bar Association, Inter-American Demo-
graphic Congress (Mexico City, 1943), First Pan American Conference on Criminal
Jurisprudence (Santiago, Chile, 1944), Conference on Cartography (Rio de Janeiro,
1944).   Not all these conferences were held under official government sponsorship.
Canada, Wartime Information Board (*Reference Paper*, No. 34, February 16, 1945),
"Canada and the Inter-American System" (Ottawa, 1945), 13–14.

[20] Miller, *loc. cit.*, 26–28.

to the Inter-American Defense Conference at Rio de Janeiro but expressed a desire to see some measure of Canadian participation. Typical was the comment of the *Victoria Daily Times:*

. . . just as the war has wrought changes in human relationships of which none of us dreamed a few years ago, so has it imparted a new and arresting significance to Canada's role as a world power in general and as a great nation of the Western Hemisphere in particular. Now more than ever before since she reached the status of full nationhood is it desirable that Canada's name be added to the roster. . . .

She is an American nation with a large and growing part of her economic life wrapped up in the development of the Western Hemisphere, an association which is bound to become more intensified after the Battle of the Continents has been won. . . .

She is not a member of the Pan American Union, and we have no knowledge that preliminary overtures looking toward her inclusion have been made; but at no time in the past has the moment for such "conversations" appeared so propitious as that which may present itself at the forthcoming meeting in the Brazilian capital.[21]

Throughout the next two years Canadian newspapers sustained an active interest in Pan Americanism. Particularly was this true in Quebec Province where L'Union des Latins d'Amerique and the Pan-American League of Canada promoted active publicity campaigns.[22] In Ottawa both of the capital's daily newspapers, the *Journal* and the *Citizen*, definitely committed themselves to the cause of the Inter-American system. "There is," wrote the former, "what the world knows as the Pan American Union. The time seems to have come when Canada should be a part of it."[23]

[21] *Victoria Daily Times*, January 10, 1942.

[22] L'Union des Latins d'Amerique, a French-Canadian organization, was founded in Montreal in 1940. In 1946–47, it had "close to 1,500 members, more than 350 of them learning either Spanish or Portuguese"; Letter from Lt. Col. Urgel Mitchell, president of the Union, to author September 10, 1947. For a complete list of its activities: sponsoring receptions for Latin American diplomats in Canada and Canadian ambassadors to Latin America, lectures, conducted tours to South or Central America, etc., see *Rapport du President, 1946–47* (Montreal, 1947), 1–3.

The Pan-American League of Canada was founded in Toronto in December, 1943. It has chapters in both Toronto and Montreal, but has moved its national office to the latter city and is concentrating its efforts there. In 1943–44 it sponsored immediate Canadian membership in the Pan American Union. Information was gathered in personal interviews with Mr. R. G. MacIsaac, president, and Mr. Marcel M. Therien, secretary, of the League, Montreal, November, 1946.

[23] *Ottawa Journal*, December 8, 1943. Cf. *Ottawa Citizen*, December 27, 1943.

What was the attitude of the Government? The extreme caution of Prime Minister King's statements makes a categorical answer difficult. A careful study of the record, however, indicates that perhaps the official view was evolving in the same direction as that of the press. Early in the thirties enquiries concerning the Dominion's membership in the Union had been dismissed with the brief comment that no invitation had been received. In 1939 Mr. King referred to technical difficulties—Canada was not a "Republic"—but admitted that this barrier could be by-passed.[24] In 1942 he told the House of Commons that "there have been times quite recently when we might have expected invitations but were given reasons why it would not be advisable to have an invitation extended. That position still exists to a certain extent for reasons which I cannot explain publicly. . . . "[25] Other government representatives were slightly more outspoken. Thus Leighton McCarthy, Canadian Minister to the United States, told a Montreal audience that "the time may come when Canada will take a larger share in the affairs of the Americas and become an active participant in Pan American Union plans for hemispheric solidarity." This would not, he thought, change Canada's "cherished position in the alliance of free British people." The two were not now contradictory "though they may have been once when Canadian policy was determined in Downing Street."[26] Brooke Claxton, Parliamentary Under-Secretary to the Prime Minister, went even farther when, speaking in Washington, he declared that "the Canadian people would like to see their country join the Pan American Union."[27] It is interesting to note, however, that in 1944 a study made by the Institute of Public Opinion revealed that 72 per cent of adult Canadians had never heard, or had no accurate knowledge, of the Pan American Union. Of those who did know what the Union was, 84 per cent favored Canadian membership,

[24] Canada, *House of Commons Debates*, March 30, 1939, p. 2420.

[25] *Ibid.*, August 1, 1942, p. 5146.

[26] *Montreal Star*, November 16, 1943.

[27] *New York Times*, September 1, 1943.

8 per cent were undecided, and only 8 per cent opposed.[28] Despite the overwhelmingly favorable reaction of the informed group, Prime Minister King concluded that the time had not come for Canadian participation, which, he felt, "could be based only upon a wise general appreciation in this country of the purposes and responsibilities of the Pan American Union."[29]

Mackenzie King's statement did not allay the rumor, still current in official and diplomatic circles, that the true reason for Canada's absence from the Pan American Union lay in United States opposition. Accordingly when at the Chapultepec Conference the following year a Chilean resolution extending an invitation to Canada was watered down to a mere expression of appreciation for the Dominion's war effort, the United States was again considered responsible.

IV

The end of the war and the developments of the next three years brought a marked recession of the tide in favor of the Union. Although a 1947 poll indicated a slight increase in the number of Canadians who were informed concerning its nature and approximately the same percentage in favor of Canadian membership,[30] those agencies which help mold public opinion—politicians, career diplomats, special interest groups and the press—were increasingly cool towards the project. The retreat from the position taken by Brooke Claxton was suggested in an address by Lester B. Pearson, Under-Secretary of State for External Affairs, before the *New York Herald Tribune* Forum on March 8, 1947:

> Perhaps our position vis-à-vis the Pan American Union . . . is not unlike the maid who having been asked why she did not marry her beau replied that he had not asked her. When pressed as to what she would do if he did ask her she hesitated and admitted coyly that though they were very close friends she wasn't sure that they were in love with each other. However, she might add, I will always feel a deep sisterly affection for

[28] Poll, Canadian Institute of Public Opinion, January 12, 1944, reported in *Ottawa Citizen*, January 14, 1944.

[29] Canada, *House of Commons Debates*, August 4, 1944, p. 5912.

[30] *Ottawa Citizen*, June 14, 1947.

him, and perhaps this might eventually grow into love and even mar-
riage.[31]

The following month a new element was injected into the situation. Senator Arthur Vandenburg, speaking to the Governing
Board of the Pan American Union on the 57th anniversary of its
founding, expressed the wish that

the time may soon come when our continental fellowship will be geographically and spiritually complete through the association with us, on
some appropriate basis, of the great and splendid Dominion of Canada.
. . . By every rule of reason we should wish her here. I would welcome
the final and total new world unity which will be nobly dramatized when
the twenty-second chair is filled, and our continental brotherhood is complete from the Arctic Circle to Cape Horn.[32]

Senator Vandenburg spoke as a private citizen but the fact that
he was at the time chairman of the Senate Foreign Relations Committee gave his words a particular significance. Did they fore-
shadow a change in American policy? If Canada now received an
invitation to join the Union what would her answer be?

No official comment was forthcoming on Senator Vandenburg's
talk. Five days later, however, one of the most prominent members
of the Liberal Party, the Right Honorable Vincent Massey, one-
time Canadian Ambassador in Washington and more recently
Canadian High Commissioner in London, begged his country not
to let herself become involved in Western Hemisphere politics.
To do so would, he felt sure, offer no practical advantage but would
lead to needless embarrassment.[33] Shortly thereafter Massey's
ideas were further elaborated in an article in *Maclean's Magazine*.
Contrary to the usual belief that membership in the Pan American
Union would promote trade and cultural relations with Latin
America it might, he thought, have the opposite effect. For
although equality of the American Republics was "established on
paper" the overwhelming economic and military strength of the
United States made it a difficult principle to apply. Many inter-

[31] *New York Herald Tribune*, March 9, 1947.
[32] *New York Times*, April 15, 1947.
[33] Statement to the Canadian Press, reported in the *Ottawa Citizen*, April 21, 1947.

American problems were controversial in nature and might place Canada in an embarrassing position of having to choose between the United States and her sister Republics. Let us, therefore, he argued, "cultivate good relations with Latin America in our own way, and not as a cog in the Pan-American machine."

Relations with the United States might also suffer:

> For us, Inter-American questions mean largely Canadian-American questions. There is no country enjoying such close and friendly contacts with the United States as we do. Canada has almost a special door in Washington. Our position will remain more dignified and also more effective by maintaining our own special relations with her, than by assimilating our position to that of a group of 20 republics, large and small. It is better for us to approach Washington as an important and respected neighbor than to go arm in arm with, say, Paraguay and Costa Rica.[34]

Finally, Massey objected to the isolationism of the Pan American Union:

> The Pan-American movement was cradled in isolationism. That was the prime reason why the South American states became closely associated in the nineteenth century. In both world wars the Pan-American movement showed its isolationist instincts. It has never outgrown a regional outlook. It is not surprising that many of those who advocate our joining it are former isolationists. The Union, in this respect is in sharp contrast with the British Commonwealth, a world association with a sense of world responsibility, and which acted accordingly in 1939.[35]

In contrast to the record of the British Commonwealth, the Pan American machinery had never worked in co-operation with the League of Nations and there was "no sign of any formal co-operation between the Pan-American states *collectively* and the new United Nations." Yet the "only real defense . . . under the conditions of modern warfare is an effective system of world security." Under these conditions to be maneuvered into joining [the Pan American Union] "would not indicate a very firm grasp of policy."[36]

---

[34] Vincent Massey, "Should Canada Join the Pan American Union?" *Maclean's Magazine*, LX (August 15, 1947), 46.

[35] *Ibid.*, 45.

[36] *Ibid.*, 45, 47.

There were many other evidences of the trend of Canadian policy. Leaders of the Co-operative Commonwealth Federation party, formerly strong advocates of Pan Americanism now expressed the opinion that the development of a strong regional group, especially if dominated by a powerful state, would undermine the work of the United Nations.[37]   A number of influential newspapers also restated their views.   Typical was the comment of the *Ottawa Citizen:*

The United Nations is fighting for its existence as the body within which all situations tending toward war should be thrashed out.   And while there is a place today for regional groupings of the kind the Pan American Union represents, there is danger also that these may be used as instruments to sidetrack or supplant it.[38]

The trend in government policy was indicated by Paul Martin, Canadian representative on the United Nations Economic and Social Council.   In opposing a move to set up a special Economic Commission for Latin America, he warned against a "hasty" embarkation on a course of regionalism that might constitute a reversal of the approach drafted at San Francisco.[39]

By the fall of 1947 close observers were inclined to believe that Canada preferred not to receive an invitation to the forthcoming Bogotá Conference.   The fact that the meeting (held from March

[37] Critics of the C. C. F. suggest that the real reason for the new policy is enthusiasm for a Labor Commonwealth generated by the advent to power of the English Labor Government.   Mr. Coldwell and other party leaders deny this.   They maintain that they were disillusioned by their experience with Latin American bloc politics at international conferences, particularly the group voting of the American states at San Francisco.   Statement based on interviews with C. C. F. leaders in Ottawa in November, 1946 and June, 1947.

[38] *Ottawa Citizen,* April 22, 1947.   For other newspapers which altered their opinion on closer political ties with Latin America see: *Ottawa Journal,* August 25, 1947; *Toronto Globe and Mail,* August 27, 1947; *La Presse,* September 5, 1947; and *La Patrie,* August 26, 1947.

[39] *Ottawa Journal,* August 25, 1947.   Martin's remarks at this time are interesting in the light of his stand in 1936 when, speaking to the House of Commons, he said: "I would suggest, while I see great difficulties in determining where the terminals of Great Britain's region would be and while I am not at all anxious to disturb our relations with her . . . that the Government might well consider the advisability of taking part in the Pan American Union.   One cannot go through the deliberations of the Montevideo conference . . . without feeling the wisdom of this kind of suggestion" (Canada, *House of Commons Debates,* June 18, 1936, p. 3884).   Martin also supported Pan Americanism in 1942 (*ibid.,* February 27, 1942, p. 913).

30 to May 2, 1948) adjourned without any formal overtures being made to Canada suggests that the Mackenzie King government had successfully avoided letting itself be maneuvered (to use Massey's phrase) into an open decision. Actually Canada had, for the moment, cast in her lot with world-wide rather than regional organization. Her choice was probably based as much on her consciousness of her position as a Northern rather than a Western Hemisphere nation as it was on her allegiance to the United Nations.

V

Even as this decision was being made forces were at work which might draw the United States and Canada into a more formal alliance—possibly into a new regional grouping. The growing menace of Soviet expansion in Europe, the world-wide threat of Soviet Communism, and the difficulties being experienced within the United Nations suggested that some form of regional organization might yet be the best guarantee of national security. In Canada, the French and English elements of the population which had found it impossible to develop a common enthusiasm for Pan Americanism were united in their distaste for and fear of imperialistic Marxism. Prime Minister Mackenzie King reflected this feeling in a speech in Ottawa on January 20, 1948:

So long as Communism remains a menace to the free world, it is vital to the defense of freedom to maintain a preponderance of military strength on the side of freedom, and to ensure that degree of unity among the nations which will ensure that they cannot be defeated and destroyed one by one.[40]

In the light of this statement the Prime Minister's reaction to the Brussels Pact was of great interest.[41] Addressing the House of Commons on the day of its signature, March 17, 1948, he said:

[40] Canada, Department of External Affairs, Information Division (*Reference Paper*, No. 33, October 29, 1948), "North Atlantic Treaty" (Ottawa, 1948), 1.

[41] The Brussels Pact binds five western European nations—Great Britain, France, Belgium, the Netherlands, and Luxemburg—in a fifty-year treaty of collective military aid and economic and social co-operation.

This pact is far more than an alliance of the old kind. It is a partial realization of the idea of collective security by an arrangement made under the Charter of the United Nations. As such, it is a step towards peace, which may well be followed by other similar steps until there is built up an association of all free states which are willing to accept responsibilities of mutual assistance to prevent aggression and preserve peace.

. . . .

The Canadian Government has been closely following recent developments in the international sphere. The peoples of all free countries may be assured that Canada will play her full part in every movement to give substance to the conception of an effective system of collective security by the development of regional pacts under the Charter of the United Nations.[42]

King's hint that his government would participate actively in a regional security pact was confirmed by the Secretary of State for External Affairs, L. S. St. Laurent. In opening a four-day debate on foreign affairs (April 29, 1948), he maintained that although Canada was not abandoning the United Nations it was seriously considering affiliation with a "Western Union" formed in accordance with Article 51 of the United Nations Charter. The purpose of such a "collective security league" he told the members of the House:

would not be merely negative. . . . It would create a dynamic counter-attraction to communism—the dynamic counter-attraction of a free, prosperous and progressive society as opposed to the totalitarian and reactionary society of the communist world. The formation of such a defensive group of free states would not be a counsel of despair but a message of hope. It would not mean that we regarded a third world war as inevitable; but that the free democracies had decided that to prevent such a war they would organize so as to confront the forces of communist expansionism with an overwhelming preponderance of moral, economic, and military force and with sufficient degree of unity to ensure that this preponderance of force is so used that the free nations cannot be defeated one by one. No measure less than this will do. We must at all cost avoid the fatal repetition of the history of the pre-war years when the Nazi aggressor picked off its victims one by one. Such a process does not end at the Atlantic.[43]

[42] "North Atlantic Treaty," *loc. cit.*, 1.

[43] *Canadian Weekly Bulletin*, III (May 7, 1948), 9. This Weekly is the official news bulletin of the Information Division of the Department of External Affairs.

The trend in policy suggested by St. Laurent was further emphasized by Lester B. Pearson, Under-Secretary of State for External Affairs, in an address to the Convention of Kiwanis International at Los Angeles, California. Speaking on June 8, the very day on which Premier Gottwald signed the new Czech constitution, Pearson set forth at some length the benefits of regional security. Referring to the Inter-American Pact of Rio de Janeiro as an example of a regional agreement within the framework of the United Nations he declared that "a wider and more powerful association" was "required to stop the aggressor. . . . an association of western European and Atlantic democracies . . . every member of which will take on equal and reciprocal obligations for collective defence and mutual aid in war, and work together for freedom and prosperity in peace." He stated categorically that Canada was ready to co-operate with the United States in translating such a program into action. Appealing to the Americans in his audience, Pearson reminded them that there were "difficulties in the way of doing this, difficulties which only the United States" could overcome. He went on to say:

It would not be appropriate for an outsider to tell you how this can be done—even if he knew! I have confidence, however, that it can and will be done. Yours is the major responsibility, because yours is the power, but you can count, I feel sure, on the support of your northern neighbor for any steady and consistent, firm and unprovocative policy to this great end. . . . [44]

Three days later, in Toronto, L. S. St. Laurent reiterated Canada's determination both to oppose communism and to support the United Nations. He added, however, that

the best guarantee of peace today is the creation and preservation by the nations of the Free World, under the leadership of Great Britain, the United States and France, of an overwhelming preponderance of force over any adversary or possible combination of adversaries. This force must not be only military; it must be economic; it must be moral. [45]

[44] *Ibid.*, III (June 11, 1948), 8.

[45] *Ibid.*, III (June 11, 1948), 8, from a speech delivered at a dinner in connection with the International Trade Fair in Toronto.

Developments in the United States were tending in the same direction. On June 11, the day of St. Laurent's Toronto address, the United States Senate by a vote of 64-4 passed a resolution favoring the principle of military aid to defensive alliances formed among the free nations of the world. Shortly thereafter discussions were begun in Washington between representatives of the United States, the United Kingdom, Belgium, Holland, Luxemburg, France and Canada on the question of western European security arrangements and the association of the United States and Canada with them. Although the discussions were carried on with complete secrecy L. B. Pearson, in his first public address after he assumed the duties of Secretary of State for External Affairs, [46] reported optimistically: "It is not possible for me to tell you today how these discussions are going. I can, however, say that the Canadian Government has every reason to believe that the discussion will be fruitful; that Canada is playing a useful part in them." He hoped that an effective "North Atlantic Regional System for security and progress would soon be formed—a regional system in which *all* members would have a voice in framing policy and not just the responsibility for its execution." [47]

Canada's desire to co-operate with the United States and the countries of the Western Union in a North Atlantic security pact was reiterated on October 25. In an important address delivered at the annual meeting of the United Nations Association of Canada in Toronto the Minister of National Defence, Brooke Claxton, stated in unequivocal terms that fear of Soviet aggression underlay Canada's deep interest in such a regional agreement:

We all know that it is much better to stand together than to fall separately. And make no mistake about it. If a war comes, if the Soviet Union commits an act of aggression, it will be an act which will break our peace and ultimately threaten our security. The only war possible today is a war of aggression by the Soviets. I have heard some people—just a few—speak about the possibility of Canada being neutral in such a war. I do not

---

[46] Pearson gave up his career service position of Under-Secretary of State for External Affairs for the cabinet post on September 10, 1948.

[47] *Canadian Weekly Bulletin*, III (September 24, 1948), 8.

believe that this is even a theoretical possibility for us. Our vital interests, even our territory could be open to attack. The choice in war would be a simple one—Communism or Canada. Our people would never tolerate a position in which we were passive while our country was being defended by others.[48]

Claxton emphasized the point that the Government's stand on a North Atlantic security pact had the support not only of his own Liberal party but also of the Cooperative Commonwealth Federation and the Progressive-Conservatives.[49] In conclusion the Secretary of Defence maintained that:

> We want to let time, not trial of war, be the determining factor.
> That is what democracies in search of peace must be working for now—time. And the only way we can gain time is to be prepared to defend our way of life and to proclaim our willingness to do just that in such unmistakable terms that no one can stumble into war without knowing where each of us will stand.[50]

Canada's stand was announced three days later, October 28, when L. B. Pearson, Secretary of State for External Affairs, told a press conference that "the Canadian Government has informed other participants in the Washington discussions that Canada is now ready to enter negotiations for a regional treaty for collective security with them and with other North Atlantic states."[51] Thus the Canadian Government which had been inclined to frown upon membership in the Pan American Union on the ground that it was a regional organization whose work competed with that of the United Nations[52] had become, in eighteen months, a strong advocate of an entirely new security group. Ottawa had apparently made her decision. The Dominion's primary interests lay in the

[48] *Ibid.*, III (October 29, 1948), 1.

[49] Resolutions adopted by the Liberals unanimously at the national convention in Ottawa, August 6, 1948; by the C. C. F. convention, August 21, 1948; and by the Progressive-Conservative party convention, October 2, 1948.

[50] *Canadian Weekly Bulletin*, III (October 29, 1948), 7.

[51] *Ibid.*, 9.

[52] The statement that Canada was opposed to membership in a regional group other than the Commonwealth of Nations is based primarily on numerous off-the-record interviews by the author with Canadian diplomats in Latin America and with cabinet members, members of Parliament, and political leaders in Ottawa, September, 1946—June, 1947.

Northern and not in the Western Hemisphere. The question remained, however, Would the United States depart so far from her traditional policy as to join her in a North Atlantic Union? Recent events have indicated that such a course of action is not unlikely. [53]

[53] Acting Secretary of State Lovett told a press conference that proposals for membership in a North Atlantic Security Treaty "if and when presented by the Brussels pact countries, would be considered by the United States in the light of the Vandenberg resolution adopted by the United States Senate last June" (Department of State, *Wireless Bulletin* No. 266, November 10, 1948, 1). Since this resolution favored "the strongest encouragement to the development under the Charter, of regional 'and other' collective arrangements for self-defense" (*New York Times*, June 12, 1948), Lovett's statement could be interpreted as favorable to United States affiliation.

Sovereignty and Imperialism in the Polar Regions

By Elmer Plischke*

In the postwar years the world has been privileged to enjoy an encouraging independence boom.[1] Nineteenth century colonialism appears to be on the decline. Autonomous Iceland and politically advanced colonial areas such as the Philippine Islands, India, Burma, the Near East Mandates of Iraq, Syria, Lebanon, and Transjordania have achieved independence. Meanwhile, the Dutch East Indies are rapidly following suit, and other areas, including Ceylon and French Indo-China, are tending towards autonomy within a dominion status. Old-fashioned overseas imperialism therefore seems to be receding from the international scene.

But the decline of colonialism does not necessarily imply a concomitant recession of economic or financial imperialism, or of competition for strategic dependencies. The current development, at least as far as strategic imperialism is concerned, is partly characterized by a shift in geographic locale toward the polar regions.

1. Rivalry in the Arctic and Antarctic

Although this struggle for territory involves both the Arctic and the Antarctic, it differs perceptibly in the two areas. In the Arctic there is little if any "unpossessed" territory, since the various known islands and archipelagoes have been legally claimed and

*Elmer Plischke is Assistant Professor, Department of Government and Politics, University of Maryland.

[1] See Elmer Plischke, "The Independence Boom," *Forum*, CVII (May, 1947), 404–11.

existing pretensions generally are uncontested today. Nevertheless a new strategic imperialism appears to be emerging in the Arctic because of the change in the power positions of the United States and the Soviet Union as a result of World War II, and because of the technological developments in the machines of mass destruction perfected during the struggle—including the atom bomb, long-range flying, jet and rocket propulsion, the guided missile, and other potential devices for the waging of intercontinental hostilities.

The chief reasons, however, for recent intensified interest in this area are trans-polar aviation and aerial defense. Geographic position and the elements of time and distance combine to render the Arctic Basin of paramount strategic value. The currently-publicized "polar projection" of the globe well illustrates these factors of location and relative distance, depicting the globe with the North Pole at its center and with the South Pole as its outer circumference. Its significance is simply that, except for India and China, the world's areas of densest population—between which polar security and imperialist competition obviously are most vital—lie immediately around the Arctic Basin. In many cases, air distances between the countries of the Northern Hemisphere are markedly shorter via the Arctic than are those of prewar established routes. Hundreds, if not thousands, of air-miles are saved along polar great circle routes between many major localities.[2] An appreciation of this geographic fact is fundamental to an understanding of the future role of the Arctic in security and war plans, as well as for peacetime, global commercial aviation.[3]

[2] Elmer Plischke, "Trans-Arctic Aviation," *Economic Geography*, XIX (July, 1943), 283–91; reprinted under same title in The Smithsonian Institution, *Annual Report* (Washington, 1944), 285–96.

[3] American awareness of the polar security problem, for example, is well illustrated by our postwar cold-climate task force maneuvers. In 1946 four such operations were undertaken, and the following winter four additional practices were scheduled. Among the more interesting are "Operation Musk-ox," a 3,100-mile joint Canadian-American snowmobile trek; "Operation Frostbite," in which carrier aircraft were tested by our Navy in Greenland; "Operation Iceberg," to test American submarines in Arctic waters to the north of Bering Strait; and "Operation High Jump," or Rear Admiral Richard E. Byrd's Fourth Antarctic Expedition.

In the Antarctic, by way of contrast, the immediate urgency of the power-politics struggle is less acute, and the imperialist race is prompted by other considerations. The Antarctic Continent is a vast frozen waste, with an ice-covered plateau some 8,000 to 10,000 feet high, broken by a number of imposing mountain ranges. It is relatively isolated, cut off by pack ice and stormy seas which render it somewhat unapproachable. It is not the focal point of important surrounding land masses. Weather changes rapidly, so that, although experimental flying has been undertaken and with some success, it is hazardous at best.

The Antarctic is almost entirely devoid of natural life, both flora and fauna, except for seals and penguins. Even they find the climatic so rigorous that all but the emperor penguin leave the continent in the winter months. There appears to be a dearth of minerals, partly perhaps because of insufficient exploration and information. It is known that there are deposits of lignite, iron, nickel, and other minerals, perhaps including uranium, but in the immediate future they very likely will remain inaccessible. The real economic value of the Antarctic at the present time centers about the whaling industry, which has been plied in subjacent waters for decades, over half of the total annual catch in recent years being taken in the vicinity of the Ross Sea and Graham Land.

Nevertheless, the Antarctic Continent constitutes the last remaining unpossessed territory on this globe, and challenges the imagination of contemporary empire builders. Its immediate value still is doubtful, especially for purposes of colonization, and even its commercial possibilities are questionable, with the exception of whaling. There therefore seems to be little reason for restive jurisdictional controversy because of economic factors. The potentialities of the area, however, are far from determined, and it is these that have stimulated much of the imperialist wrangle of recent decades. The competition for hegemony also is prompted in part by a desire to own territory for reasons of prestige. For a few peripheral states, principally Argentina and Chile, strategic factors are involved, but these are not of major global significance.

II. Jurisdiction in the Arctic

Polar imperialism in the Arctic antedates that in the Antarctic, the former dating back to the days of the search for the Northwest Passage and the discoveries and claims it engendered. But today the jurisdictional question has generally been resolved and major conflicting claims have been settled. It therefore is a relatively simple matter to understand the territorial status of most Arctic possessions.

It is readily acknowledged that the entire island of Greenland belongs to Denmark.[4] But, according to the late President Roosevelt and former Secretary of State Cordell Hull, the island lies in the Western Hemisphere, and therefore comes under the aegis of the Monroe Doctrine, which prohibits non-American states from acquiring territory in the island.[5] By and large, the same is true of Iceland, except that it enjoys complete independence and was admitted to separate membership in the United Nations in 1946. Spitsbergen, together with Bear Island, was recognized as Norwegian territory by multilateral treaty in 1920.[6] Norway also possesses Jan Mayen Island—in the Arctic between Iceland and Spitsbergen—having formally extended jurisdiction over it in 1929.[7]

Since 1920 the Soviet Government has taken a more active interest in the Arctic than any other state. Despite the Soviet decree of April 12, 1926, incorporating the sector principle into its national law as described below, the Soviet Government has adopted a policy of effective occupation, settlement, and adminis-

---

[4] "Legal Status of Eastern Greenland," *Permanent Court of International Justice*, Series A/B, No. 53 (1933); also "The Legal Status of Eastern Greenland," *Geographical Journal*, LXXXII (1933), 151–56.

[5] *New York Times*, June 6, 1940; *ibid.*, April 11, 1940; *ibid.*, April 13, 1940; and Department of State, *Bulletin*, IV (April 12, 1941), 447. Also see Lawrence Martin, "The Geography of the Monroe Doctrine and the Limits of the Western Hemisphere," *Geographical Review*, XXX (1940), 525–28.

[6] *Foreign Relations of the United States*, I (1920), 78–87; *American Journal of International Law, Supplement*, XVIII (1924), 199–208.

[7] For royal proclamation, see *British and Foreign State Papers* [hereafter cited as *State Papers*], CXXXI (1929), 582. For background, see J. M. Wordie, "Jan Mayen Island," *Geographical Journal*, LIX (1922), 180–95.

tration for the islands to the north of its mainland. In view of this display of jurisdiction no opposing pretensions, with but one or two exceptions,[8] have been raised by other states to territory lying within the geographic limits of the Soviet portion of the Arctic.

The Dominion of Canada similarly claims all the known islands lying to the north of her mainland. This pretension has not always been respected, so that in the past 20 years or more, a serious effort has been made to subject the entire polar island empire to effective state administration. The Dominion, like the Soviet Union, thus has sought to establish an absolute legal title to the polar territory adjacent to its mainland.[9]

In this manner, Denmark, Norway, and especially the Soviet Union and Canada possess, or claim to possess, all known territory within the Arctic Basin to the north of the continental mainland. Their dependent territories provide the landed areas necessary for the development of advance polar bases and strategic facilities.

With a view to future defense, however, the United States finds itself in the unenviable position of having very little Arctic domain. Our only such advance territory is Alaska, which, though a goodly portion extends beyond the Arctic Circle, is temperate rather than polar as far as strategic location is concerned. Despite active bases, such as Kodiak, Adak, Attu, and others in the Aleutians as well as on the mainland, Alaska is inadequate for complete trans-polar security for the United States. Its location is such that defensively it can scarcely be relied upon except to protect our flank against attack from the northwest.

III. Arctic Power Politics and Imperialism

The solution of our polar security problem therefore has been said to lie in close co-operation with Canada and Denmark, and

[8] Particularly Franz Josef Land in the west, for many decades claimed by Norway, and Wrangel Island in the east, in which the United States had evinced some interest.

[9] See, for example, V. Kenneth Johnston, "Canada's Title to the Arctic Islands," *Canadian Historical Review*, XIV (1933), 24–41; and James Montagues, "Canada Occupies the Arctic: Services Rendered by the Government," *Canadian Magazine*, LXXVI (December, 1931), 10, 11, 41.

perhaps Iceland, in establishing a joint defense ring over the Arctic cap of the Western Hemisphere. Since their Arctic territories may very well become the battle field of future hemispheric warfare, such co-operation naturally will accrue to their benefit as well as to ours.

Much has been achieved by way of laying the foundation for permanent American-Canadian co-operation. On August 18, 1940, some 15 months before Pearl Harbor, it was mutually agreed that a United States–Canadian Permanent Joint Board of Defense be established.[10] It served a very useful purpose during the war and still is meeting periodically to discuss mutual defense problems. Five basic principles were agreed upon by our governments early in 1947, perhaps the most important of which provides for mutual and reciprocal availability of military, naval, and air facilities in each country including the Arctic islands,[11] thus rendering Canadian polar territory susceptible to use by the United States.

Along the eastern flank of the North American polar zone, the United States, of course, retains its wartime base in Newfoundland, where a 99-year gift-site was granted to us by Great Britain in connection with the Bases-Destroyers Deal, announced on September 3, 1940.[12] But it lies too far south to be effective in our polar defense.

Of greater interest are Greenland and Iceland. During the recent war, the United States occupied both in order to forestall German control of the North Atlantic. Eight months before Pearl Harbor, on April 9, 1941, an agreement was signed with the Danish Minister in Washington, granting to the United States complete rights of occupation over the island during the war, without detriment to the sovereignty of Denmark, of course. It was further provided that when the danger to the American Continent had passed, the United States and Denmark would consult together,

---

[10] Ogdensburg Agreement, see Department of State, *Bulletin*, III (August 24, 1940), 154.

[11] *Indianapolis Star*, February 13, 1947.

[12] President Roosevelt's Message to Congress, *Peace and War: U. S. Foreign Policy, 1931–1941* (Washington, 1943), 211–14.

and either one of them might then give 12 months' notice to ter-
minate the agreement.[13]   In July, 1941, also before the Japanese
attack and on the request of the Icelandic Government, the United
States concluded a similar agreement with it, authorizing American
occupation of that island, again without prejudice to established
sovereignty.[14]

The withdrawal after the end of hostilities of our occupation
forces from Greenland and Iceland, though doubtless reluctant, is
today virtually complete.   By agreement between the American
Government and Iceland, our troops commenced to withdraw
from the island in October, 1946.   By the end of the year, in
addition to a handful of American businessmen, only a few hundred
ground personnel remained to service civilian transport planes at
airfields maintained by the United States in the island.[15]   Occupation troops similarly have been withdrawn from Greenland.   Early
in 1947, however, rumors were circulating to the effect that Denmark contemplated selling the island to the United States, but
these rumors were officially denied.[16]   Danish sale of Greenland
to the United States would be a very logical step for both countries,
as the island is considered by both to come under the Monroe
Doctrine, is vital to the United States security position, and is of
little practical value to Denmark.

The Soviet Union, meanwhile, has been displaying an active
interest in Spitsbergen, which is strategically located to the east
of Greenland, between northern Eurasia and America.   Early in
1947 the Soviet Government renewed its 1944–1945 request for
a Spitsbergen military base.[17]   The Soviet emphasis on the necessity for joint defense of the archipelago caused the Norwegian
Government secretly to wish it had never acquired the islands,
especially since they mean so little to Norway either economically

---

[13] *New York Times*, April 11, 1941.

[14] *Ibid.*, July 8, 1941.

[15] *Ibid.*, October 24 and 26, 1946.   For Soviet pressure insistent upon American
withdrawal and for our negotiations with Iceland, see *ibid.*, September 26 ff., 1946.

[16] *Ibid.*, October 17, 1947; also see *ibid.*, May 30, 1947.

[17] *Ibid.*, January 10 ff., 1947.

or geographically. In March, 1947, the Norwegian Parliament turned down the Soviet request by a vote of 101 to 11. Since Soviet commercial relations with Spitsbergen apparently fail to justify its political control and the establishment of military bases, Norway hopes to be able to pass the issue along to the United Nations when it becomes really critical.[18]

There is little doubt that American interest in Greenland and Iceland, and Soviet interest in Spitsbergen, will continue to grow in direct proportion to the development of apparent need for polar security. And each is likely to oppose the pretensions of the other to bases in these islands. If the United States acquires strategic rights in Greenland and Iceland, the imperialist struggle is likely to converge upon Spitsbergen.

IV. Polar Sector Theory

One of the more interesting features of the rivalry for polar territory is that jurisdictional claims have taken a somewhat unusual feature. A new legal doctrine has been developed, seeking to resolve, arbitrarily and in advance, the problems of polar jurisdiction. It is called the "sector principle." Geographically, a polar sector is a triangular slice of polar territory, with its apex at the pole, bounded by two meridians of longitude, and usually having a parallel of latitude or a territorial coastline as its base. All Arctic sectors therefore converge at the North Pole, while Antarctic sectors meet at the South Pole.

Sectors differ in the two polar regions for a number of reasons. In the Arctic, where there are great sub-polar landmasses, the base of the sector is formed by the northern boundary of the subjacent continental territory, and the sides of the triangle conform to the easternmost and westernmost longitudinal extremities of the territory. This is particularly true of Canada and the Soviet Union.

In the Antarctic, on the other hand, where there are no prom-

[18] *Ibid.*, March 4, 1947.

inent sub-polar landmasses—the southern coasts of Africa, Australia, and South America being neither large nor immediately subjacent—more or less arbitrary parallels of latitude are selected as the northern bases of the sectors, while the sides are extended to the widest extent possible. Thus, in the Antarctic the base of the sector bears no relation at all to the width of the possessions of the claimant state outside the Antarctic Circle.

In the Arctic, sectors have also been drawn to the pole from colonial possessions, such as Greenland and Spitsbergen, and from the Alaska Territory. This has not been done in the Antarctic, although some sectors are extended poleward in such a manner as to include minor colonial possessions, such as the Falkland, South Georgia, South Shetlands, South Orkneys, South Sandwich, Bouvet, and other islands.

A. ARCTIC SECTORS

In the past, six Arctic sectors have been delineated, one assigned respectively to each of the following: Denmark (based on Greenland and Iceland), Norway (based on Spitsbergen and Jan Mayen Island), Finland, the Soviet Union, the United States (based on Alaska), and Canada.[19] Since the poleward extension of the prewar Finnish longitudinal boundaries was interrupted by the Spitsbergen Archipelago, some sectorists eliminated Finland from this list. Today, in any case, she would be excluded by virtue of her cession of the Arctic coastal Petsamo District to the Soviet Union in the Peace Treaty of 1947.[20] Since the establishment of the complete independence of Iceland, it appears that a logical

---

[19] Charles Cheney Hyde, "Acquisition of Sovereignty Over Polar Areas," *Iowa Law Review*, XIX (1934), 289–92; Naval War College, "Jurisdiction and Polar Areas," *International Law Situations, 1937* (Washington, 1939), Situation 3, p. 116; Gustav Smedal, *Acquisition of Sovereignty Over Polar Areas* (Oslo, 1931), 54; Vladimir Leont'evich Lakhtine, *Prava na Severny Poliarny Prostranstva* (Moscow, 1928), 37–38, as cited in T. A. Taracouzio, *Soviets in the Arctic* (New York, 1938), 321. Lakhtine's study was rewritten in English under the title "Rights Over the Arctic," *American Journal of International Law*, XXIV (1930), 703–17.

[20] Article 2; see U. S., Department of State (Publication 2743), *Treaties of Peace with Italy, Bulgaria, Hungary, Roumania, and Finland* (Washington, 1947).

presentation of polar sectorism in the Arctic would have to provide a separate sector for it, so that six Arctic sectoral states would remain.

As a juridical theory, the sector principle originally was propounded on February 20, 1907, by Canadian Senator P. Poirier, who allocated sectors to Norway, Russia, the United States, and Canada.[21] Eighteen years later, the American publicist David Hunter Miller sliced the Arctic into three components—Russian, American, and Canadian.[22] On April 15, 1926, the Soviet Government issued a decree declaring that all lands and islands to the north of its mainland (between 32°4'35" E. longitude and 168° 49'30" W. longitude) belonged to the U.S.S.R.[23] Following this decree, a number of Soviet writers assumed the major brunt of the case for the principle. Its chief exponents are E. A. Korovin,[24] Leonid Breitfuss,[25] Vladimir Leont'evich Lakhtine,[26] and S. V. Sigrist.[27] These were rapidly followed by a number of other writers, including the German geographer Ernst Sorge,[28] Professor

[21] Dominion of Canada, *Senate Debates* (1906–1907), 271. Despite subsequent reliance upon sectorism by a number of Dominion officials, the Government of Canada never has based the legality of its pretensions to polar territory upon it, and neither the Canadian Parliament nor the Foreign Office has declared or implied its adherence to the principle.

[22] "Political Rights in the Arctic," *Foreign Affairs*, IV (October, 1925), 47–60. This study was combined with another on "National Rights in the Antarctic," *Foreign Affairs*, V (April, 1927), 508–10, and was published as "Political Rights in the Polar Regions," in Wolfgang L. G. Joerg, *Problems of Polar Research* (New York, 1928), 235–50.

[23] *State Papers*, CXXIV (1926), 1064–65; translating text from *Izvestia*, April 16, 1926.

[24] "Problema vozdushnoi okkupatsii v sviazi s pravom na poliarnye prostranstva" [Problems of Aerial Occupation in Connection with Rights in the Arctic], *Voprosy Vozdushnogo Prava*, I, 104 ff; "S.S.S.R. i Poliarnye Zemli" [The U.S.S.R. and the Land in the Arctic], *Sovetskoe Pravo*, III (1926), 43 ff; and "S.S.S.R. i Severnyi Polius" [The U.S.S.R. and the North Pole], *Sovetskoe Pravo*, III (1929), no. 3.

[25] "Die territoriale Sektoreneinteilung der Arktis im Zusammenhang mit dem zuerwartenden transarktischen Luftverkehr," *Petermanns Mitteilungen*, LXXIV (1928), 23–28; translated by M. B. A. Anderson and R. M. Anderson as "Territorial Division of the Arctic," *Dalhousie Review*, VIII (January, 1929), 456–70.

[26] *Supra*, note 19.

[27] "Sovetskoe Pravo v Poliarnykh Prostranstvakh" [Soviet Law in the Arctic], *Rabochii Sud* (1928), 984 ff.

[28] "Die Arktis," *Handbuch der Geographischen Wissenschaft*, ed. Fritz Klute (Potsdam, 1933), 496–543 (Ch. 8).

Bruce Hopper,[29] and the Canadian writer D. M. LeBourdais.[30] These latter, however, appear to accept the principle without attempting to justify its validity. It is interesting to note that, while all of these exponents pretend to interpret the same principle, they fail to agree on the allocation of the sectoral lines and the number and size of the sectors. As a matter of fact, there is very little agreement even among the Soviet authorities, except as far as the Canadian sector is concerned.[31]

B. ANTARCTIC SECTORAL CLAIMS

Seven sweeping sectoral areas have been claimed in the Antarctic, respectively by Great Britain and the Dominions of Australia and New Zealand, Argentina, Chile, Norway, and France, but not including the United States. The British Commonwealth thus claims almost three-quarters of the Antarctic Continent, Norway asserts possessory rights to more than one-eighth, and the small French pretension cuts through that of Australia, whose portion therefore is divided. Argentina and Chile advance mutually competing rights to the sector claimed by Great Britain. A slice comprising about one-eighth of the Continent remains unclaimed.

The British Government commenced the race on July 21, 1908, by laying claim to the "Falkland Islands Dependencies," including Graham Land, located on the Atlantic side of the Antarctic.[32] By letters patent, on March 28, 1917, this territory was more accurately defined, when specific longitudinal and latitudinal boundaries were circumscribed.[33] On the opposite side of the

---

[29] "Sovereignty in the Arctic," *Research Bulletin on the Soviet Union*, II (August 30, 1937), 81–83.

[30] "Canada's New Front Door," *Canadian Magazine*, LXXXIX (March, 1938), 9.

[31] Summarized in Elmer Plischke, "Trans-Polar Aviation and Jurisdiction Over Arctic Airspace," *American Political Science Review*, XXXVII (1943), 1008–10.

[32] This pretension also included South Georgia, the South Orkneys, the South Shetlands, and the South Sandwich Islands, lying to the south and east of the Falkland Islands. *State Papers*, CI (1907–1908), 76–77.

[33] All islands and territories were claimed between 20° and 50° W. longitude to the south of 50° S. latitude and between 50° and 80° W. longitude to the south of 58° S. latitude; hence on the Antarctic Continent, it embraced all territory between 20° and 80° W. longitude. For letters patent, see *State Papers*, CXI (1917–1918), 16–17. See also Sidney F. Harmer, "Scientific Development of the Falkland Islands Dependencies," *Geographical Journal*, LVI (July, 1920), 61–65; and "Ross Dependency," *Geographical Journal*, LXII (November, 1923), 364.

globe, the British Government staked out two further claims. On July 30, 1923, by Order in Council, the British Government created the "Ross Dependency" and placed it under the control of the Governor-General of the Dominion of New Zealand.[34] Ten years later, on February 7, 1933, a British Order in Council placed a large slice of Antarctica, constituting more than one-fourth of its total area, under the jurisdiction of the Commonwealth of Australia.[35] By parliamentary act, the Government of Australia accepted jurisdiction on June 13.[36]

The British Government specifically exempted Adélie Land from its 1933 enactment, the limits of which it did not deign to define. This reservation was founded, however, upon the pretension of France to this territory, based on the discoveries of the French navigator Dumont d'Urville in 1840. On March 29, 1924, *Le Moniteur* published a presidential decree making the French Minister of Colonies responsible for its administration, and the following November the latter placed Adélie Land, together with several islands—including Crozets, Amsterdam, St. Paul, and Kerguelen—under the Governor-General of Madagascar.[37] Although the British and Australian Governments resented this action at the time, its legitimacy subsequently was acknowledged.[38]

Between the British Falkland Islands and the Australian sectors lies the Antarctic slice claimed by Norway. Her interests are

[34] Comprising all islands and territories between 160° E. and 150° W. longitude, to the south of 60° S. latitude. *State Papers*, CXVII (1923), 91–92; also *London Gazette*, July 31, 1923.

[35] Including islands and territories to the south of 60° S. latitude lying between 160° and 45° E. longitude. *State Papers*, CXXXVII (1934), 754–55.

[36] *Ibid.*, CXXXVI (1933), 293.

[37] Between 136° 20′ and 142° 20′ E. longitude and south of 60° to 67° S. latitude. See R. N. Rudmose Brown, *The Polar Regions* (New York, 1927), 177; and A. H. Charteris, "Australasian Claims in Antarctica," *Journal of Comparative Legislation and International Law*, 3rd series, XI (1929), 226–27. Confirming French pretensions is the Madagascar citizenship decree of September 6, 1933, applying to Adélie Land and the French Antarctic Islands; see *State Papers*, CXXXVI (1933), 680.

[38] Anglo-French understanding was subsequently confirmed by an agreement, October 25, 1938, regarding aerial navigation in the Antarctic. See Jesse S. Reeves, "Antarctic Sectors," *American Journal of International Law*, XXXIII (1939), 519. The United States Government notified the British and Australian Governments that it reserved all American rights to both aviation and territorial claims in the Antarctic. Green H. Hackworth, *Digest of International Law*, I (Washington, 1940), 459.

founded upon Roald Amundsen's South Pole expedition of 1911–1912 and the Norwegian whaling industry. Although both Britain and Norway at one time competed for possession of Bouvet Island in the South Atlantic, negotiations resulted in an abandonment by Britain of her title in 1929, and the island was formally annexed by Norway on February 27, 1930.[39] The following year, on May 1, a royal proclamation also announced the annexation of Peter I Island.[40] On January 14, 1939, by Order in Council, the Norwegian Government formally defined its sector as extending from the Falkland Islands Dependency in the west to the limits of the Australian Antarctic Dependency in the east.[41]

Currently, the most troublesome area in the Antarctic is that lying in the Western Hemisphere, where both Argentina and Chile have staked out sectoral pretensions, which conflict in themselves and both of which overlap the Falkland Islands Dependency. Argentina has been in the race for some time, basing her claim on the Falkland Islands, jurisdictional rights over which she alleges never to have surrendered and the return of which she periodically demands from Great Britain. Argentina formally asserted her title to Antarctic territory in July, 1939, claiming not only the Falkland Islands, but also South Georgia, the South Orkneys, the South Shetlands, the South Sandwich islands, and Graham Land, insisting that they constitute a natural geographic dependency of South America, the southern tip of which belongs to her.[42]

The following year the Chilean Government formally announced its assertion of jurisdiction over much the same area. Her sectoral decree was issued on November 6, 1940, and the diplomatic representatives of the interested states were immediately notified to

[39] Charteris, *loc. cit.*, 227, note 1; *State Papers*, CXXXII (1930), 863; also see *ibid.*, 865–66.

[40] *State Papers*, CXXXIV (1931), 1010; also see *ibid.*, CXXXVI (1933), 27–28.

[41] Hence claiming the territory between 20° W. and 45° E. longitude, on the Continent and in the surrounding sea. Jesse S. Reeves, *loc. cit.*, 519; also see Fridtjov Isachsen, "The Norwegian Dependency in the Antarctic," *Le Nord*, II (1939), 67 ff.

[42] The Argentinian quadrant extends from 20° to 68° W. longitude. *New York Times*, July 25, 1939; also see *ibid.*, July 29, 1939, and November 7, 1940.

that effect.[43]   Inasmuch as their respective Antarctic components overlap, the Governments of Argentina and Chile set about resolving this conflict by proposing its submittal to arbitration, and a preliminary accord to this effect was signed in March, 1941.[44] But negotiations later were dropped because of the attack at Pearl Harbor and the ensuing war.   It was not until 1946 that concentrated interest again was revived, which reached a particularly critical state in the postwar years.

The United States has demanded no official territorial prerogatives in the Antarctic, and at the same time our Government has consciously avoided recognizing foreign pretensions.   Both Admiral Richard E. Byrd and Lincoln Ellsworth have unofficially claimed Antarctic territory for the United States, but these have not been confirmed by our Government.   One slice of the Antarctic—on the Pacific side, between the New Zealand and Chilean stakes— remains unclaimed.   It includes Mary Byrd Land, which Admiral Byrd unofficially claimed for the United States during his first two Antarctic expeditions.[45]   Considerable interest was aroused as his third expedition got under way in 1939.   Speculation was rife concerning the establishment of an American Antarctic sector based on his explorations and those of Ellsworth.[46]   Although a resolution was introduced into the Senate proposing that we claim all Antarctic areas discovered by Americans, it was tabled.[47] During the Fourth Byrd Expedition following World War II, the United States Navy was very emphatic in denying any intention of staking out an American dependency in the Antarctic.[48]

[43] Between 53° and 90° W. longitude.   *New York Times*, November 7, 1940; also see *ibid.*, November 8, 1940.

[44] *Ibid.*, March 27, 1941; for earlier negotiations, see *ibid.*, December 21, 1940.

[45] Byrd's claim comprised all the territory which he discovered or explored to the east of 150° W. longitude during his first two Antarctic expeditions; Hackworth, *op. cit.*, I, 454.

[46] United States, Department of Interior, *Annual Report of Secretary of Interior, 1939,* 344; also see Reeves, *loc. cit.*, 521.

[47] *Congressional Record*, 71st Cong., 2nd Sess., S. R. 310.

[48] *New York Times*, January 26, 1947; *ibid.*, March 2, 1947.   For a recent general account of American interests, see Comdr. W. J. Lederer and Stacy V. Jones, "Who Owns Antarctica?" *Saturday Evening Post*, December 13, 1947, 26–27, 153–54.

A number of important issues are involved in contemporary Antarctic imperialism. In the first place, competing jurisdictional pretensions must be ironed out. That this is possible is amply illustrated by such well-known arbitrations as those which settled the East Greenland, Clipperton Island, and Palmas Island questions.[49] But after the end of World War II—the competitive action particularly of Great Britain, Argentina, and Chile—rapidly came to a head. A second, perhaps more fundamental issue therefore concerns the legal validity of existing territorial claims, as based upon the sector principle.

In this tripartite rivalry Argentina and Chile appear to be willing to resolve their own conflicting claims by compromise or submittal to arbitration, but they present a united front against Great Britain in order to eliminate her from the contest. This attitude partly explains the action taken at the Ninth International Conference of American States held at Bogata in the spring of 1948. There the Ecuadorian proposal for the creation of a new inter-American committee on dependent areas to sit at Havana and to study pacific means for the adjustment of all colonial claims in this hemisphere was approved without a dissenting vote.[49a]

This committee was not established on September 1, the target date, however, because of the reluctance displayed by the United States. Meanwhile, on August 28, the United States Government announced a counter-proposal urging the eight interested states—Argentina, Australia, Chile, France, New Zealand, Norway, the United Kingdom, and the United States—to adopt some form of internationalization or multipartite trusteeship for Antarctica and its peripheral islands.[49b]

[49] *Supra*, note 4; *American Journal of International Law*, XXVI (1932), 390 ff; and XXII (1928), 867 ff.

[49a] Secretary of State Marshall abstained in the voting, however, because American policy opposed alienating the British Government by settling an issue in which it had an important stake but enjoyed no voice. See *New York Times*, April 23, 1948; for earlier discussions at the Bogata Conference, see *ibid.*, April 7 and 8, 1948. Also see "Antarctic Claims Raise Colonial Issue in Americas," *Foreign Policy Bulletin*, September 3, 1948.

[49b] *New York Times*, August 29, 1948.

A possible alternative would be for the interested states to submit Antarctic territory to United Nations jurisdiction, with the understanding that it would issue the necessary regulations and legislation to govern properly the territory, that natural life would be adequately protected, that any state could maintain climatological and meteorological stations in the territory provided that resulting information were made readily available, and that all states would be entitled to equal commercial and economic rights. This should satisfy the interested states, and the only factor of significance not resolved by this proposal is the matter of national pride and prestige that accompanies imperialist control.

Unless the question is settled in either of these ways, the issues noted above remain, and must then be resolved in accordance with existing principles of law. It therefore remains to examine briefly the status of the jurisdictional rights of claimant states in this imperialist contest.

V. INTERNATIONAL LAW AND POLAR JURISDICTION

The legal principles according to which states have acquired valid title to unoccupied territory (*terra nullius*) throughout the past centuries, and therefore, unless specifically modified, may be presumed to apply to the polar regions, include "effective occupation," and "prescription." Valid title does not accrue from "discovery," "symbolic appropriation," or "contiguity," while only a limited validity is accorded to "continuity."

Effective occupation has generally been accepted as the universal principle according to which territory may be legally acquired under international law. Even if effectiveness was not overtly approved universally until the nineteenth century, it nevertheless has definitely superseded all other juridical principles governing the acquisition of unpossessed territory. At most, discovery and symbolic appropriation—or the claiming of a territory by erecting a plaque, notice, or monument specifically stating or merely symbolizing an assertion of jurisdiction—today afford but an inchoate title to possession and must be confirmed by occupation within a reasonable length of time. As a matter of fact, discovery always has been little more than a fugitive, secondary argument advanced by a government which could not find a stronger claim in its state practice, and, when relied upon in an international dispute, it invariably has yielded to arguments proving the exercise of state authority.[50] The same has generally been true of claims based upon symbolic appropriation or "ceremonial occupation."[51]

Ever since the earliest classical writers, international law thinkers have universally supported the principle of effective occupation, and it made its appearance in the relations between states as early as the classical era of discovery. In the nineteenth century the principle was utilized by states in their territorial arguments and arbitrations in all corners of the globe, particularly in North America in the Guano Act of the United States,[52] the Nootka Sound controversy, the Louisiana Territory settlement, the American attitude toward Russian pretensions on the Northwest coast, and in the Oregon question.

Despite the fact that effective occupation did not attain universality during this period—since states appealed to it in one instance and denied it in another, depending upon the manner in which their particular interests were affected and also upon the strength of the case they were able to present—nevertheless the principle was rendered obligatory in colonial administration by the Berlin Act of 1885, at least as far as African coastal lands were concerned.[53] Since that time it has been widely appealed to in state practice, and a number of important arbitral awards have relied unreservedly upon it, notably those delivered in the cases

[50] Amos S. Hershey, *The Essentials of International Public Law and Organization* (New York, 1930), 285; Charles G. Fenwick, *International Law* (New York, 1934), 250.

[51] Arthur S. Keller, Oliver J. Lissitzyn, and Fred J. Mann, *Creation of Rights of Sovereignty Through Symbolic Acts, 1400–1800* (New York, 1938), 148–49, holds such acts to afford valid title; but see Friedrich A. von der Heydte, "Discovery, Symbolic Annexation, and Virtual Effectiveness in International Law," *American Journal of International Law*, XXIX (1935), 452–54.

[52] *Statutes at Large*, XI (1863), 119–20; *U. S. Code* (1940), Title 48, secs. 1411–19.

[53] See Article 35; *American Journal of International Law, Supplement*, III (1909), 24.

concerning Eastern Greenland, the Venezuela–British Guiana boundary, and Clipperton and Palmas islands.[54]

But universal reliance upon effective occupation in international practice since 1885 does not necessarily mean that it must be applied to the more inaccessible regions in exactly the same manner and to the same extent and degree as it must be applied in more accessible areas. A series of recent studies and arbitral decisions have reinterpreted the requirements of effectiveness in order to meet the exigencies of each particular case, relying more upon the establishment of an administration and enforcement of law than upon actual colonization, settlement, and the cultivation of the soil, which were stressed in the earlier disputes over American and African territory. According to this new view, it is sufficient for the possessory state to make its authority felt, whether or not this authority is exercised at every moment and in all corners of the territory.[55] This liberalized interpretation, of course, renders the principle of effective occupation applicable to polar territory.

In addition to occupation, the principle of prescription—that is, continuous and unchallenged possession of a territory for such an extended length of time that possession becomes an accepted fact in the international order and cannot be questioned under international law—is recognized as according juridical title to unoccupied territory, and for several centuries has been utilized both in international thinking and in state practice.[56] There are few statesmen and writers who in the past have denied or who presently refuse to recognize its validity. The actual length of time required to render a prescriptive title certain as between conflicting claims, however, has not been definitely established. It is rather believed to vary according to the circumstances attending

[54] For Eastern Greenland, Clipperton Island, and Palmas Island awards, see *supra*, notes 4 and 49, for British Guiana—Venezuela dispute, see arbitration treaty, Article 4 (c), *State Papers*, LXXXIX (1896–1897), 60–61, and arbitral award, *ibid.*, XCII (1899–1900), 160–62.

[55] See especially Mark Frank Lindley, *The Acquisition and Government of Backward Territory in International Law* (London, 1926), 157, 159; also Clipperton Island award, *State Papers*, CXXXIV (1931), 845–46.

[56] Hershey, *op. cit.*, 276; Fenwick, *op. cit.*, 259–261.

each particular case, although, on a few occasions, as in the Venezuela–British Guiana dispute, the length of time was fixed at
50 years.[57]

States which appear to benefit thereby are prone to support and
condone the principles of contiguity—that is, the extension of
jurisdiction over properly possessed territory to adjacent island
territory by virtue of its geographic proximity—and continuity
or hinterland—that is, the extension of title to coastal territory also
to the hinterland. States which do not so benefit by these principles, however, have traditionally relied rather upon effective
occupation. Interpretations have varied considerably with respect
to the validity to be ascribed to these principles.

As far as islands are concerned which lie within territorial
waters, or which belong to definitely prescribed archipelagoes of
which the principal islands are effectively occupied, they are
admittedly recognized as belonging to the possessory state.[58]
But, by and large, the principle of contiguity is otherwise denied
juridical legitimacy under international law, the Palmas Island
award categorically refusing to accord it any authority whatever.[59]
Recently this principle was revived in its broadest implications as
the sector principle with particular reference to the islands of the
Arctic, and, to say the least, has failed to achieve general approval.

The principle of continuity or hinterland, on the contrary, has
frequently been utilized in state practice, especially in the classical
days of discovery, during the first half of the nineteenth century in
the arguments of the American Government concerning the Louisiana and Oregon territories, and in the late nineteenth century
when African territory was being divided. But states whose
interests are prejudiced by its application are inclined to reject
it, as indicated by the action of the United States in the Venezuela–

---

[57] *State Papers*, LXXXIX (1896–1897), 60. The same length of time was proposed
by the Russian Government in the controversy over Northwest North America, *ibid.*,
IX (1821–1822), 485.

[58] Hershey, *op. cit.*, 287–88.

[59] *State Papers*, CXXVIII (1928), 890–91, 909.

British Guiana controversy.[60]   At most, therefore, continuity can afford merely an inchoate title and then only under prescribed geographical circumstances.   Currently the principle, along with that of contiguity, has been revived in the scramble for Antarctic territory, where, likewise identified as the sector principle, it is based upon nothing more than the nebulous claims derived from discovery, exploration, and symbolic appropriation.

It therefore is apparent that, since effective occupation still constitutes the basic principle *par excellence* governing the acquisition of territory under international law and practice, it can continue to be applied even to the more inaccessible remaining unpossessed territory in the Antarctic.   Prescription is likewise recognized under international law, and while contiguity is definitely rejected in both thought and practice, the status of the principle of continuity is not clearly defined and is not recognized in international arbitration and adjudication, although it appears to be resorted to by states if no stronger claim can be presented.

VI. VALIDITY OF THE SECTOR PRINCIPLE

The acceptance by Soviet and Canadian writers of polar sectorism as applied in the Arctic is not difficult to understand, since, more than any other interested states, the Soviet Union and the Dominion of Canada are its immediate beneficiaries.   Perhaps this matter of individual benefit also may explain why thinkers in the remaining interested states, especially Norway and the United States, refrain from accepting the principle.   It is interesting to note that, by comparison, publicists have not generally undertaken to defend the validity of Antarctic sectors.

As far as state practice in the Arctic is concerned, only the Soviet Government, in its 1926 decree, described above, incorporated polar sectorism into its municipal law.   A number of Canadian officials have recognized it in their speeches and official acts,[61] but

[60] John Bassett Moore, *A Digest of International Law* (Washington, 1906), I, 268–69.

[61] Senator P. Poirier (1907), Secretary of the Interior Charles Stewart (1924–1926), Secretary of the Interior Thomas G. Murphy (1931), and Minister of Mines T. A. Crerar (1938).

no particular legislative or administrative enactments of the Canadian Government can be singled out in which the principle is applied as it is interpreted by the Soviet school of thought.

The remaining interested Arctic states refuse to accept sectorism as a valid juridical principle in their state practice. Finland and Denmark have remained silent upon the question, while Norway expressly refuses to recognize it,[62] and the United States—by repeated insistence upon effective occupation and by the promotion of active interests beyond its hypothetical Arctic sectoral limits, particularly in Wrangel Island, Ellesmere Island, and Greenland—at least rejects the principle by implication.

Moreover, the practice of not only those states which do not condone sectorism, but also of the Soviet Union and Canada as well, indicates very clearly a universal reliance upon effective occupation. The activity of the Soviets in establishing permanent, large-scale polar institutions, in erecting Arctic stations, in regularizing icebreaker and aerial services, and in effecting economic, political, and judicial polar administration—all evidence a confidence in the juridical significance of effectiveness. The same is true of Canadian state practice, which embraces a system of licensing control and effective administration by the Royal Canadian Mounted Police and the Eastern Arctic Patrol.

As far as Arctic sectorism is concerned, it consequently may be concluded that only a small minority of thinkers favor the principle, and even some of these are unable to substantiate its validity. State practice is confused and contradictory on the part of the two states which are said to condone the principle, whereas practice is consistent only among those refusing to recognize it. The sectoral decree of the Soviet Union received no official recognition by other members of the Family of Nations, and as yet its validity under international law has not been tested by arbitration or adjudication.

The situation in the Antarctic, however, is quite different. There seven states have laid out claims based on official sectoral decrees.

---

[62] See, for example, Norwegian note to Great Britain, 1930, in *American Journal of International Law, Supplement*, XXVII (1933), 93.

State action is clearly in support of the principle. Other states, however, led by the United States, have definitely rejected these claims,[63] and it is highly questionable whether an international arbiter or tribunal would be able to recognize these pretensions unless they have been amply substantiated by additional evidences of state administration. That the interested states are fully cognizant of this is clearly evidenced by the fact that Antarctic territories are administered by colonial executives and that various laws of such colonial areas are specifically made applicable to the Antarctic dependencies. In any case, if the issue were submitted to adjudication, it is not without reason to expect that the award either would recognize as valid only the possessions that are effectively occupied or would accept the sectoral decrees merely as inchoate.[64]

[63] In 1946 the Department of State specifically refused to recognize other states' sectoral claims and reserved its own territorial rights; *New York Times*, December 28, 1946. Also see Hackworth, *op. cit.*, I, 452 ff.

[64] The problem of jurisdiction over polar airspace is discussed by the author in the article cited above, note [31].

United States Immigration Policy, 1882-1948

By J. P. SHALLOO*

Prior to 1882 immigration laws and regulations were under the control and direction of the states. The inability of state immigration departments to cope with the increasing volume of immigrants from Europe and Asia and the need for uniformity of procedure and administration called for action which would unify the service and effectively exclude undesirable immigrants who were becoming both a burden and a problem, especially at the main ports of entry. In answer to insistent protests against the indiscriminate admission of inadequately examined foreigners by labor, civic, and humanitarian organizations, Congress assumed jurisdiction over all problems of immigration under the supervision of the Secretary of the Treasury on August 3, 1882.

The immigration law of 1882 marks the turning point in the history of immigration to the United States. Since that date there has grown a complicated body of Federal law and administrative regulations designed to check the rising tide of foreigners seeking entry into the United States. The doctrine of refuge and asylum as epitomized by Emma Lazarus in "The New Colossus," inscribed at the base of the Statue of Liberty, was superseded by the beginning of a master plan within which a definite policy could be developed. One phase of the regulative plan may be seen, for example, in the suspension of immigration of Chinese laborers to the United States in 1882, which eventuated in Chinese exclusion in 1904.[1] The policy initiated by the Act of 1882 was based upon the concept of assimilation. The "old" immigration (from

---

*J. P. Shalloo is Assistant Professor of Sociology, University of Pennsylvania.

[1] The Chinese were restored to eligible-to-citizenship status in December, 1943, and may now enter as quota immigrants at the rate of 105 per year.

northern and western Europe) was rapidly declining, while the "new" immigration (from southern and eastern Europe) was beginning to overwhelm the immigration facilities at ports of entry on the Atlantic seaboard. The need for action was urgent if the United States was to escape a veritable flood-tide of aliens about whom practically nothing was known.

The most important point of the Act of August 3, 1882, was the transfer of jurisdiction from the states to the Federal Government where authority was exercised by the Secretary of the Treasury, although inspection and examination remained in the control of state boards. Furthermore, the act provided that "any convict, lunatic, idiot, or any person unable to take care of himself or herself without becoming a public charge" was not to be permitted to land. Another important innovation was the establishment of the Immigrant Fund by levying a duty of fifty cents on every "passenger not a citizen of the United States," who came "from any foreign port to any port of the United States by steam or sail vessel." This duty was "to constitute a lien upon the vessel until paid."[2]

The establishment of the Fund by congressional action was a direct result of vigorous protests by American taxpayers and by earlier arrivals from Europe against the wholesale dumping of undesirables by foreign governments, and against such practices as that of The Prisoners' Aid Society of London which prepaid the passage of ticket-of-leave men to the United States. In one notorious case the Cantons of Switzerland by public subscription paid the passage of a chronic drunkard to the United States simply to get rid of him, although the Swiss Government apologized after he had been returned. The Fund, moreover, defrayed the expenses of the immigration administration. Herman Stump, a former Commissioner-General of Immigration, testifying before the Industrial Commission on January 10, 1899, told the Commission that the Immigrant Fund had a surplus during his administra-

---

[2] Henry Pratt Fairchild, *Immigration: A World Movement and Its American Significance* (New York, 1920), 107.

tion of $200,000 to $250,000 and that "not one of the immigrants nor the administration of the law has ever been a charge on the people of the United States."[3]

The year 1882 is important not merely for the Immigrant Fund, the assumption of Federal control of immigration, the exclusion of Chinese labor, and the beginning of a list of excluded classes, but also because of the change in the ethnic composition of the immigrant population. In the decade 1881–1890 immigrants from northern and western Europe constituted 72.0 per cent, while immigrants from southern and eastern Europe were only 18.3 per cent of the total European immigration. However, in the decade 1891–1900 the latter were more than one-half of the total European immigration (52.8 per cent). By 1910 southern and eastern Europe contributed 71.9 per cent of the immigration from Europe. The shift from northern and western Europe was more than a mere change in the national and ethnic character of immigration. It was more than an increasing cultural difference between the American population and the accelerating tide of new immigrants. Those who came in from eastern Europe, the Balkans, and the Mediterranean regions were for the most part poverty-stricken, diseased, illiterate, and unskilled. The social, political, and economic conditions of the lands from which they came were the least advanced of all European countries, and most certainly far below the living standards of northern and northwestern Europe in 1882. Even as late as 1897, when illiteracy was 13.43 per cent in the United States, it was 77 per cent in Portugal, 54 per cent in Italy, 46 per cent in Hungary, and 41 per cent in Russia. It is obvious that illiteracy is a function of poor educational facilities, but it is equally true that illiterate immigrants were regarded as essentially undesirable and inferior by American labor organizations and by advocates of restrictive legislation. Furthermore, the fact that an increasing number of "new" immigrants settled in New York and other ports of entry made possible a concerted

[3] *Reports of the Industrial Commission on Immigration, Including Testimony, with Review and Digest, and Special Reports, and on Education, Including Testimony, with Review and Digest,* XV (Washington, 1901), 12.

and organized protest against any further increase and a demand for selective criteria to screen the arriving immigrants much more rigidly. Examinations for diseased, insane, paupers, criminals, and other undesirables were perfunctory on both sides of the Atlantic.

II

At the insistence of the Knights of Labor, the Contract Labor Law was passed on February 26, 1885, making it "unlawful for any person, company, partnership, or corporation, in any manner whatsoever, to prepay the transportation, or in any way assist or encourage the importation or migration of any alien or aliens, any foreigner or foreigners, into the United States, its Territories, or the District of Columbia, under contract or agreement, parol or special, express or implied, made previous to the importation or migration of such alien or aliens, foreigner or foreigners, to perform labor or service of any kind in the United States, its Territories, or the District of Columbia."[4] Such contracts were to be void, and fines of $1,000 were provided against contractors and shipmasters knowingly bringing in such laborers. Also, shipmasters might be imprisoned for not more than six months. Exceptions to the law were secretaries, servants, and domestics of foreigners temporarily residing in the United States; skilled workmen for industries not yet established, if such labor could not otherwise be obtained; and actors, artists, singers, and lecturers. Giving assistance to relatives and personal friends was not forbidden. As the law was framed, no enforcement machinery was set up. To correct this deficiency an amendatory act was passed on February 23, 1887, empowering the Secretary of the Treasury to carry out the provisions of the Act of 1885 and to return all contract laborers in the same manner as other excluded classes.

These two laws were fatally defective in that no provision was made to take action against the contract laborer himself. Contractors and shipmasters could be penalized, but knowledge of

[4] *Ibid.*, 648. Cf. Fairchild, *op. cit.*, 108.

the contract laborer could come to light only through investigation of labor agents' activities and evidence of a definite contract. Immigrants were thoroughly indoctrinated to give the right answers to the questions by inspectors with reference to jobs promised them or arrangements made by padrones, steamship agents, or relatives, so that when the Act of 1887 was amended it provided that any person who entered this country contrary to the Contract Labor Law might be deported within one year at the expense of the owner of the importing vessel or, if he came by land, of the person contracting his services. Thus, contract laborers were not at this time placed in the excluded classes but rather in the deportable classes.[5] This distinction gave wide discretion to administrative officials, since proof of existing contracts was established by the immigration inspectors.

On March 3, 1891, Congress extended the list of defectives in the excluded classes by the addition of paupers or persons likely to become a public charge, persons suffering from a loathsome and contagious disease, polygamists, and any person whose ticket or passage was paid by others, unless it could be proved specifically that he did not belong to one of the excluded classes or to the category of contract laborers. Advertising and soliciting by steamship companies were forbidden; ministers and professors were excepted from the Contract Labor Law; but—and this is an important change—"relatives and friends of persons in this country are not hereafter to be excepted."[6] Complete manifests of passengers must be kept, giving name, nationality, last residence, and destination. Inspection service was assumed by the Federal Government and public charges were liable to deportation within one year if the causes of such dependence existed prior to landing. It may be seen that promises of employment or prepaid passage of relatives and friends in Europe were now prohibited and immigrants who came to the United States under such conditions could

[5] Fairchild rightly points out that the principle of deportation after landing must be distinguished from exclusion, *op. cit.*, 110.

[6] *Ibid.*, 111.

be deported both as contract laborers and as members of an excluded class.

In the same law provision was made for listing alien passengers in groups of thirty and tickets were given corresponding to their numbers on the manifests. Also the shipmaster must certify that he and the ship's surgeon had examined the immigrants before sailing and believed none of them belonged to the excluded classes. If there was any doubt about their right to land, a board of special inquiry of not less than four inspectors should pass on the case.

The Committee on Immigration in 1902 stated that the time had come to view the future of our immigration legislation and policy with great care. The millions of immigrants with different national and cultural backgrounds entering the United States each year provided material which could easily cause a change in the American form of government and way of life that would prove disastrous to the United States. The free institutions of this country might be so affected by the imported rivalries of the Old World as to destroy the moral and legal foundations of freedom and security. Further, the possibility of intermarriage of such diverse racial stocks as must necessarily occur made it mandatory that "measures . . . be adopted to avoid the risks of altering completely the complexion of our population by admixture with another."[7]

Without enumerating all the provisions of the Act of March 3, 1903, it may be noted that the excluded classes were again enlarged to include epileptics; persons insane within five years, and persons who had had two or more attacks of insanity at any time previously; professional beggars; anarchists, or persons who believed in or advocated the overthrow by force or violence of the government of the United States, or of all government or of all forms of law, or the assassination of public officials; prostitutes and persons who procured or attempted to bring in prostitutes or women for the purpose of prostitution; and those who, within one year, had

[7] U. S., *Senate Documents* (57th Cong., 2d Sess., Doc. No. 62): *Regulation of Immigration* (Report of the Committee on Immigration on the Bill to Regulate Immigration of Aliens into the United States. Washington, 1902), v–vi.

been deported under the contract labor clause. The importation of prostitutes carried a penalty upon conviction of five years' imprisonment (maximum) and a fine of $5,000.[8] Anarchists and other political undesirables were forbidden naturalization. This last provision was directly related to the Haymarket bombings in Chicago in 1886. Aliens illegally entering this country and those becoming public charges could be deported within two years instead of one as provided in the Act of 1891.

In 1903, on February 14, the Department of Commerce and Labor was established and the Commissioner-General of Immigration was transferred to it from the Treasury Department. With the establishment of the Department of Labor in 1913, the Bureau of Immigration and Naturalization was transferred to the new department; and in 1940, it was placed under the control of the Attorney General in the Department of Justice.

In 1907 the immigration laws were consolidated and sections of earlier laws repealed if inconsistent with the new law. The excluded classes were further extended to include:

imbeciles, feeble-minded persons, persons afflicted with tuberculosis, persons not included in any of the specifically excluded classes who have a mental or physical deficiency which may affect their ability to earn a living, persons who admit having committed a crime involving moral turpitude, persons who admit their belief in the practice of polygamy, women or girls coming into the United States for the purpose of prostitution, or for any other immoral purpose, or persons who attempt to bring in such women or girls, and all children under the age of sixteen unaccompanied by one or both of their parents, at the discretion of the Secretary of Commerce and Labor. Persons whose tickets are paid for with the money of another must show affirmatively that they were not paid for by any corporation, society, association, municipality, or foreign government, either directly or indirectly. This is not to apply to aliens in continuous transit through the United States to foreign contiguous territory.[9]

From the foregoing analysis of the legislation from 1882 to 1907 it becomes apparent that no specific policy had been formulated

---

[8] This section dealing with prostitutes was inspired by and directly aimed at the Chinese.

[9] Fairchild, *op. cit.*, 115–16.

but rather that the Congress in response to sectional and organizational pressures had added piecemeal to the volume of complicated and ambiguous laws and regulations. Probably the most inconsistent legislation was that relating to contract labor. In order to prosecute the importer it was necessary to depend upon district attorneys and judges who followed strict rules of evidence and who held themselves to exact definitions of a contract. "But," as the Industrial Commission on Immigration pointed out, "the deportation of an immigrant turns upon the circumstantial evidence presented to administrative authorities and the inferences which may be drawn therefrom." [10] The result of this type of dual jurisdiction—in fact, mutually exclusive authorities—may be seen in the fact that 8,000 immigrants were deported by administrative ruling of inspectors, but there were "very few cases in which the importer was fined." [11]

Viewing the laws prohibiting certain classes from entry into the United States as immigrants it appears clear that the exclusion of prostitutes, criminals, polygamists, anarchists, contract laborers, and even those suffering from certain types of insanity, was a practical impossibility. Thousands who could not pass inspection at American ports came in across the Canadian border at isolated places. The main difficulty during this period of heavy immigration, when thousands each day entered through the port of New York alone, was insufficient personnel. This is equally true in 1948. While Congress passed stringent restrictive legislation at the demand of organized labor and restrictionist organizations, it did not provide funds for proper enforcement, with the result that for the most part these laws were merely emphatic pronouncements without substance.

III

The emphasis upon the labor aspect of our immigration legislation is deliberate. It indicates the confusion and uncertainty

---

[10] *Reports of the Industrial Commission on Immigration*, XV, 648.
[11] *Ibid.*

as to what our policy should be. Prior to 1882 labor was weak as a pressure group. With the organization of the Knights of Labor and its successor, the American Federation of Labor, the imported, tractable foreigner who had been used largely to break strikes and who frequently refused to join any organization of others from different and ofttimes antagonistic national origin, assumed menacing proportions to the ambitions of native labor. Testimony before congressional committees on immigration makes amply clear that the so-called poverty clause—"likely to become a public charge"—could be invoked against any immigrant, regardless of his potential value, if he could not be barred as a member of the excluded classes. Every minority, whether European, Oriental, or native Negro American, has heard the charge of undermining the American standard of living, destroying the wage structure, or displacing native white workers. There is little foundation to the charge that immigrant labor displaced native labor, but the specter of competition was sufficiently real to warrant restrictive measures on the part of Congress. Patriotic organizations and otherwise discerning and intelligent Americans feared the importation of radical and even monarchical ideas. To them, these "scum" of eastern and southern Europe, crowded into filthy tenements in alleys of the great cities and reeking with disease, provided tangible evidence of inherent inferiority and undesirable character.

Huge sums of money sent to their homelands were taken as further evidence of their lack of faith in the United States. A total of $214,000,000 was sent abroad by Italian immigrants in this country in the two-and-one-half-year period 1907 to June 30, 1909. The amount sent in 1907 was $92,600,000; in 1908, $76,000,000; and $45,400,000 for the first six months of 1909.[12] The value of international money orders issued in the United States and paid in foreign countries from 1900 through 1909 was $498,971,031.06. This amount includes all countries in both

[12] U. S., *Senate Documents* (61st Cong., 2d Sess., Doc. No. 381): *Immigrant Banks* (February 24, 1910), 79–80.

hemispheres.[13]   Regardless of the international economic theory that these sums of money represented credit and thus provided dollars for foreign countries to buy goods from the United States, the sending of *money* to their homelands by immigrants was regarded as an attempt to impoverish the United States and to enrich their own countries.

Thousands returned to Italy every winter only to return the following spring to gather more American dollars in order to pay off mortgages on their homes and farms in Italy.   To the opponents of unrestricted immigration, the extremely low rate of naturalization could mean only one thing: America is good enough to earn money in, but not good enough to stay in.   By 1907 agitation in this country reached proportions which could not be ignored.   The period when a free labor policy was needed was drawing to a close.

From 1882 to 1914 the "new" immigration reached a total of 11,960,122 while the "old" immigration was only 7,566,041. Perhaps the increase may better be seen by comparing the "new" and "old" immigration from 1897 to 1914.   In those eighteen years 2,983,548 immigrants came from north and northwestern Europe, but 10,057,576 immigrants were admitted from south and eastern Europe.   The peak years were reached in the decade preceding World War I.   In 1905, 1906, 1907, 1910, 1913, and 1914 "more than a million immigrants landed each year, while immigration averaged about 800,000 for each year not mentioned. . . .   Indeed, more than half the approximate 35,000,000 immigrants who have come to our shores since 1820 have come within the last thirty-five years" (1892–1927).[14]

Before proceeding further to examine and analyze our immigration legislation it may be desirable to point out certain general principles which appear to underlie the intentions of Congress and the demands of the American public, at least the politically influential segments of the public.   The rising clamor for restriction

[13] *Ibid.*, 83.
[14] Roy L. Garis, *Immigration Restriction* (New York, 1927), 205–7.

would appear to be related to the urbanization and industrializa-
tion of the United States. The concentration of the foreign born
in the cities gave rise to serious questions of public health, sanita-
tion, full and continuous employment, as well as problems of
relief. The Americanization movement, with emphasis upon
assimilation, called attention to the islands of foreign born in our
large cities who might be responsible for serious conflict. The
feeling was common that homogeneity of national stock and ideals
must remain unrealized if more aliens were added to the already
large number of identifiably different peoples. The Immigration
Commission made it clear in 1911 that

in framing legislation emphasis should be laid upon the following principles:
   1. While the American people, as in the past, welcome the oppressed
of other lands, care should be taken that immigration be such both in
quality and quantity as not to make too difficult the process of assimilation.
   2. . . . further general legislation concerning the admission of aliens
should be based primarily upon economic or business considerations
touching the prosperity and economic well-being of our people.[15]

We see in these recommendations two basic policies: welcome
for the oppressed, and improvement of the general welfare of the
United States with emphasis upon economic conditions in this
country.

The "new" immigration with its high proportion of Roman
Catholics and Jews differed radically in background from the
older stock whose basic political and social philosophy was derived
from Protestant and Anglo-Saxon origins. Historians, in the
period 1875 to 1925, faithfully reflected the conviction that the
noble and inspiring heritage created by Teutonic, Aryan, and
Anglo-Saxon founders of the Republic was in the process of destruction by the hordes of undesirable Slavic, Hebrew, and Mediterranean peoples. Such writers as Herbert Baxter Adams, John
Fiske, John W. Burgess, Henry Cabot Lodge, and James K. Hos-

[15] U. S., *Senate Documents* (61st Cong., 3rd Sess., Doc. No. 747): *Abstracts of Reports
of the Immigration Commission, with Conclusions and Recommendations and Views of the Minority*
(December 5, 1910), I, 45.

mer gave vigorous and "scientific" support to the doctrine of Nordic superiority. Edward Channing was more specific in his assertion that American political evolution was obviously a characteristic of the "English race."[16] Perhaps the most influential historian of the period was Edward Augustus Freeman who believed that the Teutons were the last of the Aryan peoples chronologically and were destined to be the rulers and teachers of the world. The Teutonic character achieved its highest development in England; and the English people had three homes: "originally on the European mainland, then in England and, finally, in the United States."[17]

In the first decade of the twentieth century eastern Europeans, especially Jews from Russia and Rumania, were customarily looked upon as avowed socialists, radicals, and atheists. Organizations such as the Workmen's Circle espoused the cause of the oppressed and the exploited. Sweatshops increased, and low wages, deplorable working conditions, as well as a mild contempt for the American middle-class economic and political philosophy, tended to separate these aliens still further from the processes of assimilation and integration.[18] Ghettos and foreign colonies became suspect in the eyes of native-born Americans of northern and western European ancestry. World War I was looming larger and at its outbreak considerable doubt was felt as to the loyalty of Germans, Austrians, and Italians.

Such a situation gave rise to further study and investigation by Congress, which resulted in the Immigration Act of 1917. Among the many changes and revisions effected was the revival of the literacy test for immigrants. The literacy test had been before Congress in several sessions. In fact, before it was passed over President Wilson's veto in 1917 there had been sixteen re-

[16] Edward N. Saveth, *American Historians and European Immigrants, 1875–1925* (New York, 1948), 23, 27. See also Harry Elmer Barnes, *A History of Historical Writing* (Norman [Oklahoma], 1938), 233–35; and Merle Curti, *The Growth of American Thought* (New York, 1943), 568.

[17] Saveth, *op. cit.*, 19.

[18] Cf. Bernard D. Weinryb, "The Adaptation of Jewish Labor Groups to American Life," *Jewish Social Studies*, VIII (October, 1946), 219–44.

corded votes in either the House or the Senate. This literacy test, introduced by Senator Henry Cabot Lodge of Massachusetts in 1896, had been repeatedly vetoed, although passed three times by both houses. President Cleveland saw no patriotic value in being able to read and write. Attached to his veto was an astute remark to the effect that we could better afford one hundred thousand law-abiding illiterates than one literate agitator.

The original literacy bill required reading in some recognized national language. Such a bill would exclude automatically a large proportion of Jews.[19] In its final form the bill provided that all aliens over sixteen years of age, physically capable of reading, who could not read the English language, or some other language or dialect, including Hebrew or Yiddish, with certain exemptions for specific relatives of immigrants, were inadmissible. The test consisted of not less than thirty or more than forty words in ordinary use. Uniform slips were furnished inspectors, printed in plainly legible type. No numerical restriction was contemplated but merely qualitative selection. It is obvious that such a test is practically worthless if the intent is to screen out genuine illiterates and admit genuine literates. An educational qualification would have been more effective if the purpose was to improve the intellectual standards of admission. Unless the prospective immigrant were clearly defective he could easily learn to pass such a test in a very short time before applying for a passport. Thus one more class of immigrants was added to the excluded classes—the illiterates. By the Immigration Act of 1917 people from the so-called Barred Zone (an area in the southwest Pacific) were declared inadmissible as immigrants, thus excluding virtually all Asiatic immigration not already barred by the Chinese Exclusion Act or by the Gentlemen's Agreement of 1907 concerning Japanese laborers.

The passage of the literacy bill was but another effort in a long series to exclude south and southeastern Europeans. The Barred

---

[19] For the text of the original bill see Prescott F. Hall, *Immigration* (rev. ed., New York, 1908), 367-68.

Zone law was more forthright and honest. Both groups, European and Asiatic, were regarded as more difficult to assimilate because of the great difference in language, religion, institutions, and general legal philosophy than the immigrants from north and northwestern Europe. The French Canadians and Mexicans are considered undesirable today for the same reasons. It is difficult to assimilate them into the American population culturally and biologically. Superficially, our immigration policy appears after long travail to be oriented toward a consciousness of kind and a consciousness of difference. These two attitudes, positive and negative, will be clearly evident in the congressional action and the pressure which practically forced such action in 1921.

During World War I, one hundred per cent Americanism became even more pronounced than it was during the anti-alien agitation of the American Protective Association, an anti-foreign, anti-Catholic organization formed in 1887. "Private organizations with hundreds of thousands of members were set up to investigate and report disloyal acts and utterances."[20] The Department of Justice assumed the role of clearinghouse for reports of disloyalty. Raids and wholesale arrests were made. The American Protective League, a volunteer organization, emerged in 1917 to safeguard and preserve American freedom and institutions. Attorney General Thomas Watt Gregory and later his successor, A. Mitchell Palmer, encouraged the League. Indeed, the "Secret Service Division" of this extra-legal, alien-baiting organization was defended by Gregory, but when Secretary of the Treasury William Gibbs McAdoo criticized the badge and identification card of this "Secret Service" the title "Auxiliary to the U. S. Department of Justice" was adopted. After the end of the war in Europe, aliens, especially Jews, Catholics, and eastern and southern Europeans, were to feel the full weight of suspicion and hostility as isolationism mounted and disillusioned American soldiers returned home.

An act approved October 16, 1918, and amended by an act

[20] Homer Cummings and Carl McFarland, *Federal Justice* (New York, 1937), 420.

approved June 5, 1920, was entitled "An Act to Exclude and Expel from the United States Aliens Who Are Members of the Anarchistic and Similar Classes." In this act there was provision for expulsion and exclusion of a remarkably wide variety of radicals. Not only aliens who were members of or affiliated with radical groups but all aliens who wrote, published, or caused to be published, circulated, distributed, printed or displayed, advised or taught, or advocated any doctrines against the American form of government were excludable and deportable. Further, giving, loaning, or promising money or anything of value to promote such doctrines would result in deportation and exclusion.

IV

From 1882 to 1920, with the exception of Chinese exclusion and the Barred Zone law of 1917, the increasing number of restrictive measures were qualitative, that is, they were designed to subject the individual alien to definite criteria of admissibility. While the over-all purpose and effect was numerical restriction, such quantitative limitation was not specifically declared. Except for the Chinese and other Asiatics, national origin did not appear in the legislation. Numerical restriction on the basis of nationality was first introduced in the quota law of 1921 and is the basis of our present policy.

The first serious attempt in the history of the United States to limit the number of immigrants generally, and the southern and eastern European immigrants specifically, was incorporated into the temporary Act of May 19, 1921. This law, which was extended by the Act of May 11, 1922, to July 1, 1924, applied the quota principle on the basis of place of birth. It provided that in any fiscal year the number of immigrants of any nationality to be admitted under quotas to the United States was to be limited to 3 per cent of the number of foreign-born persons of such nationality resident in the United States as determined by the United States Census of 1910. That this law sought to decrease the proportion of the "new" and increase the proportion of the "old" immigration was generally admitted, although the general welfare of the United States was the most articulate reason given.

This stop-gap law would give Congress time to formulate a permanent immigration program for the future. We may speculate on the proposition that had this law been effective in its purpose there might have been no need for any other type of legislation, but, as it happened, in 1922 only 46.4 per cent of the north and northwestern European quotas were filled while 95.6 per cent of southern and eastern European, including Turkish and other Asiatic, quotas were filled. Total quota immigration under this act was 356,995. Approximately two-thirds of all aliens admissible were admitted in 1921–1922 (68.3 per cent). Quotas for the five leading countries and percentage filling of quotas for 1921–1922 were: United Kingdom, 77,342 (55.2 per cent); Germany, 68,059 (28 per cent); Italy, 42,057 (100.2 per cent); Russia, 34,284 (84.4 per cent); and Poland, 25,827 (101.1 per cent). It is clear that the process of assimilation was not being facilitated or accelerated by the first year's experience under this act.

In the fiscal year 1922–1923 the northern and western European countries filled 90 per cent of their quotas as against 46.4 per cent in 1921–1922; however, southern and eastern European countries filled 98.3 per cent of their quotas. The two most notable decreases in admissions were southern Italians from 195,037 in 1920–1921 to 47,633 in 1923–1924 and Hebrews from 119,036 in 1920–1921 to 49,989 in 1923–1924; while the English increased from 54,627 in 1920–1921 to 93,939 in 1923–1924 and the Germans increased from 24,168 in 1920–1921 to 95,627 in 1923–1924. In the same years northern and western European admissions increased from 25.7 per cent to 55.7 per cent while southern and eastern European admissions fell from 66.7 per cent to 27.2 per cent.[21]

One further fact should be noted. In 1914 English-speaking

[21] Garis, *op. cit.*, 166–67.

"races" comprised only 8.8 per cent of the total admissions, but in 1924 these people were 28.3 per cent of total admissions, whereas non-English-speaking immigrants declined from 91.2 per cent of immigrant admissions in 1914 to 71.7 per cent in 1924. As Garis phrases it: "In 1913–14 the number of non-English-speaking peoples admitted was more than 1,000,000 in excess of the peoples whose customary language was our own, but in 1923–24 this difference was reduced to about 300,000."[22]

For the first time the factor of nationality became important. In fact, nationality and racial character were regarded as identical for restrictive purposes. The inability to assimilate aliens was no longer strictly cultural; it was emphatically biological. The theories of racial superiority proclaimed by Houston Stewart Chamberlain,[23] the racial chauvinism of Madison Grant,[24] the racial fears of Lothrop Stoddard,[25] as well as the racial philosophy of Edward A. Ross,[26] were given implicit and later explicit expression in the Johnson Act of 1924. Fear of hybridization or mongrelization superseded the threat of economic competition or the violent overthrow of government. From now on the fundamental basis of our immigration policy was to be eugenic, that is, sound family stock.

On March 8, 1924, Dr. Harry H. Laughlin, of the Carnegie Institution of Washington, stood before the Committee on Immigration and Naturalization of the House of Representatives and pronounced the eugenic ideal as the most desirable basis for immigration legislation and policy. Laughlin had submitted his report on the population found in state and Federal penal and eleemosynary institutions entitled *Analysis of America's Modern Melting Pot*, which revealed the relative social inadequacy of the several nativity groups of the United States. Laughlin testified that in 1741 Benjamin Franklin estimated the total number of

[22] Garis, *op. cit.*, 168.
[23] *Foundations of the Nineteenth Century* (New York, 1910), 2 v.
[24] *The Passing of the Great Race* (New York, 1916).
[25] *The Rising Tide of Color* (New York, 1920).
[26] *The Old World in the New* (New York, 1914).

immigrants who had arrived in the Colonies up to that year to be 80,000 and the total population of the Colonies to be 1,000,000. The Bureau of Immigration in 1919 estimated that 250,000 immigrants arrived from 1776 to 1820. The number of immigrants to the United States from 1820 to 1919 was 33,200,103. Laughlin then made the following statement: "No one doubts that the influence in establishing the American character and race and traditions, given by the 80,000 first immigrants, is more important than that given by the 33,000,000 of the last century."[27] Theodore Roosevelt declared: "The crucible in which all the new types are melted into one was shaped from 1776 to 1789, and our nationality was definitely fixed in all its essentials by the men of Washington's day."[28]

Laughlin's "Melting Pot" study will not be analyzed here, but it may be noted that the desirability of the old New England stock was confirmed and the undesirability of the "new" immigration "scientifically" demonstrated. In his analysis he stated: "The outstanding conclusion of all of the investigations so far is that immigration into the United States, in the interests of national welfare, is primarily a biological problem, and secondarily, a problem in economics and charity."[29]

The testimony of Laughlin carried tremendous weight and conviction and very neatly buttressed the evidence and arguments of E. A. Ross, Lothrop Stoddard, Madison Grant, Henry Adams, Henry Cabot Lodge, and a host of minor publicists and statesmen. Most of the avowed advocates of racial homogeneity and admirers of the sound integrity and creativeness of the Anglo-Saxon and Teutonic peoples had studied extensively in German universities, especially in the seminars of Droysen, Treitschke, and Mommsen. The Immigration Restriction League, whose

[27] U. S., House of Representatives (68th Cong., 1st Sess.): *Europe as an Emigrant-Exporting Continent and the United States as an Immigrant-Receiving Nation* (Hearings Before the Committee on Immigration and Naturalization, H. R., Serial 5-A, Statement of Dr. Harry H. Laughlin. March 8, 1924), 1295.

[28] Quoted in Saveth, *op. cit.*, 121.

[29] *Europe as an Emigrant-Exporting Continent and the United States as an Immigrant-Receiving Nation, loc. cit.*, 1339.

president in 1894 was John Fiske and whose secretary was Prescott F. Hall, contributed heavily to the development of the Anglo-Saxon emphasis which became the basis of the immigration policy in 1921 and later.

The immigration law of 1924, known as the Johnson Act, retained many of the features of the immigration law of 1917 but established many new procedures, definitions, and regulations. In Section 11 (a) the law provided that "the annual quota of any nationality shall be 2 per centum of the number of foreign-born individuals of such nationality resident in continental United States as determined by the United States census of 1890, but the minimum quota of any nationality shall be 100."[30]   It may be pointed out that this section made two notable changes in the Act of 1921. The 3 per cent of 1910 was changed to 2 per cent of 1890, a reduction in the quota percentage and a change of the base year. The change to 1890 was perfectly consistent with the trend toward stabilizing the population of the United States on an "old" immigrant basis. It was believed that 1890 as the base year would eliminate effectively the disproportions of southern and eastern Europeans who had come in after 1890. The total annual quotas under this bill for 1925 and 1926 were 164,667. The Japanese were declared ineligible to citizenship in 1924, and on this ground, though not by name, were excluded from entry into the United States as immigrants.

Subdivision (b) of Section 11, however, was the most important change, and, despite heroic efforts to amend or change and even eliminate its provisions, it became the immigration law which defines and controls our immigration policy today:

The annual quota of any nationality for the fiscal year beginning July 1, 1927, and for each fiscal year thereafter, shall be a number which bears the same ratio to 150,000 as the number of inhabitants in continental United States in 1920 having that national origin (ascertained as hereinafter provided in this section) bears to the number of inhabitants in

[30] *Ibid.*, 1401.

continental United States in 1920, but the minimum quota of any nationality shall be 100.[31]

This act, generally known as the National Origins Law, further provided for examination of quota immigrants at European ports of exit rather than American ports of entry and provided further that the burden of proof for legal entry rested upon the immigrant. This latter requirement was to create unusual hardships for immigrants, who were hospitalized with, say, tuberculosis, to prove affirmatively that they contracted the disease subsequent to entry. The same type of situation arose for those who became public charges to prove that the causes of their incapacitation did not exist prior to entry. In other words, the immigration authorities did not have to prove that the causes of inadequacy were of Old World origin but the immigrant did have to prove affirmatively that they were of New World origin.

The derivation of national origins gave rise to endless controversies. A joint committee of the Secretaries of State, Commerce, and Labor, working with the Bureau of the Census, was to determine the national origins of the population of continental United States on the basis of the Census of 1920. The technical details of the formula for deriving national origins will not be discussed beyond stating that tracing the origin of the 1920 population from the founding of the Colonies to the date of publication of the Census was a complicated, incomprehensible, and in many respects an occult and abstruse exercise in bias, speculation, statistical sleight of hand, and scientific nonsense. Not the method of identifying the origin of persons long gone to their reward in the eighteenth century by simply assigning them their nationality because their names were O'Brien, Cutler, Abrahams, or Swenson, but rather the purpose and the results are important. The heroic labors of the antagonists of the "new" and the champions of the "old" immigration are of importance in a discussion of policy.

---

[31] *Ibid.*, 1401. The effective date of the National Origins provision was 1927, but because Presidents Coolidge and Hoover failed to sign or veto, the law became effective two years later than the date set by Congress.

The woods around the North Sea became enshrined as the original homeland of all who love freedom, public order, sobriety, thrift, independence, democracy, honesty, true Christianity, the American way of life, and an unyielding and imperishable devotion to the ideals of the Founding Fathers and the reliable and incontrovertible moral values of the American Protestant Gentile white middle class. The trend at last reached its inevitable objective. Family stocks were of the greatest importance. We must now assimilate the millions of strange aliens, forbid any further additions, and establish homogeneity on the basis of common instincts and common origins. This law was a sort of act of penance and a purification rite. It represented a belated return to sound biological and moral principles. Eugenics had triumphed. Under national origins, northern and western Europe might now furnish 83.3 per cent of the future quota immigrants, southern and eastern Europe 14.3 per cent, and "other" 2.4 per cent.

From July 1, 1929, the effective date of the national origins provision of the Act of 1924, to June 30, 1947, the average annual number of quota immigrants has been approximately 35,000. Unused quotas, which are neither transferable from one nationality to another nor cumulative, are accounted for by the quota deficiencies of the large quota countries. The eighteen-year period during which 2,700,000 legally could have entered the United States as quota immigrants thus showed an over-all deficiency of approximately 2,070,000. "The total unused quotas for the last nine years (from 1939 to 1947, inclusive) for the six countries from which displaced persons, exclusive of the German Jews, have come, is only 30,342."[32] It is clearly apparent that areas of origin of Displaced Persons have filled their quota allotments almost one hundred per cent, thus destroying the logic that they should be permitted to enter at a rate to fill unused quotas of their own countries in previous years.

[32] U. S., *Senate Reports* (80th Cong., 2d Sess., Report No. 950): *Displaced Persons in Europe* (Report of the Committee on the Judiciary Pursuant to S. Res. 137, a Resolution to Make an Investigation of the Immigration System. March 2, 1948), 44.

The year 1947 accounted for 70,701 quota immigrant arrivals, the highest since 1930. This number constituted 46 per cent of 153,929 total admissible quota immigrants from all countries, or, stated in another way, 37 per cent of the 125,853 quota immigrants allocated to northern and western Europe and 89 per cent of the 24,648 allocated to southern and eastern Europe.[33]

Under the President's directive of December 22, 1945, 19,965 Displaced Persons had been admitted as of June 30, 1947. The first ship with Displaced Persons arrived in this country on May 20, 1946. These were persons born in central and eastern Europe who could not or would not return to their prewar homes and were given priorities in their quotas. Later other European and Asiatic countries were included. On January 1, 1948, nearly two-thirds of all Displaced Persons were coming from Germany.[34]

V

The eugenic basis of the immigration policy of the United States is well exemplified in the controversy over the admission of Displaced Persons. The Stratton Bill of 1947 providing for the admission of 400,000 Displaced Persons in a period of four years was rejected by Congress.[35] This bill was in effect an attempt to substitute refuge and asylum for the national origins basis adopted in 1924. On March 2, 1948, S. 2242 was introduced into the Senate by Senator Alexander Wiley of Wisconsin providing for the admission of 100,000 Displaced Persons for permanent settlement in the United States, half of whom were to be admitted in 1949 and half in 1950. Displaced Persons were defined in Section 2 (b) as "any displaced person or refugee as defined in

[33] *Monthly Review of the Immigration and Naturalization Service*, V (January, 1948), 82.
[34] *Ibid.*, 82–83.
[35] "A Bill to authorize the United States during an emergency period to undertake its fair share in the resettlement of displaced persons in Germany, Austria, and Italy including relatives of citizens or members of our armed forces by permitting their admission into the United States in a number equivalent to a part of the total quota numbers unused during the war years," 8oth Congress, 1st Session, H.R. 2910 (April 1, 1947).

Annex I of the Constitution of the International Refugee Organization and who is the concern of the International Refugee Organization." "Displaced person or refugee" as defined in Annex I of the Constitution of IRO reads:

a person who, as a result of the actions of the authorities of the regimes mentioned in Part I, section A, paragraph 1 (a) of this Annex has been deported from, or has been obliged to leave his country of nationality or of former habitual residence, such as persons who were compelled to undertake forced labour or who were deported for racial, religious, or political reasons.[36]

The Displaced Persons Act of 1948 in sub-section (c) of Section 2 defines "eligible displaced person" as anyone defined in Section 2 (b) above:

(1) who on or after September 1, 1939, and on or before December 22, 1945, entered Germany, Austria, or Italy and who on January 1, 1948, was in Italy or the American sector, the British sector, or the French sector of either Berlin or Vienna or the American zone, the British zone, or the French zone of either Germany or Austria; or a person who, having resided in Germany or Austria, was a victim of persecution by the Nazi government and was detained in, or was obliged to flee from such persecution and was subsequently returned to, one of these countries as a result of enemy action, or of war circumstances, and on January 1, 1948, had not been firmly resettled therein, and (2) who is qualified under the immigration laws of the United States for admission into the United States for permanent residence, and (3) for whom assurances in accordance with the regulations of the Commission have been given that such person, if admitted into the United States, will be suitably employed without displacing some other person from employment and that such person, and the members of such person's family who shall accompany such person and who propose to live with such person, shall not become public charges and will have safe and sanitary housing without displacing some other person from such housing. The spouse and unmarried dependent child or children under twenty-one years of age of such an eligible displaced person shall, if otherwise qualified for admission into the United States for permanent residence, also be deemed eligible displaced persons.[37]

---

[36] The regimes mentioned in Part I, Section A, paragraph 1 (a) are "victims of the nazi or fascist regimes or of regimes which took part on their side in the second world war, or of the quisling or similar regimes which assisted them against the United Nations." See *Senate Reports*, No. 950, *Displaced Persons*, p. 9.

[37] *Public Law 774*, Chapter 647 (80th Cong., 2d Sess., S. 2242), 1.

and Section 2 (e) states that

"Eligible displaced orphan" means a displaced person (1) who is under the age of sixteen years, and (2) who is qualified under the immigration laws of the United States for admission into the United States for permanent residence, and (3) who is an orphan because of the death or disappearance of both parents, and (4) who, on or before the effective date of this Act, was in Italy or in the American sector, the British sector, or the French sector of either Berlin or Vienna or the American zone, the British zone or the French zone of either Germany or Austria, and (5) for whom satisfactory assurances in accordance with the regulations of the Commission have been given that such person, if admitted into the United States, will be cared for properly.[38]

This act, with a number of amendments, was finally passed by Congress, becoming effective June 25, 1948, and was legislatively designated as the Displaced Persons Act of 1948. Section 2 (d) of the original act was amended in the final bill to read: " 'Eligible displaced person' shall also mean a native of Czechoslovakia who has fled as a direct result of persecution or fear of persecution from that country since January 1, 1948" and who is in the sectors noted above on the effective date of this act. The age of "eligible displaced orphan" is raised to "under sixteen years" in place of age fourteen as originally proposed.

Section 3 of the act provides for the admission of 205,000 during the two fiscal years following the passage of this act, and such visas as are issued by consular officers are to be charged against the quota of the country of the alien's nationality. Thus, an Esthonian Displaced Person meeting all other immigration requirements who received a visa for entry into the United States becomes a quota immigrant from Esthonia rather than a Displaced Person, despite the fact that Esthonia has ceased to exist as an independent country. Since the United States has not recognized Russian annexation of the Baltic countries, Displaced Persons from those countries still must have quota accreditation to the country of their nationality. Eligible displaced orphans are admissible by special non-quota immigration visas not to exceed three thousand.

[38] *Ibid.*, 2.

The total number of 205,000 in two years (although 105,000 more than in the original bill), as compared to H.R. 2190 allowing 400,000 in four years, was condemned as anti-Semitic and anti-Catholic by press, pulpit, and all 1948 candidates for the presidency of the United States. The objectionable sections are those concerning the effective dates for determination of eligibility by specific sectors and zones and the reduction of admissible Displaced Persons under quota regulations. The reason for the protest against this act by Jewish, Catholic, and liberal persons and organizations was their claim that the overwhelming number of Displaced Persons in the zones and sectors defined by the law did not enter those areas until *after* 1945, thus being disqualified for "eligible Displaced Person" status. Governor Thomas E. Dewey of New York, the Republican nominee for President, attempted to persuade the Senate Subcommittee to Investigate Immigration and Naturalization, consisting of Chapman Revercomb, chairman (West Virginia), Forrest C. Donnell (Missouri), John Sherman Cooper (Kentucky), Pat McCarran (Nevada), and J. Howard McGrath (Rhode Island), to change these provisions. The result was a 2–2 vote by the Committee, Chairman Revercomb breaking the tie vote by sustaining the act as written. The Displaced Persons Act of 1948 was "reluctantly" signed by President Truman and was one of the items listed by him for action by the Special Session of Congress which was called for July 26 and adjourned on August 7, 1948. No effective action was then taken.

Analysis of this act indicates consistency with the established immigration policy of 1924. Suggestions that Displaced Persons be admitted "in a number equivalent to a part of the total quota numbers unused during the war years" as set forth in the opening statement of the Stratton Bill, or suggestions that quota deficiencies of the United Kingdom and other large quota countries be utilized to equal 150,000 for the years in which there were over-all quota deficiency admissions, or suggestions to admit Displaced Persons on a nonquota basis, or outside the quotas, would in effect destroy the present immigration policy. Every person must be sympathetic to human suffering and misery, but whether such an emotional reaction is a sufficient and wise basis for American immigration policy is at least debatable. There is little reason to believe that the eugenic, national-biological policy of 1924 will be completely repealed in the foreseeable future. In addition to the basic eugenic philosophy at present in effect in our immigration policy, the concern of Congress with respect to the political and economic ideologies of certain classes of Displaced Persons permits the speculation that to the essential biological selection may be added a rigid and well-nigh inflexible denial of entry to *all* immigrants about whose political and economic beliefs there is even the shadow of a doubt from the American point of view. In fact, Senator Wiley, on August 14, 1948, took the position that revision of the Displaced Persons Act may be necessary but that "one of the prime objectives of the act was the exercise of vigilance lest Communist agents 'sneak into our country in the guise of displaced persons.' "[39]

VI

The analysis of the immigration policy of the United States which has been presented permits, in the judgment of the author, the following generalizations: (1) Prior to 1882 there appears to have been a number of contradictory and confusing laws and policies depending upon the needs and attitudes of the states with reference to immigration. (2) From 1882 to 1924 legislation served a twofold purpose: (a) to develop a coherent and consistent selective policy and (b) to satisfy the demands of labor organizations and socially minded and patriotic groups who feared the effects of dysgenic and radical infiltration upon the security and freedom of the American people. (3) From 1924 to 1948 there has been a further extension and refinement of policy with emphasis upon restriction of immigration generally and upon admission of qualified immigrants through a careful screening process to promote biological and cultural homogeneity in this

[39] *The New York Times*, August 15, 1948, Section 4, p. 10.

country. (4) Future legislation will follow the trend since 1882 with emphasis on those immigrants who possess attitudes, characteristics, qualifications, and skills which will be beneficial to the further development of American economic, political, and moral welfare.

Probably the best statement of the present and future immigration policy of the United States was made by Dr. Harry H. Laughlin in 1924 to the Committee on Immigration and Naturalization of the House of Representatives: "If 'America is to remain American,' we shall have to perfect the principle of selective immigration based upon high family stock standards. By national eugenics we shall have to correct the errors of past national policies of immigration, but by new statutes which are sound biologically we can cause future immigration to improve our native family stocks."[40]

---

[40] *Europe as an Emigrant-Exporting Continent and the United States as an Immigrant-Receiving Nation, loc. cit.,* 1238.

The Two Paris Peace Conferences of the Twentieth Century

By F. Lee Benns*

History-making peace conferences, in which the United States played a significant role, have been convened in Paris twice within the past generation as an aftermath of two bloody and destructive world wars. An examination of the procedure and organization of these conferences of 1919 and 1946 reveals several significant differences and some similarities.

The first major difference to be noted is that the treaties considered and approved by the peace conference in 1919 were drafted *after* the statesmen had gathered in Paris for that purpose. To a large extent, in 1919, the plenipotentiaries and their experts had to build the treaties from the ground up during the peace conference. This was not so in 1946. At the Potsdam Conference (July 17–August 2, 1945), following the collapse of the Nazis and the military defeat of Germany, President Truman, Prime Minister Attlee, and Premier Stalin agreed that the peace treaties with Italy, Rumania, Bulgaria, Hungary, and Finland should be drafted by the Council of Foreign Ministers *before* a peace conference was convened.[1] This Council, according to the original plan, was to be composed of the foreign ministers of Great Britain, Russia, the United States, France, and China. In the drafting of the several treaties, however, it was agreed that the Council was in each case to consist only of representatives of those states which had signed the armistice terms imposed upon the enemy state concerned, with one exception, namely, that France was to be regarded as a signatory of the armistice with Italy.[2]

*F. Lee Benns is Professor of History, Indiana University.
[1] James F. Byrnes, *Speaking Frankly* (New York and London, 1947), 71.
[2] *Ibid.*, 72.

The Council of Foreign Ministers, at its first meeting in London (September 11–October 2, 1945), almost at once became dead-locked over the matter of procedure and adjourned without tangible achievements.[3] To break the deadlock the foreign ministers of the Big Three—James F. Byrnes, Ernest Bevin, and Vyacheslav M. Molotov—were obliged to convene again and met this time in Moscow (December 16–December 26, 1945). These three men there agreed that the terms of the treaty with Italy should be drafted by the foreign ministers of Great Britain, the United States, Russia, and France; the terms of the treaties with Rumania, Bulgaria, and Hungary, by the foreign ministers of Great Britain, the United States, and Russia; and those of the treaty with Finland, by the foreign ministers of Great Britain and Russia. China was not to attend the Council meetings when these five treaties were being discussed but the United States and France were to attend and to be permitted to discuss even in those cases in which they were not permitted to vote.[4]

At the Moscow Conference it was further agreed that, upon the completion of the draft treaties, a general peace conference would be convened for the purpose of considering them, the conference to consist of representatives of the five members of the Council of Foreign Ministers—Russia, Great Britain, the United States, France, and China—and of representatives of the sixteen other states which had actively waged war with substantial military force against the European enemy states. At the conclusion of this peace conference the states which had drawn up the original draft treaties should consider the recommendations of the conference and then draft the final texts of the several treaties.[5]

During the first seven months of 1946 the foreign ministers of the United States, Great Britain, Russia, and France, and their deputies, carried on negotiations in an attempt to reach agreement

---

[3] *Ibid.*, 102–06.

[4] *Ibid.*, 111–15.

[5] *Chronology of International Events and Documents*, II, new series (Supplement to *The World Today*, Royal Institute of International Affairs, 1945–46), 22. Hereafter cited as Royal Institute, *Chronology*.

on the terms of the treaties to be presented to the future peace conference, and ultimately full and almost complete treaties were drafted for each of the five defeated powers. Where agreement was not reached on any specific point alternative articles were prepared.[6] The task of the peace conference of 1946, therefore, was one of accepting or rejecting or amending articles already drafted by the Council of Foreign Ministers. After the First World War, on the contrary, no such efforts to reach preliminary agreements were made, and to a large extent each of the representatives of the major powers brought to Paris his own ideas and programs, which all too frequently clashed with those of the other leading plenipotentiaries.[7]

II

And that brings up the matter of the so-called Big Four, for one similarity in peace-making after the two world wars is that on each occasion negotiations were dominated by a Big Four. In 1919 they were Wilson, Lloyd George, Clemenceau, and Orlando;[8] in 1946 they were Byrnes, Bevin, Molotov, and Bidault.[9] In the former case they were the heads of the governments which they represented; in the latter they were only the foreign ministers, for after the Second World War, except for the preliminary conference at Potsdam, the heads of the major powers did not participate in person in the peace negotiations. So far as countries are concerned Russia was not in the first Big Four and Italy was not in the second. In the Big Four of 1919 Italy, represented by Orlando, played a relatively minor part;[10] in the Big Four of 1946 France, represented

[6] For an example see the alternative wordings of Article 71 of the draft treaty with Italy, in United States, Department of State (Publication 2868, Conference series 103), *Paris Peace Conference, 1946: Selected Documents* (Washington, 1948), 119–20. This volume of documents, which were selected from a set compiled at the conference for the use of Secretary of State James F. Byrnes, will hereafter be cited as *Paris Conference, 1946.*

[7] H. W. V. Temperley, ed., *A History of the Peace Conference of Paris,* I (London, 1920), 237–41.

[8] Robert Lansing, *The Big Four and Others of the Peace Conference* (Boston and New York, 1921), 4, 10–134.

[9] Royal Institute, *Chronology,* II, new series, 364–67.

[10] Lansing, *The Big Four,* 125–26.

by Georges Bidault, was similarly relegated to a minor role. One difference between the Big Four of 1946 and that of 1919 is fairly obvious. After the Second World War the Big Four emerged, met, clashed, struggled, and compromised for months before the actual peace conference convened and continued to clash and compromise even after it had adjourned. In 1919, on the other hand, the clashes and struggles and compromises of the Big Four were limited, for the most part, to the peace conference itself.

In the Big Four of 1946 there was probably a deeper distrust of one another's fundamental aims than in that of 1919, for Wilson, Lloyd George, Clemenceau, and Orlando had at least one basic common bond in that they all represented capitalistic democracies. In 1946, on the other hand, the political and economic ideologies of the three Western democracies were far different from those of the Soviet Union. In consequence the members of the Big Four in 1946 were soon caught in the vicious circle of fear and distrust—on the one hand, fear of Communism with its threat of "world revolution"; on the other, fear of "capitalistic imperialism" with its threat of encirclement. Byrnes, Bevin, and Bidault accordingly sought to provide national security against the alleged or suspected "plots of the Communists," while Molotov used his veto to try to check the "machinations of the greedy imperialists." Though not openly expressed, these fears were ever-present and the search for security by each side in turn only intensified national suspicions.[11]

These national suspicions after the Second World War, in turn, probably account for another significant difference between peace-making in 1946 and peace-making in 1919. After the First World War the Allies turned their attention at once to the drafting of the most important treaty, namely, the treaty with Germany. The Treaty of Versailles then served as the model for the four minor treaties with Austria, Hungary, Bulgaria, and Turkey.[12] In 1946, on the contrary, the Allies gave their attention first to the drafting

[11] For examples of these suspicions, see Royal Institute, *Chronology*, II, new series, 295; *New York Times*, April 16, 1946.
[12] Temperley, *History of the Peace Conference*, I, 261.

of the minor treaties. The crucial question for all Europe—the fate of Germany—was postponed. The reason given for the postponement was that a peace settlement could not be made for Germany until that country had a government ready to accept it and adequate to execute it. But behind the announced reason for delay probably was the Big Four's realization of the difficulty which would confront them in agreeing upon terms.[13]

III

Even though the treaty with Germany was more or less indefinitely postponed in 1946, unanimity among the Big Four was not easily or quickly attained on all the terms of the treaties with the lesser states. The crisis which gained the greatest notoriety and which probably took up more time than any other one problem, both in 1946 and in 1919, arose from the conflict over the boundary between Yugoslavia and Italy.[14] In 1919 the city involved was Fiume;[15] in 1946 it was Trieste.[16] In 1919 Italy, largely for strategic reasons, sought a boundary which transgressed ethnic principles. At that time the United States opposed Italy's demands and President Wilson drew a boundary line which the Italians then bitterly denounced as grossly unfair[17] but which in 1946 they themselves put forward as a just solution of the boundary question.[18] In 1946 Yugoslavia, from motives very similar to Italy's in 1919, sought to push her boundary farther west, also at the expense of ethnic principles.[19] This time the United States opposed Yugoslavia for ethnic reasons and also, probably, because it desired to prevent the control of the important port of Trieste

---

[13] Byrnes, *Speaking Frankly*, 70–71.

[14] Byrnes, *Speaking Frankly*, 127; René Albrecht-Carrié, *Italy at the Paris Peace Conference* (New York, 1938), 86–183.

[15] Albrecht-Carrié, *Italy at Paris*, 98–103.

[16] Byrnes, *Speaking Frankly*, 97, 127–28, 133–34, 147–48.

[17] Albrecht-Carrié, *Italy at Paris*, 117–19, 123–28; Ray Stannard Baker, *Woodrow Wilson and World Settlement*, III (Garden City, New York, 1922), 274–77.

[18] *New York Times*, May 2, 1946.

[19] Byrnes, *Speaking Frankly*, 127–28.

from falling into the hands of a state considered to be a Soviet satellite. [20]

The Trieste problem in 1946 also somewhat resembled the Danzig problem in 1919. After the First World War Poland desired Danzig as an outlet to the sea, though Danzig's population of some 300,000 was overwhelmingly German. [21] In 1946 Yugoslavia similarly desired Trieste as an outlet to the sea for its northwestern territories even though the city's 250,000 population was predominantly Italian. [22] In 1919 France looked to Poland as a possible postwar ally against Germany; Clemenceau therefore desired to strengthen that state and accordingly fought in the Big Four to have Danzig given to Poland. [23] In 1946 Russia considered Yugoslavia as an ally and an outpost on the Adriatic, and Molotov consequently supported Yugoslavia's demand for Trieste. [24] In 1919 Lloyd George opposed Poland's claim to Danzig, giving as his reason the fact that Danzig's population was German. [25] But Lloyd George's deep concern for Germans seemed open to question, in view of his willingness at that time to turn over to Italy 250,000 Germans in the South Tyrol. In 1946 the Western powers opposed giving Trieste to Yugoslavia, ostensibly for ethnic reasons; but in 1946 these same Western powers also ignored ethnic principles when they refused to return the South Tyrol with its German population to Austria. [26] In 1946 as in 1919 a compromise had to be reached, and in each case it resulted in the establishment of a Free City—Danzig under the League of Nations, Trieste under the United Nations.

Aside from the much publicized Italian-Yugoslav boundary dispute four other major differences were still unresolved by the Council of Foreign Ministers up to the time of the meeting of the

[20] "Draft Treaties of Peace," *World Today*, II (December, 1946), 580–81.

[21] E. M. House and Charles Seymour, *What Really Happened at Paris* (New York, 1921), 78.

[22] Byrnes, *Speaking Frankly*, 127.

[23] House and Seymour, *What Really Happened at Paris*, 70.

[24] Byrnes, *Speaking Frankly*, 97; *New York Times*, April 11, 1946.

[25] House and Seymour, *What Really Happened at Paris*, 70.

[26] *New York Times*, April 22, 1946 and May 1, 1946.

Paris Peace Conference of 1946. First, the three Western powers sought to insert terms in the peace treaties which would assure to all countries equality of opportunity in the economic life of the five defeated states, or—to put it in another way—they sought to prevent Russia from gaining a privileged position in those states; Russia, on the other hand, appeared to wish to leave some loopholes for discriminatory or monopolistic agreements regarding commerce, industry, and commercial aviation.[27] Second, in the matter of treatment of enemy property in Germany and in the Allied countries and in the matter of compensation to Allied nationals for loss of, or damage to, property in the enemy countries, Russia wished to be more lenient to the defeated countries than did the three Western powers.[28] Third, in regard to the Danube, the three Western powers wished to insert articles in the treaties with Hungary, Rumania, and Bulgaria stating that within six months after the treaties became effective a conference of the interested states would be convened to establish a new permanent international regime of the Danube; while Russia maintained that the question of internationalizing the Danube should not be included in these treaties since it concerned other Danubian states also.[29] Fourth, in the matter of future disputes over the interpretation or execution of the treaties, the Western powers desired final recourse to the International Court of Justice, while Russia wished disputes to be settled by direct diplomacy, or, in the last resort, by the Big Four.[30]

In 1946 these disagreements among the Big Four seemed likely to entail the indefinite postponement of the general peace conference, for Molotov maintained that the latter should not be convened until at least Great Britain, the United States and Russia

[27] See, for example, the alternative wordings of Article 71 of the draft treaty with Italy, *Peace Conference, 1946*, 119–20.

[28] See, for example, the alternative wordings of Articles 24–27 of the draft treaty with Rumania, *ibid.*, 664–69.

[29] See, for example, the alternative wordings of Article 34 of the draft treaty with Rumania, *ibid.*, 675–76.

[30] See, for example, the alternative wordings of Article 16 of the draft treaty with Italy, *ibid.*, 86–90.

had reached agreement on fundamentals. Eventually, however, it was decided, that the unfinished drafts, with alternate articles in some cases, should be allowed to go to the peace conference on the strict understanding that the Council of Foreign Ministers must agree afterwards upon the specific and final terms of each treaty.[31]

IV

With the way finally opened for the convening of a peace conference in 1946, the Council of Foreign Ministers next unanimously agreed on the rules of procedure to be recommended to the conference. First, the plenary conference of the twenty-one nations should consider the treaties and refer to the various commissions relevant parts of them. The reports of the commissions should then be referred back to the plenary conference which might adopt such recommendations as it pleased. Second, a Committee on Procedure, including representatives of each of the twenty-one states, should act as a sort of steering committee, assisting the plenary conference and co-ordinating the work of the commissions. Third, nine special commissions should be appointed. Five of these should be political and territorial, one for each of the five treaties. Four of them should be functional: namely, a military commission to consider the military terms of all of the treaties; a legal commission to consider the legal terms of all; and two economic commissions—one to consider economic aspects of the treaty with Italy, and the other to do the same for the treaties with Finland, Rumania, Bulgaria, and Hungary. Fourth, voting in the plenary conference and in the commissions was to be carried by a two-third's majority, but the minority view of a commission should also be heard by the plenary conference. Byrnes, Bevin, Molotov, and Bidault all agreed to support unitedly at the peace conference the chief features of these rules.[32]

In the matter of procedure at the peace conferences of 1919 and

[31] Royal Institute, *Chronology*, II, new series, 297.
[32] *Ibid.*, II, new series, 426.

1946 a number of similarities and differences are easily discernible. The decisions regarding the states to be represented and the general rules to be followed in the conferences were in both cases made by the major powers. In 1919 the Big Four, in an informal meeting preceding the opening of the peace conference, decided that any state which had declared war on, or broken diplomatic relations with, the Central Powers was eligible.[33] The result was that many states[34] which had played no important roles in the war were represented. At the Moscow Conference in December, 1945, the Big Three decided, on the other hand, that only those states which had actually waged war with substantial military force should attend the peace conference.[35] As a result, only one Latin-American country, Brazil, was represented instead of ten as in 1919. Because of this difference, perhaps, still another contrast between the two conferences is noticeable. In 1919 the votes of national delegations were weighted, the five great powers having five votes each in the Plenary Conference, the other powers being graduated from three down to one.[36] In the 1946 conference each state had one vote only.

Both peace conferences had steering committees. In 1919 for the first two months the committee was the Council of Ten, consisting of the two ranking delegates of the United States, Great Britain, France, Italy, and Japan. During the last three months the steering committee consisted of only Wilson, Lloyd George, Clemenceau, and Orlando. Nearly all the important final decisions in 1919 were made by this steering committee.[37] In the conference of 1946 the steering committee was the Committee on Procedure which consisted of representatives of each of the twenty-one states,

[33] Temperley, *History of the Peace Conference*, I, 247.
[34] Notably Hejaz, Siam, Bolivia, Cuba, Ecuador, Guatemala, Haiti, Honduras, Liberia, Nicaragua, Panama, Peru, and Uruguay.
[35] Royal Institute, *Chronology*, II, new series, 22. In 1946 the states represented were Great Britain, the Soviet Union, the United States, China, France, Australia, Belgium, Brazil, Canada, Czechoslovakia, Ethiopia, Greece, India, the Netherlands, New Zealand, Norway, Poland, the Union of South Africa, Yugoslavia, the Ukraine, and White Russia.
[36] Temperley, *History of the Peace Conference*, I, 248.
[37] *Ibid.*, 248-49, 262-65.

and it possessed no power to make final decisions regarding the terms of the treaties.[38]   Both peace conferences resorted to the use of commissions to carry on studies and investigations and make reports.   In the conference of 1919 these reports were made to the Big Four which then made its own decisions.[39]   In 1946 these reports were made instead directly to the plenary conference which accepted or rejected them.[40]   In 1919 the chairman of the plenary conference, Clemenceau, was elected by the members of the conference upon the nomination of President Wilson, and Clemenceau served throughout the conference.[41]   In 1946 by the decision of the Big Four the chairmanship was rotated among the five members of the Council of Foreign Ministers.[42]

In contrast with the relative speed with which the Paris Peace Conference was convened after the First World War, it was not until July 29, 1946—nearly fifteen months after the German armistice of May 7, 1945—that the peace conference following the Second World War was opened by French Foreign Minister Bidault.   The latter formally assured the delegates of the twenty-one states that they would have an opportunity for the fullest possible discussion of the five treaties which had been drafted by the Council of Foreign Ministers, and that the final drawing up of the treaties would take place only after the recommendations of the conference had been given full consideration.[43]   The opening days of the conference were given over to organization and to speeches by the heads of the twenty-one national delegations, in the course of which differences of viewpoint became obvious and verbal clashes frequently resulted.[44]

[38] Royal Institute, *Chronology*, II, new series, 426.
[39] Temperley, *History of the Peace Conference*, I, 265, 276.
[40] See, for example, *Paris Conference, 1946*, 404–50.
[41] Lansing, *Big Four*, 13.
[42] Royal Institute, *Chronology*, II, new series, 476.
[43] Royal Institute, *Chronology*, II, new series, 470.
[44] *Ibid.*, 470–83, 511–19.

V

In 1946, just as in 1919, a dispute arose at the very first meeting of the plenary conference when the smaller states attempted to revolt against domination by the Big Four. The Australian foreign minister, Herbert V. Evatt, objected to the proposed two-thirds vote which the Big Four had ruled should be necessary to have a recommendation of the peace conference considered subsequently by them. Some of the states which were not of the four had, he asserted, "as much right as some of the four to take part in the final drafting of the treaties." In the conference, he declared, each of the twenty-one states should have equal rank and voice. His view was supported by others, including the Dutch delegate who maintained that a vote by a simple majority should be sufficient to make a recommendation effective. [45] This question of the two-thirds rule was referred to the Committee on Procedure where the fight was waged until August 7 when, at two o'clock in the morning, a compromise was finally passed by a vote of 15 to 6, the latter representing the so-called Slav bloc—Russia, White Russia, the Ukraine, Poland, Czechoslovakia and Yugoslavia. [46]

According to this compromise, recommendations of the plenary conference should be of two kinds: those adopted by a two-thirds majority vote, and those which obtained a majority of more than one half but less than two thirds. Both types of recommendation should be submitted to the Council of Foreign Ministers for their consideration. [47] The fight next shifted back to the plenary conference where the recommendation of the Committee on Procedure came up for adoption. Molotov at once opposed the Committee's recommendation and criticized the British and American delegations which, he asserted, despite Bevin's and Byrnes' earlier agreement to support unitedly the rules recommended by the Big Four, [48] had "joined hands to carry this decision in the Committee." He

[45] Royal Institute, *Chronology*, II, new series, 470–74.
[46] *Ibid.*, 476–79; *Paris Conference, 1946*, 40–42.
[47] *Paris Conference, 1946*, 46–47.
[48] *Cf. ante*, p. 160.

claimed that what was desired were decisive votes on the part of the conference to assist the Council of Foreign Ministers in reaching decisions, and questioned whether a vote of 11 to 10 would be helpful. The Australian delegate, however, at once returned to the fray. Molotov was voted down 15 to 6 and the recommendation of the Committee on Procedure was adopted, also by a vote of 15 to 6.[49] The small powers thus won a small concession.

But the latter continued to revolt against the rules of the Big Four. The Dutch delegate demanded that delegations from all states should have a full and equal share in the work of all the commissions instead of only those which had declared war on a given state. His motion, however, was defeated in the Committee on Procedure.[50] Molotov then suggested that those delegations which wished to take part in the commissions might do so without voting just as the United States had joined (without voting) in discussions of the Finnish Treaty in the Council of Foreign Ministers. This was agreed to.[51] The New Zealand delegate then led a revolt against the Big Four's decision that the chairmanship of the Plenary Conference should rotate among members of the Council of Foreign Ministers. He proposed that French Foreign Minister Bidault should be made permanent chairman of the conference as Clemenceau had been made in 1919. He was voted down.[52] The Dutch delegate thereupon proposed that the conference should elect its chairman. He, too, was voted down. Whenever the Big Four stood together and opposed the smaller powers the latter were defeated.[53]

In general, however, the small powers were better treated in 1946 than they had been at Paris after the First World War. In 1919 Clemenceau had bluntly informed them that the great powers, backed by 12,000,000 soldiers, would have to be responsible for

[49] *Paris Conference, 1946,* 49–52.
[50] Royal Institute, *Chronology,* II, new series, 474.
[51] *Ibid.*
[52] *Ibid.,* 475, 476, 479.
[53] *Ibid.,* 476–77.

the execution of the treaties and that they would therefore control the conference.[54] In 1919 only six plenary sessions were held before the Treaty of Versailles was signed. The full text of this treaty was not presented to the small powers until the day before it was presented to the Germans, and then Clemenceau did not permit the plenary conference to vote on its acceptance or rejection.[55] In fact, Lansing characterized the plenary sessions of 1919 as farces which permitted no "frank exchange of views" but which were called together merely to register their approval of the decisions of the Big Four and not to criticize or object.[56] The procedure followed in 1946 was obviously quite different, for then the plenary conference was permitted to vote article by article on all five of the treaties.[57]

One very noticeable difference in the conferences of 1946 and 1919 was the treatment—at least the superficial treatment—of the defeated powers. In 1919 the peace treaties were completed before representatives of the defeated states were permitted to come to the conference and they were then allowed to make only written observations regarding them.[58] In 1946 the Committee on Procedure decided that representatives of the defeated powers should be invited to attend the plenary conference to present their views before the different commissions began their work.[59] Subsequently speeches were delivered before the conference by the Italian and Rumanian premiers and by the Bulgarian, Hungarian, and Finnish foreign ministers.[60] Probably the speeches of these representatives had little effect on the eventual treaties, but the defeated powers were at least given a chance to be heard by the whole conference.

[54] Temperley, *History of the Peace Conference*, I, 249.

[55] *Ibid.*, 249–50, 269.

[56] Lansing, *Big Four*, 19–20.

[57] See, for example, the discussions and decisions of the plenary conference on the treaty with Italy, *Paris Conference, 1946*, 596–612.

[58] Temperley, *History of the Peace Conference*, I, 269–70.

[59] Royal Institute, *Chronology*, II, new series, 477.

[60] *Paris Conference, 1946*, 397, 729, 898, 1104–05, 1274–75.

VI

During the summer of 1946 many gained the impression that the peace conference then meeting in Paris faced more crises and came nearer breaking up than the one in 1919. This is not true. The tension in Paris in 1919, especially between Clemenceau and Wilson and between Wilson and Orlando,[61] was probably greater than that between Byrnes and Molotov or between Molotov and Bevin. In 1919 so great was the tension on one occasion that President Wilson ordered his ship, the *George Washington*, to come for him.[62] On another occasion the Japanese threatened to leave the conference and refuse to join the new League of Nations unless they were granted certain of their demands.[63] And at still another time the Italian delegation actually went home because of Wilson's opposition to its demand for Fiume.[64] During the peace conference of 1946, it is true, there were threats that the Yugoslav government would not sign the Italian treaty if its demands were not met;[65] but in 1919 China actually did refuse to sign the Treaty of Versailles because it granted Japan rights in Shantung.[66] The crises and clashes were no worse in 1946 than in 1919.

But the publicity in 1946 was much greater than in 1919. In the earlier conference the meetings of the Council of Ten and of the Big Four were secret; no press representatives were allowed to be present. Although some information leaked out, the public had no certainty that such information was not merely the opinion of some journalist.[67] Even after the treaty of Versailles had been approved and presented to the German delegation, the full text was kept secret in the Allied countries.[68] In 1946, on the other hand, the preliminary draft treaties were published when presented

---

[61] Lansing, *Big Four*, 67, 110, 116; Baker, *Woodrow Wilson and World Settlement*, II, 35.
[62] Baker, *Woodrow Wilson and World Settlement*, II, 57–58.
[63] *Ibid.*, II, 241, 257–58.
[64] Temperley, *History of the Peace Conference*, I, 268.
[65] Byrnes, *Speaking Frankly*, 135.
[66] Temperley, *History of the Peace Conference*, I, 271.
[67] Temperley, *History of the Peace Conference*, I, 277–78.
[68] *Ibid.*, 270.

to the peace conference, and the meetings of the Committee on Procedure, all of the commissions, and the plenary conference itself were open to the press.[69] That is undoubtedly one reason the public got the impression in 1946 that there were so many disputes. Differences of opinion among the delegates, especially if between the Western powers and Russia, were frequently played up by sensation-seeking reporters as real crises or near-crises.

Eventually, however, on October 7, 1946, after the plenipotentiaries had been in session ten full weeks, the various commissions finished their study and discussion and had reports ready to submit to the plenary conference. The latter thereupon unanimously adopted rules of procedure, suggested by the Big Four, which set up a rigid timetable to be followed. Each national delegation was to be limited to a 30-minute speech on each of the five treaties. Following these half-hour speeches the plenary conference was to start voting on the various articles and amendments of the treaty under consideration. Three days were allowed for the Italian treaty and one day each for the Rumanian, Bulgarian, Hungarian, and Finnish treaties.[70] By adhering to this rigid schedule, it was hoped, the peace conference could adjourn in time for the meeting of the General Assembly of the United Nations in New York on October 23.

In accordance with this schedule the plenary conference completed the approval of a draft treaty for Italy at 3:15 o'clock on the morning of October 10. Innumerable votes had been taken and in general the outcome in each case had been 15 to 6 in favor of the views of the Western powers and 15 to 6 against those of Russia or Yugoslavia.[71] At 2 o'clock on the morning of October 11 a Rumanian treaty was likewise approved by a vote of 15 to 6, incorporating over Russia's opposition the views of the Western powers regarding the internationalizing of the Danube and the requirement of most-favored-nation treatment for the Allies.[72]

[69] Royal Institute, *Chronology*, II, new series, 471–72.
[70] *Paris Conference, 1946*, 69–70.
[71] For the discussions and decisions on the Italian treaty, see *ibid.*, 597–648.
[72] For the discussions and decisions on the Rumanian treaty, see *ibid.*, 816–33.

Early in the morning of October 12 a Bulgarian treaty was similarly approved except for the first article, which, as drafted by the Big Four, stated that Bulgaria's frontiers with Greece should be those existing on January 1, 1941. At the peace conference, however, Greece had asked for frontier changes at the expense of Bulgaria, changes which had been denied by the Bulgarian Political and Territorial Commission. Although before the conference the Big Four had pledged themselves to support in the conference those articles of the treaties upon which they had agreed, in this case Bevin did not stand by his earlier commitment. Since Great Britain and eleven other states, including Australia, Canada, India, New Zealand, and South Africa, abstained from voting, the article failed to obtain a majority. This issue was left open, therefore, to be settled later by the Big Four.[73] During the night of October 12-13 the plenary conference approved a Hungarian treaty which closely resembled that with Rumania,[74] and a treaty with Finland was then quickly approved on the night of October 14.[75] On the next day the conference adjourned, following a farewell address by Bidault.[76]

VII

The adjournment brings up a final and very important difference between the peace conference of 1946 and that of 1919. At Versailles after the First World War the plenary conference witnessed the signing of the German peace treaty with its definitive terms. In 1946, since the peace conference closed with the passage of recommendations on the terms of each of the five treaties, the definitive terms still remained to be decided. For it must be emphasized that the Paris Peace Conference of 1946 was only an advisory body and that the final treaties still had to be approved by those members of the Big Four which had signed the armistices with the respective enemy powers. About all that the conference

---

[73] For the discussions and decisions on the Bulgarian treaty, see *ibid.*, 993–1010.
[74] For the discussions and decisions on the Hungarian treaty, see *ibid.*, 1191–1214.
[75] For the discussions and decisions on the Finnish treaty, see *ibid.*, 1330–43.
[76] *Ibid.*, 1346.

had done, therefore, was to indicate by votes that, in general, those fifteen states which had capitalistic, democratic institutions uniformly supported Byrnes, Bevin, and Bidault against Molotov, and that the Slav bloc of six states—dominated by Russia with her communistic, totalitarian institutions—uniformly supported Molotov. The problem of unanimous agreement among the Big Four still remained unsolved.

In a last attempt to reach a solution another session of the Council of Foreign Ministers was held, this time in New York (November 4–December 12, 1946).[77] On the majority of issues the agreements of the Big Four reached in that session were based upon recommendations made by the Paris Peace Conference. According to Secretary of State Byrnes, of the 53 recommendations which the peace conference had adopted by at least a two-thirds majority, 47 were incorporated with little or no change in the final texts of the treaties, and of the 41 recommendations which the peace conference had adopted by a majority of less than two-thirds, 24 appeared in the final texts.[78] The five treaties were ultimately signed in Paris on February 10, 1947, by representatives of the enemy states and by representatives of the states which had participated in the Paris Peace Conference with the exception of the United States.[79] Mr. Byrnes had already signed for the United States in Washington on January 20, the day before George C. Marshall succeeded him as secretary of state.[80]

It is obvious, from what has been written above, that in matters of procedure and organization the two Paris Peace Conferences of the twentieth century differed significantly in more than a score of ways and that, on the other hand, they resembled each other in approximately a dozen particulars. The most significant similarity, of course, was that in both 1919 and 1946 the terms of the peace treaties were decided in the last analysis by the Big Four

[77] Royal Institute, *Chronology*, II, new series, 678–79, 717–19, 749–51, 788.
[78] *Paris Conference, 1946*, iv.
[79] Royal Institute, *Chronology*, III, new series, 96.
[80] *Ibid.*, III, new series, 51.

or, more truly, the Big Three—the United States, Great Britain, and France in 1919, and the United States, Great Britain, and Russia in 1946. The most significant difference between the two occasions, obviously, was the presence within the Big Three in 1946—and the absence in 1919—of a deep-seated fear and distrust arising from the existence within the three states of fundamentally different political and economic institutions. It is the absence in 1919 and the presence in 1946 of this profound suspicion and resultant desire for national security which account for the contrasting fact that the peace treaty with Germany was the first to be drafted and signed after the First World War but is apparently destined this time to be the last.

The Supreme Allied Command in Northwest Europe, 1944-45

By FORREST C. POGUE*

General Dwight D. Eisenhower, Supreme Commander, Allied Expeditionary Force, was ordered by the British and American Chiefs of Staff on February 12, 1944 to enter "the Continent of Europe and, in conjunction with the other United Nations, undertake operations aimed at the heart of Germany and the destruction of her armed forces." To make possible the successful execution of the directive, the Allied Powers found it necessary to grant broad military and political powers to the Supreme Commander. This break with the tradition of separation of political and military functions arose from the complexity of the task in Northwest Europe which required of General Eisenhower not only command

*Forrest C. Pogue is writing the official history of the Supreme Command, European Theater of Operations, for the Department of the Army, and is basing it upon the official documents of the Department and of Supreme Headquarters, A. E. F. The views expressed in this essay, however, are those of the author and are not official. Published works of value for the subject of this essay are: Col. Robert S. Allen, *Lucky Forward, the History of Patton's Third U. S. Army* (New York, 1947); Lt. Gen. Lewis H. Brereton, *The Brereton Diaries* (New York, 1946); Lt. Col. Alfred H. Burne, *Strategy in World War II* (Harrisburg, Pa., 1947); Captain Harry C. Butcher, *My Three Years with Eisenhower* (New York, 1946); Kenneth S. Davis, *Soldier of Democracy, a Biography of Dwight D. Eisenhower* (Garden City, N. Y., 1945); Maj. Gen. Sir Francis W. de Guingand, *Operation Victory* (New York, 1947); Gen. Dwight D. Eisenhower, *Crusade in Europe* (Garden City, N. Y., 1948); Gen. Dwight D. Eisenhower, *Report by the Supreme Commander to the Combined Chiefs of Staff on the Operations in Europe of the Allied Expeditionary Force, 6 June 1944 to 8 May 1945* (Washington, 1946); *History of the Psychological Warfare Division (SHAEF)* (Hq. USFET, 1945); Ralph Ingersoll, *Top Secret* (New York, 1946); William L. Langer, *Our Vichy Gamble* (New York, 1947); John J. McCloy, "Great Military Decisions," *Foreign Affairs,* XXVI (October, 1947), 52–72; Gen. George C. Marshall, *Biennial Report to the Secretary of War, July 1, 1943 to June 30, 1945* (Washington, 1946); Viscount Montgomery, *Normandy to the Baltic* (London, 1947); Allen Moorehead, *Montgomery, a Biography* (New York, 1946); Lt. Col. G. A. Rowan-Robinson, "The Role of Supreme Allied Commander, Foch and Eisenhower," *The Fighting Forces,* XXIV (London, April, 1947), 68–72; Robert E. Sherwood, *Roosevelt and Hopkins, an Intimate History* (New York, 1948); Henry L. Stimson and McGeorge Bundy, *On Active Service in Peace and War* (New York, 1948).

of the combined Allied army, navy, and air forces, but also control of military government, civil affairs, press relations, and psychological warfare in the European Theater of Operations.

To understand the nature of the Supreme Command in Northwest Europe, it is helpful to examine first the somewhat involved machinery of the Combined Chiefs of Staff created by the United States and Great Britain early in 1942. Unlike the Supreme Allied War Council, which was belatedly established in World War I after costly defeats had proved the need of a body to determine combined strategy, the Combined Chiefs of Staff organization was set up in Washington shortly after the entry of the United States into the war with the purpose of co-ordinating all Allied military strategy so that the full Allied resources could be directed with maximum effectiveness against the enemy. This body was made up of the Chiefs of Staff Committee in Great Britain, consisting during the latter part of the war of Chief of the Imperial General Staff, General Sir Alan Brooke; Chief of the Air Staff, Sir Charles Portal; and First Sea Lord, Sir Andrew Cunningham; and the Joint Chiefs of Staff in the United States, which included Admiral William D. Leahy, General George C. Marshall, Admiral Ernest J. King, and General H. H. Arnold. When not acting together in special conferences, the Combined Chiefs of Staff sat in Washington, where the British members were represented through the Joint Staff Mission, headed by Field Marshal Sir John Dill (and later General Sir Henry Maitland Wilson). At Casablanca, Washington, Quebec (twice), Tehran, Cairo, and Yalta, the Combined Chiefs of Staff met President Roosevelt and Prime Minister Churchill to determine strategy, allocate resources, and grant directives to the Allied commanders. Occasionally, as at Tehran and Yalta, heads of other states were consulted, in order to co-ordinate operations.

In strategic matters the Combined Chiefs of Staff exercised careful control, but on operational matters they gave considerable autonomy to the Supreme Commanders. A careful study of the actions of the Combined Chiefs of Staff shows that they did not attempt to influence the detailed conduct of the battles from Washington. It is true that in the period prior to D-Day the British Chiefs of Staff, being charged with special responsibilities in connection with the planning for Operation OVERLORD (the operation for the cross-channel invasion of northern France), did exercise considerable control. It is equally true that the United States Joint Chiefs of Staff, through their control of United States supplies and forces in Europe, were able to direct activities of General Eisenhower in his capacity as commander of United States Forces in Europe. But the view that the Combined Chiefs of Staff were in such day-to-day control of the battle that they decided the direction in which troops should go, and the means allotted to the various armies, is incorrect. On the one occasion when it appeared that such intervention would be recommended, the United States Chiefs of Staff resisted the proposal so firmly that it was quickly dropped.

In their grants of power to the Supreme Commander, the United States and British Chiefs of Staff tended to be more generous than either group likely would have been to the commander of their purely national forces. Thus it was that Britain handed over broad powers to an American Supreme Commander to deal with military and diplomatic questions. On several occasions when the British War Cabinet was unwilling to yield to requests of Lieutenant General Frederick E. Morgan, head planner for the invasion of Northwest Europe, and General Sir Bernard L. Montgomery, head of 21st Army Group, the British commanders asked General Eisenhower to intercede as Supreme Commander. Usually these requests met with success. General Eisenhower by his insistence on certain decisions, such as the imposition of a visitors' ban in coastal areas of the United Kingdom, the furnishing of land for maneuver purposes, and the imposition of a ban on diplomatic mail just prior to D-Day, was able to win the approval of the War Cabinet on matters charged with possible unpleasant political consequences. In the same way, his emphasis on the need of bombing railway centers in Belgium and France finally

brought approval from British authorities, although the Prime
Minister and most of his Cabinet believed that the ill-feeling which
would probably be created would make bad relations between
the United Kingdom and France.   On more than one occasion
when the Supreme Commander asked for troops, landing craft,
planes, and supplies earmarked for the Pacific, he was allowed
his request although it might work a hardship on that theater.
This was due, in part, at least, to the decision taken early in the
war to press the attack in the European Theater at the expense of
other campaigns.   The United States Chiefs of Staff, being remote
from the planners in London, occasionally granted General Eisenhower broad powers of decision in agreements with the British.   In
the controversy of March and April, 1944 over the proposed invasion of southern France, the Joint Chiefs of Staff named the
United States commander as their representative in meetings with
the British and, after indicating their viewpoint, gave him the
power to make the final decision.   So clear was this influence that
when, later, Prime Minister Churchill sought to change the southern France operation to the Bordeaux area, he was advised that
the United States Chiefs of Staff were prepared to listen only if
General Eisenhower would declare that it was the sole plan which
would give success.

The concept of Supreme Command, achieved late in the campaigns of World War I, was adopted in 1939 by the British when
they sent troops to France.   The United States, on its entrance
into the war, agreed with Great Britain on the idea of appointing
Allied commanders-in-chief.   In accordance with this action,
General Wavell was given broad powers over Allied forces in
parts of the Far East, General MacArthur was given command
over American and part of the Dominion forces in the Southwest
Pacific, and General Eisenhower was named commander in the
Mediterranean Theater.   By the time he became Supreme Commander in Northwest Europe, the concept of Supreme Command
was well established.

The American leader was chosen for his European post in

December, 1943 at Cairo by President Roosevelt, and confirmed in his appointment by Mr. Churchill. Under the new commander was placed General Montgomery's 21st Army Group with its Second British and First Canadian Armies, consisting altogether of eighteen divisions. This was in addition to Lieutenant General Omar N. Bradley's 12th Army Group, made up at the end of the war of the First, Third, Ninth, and Fifteenth Armies, and the 6th Army Group, consisting of the First French and Seventh U. S. Armies. The total Allied Forces in Northwest Europe numbered some ninety divisions in May, 1945. Also entrusted to the chief commander were the air and naval forces to be used in the cross-channel invasion. In addition, General Eisenhower, as senior United States officer, commanded Headquarters, European Theater of Operations, United States Army (ETOUSA), which controlled all American forces in the European Theater.

Much of General Eisenhower's early training was that of the typical professional soldier. Later assignments, such as that of special assistant in the office of General Douglas MacArthur, while the latter was Chief of Staff of the Army, special assistant to General MacArthur in the Philippines, and assistant chief of staff, War Plans Division of the War Department, gave him the opportunity to observe the broader aspects of military policy. The real school for the future commander of Supreme Headquarters, Allied Expeditionary Force (SHAEF), however, was in the Mediterranean Theater where, as Allied Commander-in-Chief, he came into contact with most of the political and military problems which were to be found later on a greater scale in the European Theater of Operations. It was at Allied Forces Headquarters (AFHQ) in the Mediterranean that he became familiar with the great burdens of a military leader of a coalition. There he had to deal with civil affairs in a friendly country and military government in enemy territories, arrange for the feeding of a hungry nation while fighting a battle, deal with political representatives of the French Committee of National Liberation which was not recognized by the United States but from which he had to get troops, handle psychological warfare and press relations programs without offending British and American political leaders and publishers, and plan campaigns which were deeply involved in discussions of global importance. There, if he had not learned it before, the future SHAEF commander learned that war was not a simple matter of planning and executing tactical operations, but one of balancing many national and international forces against a military objective.

II

When General Eisenhower reached London in mid-January, 1944, to assume control of Supreme Headquarters, he found the broad outlines of his command formed, and the main elements of the assault plan ready. The basic ideas of the cross-channel attack plan were known to the new commander, since they had been presented in memoranda which General Eisenhower had helped write in the War Department in 1942. Lieutenant General Frederick E. Morgan had been appointed to head an organization known as COSSAC (Chief of Staff to the Supreme Allied Commander) in April, 1943 and directed to prepare plans to be used in case of the collapse of Germany and for a cross-channel invasion. The latter plan, called OVERLORD, was submitted to the Combined Chiefs of Staff at the Quebec Conference in August, 1943. There the plan was adopted, subject to minor revisions, and General Morgan was instructed to continue planning for a target date of May 1, 1944. Despite this action, the Prime Minister and the British Chiefs of Staff continued to favor the operations being conducted in the Italian Theater. In this controversy, which continued with some vigor until the Tehran and Cairo Conferences of November and December, 1943, General Eisenhower supported the concept of a cross-channel attack.

It is important to recall that many of the personnel of SHAEF were chosen six to eight months before the appointment of General Eisenhower, and were selected by General Morgan with the idea that either General Brooke or General Marshall would lead the Allied forces. The new commander remade the head-quarters by bringing many of his key officers from Allied Force Headquarters in the Mediterranean. Following normal army practice, General Eisenhower brought his own Chief of Staff, Lieutenant General Walter Bedell Smith, instead of using the Chief of Staff Designate, General Morgan, who remained as one of the three deputy chiefs of staff. The other two deputies, Lieutenant General Humfrey M. Gale (Administration) and Air Vice Marshal James M. Robb (Air), had served under General Eisenhower at AFHQ. While the American commander did not select his deputy Supreme Commander, a choice for the British to make, he was pleased at the selection of Air Chief Marshal Sir Arthur W. Tedder, his chief airman in the Mediterranean. For the Intelligence (G-2) post he insisted on retaining Major General Kenneth W. D. Strong, and he brought to London as deputy director of operations, Major General J. F. M. Whiteley, who had been deputy chief of staff at AFHQ. The director of operations, Major General H. R. Bull, while a COSSAC appointee, had served for a time in the Mediterranean Theater. AFHQ members filled the posts of Adjutant General, director of Press Relations, director of Psychological Warfare activities, and assistant director of Civil Affairs. The task of dealing with field commanders was simplified by the fact that many of the British and United States leaders had fought under the SHAEF commander in earlier campaigns. General Montgomery, the 21st Army Group commander, Lieutenant General Miles C. Dempsey, commander of the Second British Army, Lieutenant General Omar Bradley, and Lieutenant General George S. Patton, all brought with them the staffs which they had used in the Mediterranean campaigns. These ground commanders were joined by many of their air and naval colleagues from the south—Air Marshals Arthur Coningham, H. E. P. Wigglesworth, and H. Broadhurst, Generals Carl Spaatz and James Doolittle, and Admiral Bertram H. Ramsay.

It is not surprising that the AFHQ personnel made their imprint on the organization which COSSAC had furnished ready-made for the new commander. While General Eisenhower was quick to compliment the COSSAC planners, to ask for their guidance, and to demand an integration of staff members from the two theaters, he and the other newcomers made numerous changes in the SHAEF organization. Feeling that they had "mud on their boots" from many campaigns, the Mediterranean veterans were sometimes impatient with the COSSAC planners who had often been forced to proceed along academic lines. The arrival of the Supreme Commander gave a touch of reality to OVERLORD planning which had not been present before. General Morgan had been told to produce a plan to make use of a limited number of craft and soldiers. Not until the actual leader of the expedition was appointed was it possible to approach the problem of the specific resources essential to a successful operation. In this role, General Eisenhower was aided in securing backing by the prestige he had gained in the Mediterranean, the strong support of the United States for the cross-channel operation, and the close relations between himself and the Prime Minister.

Most important of the ideas which General Eisenhower brought from AFHQ was the concept of an integrated headquarters in which British and American officers worked side by side without any question of national considerations. It was in the Mediterranean Theater that he had settled the question that troops once placed under the Supreme Commander were truly subject to his control. Early in the North African campaign, the British had given Lieutenant General K. A. N. Anderson orders, similar to those issued to their commanders serving under the French in 1918 and in 1939, by which the British leader could appeal directly to his superiors at home. General Eisenhower strongly protested this directive, and succeeded in having a second one written which left to the commander only the right to bring his objections to the attention of the Allied Commander-in-Chief.

While there were dozens of detailed problems of a tactical nature which had already been delegated to the corps and division commanders who were to lead assault forces into Normandy, the

Supreme Commander found it necessary to intervene decisively in several issues which involved strategic as well as tactical considerations. These included: the broadening of the assault front, the securing of additional landing craft, the postponement of the invasion of southern France, the command of strategic air power for OVERLORD, the transportation bombing scheme, and the airborne drop on D-Day. The purely military decision to expand the assault area from the Caen to the Cotentin beaches required a reallocation of landing craft which involved strategic commitments in the Mediterranean. Before a change could be made to increase the margin of victory on D-Day, it was essential to make decisions involving a promise to Marshal Stalin of a southern France invasion, commitments in the Pacific, and the military policy of the United States. In the final settlement of the matter, as we have seen, the United States Chiefs of Staff appointed General Eisenhower their representative to meet with the British and seek the best military settlement under the circumstances. In the matter of the transportation bombing plan, the question of the best means to insure the success of the landings became entangled in the broader question of control of strategic bombers, British fears for their air defense, and the reaction of the French to Allied bombings. In both the landing craft and bombing decisions, involving political overtones, General Eisenhower followed the same rule he laid down for the airborne drop on D-Day. In the face of dire predictions of heavy losses made by his Air Commander-in-Chief, the Supreme Commander declared that all means necessary to insure the success of the Normandy landings must be used. Thus, he attempted to hold to solutions on purely military grounds, although he never ceased to be aware of their political implications, and could not escape the pressure of political and diplomatic forces.

While the Allied planners made clear from the beginning of their combined efforts their intent to appoint a Supreme Commander for their operations, they did not state precisely the extent to which he would exercise command in the field. In the North African operation General Eisenhower exercised command over task forces, and had Allied Naval and Air commanders as his assistants. In the later Mediterranean operations he occasionally made use of an Allied Army Group commander who served as ground commander. In early OVERLORD planning, the COSSAC staff proposed that the Supreme Commander exercise command on a political level while three commanders-in-chief of air, ground, and naval forces directed the actual fighting. General Eisenhower was willing to accept this arrangement in regard to naval and tactical air forces, but rejected it in regard to the ground command, since he believed firmly that personal command of ground operations was essential to proper co-ordination of air and sea support with the ground forces' efforts. The British continued to urge that a ground commander be appointed, a view opposed by the War Department, especially when it became clear that an American would be chosen Supreme Commander. The only concession to the British view was the placing of United States and British assault forces under General Montgomery for the first phase of the invasion of northern France.

The COSSAC planners had agreed that General Montgomery's control of assault troops would continue only until the Supreme Commander took direct command of ground operations on the Continent. At the same time the command of United States forces was to revert fully to the American Army Group. General Bradley's 12th Army Group, which had been engaged in planning and administrative activities since October, 1943, became tactically operational in Normandy on August 1, 1944. It did not achieve full equality with the 21st Army Group, however, until September 1 when General Eisenhower assumed direct control of the Allied Ground Forces in Northwest Europe. On September 15 General Eisenhower took command of the 6th Army Group which was headed by Lieutenant General Jacob L. Devers. During the Ardennes counterattack in December, 1944, when General Montgomery for a time was given control of the American First and Ninth Armies, the proposal for the appointment of a ground forces commander was renewed. The United States Chiefs of

Staff and General Eisenhower vigorously opposed this revival of an old issue, and the idea was rejected. When, once more, in February, 1945, the British brought it forward for the last time, the American Chiefs of Staff refused to consider the suggestion.

In the early planning for the assault, the planners had assumed that the British would furnish all the naval support ships for the attack. In accordance with this view, the British directed early planning for the naval part of OVERLORD. Even though it later proved necessary to bring in a considerable United States naval force, the Combined Chiefs of Staff agreed that a British officer should command the Allied Naval Expeditionary Force, and at Quebec in the fall of 1943 named Admiral Sir Charles Little to that command. He was later succeeded by Admiral Ramsay, the naval commander who had directed the evacuation from Dunkirk.

The air command was far more complicated. Air Chief Marshal Sir Trafford Leigh-Mallory was tentatively appointed to plan for Allied air operations in support of OVERLORD in the summer of 1943. At Quebec, the Combined Chiefs of Staff named him commander of the Allied Expeditionary Air Force with control of all Allied tactical air forces in support of the cross-channel operation. Directives were issued in November and December, 1943, placing the Second British Tactical Air Force and the Ninth U. S. Air Force under Air Marshal Leigh-Mallory. When these directives were issued, however, the Combined Chiefs of Staff were unable to reach an agreement on the command of strategic air forces to be used in support of OVERLORD, and it was not until the following April that a solution to the problem was reached. Difficulty was raised in particular because of the fear on the part of the British that their air power would not be available for British air defense if the planes were placed under an operational head-quarters. General Eisenhower, in a series of discussions with the British Chief of the Air Staff, Portal, succeeded in allaying the fears of British airmen, and received a directive placing under SHAEF those portions of Air Chief Marshal Harris' Bomber Command and General Spaatz' United States Strategic Air Forces which were to support OVERLORD, with Air Marshal Tedder co-ordinating their activities. The decision made the Deputy Supreme Commander's role a most important one in the air operations. As former commander of British air forces in the African Desert campaign and as chief of the Allied Air Forces in the Mediterranean, he had the confidence of British and American airmen, and the full backing of the Supreme Commander. In his role as co-ordinator and conciliator, he played an important part in Allied victory. The bomber forces remained under SHAEF's control until August, 1944 when they reverted to Bomber Command and Headquarters, United States Strategic Air Forces. The tactical air forces remained under Allied Expeditionary Air Force until October, 1944 when Air Marshal Leigh-Mallory was assigned to another post. The control was then transferred to Air Staff (SHAEF).

III

Much of the influence of Supreme Headquarters was exercised through a number of councils and committees which met alternately in London and in General Eisenhower's headquarters (located successively in Kingston-on-Thames, Portsmouth, Jullouville, Versailles, Reims). A partial list of these will indicate the varied nature of the efforts which SHAEF attempted to coordinate. They included: Propaganda, Civil Affairs, Railways, Liberated Manpower, Civilian Supply, Railway Targets for Bombing, Strategic Bombing Policy, Displaced Persons, Allocation of Critical Supplies, Petroleum, and Surrender Terms. The members frequently included representatives of the War Office, Foreign Office, Admiralty, Air Ministry, Ministry of Supply, and the various air, naval, and ground commands, including SHAEF and the supply headquarters. As commander of ground forces, General Eisenhower kept in close touch with the Allied Naval and Air commanders, and his Army Group chiefs. Planning for operations was carried on more or less simultaneously by SHAEF and lower echelons, with broad policy being stated by Supreme Headquarters and the technical arrangements being worked out by Army Groups and their subordinate commands. Liaison was maintained at all stages of planning between SHAEF and the next lowest echelon of command, so that constant interchange of ideas might be effected regarding operations. This was true, at least, of advance planning, and of activities in a static period. In the case of rapid advances, the role of the Supreme Commander was to keep in close touch with his Army Group commanders, offer suggestions, and make quick decisions on recommendations which they might present. An effort was made to send SHAEF personnel forward to the commanders, instead of requiring the latter to come back for conferences. In those cases where parallel planning was going on, the directors of operations of the various headquarters attempted to exchange views by reciprocal visits and by frequent telephone conferences.

Particularly vital in SHAEF's work was the allocation of supplies to the various forces. This was important because General Eisenhower, as head of United States Forces in the European Theater, the chief pool of manpower and supplies for the campaigns, had to reinforce his decisions as Supreme Commander by allotting personnel and equipment to the various armies in support of their attacks. General Eisenhower was Commanding General and General Smith was Chief of Staff of Headquarters, European Theater of Operations, United States Army (ETOUSA), which had a staff apart from the American members of SHAEF. General Eisenhower left detailed control of supplies to his sometime deputy theater commander, Lieutenant General John C. H. Lee, commander of Headquarters, Communications Zone. After this headquarters reached the Continent, it and Headquarters ETOUSA had the same staff. Some difficulties arose because of disagreements between the United States members of Supreme Headquarters and the staff of Communications Zone headquarters as to whose duty it was to advise General Eisenhower concerning personnel and supply matters relating to the American forces. He insisted that while his ETOUSA staff was supreme in matters of United States supply, he would feel free to seek advice from the American members of the SHAEF staff whenever he needed it. General Eisenhower, of course, acted as a court of last appeal for the Army Group and Army commanders who felt on occasion that they were not being given adequate supplies from the stores of the Communications Zone commander. He was also called on frequently to intervene in the allocation of supplies for the feeding and equipping of civil populations which were supplied by units in the forward echelons from stores allocated by the Supreme Commander and moved by the Communications Zone personnel.

The British Forces had their own Lines of Communications organization which General Montgomery controlled. He was able to go directly to the War Office in London for allocations from British stocks and for American materials provided through Lend-Lease, whenever British materials were sufficient for his plans. Otherwise it was essential to apply to SHAEF's supply division (G-4) for an allocation of supplies from United States stocks which General Eisenhower as Theater Commander could make available through the normal Communications Zone channels. In case troops were needed to back an attack led by the 21st Army Group commander, still another problem arose. The principle was well established that except in an emergency troops could not serve under a commander of another nationality in units smaller than a corps. For the assault and the first weeks of the invasion, United States troops were placed temporarily under General Montgomery. American airborne forces were placed at his disposal for the Arnhem operation in late September, 1944, and American units aided in the operations to open the port of Antwerp. During the Ardennes operation, when General Eisenhower feared that General Bradley's lines of communications with his northern forces would be severed, the First and Ninth Armies were placed under General Montgomery's command. For the spring attack towards the Rhine, and for the Rhine crossing, the Ninth Army was attached to the 21st Army Group.

Second in importance to operational command were SHAEF's activities in regard to Civil Affairs and Military Government. Experience in the Mediterranean had made clear the importance of careful preparation for this control in order to leave military commanders free to deal with military problems, and to make certain that the situation in rear areas did not interfere with the battle. It was impossible, however, to copy outright the system used in Sicily and Italy since AMGOT had been created to deal with enemy areas. In most of the liberated countries it could be expected that the main machinery of civil government would be operating, and that with minor changes it could be kept going. Broad guidance was given in civil affairs matters to the Supreme Commander by the Combined Civil Affairs Committee in Washington and by a London Subcommittee which represented the American and British services and agencies interested in these problems. So far as COSSAC and SHAEF planners were concerned the main problems were: (1) the type of control to be exercised by civil affairs administrators and (2) the recognition of governments in liberated countries. One group held that there should be a strong civilian civil affairs organization which should control the units attached to armies and lower echelons, while the other, which won its point, thought that the military commanders should handle these matters through civil affairs members of their staffs in accordance with rules established by the Civil Affairs Division of SHAEF. A second point of difference involved the type of governing bodies to be established: one group wished to set up a single civil affairs staff which would attempt to deal broadly with the civil affairs groups sent to various countries, while the second desired the establishment of sections for each country which would provide personnel especially trained in the problems of each area. The second alternative was ultimately adopted. Personnel from military government schools in the United States and Great Britain were sent by SHAEF to Army

Groups and lower echelons. The sections at SHAEF which were charged with planning for the specific countries ultimately were used to form the Civil Affairs (G-5) sections of the SHAEF Missions sent to France, Belgium, Holland, Norway, and Denmark after they were liberated. The French Mission (SHAEF), set up shortly after the liberation of Paris, acted not only as the chief liaison agency between SHAEF and the French Provisional Government, but also helped to implement agreements for rearming liberated manpower in France and other liberated areas. Agreements to regulate relations between the Allied armies and liberated peoples were concluded before D-Day by the United States and Great Britain with the governments in exile.

SHAEF was handicapped severely in its dealings with the French because of the failure of the United States and Great Britain to agree before D-Day on a policy to be followed towards the French Committee of National Liberation and General de Gaulle. Because of a feeling that General de Gaulle might not represent the wishes of the French people and an unwillingness to interfere with the determination of a government for France, President Roosevelt opposed any final agreement with the French Committee before the assault began. As a result many matters, such as the issuance of invasion currency and the use of French liaison officers in civil affairs units, were not settled until after the liberation of Paris in August, 1944. Control of French troops was handled temporarily under an agreement made in North Africa by which the United States Government promised to arm certain French units, and the French, in turn, agreed to place them at the disposal of the Allied commander. This arrangement was confirmed after the recognition of the French Provisional Republic in the fall of 1944, when General de Gaulle promised that he would not interfere directly with the purely military control of French troops. This pledge was not fully kept since, on several occasions, in order to emphasize political views of France which he believed could not be expressed otherwise, the French leader gave orders to his troops which were contrary to those of Allied commanders under whom they were fighting. If the question was purely military, General Eisenhower attempted to settle it by direct reference to General de Gaulle. Once it became clear that it was political, however, he referred it to the heads of the British and American Governments for settlement. In the case of the withdrawal from Strasbourg, which General Eisenhower ordered to shorten and strengthen his line in that area, the Supreme Commander reversed his decision, made on a purely military basis, when General de Gaulle held that he could not agree to it because of the possible political effects in France.

In order that the Supreme Commander might be kept informed of the diplomatic views of Great Britain and the United States, Political Advisers were attached to his staff by the Foreign Office and State Department. A European Allied Contact Section existed at Supreme Headquarters for the purpose of dealing with governments-in-exile. Planning of German surrender terms which went beyond the military phase was handled by the European Advisory Commission established in London by the United States, Great Britain, and Russia in accordance with a decision at the Moscow Conference in October, 1943. SHAEF maintained liaison with this body while SHAEF planning sections outlined the technical processes for Military Government in Germany. The Civil Affairs Division drew up military government handbooks to cover the various topics with which the occupying forces would have to deal, and developed provisional machinery to put these rules into effect. In addition to drawing up plans for dealing with the enemy in the post-hostilities period, the Supreme Commander had the task of providing a smooth transition from an Allied staff to separate British and American organizations for the occupation of Germany, of putting into operation the first phases of the occupation, and of enforcing initial military government decrees immediately following the surrender of German armies.

A third field in which the Supreme Commander held great authority and responsibility was that of public relations and psychological warfare. In the former it was his task to provide general lines of guidance for nearly 600 newsmen and photographers assigned to the European Theater and to prepare rules of censorship which could be easily administered. As an example of the problem which confronted the censors, one notes that the wordage submitted for D-Day ran to more than 700,000 words. General Eisenhower's policy, repeatedly explained, was that the correspondents were to have the maximum amount of news consistent with security of operations. He made clear that no censorship was to apply to reports of his personal actions, since he believed the newsmen should be protected against arbitrary acts by the Supreme Commander. His orders to lower echelons were quite explicit in affording access by newsmen to all phases of the operations. He believed that members of the press were, in a sense, a part of the military staff, helping to win campaigns by informing the civilian readers of the work of the armed forces.

The work of psychological warfare experts was well under way before the arrival of General Eisenhower in London in 1944. By that time, four civil agencies—the Office of Strategic Services, Office of War Information, Political Warfare Executive, and Ministry of Information—had their special programs in operation designed to determine the state of German opinion, to build enemy confidence in the accuracy of Allied information, to encourage the peoples in occupied countries, and ultimately to disseminate propaganda which would break enemy morale. The task of co-ordinating these efforts for OVERLORD was given to the Supreme Commander, who appointed representatives of the four civil agencies to aid him in bringing the full force of press, radio, and leaflets to bear on the enemy.

IV

Among the many burdens of the SHAEF commander one must list the problem of dealing with some of the field commanders. Part of the difficulty arose from misunderstandings on the part of some generals of the nature of the war which was being fought under the Supreme Command. The cross-channel operation was planned in the full knowledge that the British would commit nearly all their reserves of manpower within the first few weeks of the invasion and that, thereafter, their proportionate contribution would decline. Secretary of War Stimson and others have made clear that no effort was made to apportion influence or command on the basis of total manpower furnished to the combined effort. Instead, the United States Chiefs of Staff held to the view that the war was one which must be fought with Allied co-operation, that no operation was to be undertaken unless both partners were fully ready to back it, and that the two armies were to have their views equally respected in the field. The main consideration was that of carrying out the plan which was the most likely to bring military success.

General Patton, in *War As I Knew It*, declares that he originally believed that gasoline was taken from him in late August, 1944, as "a backhanded way of slowing up Third Army," but later found that the delay on his front was due to a change of plan by the High Command which he believed to be influenced by General Montgomery. Actually, in the spring of 1944, before the invasion of Normandy, the SHAEF planners had studied alternate routes for the advance into Germany, investigating such matters as terrain, importance of various centers to the enemy, the areas whose capture would most strongly affect enemy morale, nearness of various areas to ports of supply, and territory which the enemy was most likely to defend. After making a number of studies, the SHAEF planners concluded that the Germans were most likely to defend the Ruhr Valley, which was believed to be the most important economically, the one whose capture would most adversely affect German morale, the one nearest an excellent port—Antwerp, and an area which afforded excellent terrain for a battle. On the other hand, they did not consider a single thrust here the most feasible plan of operation, and proposed that a secondary blow be made south of Frankfurt. Both of these operations, they believed, could not be supported from Normandy or Brittany ports, and would require the capture of the port of Antwerp, together with its approaches.

In the late summer of 1944, it was the British Army Group which held the flank nearest the Ruhr Valley and which was favored in the granting of supplies. The British forces had been assigned that flank before the selection of Generals Eisenhower, Montgomery, Bradley or Patton because of the belief that the right flank, being nearest the United States and the Cherbourg and Brittany ports, would be more suitable for American supply communications. By taking the left flank, the British could deal with the dreaded V weapon sites in the Pas de Calais, and with the liberation of Belgium, a country with whom they had long maintained special ties of friendship. The logic of the situation, so far as the SHAEF planners were concerned, dictated the choice of the Ruhr Valley as the chief center of attack, and the weight of the British, Canadian, and First U. S. armies were thrown in that direction, although Third Army was permitted to make limited advances towards the Rhine. General Montgomery believed that because Third Army was not completely immobilized and all resources thrown into a single thrust by the Northern Forces across the Rhine, the Supreme Commander missed an opportunity of winning a decisive victory before winter. On the other hand, General Patton held that the most momentous error of the war lay in the failure to halt all other advances while he made a lightning dash to the Rhine.

Not until historians can go into many problems of German strength, mobility of German reserves, the state of enemy morale, the extent to which the proposed drives would have exposed the Allied troops to attacks on their unguarded flanks, can one know the true answer to the problem presented to the Supreme Commander in late August and early September, 1944. From his standpoint, however, certain things are clear. The plan of SHAEF, approved by the Supreme Commander before D-Day, required the capture of Antwerp for a successful prosecution of the attack against Germany. Unless General Eisenhower could gamble in early September that a single thrust would bring the quick overthrow of the German Government and a complete surrender in the field, something which appeared doubtful then and more doubtful in the spring of 1945, then it was essential to take Antwerp. An extremely bold or, perhaps, rash commander might have taken the gamble and won. The decision made was a reasoned one, based on the belief that a battle could be won without great risk by developing a port at Antwerp, moving all Allied forces to the Rhine, and concentrating supplies for the final assault.

A second point on which the Supreme Commander has been criticized is that concerning the spring campaign between the Rhine crossing and the halt on the Elbe. Some observers, holding that the military commanders should have acted on the assumption that a period of tension would ensue between the United States and Russia in the postwar period, believe the Supreme Commander should have driven directly for Berlin without halting at the Elbe. In late February and early March when plans for the last phase of the Central German campaign were made, General Eisenhower decided that his best policy was to stop at the Elbe, while part of his forces aided the British in seizing the northern ports, and another part went southward to prevent the Germans from staging a last ditch stand in the Southern Redoubt. In making these plans he had the backing of the United States Chiefs of Staff who were averse to any move across the Elbe resting solely on grounds of political expediency. On the basis of a directive from the Combined Chiefs of Staff to work out a formula for meeting the Russians, in order to avoid clashes which might arise out of mistaken identity, General Eisenhower selected the line of the Elbe and the Mülde as a well-defined natural line of demarcation where the forces would stop. This proposal was accepted by the Russian General Staff as a satisfactory solution of a difficult problem. South of the line of the Elbe and the Mülde, the American forces went into Czechoslovakia as far as Pilzen where, on May 5, they stopped at the request of the Russians who asked that they hold to the line Karlsbad-Pilzen-Budejovice.

V

In the SHAEF organization one finds the most ambitious effort made in modern times to control the military operations of Allies in the field and deal with political and diplomatic problems bearing on military campaigns. Not only did the Supreme Commander direct the military operations of one British, one Canadian, one French, and five American armies in battle, but he also acted as Theater Commander of more than three million American troops in the European Theater of Operations, and was responsible for the planning and executing of civil affairs and military government responsibilities in five liberated countries and Germany. His duties involved acting for the United States and Great Britain on crucial diplomatic issues. Both the Allied governments called on him for recommendations and advice as to the settlement of questions of political, as well as military, import. So great were his tasks and so extended his functions that some historians have asked whether or not such a burden should be imposed on a commander in another war. Admiral Cunningham, who served with General Eisenhower in the Mediterranean before becoming a member of the British Chiefs of Staff, when asked this question, remarked: "A Supreme Commander is a grab bag proposition, but I would always want one if I could get Ike." General Eisenhower, through his efforts to build a truly integrated staff, in which a member of a staff division could act for the general Allied good regardless of the national interests involved, and in his insistence that no one should be able to determine when examining a decision of SHAEF whether it was given by a British or American officer, developed a true Allied Command and contributed decisively to Allied victory.

Influence of Pro-Fascist Propaganda on American Neutrality, 1935–1936

By JOHN NORMAN*

Fascist propaganda, purveyed by Italian-American publications and organizations, noticeably affected the course of American neutrality during the Ethiopian crisis. About a hundred publications, consisting of pro-Fascist dailies, weeklies, and monthlies, had built up their influence by nationalistic appeals to some 5,000,000 persons of Italian origin, of whom approximately 850,000 could vote. They prompted rather than echoed the sentiments of their readers, who were really more pro-Italian than pro-Fascist.[1] The pro-Fascist tone of their appeals was determined by the propaganda activities of the Italian consular authorities, who exercised a controlling influence over the Italian-American press and societies.[2]

II

Before it was known how the Joint Resolution on neutrality, signed by President Roosevelt on August 31, 1935, might operate

*John Norman is Associate Professor of Political Science, Pennsylvania College for Women.

[1] "The War of Nerves: Hitler's Helper," *Fortune*, XXII (November, 1940), 112, states that the overwhelming majority of Italian Americans "are probably more or less apathetic about fascism, while retaining a sentimental attachment to Italy." According to a W.P.A. study, the great majority of Italian Americans in New York City were "neither Fascist nor anti-Fascist, but in general favor Italy and its international policies." Works Progress Administration: Federal Writers' Project, *The Italians of New York* (New York, 1938), 100.

[2] "Italian consular officials and secret Fascist agents are spreading Fascist propaganda throughout the ranks of some 200 Italian-American organizations in the United States. . . . Propaganda is also being carried on by the agents of the Italian Fascist Government through numerous publications, radio stations, schools, churches, as well as through the theatre." Testimony of Girolamo Valenti, anti-Fascist editor of the New York daily *Stampa Libera*, in U. S., House of Representatives (75th Cong., 3d Sess.): *Investigation of Un-American Propaganda Activities in the United States* (Hearings before a Special Committee on Un-American Activities on H. Res. 282. Washington, 1940), II, 1183, 1194. See also California, Senate, Joint Fact-Finding Committee on Un-American Activities, *Report* (Sacramento, 1943), 284–321; and Gaetano Salvemini, *Italian Fascist Activities in the United States* (Washington, 1940), 9 and *passim*.

to Italy's disadvantage, articulate Italian Americans voiced immediate and complete approval of the neutrality legislation. Three days before it went into effect, the Italian Union of America sponsored a meeting of representatives of various societies and newspapers at the Italian Palace of Rockefeller Center (which, incidentally, housed the Italian consulate general). This gathering passed a unanimous resolution to the effect that the presidents of fifty Italian-American organizations of New York, representing over 250,000 members, affirmed their "loyalty to the United States" and their "unfailing devotion to the Italian Fatherland" and that they adhered unconditionally to the spirit animating the proposed Neutrality bill.[3] Favorable sentiment continued for a few weeks after the bill's passage, but only for a few weeks.[4] The actual application of the law when Italy invaded Ethiopia began to alienate Italian-American opinion.

President Roosevelt invoked the Neutrality Act on October 5 two days after the outbreak of hostilities between Italy and Ethiopia. In accordance with the Act, he issued two proclamations: in the first, he declared a state of war existed between Italy and Ethiopia (two days before the League of Nations Council did so), thereby calling into effect the novel mandatory embargo on shipments to both belligerents of certain previously enumerated military articles; in the second, he warned American citizens against traveling on belligerent ships except at their own risk. (Impartiality on paper produced only discrimination in fact, for Italy had ships while Ethiopia had none. Also, a *discretionary* embargo, such as the President had sought in vain, would have given him the power to withhold arms from the aggressor while supplying them to the victim.) The President then went beyond the letter of the law by accompanying the proclamations with a declaration that any Americans engaged in any kind of transactions with either of the belligerents did so at their own risk.[5]

[3] *La Libera Parola* (Philadelphia), September 5, 1935.

[4] *Ibid.*, October 5, 1935; *Il Popolo Italiano* (Philadelphia), October 2, 1935; and *Il Progresso Italo-Americano* (New York), October 6, 1935. The last mentioned was the largest and most influential pro-Fascist paper; to be henceforth cited as *Il Progresso*.

[5] Department of State, *Press Releases*, XIII (October 5, 1935), 251–57.

Oblivious of the advantages afforded by the new neutrality to the aggressor, Italian-American opinion angrily noted only the disadvantages. The Philadelphia *Popolo Italiano* inquired sarcastically if Roosevelt's warning proclamation was issued because of fear of Ethiopian submarines.[6] The big New York daily *Il Progresso*, the most authoritative of all pro-Fascist organs, also objected to the warning on the ground that Ethiopia did not even possess a "caravel." This paper further resented the President's declaration of a state of war to be in existence before either Italy or Ethiopia had done so.[7]

On October 10 Secretary of State Hull, declared that though there was no legal prohibition, apart from the arms embargo, on transactions with the belligerents, the President's warnings were intended to keep us out of war, and certainly not to encourage these transactions.[8] *Il Popolo Italiano* considered the discouragement of trade with Italy as neutrality in name only.[9] *La Libera Parola* complained that the administration had applied sanctions against Italy even before England had. Why, the paper asked, had the head of the Democratic Party, which had profited so much from the Italian vote, shown such partiality? The only explanation was English influence in Washington, the paper concluded.[10] *The Italian Echo* viewed Hull's statement as simply one instance out of a thousand of the administration's hostile attitude towards Italy.[11] *Il Progresso* urged the administration to abstain from "economic sanctions against either of the warring factions."[12]

At the end of October Secretary Hull and President Roosevelt re-emphasized their policy of discouraging trade with the belligerents. The President expressed the belief that Americans would not wish to prolong the conflict by extending their trade in essentials

[6] October 8, 1935.
[7] October 8, 1935.
[8] Department of State, *Press Releases*, XIII (October 12, 1935), 303–4.
[9] October 13, 1935.
[10] October 19, 1935.
[11] (Providence), October 25, 1935.
[12] October 27, 1935.

of war for the sake of profit accruing to a relatively small number of citizens.[13] These citizens, nevertheless, ignored the President's plea. Their shipments of essential war materials such as cotton, oil, and scrap iron to Italy and her colonies rose sharply in October and November, and it was all legal because these materials were not on the official embargo list. Pro-Fascist reaction to the administration's latest statement was best embodied in a lengthy editorial in the influential *Il Progresso* entitled "American Neutrality." It accused the administration of violating the spirit of the Neutrality Act and of arraying itself with the League of Nations sanctionists, for, when one spoke of belligerents, one really spoke of Italy, since Ethiopia had no commercial relations worth speaking of with the United States.[14]

Another objection to the Neutrality Act was made on the ground that its embargo provision constituted a breach of the Treaty of Commerce and Navigation of 1871 between the United States and Italy.[15] *La Stella di Pittsburgh* quoted a pertinent portion of the treaty, which was still in effect: "Nor shall any prohibition be imposed on the importation or exportation of any articles, produce or manufactures of the United States or Italy to or from the territories of Italy, which shall not extend to all other nations." *La Stella* then reported that State Department officials were inclined to think that implements of war could scarcely be classed as ordinary articles of commerce as originally meant by the treaty; in other words, the embargo did not really contravene the 1871 treaty in the opinion of the aforementioned officials.[16] This latter view was upheld by an authority on international law, Professor Edwin M. Borchard of Yale. Testifying before the House Foreign Affairs Committee in January, 1936, the professor asserted that a neutral "is privileged to cut off trade in munitions of war. The Italian Treaty [Article XV] so limits the definition of contra-

[13] Department of State, *Press Releases*, XIII (November 2, 1935), 338–39.

[14] *Il Progresso*, November 2, 1935.

[15] *Ibid.*, November 20, 1935; *Il Popolo Italiano* (Philadelphia), January 29, 1936; and *La Stella di Pittsburgh*, November 29, 1935.

[16] November 29, 1935.

band." [17] On the other hand, the professor did say this: " . . . I think we were violating the treaty with Italy by officially discouraging trade with Italy. That stated that reciprocal trade should be free. That means not discouraged by one of the parties." [18] The latter opinion was quoted and approved by the *Corriere del Connecticut.* [19] Italian Americans also regarded the administration's warning against traveling on belligerent ships as a violation of Article XVI of the treaty, which guaranteed to every nationality equal rights in the exercise of commerce and industry. [20]

On November 15 Secretary Hull declared that such articles as oil, copper, trucks, tractors, scrap iron and scrap steel, which were essentially war materials though not actually arms, ammunition, or implements of war, were being exported in greater quantities for purposes of war contrary to government policy and to the spirit of the Neutrality Act. [21] A week later Secretary of the Interior and Federal Oil Administrator Harold L. Ickes urged the American oil industry to stop selling oil to Italy. [22] The Commerce Department, acting through the Shipping Board, notified steamship companies in debt to the government that the transportation of essential war supplies to countries at war was against national policy. It actually prevented an oil tanker from sailing to Italy by threatening to foreclose on a mortgage which the government held on the ship. [23] *Il Progresso* reacted vehemently in a double column editorial on the front page. Yes, Hull and Ickes called for only a voluntary suspension of shipments, the paper observed,

[17] U. S., *House of Representatives* (74th Cong., 2d Sess.): *American Neutrality Policy* (Hearings before the Committee on Foreign Affairs on H. R. Res. 422. Revised print, Washington, January, 1936), 66.

[18] *Ibid.*, 65.

[19] January 17, 1936.

[20] *La Libera Parola* (Philadelphia), November 2, 1935; and *Il Popolo Italiano* (Philadelphia), January 27, 1936.

[21] Department of State, *Press Releases*, XIII (November 16, 1935), 382.

[22] Whitney H. Shepardson and William O. Scroggs, *The United States in World Affairs, 1936* (New York, 1936), 20.

[23] *Ibid.*, 20–21.

but when moral pressure reached the point of threatening to withdraw credit from shippers who dared to transport oil, copper, cotton, etc., to Italy, it was tantamount to a prohibition. It injured our commerce and violated our neutrality; and this violation was rendered more grievous when one realized that while the administration was asking for a halt to exports of essential war materials, Italy was buying these materials from England, Russia, Egypt, Rumania and other sanctionist countries.[24]

News of the Hoare-Laval Peace Plan, designed by the British and French foreign ministers to appease, Premier Mussolini's ambitions in Ethiopia, plus the League's postponement of action on oil sanctions served to moderate the administration's zeal in seeking to restrict exports of oil. An article in *Il Progresso* expressed satisfaction over the peace plan and the government's relaxation of efforts to limit the flow of oil. The article then quoted the renowned authority on international law, John Basset Moore, who compared the new neutrality with the "new chastity, which encouraged fornication in the hope that it might reach the stage of legalized prostitution." Embargo was not neutrality, the article continued; neutrality was the right of a nation under international law to trade with any belligerent.[25]

Pro-Fascist influence was beginning to make itself felt in Washington. Professor Borchard declared to the Senate Foreign Relations Committee that the administration's efforts to discourage trade with Italy "began to split our own people" and that "up to the middle of November the discouragement of trade had not made a distinction between normal and abnormal. . . . That was rather a sudden inspiration . . . perhaps to appease the protests that had been made either because of the limitation of trade or because of the Italian-American objection."[26] In the middle of

[24] *Il Progresso*, November 26, 1935. Similar sentiments were expressed in the *Corriere del Connecticut* (New Haven), November 29, 1935.

[25] *Il Progresso*, December 15, 1935; reprinted in *The Italian Press* (Kansas City), January 17, 1936.

[26] U. S., Senate (74th Cong., 2d Sess.): *Neutrality* (Hearings before the Committee on Foreign Relations on S. 3474, January 10 to February 5, 1936. Washington, 1936), 209.

November, according to Herbert Feis, adviser on international economic affairs in the State Department, there was some fear that conclusive action to encourage the League might invite Italy's retaliation against the United States. "Confidence was lacking that American opinion would support the Government if such a quarrel with Italy took place; Italian minorities in eastern cities were blackening the record of events at Geneva and pleading the Italian cause."[27] *Il Progresso* attributed the administration's relaxation of restrictions on exports of oil and other essentials of war in December to the numerous protests sent by Italian Americans to government officials. Italian Americans therefore represented a "conspicuous force," and were advised to remain on the alert.[28] It was not until the President sought to have the Neutrality Act modified in January, 1936 that pro-Fascist pressure was strongly felt in official quarters.

III

The new neutrality was taken up by President Roosevelt on January 3, 1936 in his message to Congress dealing for the most part with international affairs. He declared that the temper and purposes of certain rulers in Europe and Asia did not point the way to peace and that a small minority of the world's population had impatiently placed its trust in the law of the sword. After noting the American Government's efforts to promote peace, the President stated that in the event of wars which were not of immediate concern to the Americas, the administration would pursue a twofold neutrality: first, it would not allow the belligerents to obtain arms and ammunition in the United States; second, it would try to discourage the use of American goods exceeding normal peacetime exports when found to be useful in carrying on a war. Congress was asked to enact this policy.[29]

The word "impatiently" in the President's address was im-

[27] Herbert Feis, *Seen from E. A.* (New York, 1947), 256.
[28] *Il Progresso*, December 7, 1935.
[29] Department of State, *Press Releases*, XIV (January 4, 1936), 11–19.

mediately seized upon.   The day following the speech *La Libera
Parola* recalled that when Italy had awaited her turn in 1919 she
had been betrayed by England, France, and an American President.[30]   How much longer must one wait, this paper asked a week
later, until judgment day?   Italy had resorted to force because she
knew she would get nothing peacefully.   America was pacific
because she was rich; but she too had fought once in Mexico,
Cuba, and Nicaragua.[31]   *Il Progresso* reminded the President that
an "incommensurable patience" had characterized Italian policy
in East Africa for forty years.[32]   The *Corriere del Connecticut* and
La Stella di Pittsburgh considered the speech a serious offense to
millions of Italian Americans,[33] thereby underlining the comment
of *Il Popolo Italiano:* "Let us register another enemy." [34]

On the day of the President's message a new neutrality bill,
sponsored by the administration, was introduced in both houses
of Congress by Senator Pittman and Representative McReynolds.
Inasmuch as most of the provisions of the hastily drafted Resolution
of August, 1935 would expire at the end of February, it was deemed
urgent to enact a new law, permanent in character, to meet the
exigencies of a war-threatened world.   The Pittman-McReynolds
Bill included a substantial portion of the existing legislation and
broadened its scope.   It retained the mandatory embargo on
exports of arms, munitions, and implements of war to belligerents,
but granted the President discretionary power (abominated by
Italian Americans) to restrict to a normal volume exports of other
articles and materials useful for purposes of war, except food and
medical supplies.   The President was to extend the embargo to
all new belligerents as soon as they became involved in conflict.
Loans or credits to belligerent governments were forbidden, except
for commercial credits and short-time obligations which could
be exempted from the operation of this section at the President's

[30] January 4, 1936.
[31] *La Libera Parola* (Philadelphia), January 11, 1936.
[32] January 5, 1936.
[33] Both dated January 10, 1936.
[34] January 5, 1936.

discretion. And the President was permitted to warn American citizens against trading with countries at war except at their own risk.

On January 5 a rival bill known as the Nye-Clark-Maverick Bill was introduced in Congress. It was more drastic than the other in two main respects: the arms embargo would automatically come into effect the moment war broke out, and the restriction of trade in essentials of war to normal levels, which would be reckoned on a five-year average, would be mandatory and not discretionary. Other bills came up for consideration, but the Italian-American press focused its attention primarily on these two.

Directed and assisted by their publications and organizations Italian Americans brought full pressure to bear against the pending legislation. Representative Maury Maverick of Texas, in a speech before the Foreign Policy Association in Philadelphia, deplored the "powerful representations of the Italo-American groups who have protested the enactment of any bill." The congressman, whose own neutrality bill was involved, and who was therefore in a good position to know whereof he spoke, said: "Many of these who claim to lead millions of Italians, some of them who claim to control 'one, two, three, four, or five million votes,' others who speak before congressional committees, with the obvious desire to put pressure on Congress asking preferential treatment for Italy, are doing themselves, their own people and the cause of peace a disservice. Many of these gentlemen insist that the present belligerents be exempted from embargoes under American neutrality. I see no reason for this." [35]

Representative Vito Marcantonio of New York replied to Maverick in the House. His leftist sympathies did not prevent him from delivering a speech that any pro-Fascist would have been proud to call his own. Marcantonio denied that Americans of Italian extraction were requesting special consideration. They sought only the welfare of the United States, which they had shown

[35] Speech delivered February 1, 1936; printed in U. S., *Congressional Record* (74th Cong., 2d Sess., January 30 to February 18, 1936), 80, Part II, 1407-8.

by working, dying, and fighting for their country. They wanted to keep the country out of war. "They are opposed to any scheme which would make our Nation the tool of either the international racketeerism of the League of Nations or the imperialistic interests of any foreign nation. They also believe that neutrality policies should be fixed by Congress and not by the Executive. This is the cause they espouse. Who can say . . . that it is not for the cause of peace? [Applause.]"[36] Representatives Healey and Higgins, both of Massachusetts, spoke in like accents, praising the patriotism of Italian Americans and the debt owed to Italy for her contributions to civilization, which debt could be repaid by nonpassage of the pending neutrality legislation.[37]

According to current reports Americans of Italian extraction, fearing that Mussolini's chances in Ethiopia might suffer if the President's embargo power were enlarged, "began quietly to slip notes to members of Congress with large Italian-born constituencies reminding them that an election would be taking place later on in the year!"[38] Charles Warren, former Assistant Attorney General during World War I and a noted proponent of the new neutrality, uttered the following warning to the Senate Foreign Relations Committee: ". . . If you yield to Italo-American pressure or to English or French or Abyssinian or League pressure to make a bill which will suit the one or the other, you had better not pass any bill at all." He went on to say that: "With the arrival of delegations of Italo-Americans or other hyphenates opposing or favoring this [Pittman-McReynolds] bill, I see the beginning of a repetition of conditions which prevailed from 1914 to 1917. At that time, the German Americans violently demanded an embargo on arms and ammunition, while the advocates of the allied cause opposed such an embargo. . . ."[39]

---

[36] *Ibid.*, 2221.
[37] *Ibid.*, 2247 and 2268–72.
[38] Shepardson and Scroggs, *op. cit.*, 142.
[39] U. S., Senate, *Neutrality* (as cited), 250–51.

III

Italian-American organizations had often voiced their protests collectively as well as singly. By November, 1935, hundreds of them in all parts of the country were acting in concert primarily through the American Friends of Italy. Pro-Fascist editors eagerly extended the facilities of their newspapers to help along the grandiose propaganda campaign against the administration's policy.[40] The movement displayed a resourcefulness equalled only by its thoroughness, as the following manifesto, published with minor variations in many Italian-American publications, amply demonstrates:[41]

FELLOW AMERICAN CITIZEN:

Write a separate letter to President Roosevelt, to United States Senator Royal S. Copeland, to United States Senator Robert F. Wagner, and to your local Congressman—all in Washington, D. C., protesting against certain activities of the present administration.

Make two or more copies of this entire sheet and give them to at least two other Americans having similar views.

See to it that these two friends write letters at once to Washington.

Everyone who protests must secure at least two others in an unending chain until all Americans sharing these views have acted.

Send a card with your name and address to the Committee. This will entitle you to free literature regarding the progress of this movement.

One million letters of protest are expected to reach Washington before January, when Congress meets.

> AMERICAN FRIENDS OF ITALY
> 157 East 49th Street
> New York, New York

[40] *Il Popolo Italiano* (Philadelphia), November 3, 1935.

[41] The variations appeared chiefly in the names of senators and congressmen, which were made to correspond with the different states and districts wherein the manifesto was published. *Columbus*, LVIII (New York, November, 1935), 66; *Il Progresso*, November 25, 1935; *L'Alba* (Newport, R. I.), December 14, 1935; *La Tribuna Italiana d'America* (Detroit), December 20, 1935; and *Corriere del Connecticut* (New Haven), January 3, 1936.

(Copy or write letter similar to following):

(Name)   Date
Washington, D. C.

HONORABLE SIR:

I protest against American association with League of Nations sanction activities. I protest against statements of members of the present administration in Washington showing co-operation with the schemes of the British Government as regards sanctions and embargoes. I protest against our Government meddling with European sanctions and embargo policies.

Very respectfully,
(Signature)
(Address)

After the Pittman-McReynolds Bill had come up for discussion in Congress, the form letter was altered to suit the circumstance. It now included the following statement: "I am strongly against any modification of the Neutrality Act, which would give the President discretionary power."[42]

The chain-letter idea was enthusiastically taken up. *Il Progresso* was pleased to report its rapid progress, especially in the New England States, but also in all the states where Italian-American communities flourished.[43] One congressman was so overwhelmed by the flood of protests, that he resorted to circular replies in acknowledgment.[44] It was said that 12,000 telegrams were sent to Washington from Pennsylvania alone.[45] An Italian-American lawyer in New York was praised at a meeting of the American Friends of Italy for sending innumerable letters to the Bar Association of various states asking them to send protests to Washington. An Italian-American justice of the Massachusetts Superior Court said

[42] *La Stella di Pittsburgh*, January 24, 1936. See also *Il Popolo Italiano* (Philadelphia), January 21, 1936, for the same sentiment expressed slightly differently in a form letter.

[43] *Il Progresso*, December 22, 1935. This issue of the paper also advised its readers that these form letters, requiring only one's signature, would be distributed in 400 drug stores in New York.

[44] Representative Rabaut in a letter to the editor of *La Tribuna Italiana d'America* (Detroit), February 7, 1936.

[45] *La Libera Parola* (Philadelphia), February 22, 1936.

that, after receiving a letter from the New York lawyer, he began a protest movement among the professional and business element of Boston which spread to the states neighboring Massachusetts.[46]

The above-mentioned justice was one of the organizers of the League for American Neutrality which, according to him, could depend for support on 150,000 Italian-American citizens of Massachusetts.[47] Towards the end of January, a meeting sponsored by the League was held in Faneuil Hall in Boston. The program consisted of a speech by Colonel Cyril Rocke, former British attaché in Rome, who defended the right of Italy to expansion in East Africa, and a speech by Governor Curley, who referred to Mussolini as a lover of peace, the savior of Europe from the pestilence of bolshevism, and the savior of Christianity. The meeting, of course, did not end without a resolution to send letters of protest to Washington.[48]

A letter from the League for American Neutrality to Representative Higgins was placed by him in the *Congressional Record* with the remark that it set forth "the views held by me and other Members on the important matter of neutrality. . . . " In the letter the League pointed out that the Pittman-McReynolds Bill would enable the President to embargo such materials as would "shorten the war, in his opinion, by bringing defeat to one side. This is the antithesis of neutrality. . . . " The League favored a law that would simply extend the period of the embargo on arms, ammunition, and implements of war. This law might also restrict loans to belligerents and provide that Americans traveling on belligerent ships did so at their own risk. No discretion was to be allowed the President in issuing passports.[49]

Other Italian-American organizations and individuals still continued to send letters which were not verbatim copies of the ones distributed by the American Friends of Italy. The Italian-

[46] *Il Progresso*, December 30, 1935.
[47] *Ibid.*
[48] *Ibid.*, January 28, 1936.
[49] U. S., *Congressional Record* (as cited), 1945.

American Republican National League forwarded a letter to Senator Key Pittman objecting to the bill of which he was co-sponsor.[50] The National Association of Italian Servicemen, comprising 20,000 members, approved and sent to Washington a resolution that Congress and the administration be requested to unite their efforts to maintain friendly relations between the United States and Italy.[51] Meanwhile, individual writers were admonished by *Il Progresso* not to let their ardent patriotism carry them to extremes in language, for threats and insults could create more enemies than friends.[52]

The presidents of several hundred organizations in New York, New Jersey, Pennsylvania, Connecticut, Rhode Island, and Massachusetts, acting through the Italian Union of America (or the American-Italian Union as it came to be called) in New York City on January 16, unanimously adopted a resolution, a copy of which was sent to all the members of Congress and the administration. The resolution opposed the Pittman-McReynolds Bill, because it granted the President power to regulate commerce with foreign nations; it forced America to take sides in every war; and it contained the "germ of potential wars" in that under the guise of neutrality and at the President's "discrimination," it allowed normal current credit relations between the United States and the belligerents. The Nye-Clark-Maverick Bill was opposed on the grounds that it arbitrarily designated the five years preceding the outbreak of war as a period of normal trade between the United States and the belligerents; it surrendered the American doctrine of freedom of the seas; and it allowed normal credit relations with the belligerents. Hence, it was resolved that the only safe and neutral policy for America to pursue was one based on accepted international law, and that Congress was thereby urged to re-enact the existing law.[53]

[50] *Il Progresso*, January 18, 1936.
[51] *Ibid.*
[52] *Ibid.*, January 9, 1936.
[53] *Ibid.*, January 19, 1936.

The Italian Union of America reportedly comprised 400 societies with a total membership of more than 400,000.[54] By the beginning of April, 1936, this Union, with headquarters in Rockefeller Center, claimed to have accomplished the following tasks toward counteracting British and League of Nations "propaganda": it had held over 100 conferences with American clubs and organizations; had arranged more than 75 radio addresses; had sponsored over 150 articles; had distributed over 300,000 pamphlets and circulars; and had made important personal contacts in the world of American politics and journalism.[55]

IV

The effects of the protests were soon evident. Numerous senators and representatives reacted favorably while others simply acknowledged receipt of the letters without committing themselves. On the whole, the pro-Fascist press was gratified with the response.[56] Generoso Pope, the once pro-Fascist publisher of *Il Progresso* and an influential Democrat of New York, added the weight of his personal prestige to the general campaign against the new neutrality. He made contacts with various men of influence like Senator Robert F. Wagner, Alfred E. Smith, Representative Sirovich, Representative Marcantonio, and Judge John J. Freschi, from all of whom he elicited comments aimed to please his readers.[57] At the end of January, Pope decided to go to Washington where he interviewed the political leaders of the nation.

First he called on President Roosevelt. The interview got under way as soon as Pope asked to know the President's views on neutrality. According to the publisher, the President replied, "Gene, America honestly wishes to remain neutral; and I want you to

[54] *Il Popolo Italiano* (Philadelphia), May 8, 1936.
[55] *La Capitale* (Sacramento), April 4, 1936.
[56] *Il Progresso*, January 3, 9, and 16, 1936; *The Italian Echo* (Providence), January 24, 1936; *La Tribuna Italiana* (Detroit), January 24, 1936; and *La Libera Parola* (Philadelphia), January 25, 1936.
[57] Respectively reported, *Il Progresso*, December 10, 29 and 31, 1935; January 2 and 8, 1936.

tell the Italians, through your newspapers, that our neutrality will in no way imply discrimination at the expense of Italy and in favor of any other nation." Italy, he went on, could buy anything she wanted in the United States save arms, munitions, and contraband of war. Pope inquired whether Italy could make unlimited purchases of other materials. The President said yes, except when there was danger of our being drawn into war, in which case it would be necessary to restrict exports of essential war materials to a normal volume—a normal volume to be figured from the period of most active trade between the two nations. Finally, Pope asked whether it would not be better to prolong the present Neutrality Act for another year since it had served so well the purpose for which it had been voted. "Perhaps this could be a good solution," replied the President. The interview closed with the President complimenting the Italians of America for their great contributions to the country's well-being and for their devotion to American institutions.[58]

Pope also had important conversations with Vice-President Garner, Speaker Joseph Byrnes, Assistant Secretary of State H. Walton Moore, Secretary Ickes, Majority Leader Bankhead, Representative Fred Vinson of Kentucky, Representative John R. McCormack of Massachusetts, Senator Joshua Bailey of New York, Representative Robert Doughton who was Chairman of the Ways and Means Committee, Senate "Whip" James H. Lewis, Representative Samuel McReynolds who was Chairman of the House Foreign Affairs Committee, and others. In the evening Pope gave a dinner at the Mayflower Hotel, which several of the above-named personages attended as invited guests.[59]

The next day, January 31, Pope was received by Secretary Hull at the State Department. The Secretary took this opportunity to deny that he harbored any anti-Italian prejudices. He counted among his friends some of the most eminent public officials of Italian extraction in this country, and he had only admiration

[58] The interview took place on the 30th, *Ibid.*, January 31, 1936.
[59] *Ibid.*

for the Italian people. As on the previous day, Pope asked the same questions and received the same answers regarding the Pittman-McReynolds Bill. Hull wanted the Italians to know that America had no agreement with any nation concerning war and neutrality. Pope inquired as to how one could make a distinction between oil destined for Italy's peaceful industries and oil destined for her armed forces. The Secretary admitted that the distinction was impossible or at least difficult. The question of what constituted implements of war had given cause for considerable thought, because Congress was reluctant to define them. At any rate, oil was not considered an implement of war or a material of war in the present Neutrality Act. Pope then suggested the continuation of the present law for another year. Several members of Congress with whom he had conversed declared themselves in favor of its continuation. Hull assured him that he had no personal objection to the idea if Congress should decide to accept it. Then he added that he wanted to see an increase of trade between the United States and Italy, because it would also help relieve the problem of unemployment. [60]

During the Christmas holidays, another prominent Italian American, Judge Salvatore A. Cotillo, a justice of the New York State Supreme Court, had visited Washington. He discussed the neutrality legislation with Senator Pittman, Representative McReynolds, Secretary of War Dern, Speaker Byrnes, Vice-President Garner, and many others. The judge also submitted a brief on neutrality to every member of the House and Senate. Representative Kennedy of New York, referring to the brief as a "scholarly document," had an abstract of it printed in the *Congressional Record*. [61] At the request of Senator Wagner of New York, a lengthy memorandum on neutrality by the judge was published in the *Hearings* of the Senate Foreign Relations Committee. In it the judge criticized in detail the new bills along the usual lines, being especially averse to Presidential discretion. He recommended

[60] *Ibid.*, February 1, 1936.
[61] U. S., *Congressional Record* (as cited), 1595.

either the enactment of Representative Tinkham's proposed bill exempting the present belligerents from the new neutrality legislation, or the enactment of Senator Thomas' resolution prolonging for one year the present Neutrality Act.[62]

Still other Italian-American leaders journeyed to Washington. In January a delegation of the American Friends of Italy approached members of the Senate Foreign Relations Committee to express their apprehension about certain aspects of the pending neutrality bills.[63] The Supreme Venerable and the Grand Venerable of the Order of the Sons of Italy, a permanent organization of some 300,000 members, headed a delegation from Pennsylvania, New York, and New Jersey to testify before the House Foreign Affairs Committee.[64] The League for American Neutrality was also well represented at the hearings of the committee. Indicative of the importance of these delegations was the fact that among those who testified were two judges, a former secretary of state of Connecticut, and an ex-mayor and president of the Mayors' Guild of Massachusetts. All the witnesses except one created a very favorable impression on the members of the committee. In general they expressed their willingness to accept the Pittman-McReynolds Bill if it were rendered inapplicable to the present belligerents; otherwise, they opposed the granting of discretionary power to the President and favored the extension of the existing Neutrality Act.[65]

V

The course of events in Washington afforded Italian Americans good cause to congratulate themselves. Since it was becoming increasingly evident that there was not enough time to formulate a permanent policy before the existing law expired, Senator Thomas of Utah proposed on January 16 that the existing law

[62] U. S., Senate, *Neutrality* (as cited), 259–83.

[63] *Il Popolo Italiano* (Philadelphia), January 23, 1936, and *Il Progresso*, February 2, 1936.

[64] *La Libera Parola* (Philadelphia), January 18, 1936.

[65] U. S., House of Representatives, *American Neutrality Policy* (as cited), 177ff.

be renewed for a year. The proposal was approved by the administration on February 8. A resolution extending the Neutrality Act until May 1, 1937 was passed by the House on February 17 and by the Senate on the 18th. It was signed by the President on the 29th. In the process of renewing the law, Congress amended it somewhat. Loans and credits to belligerents were prohibited, save that the President could exempt ordinary commercial credits and short-term obligations (which discretionary power Italian Americans had opposed in the Pittman-McReynolds Bill), and the President's existing optional power to extend the arms embargo to other states that became involved in any war was made mandatory. When the President signed this law, he urged Americans to limit their war trade to the normal peacetime level even though they had a legal right to exceed it. Abnormal trade would help the carrying on of war, he added, and this would defeat the very purpose of the legislation. [66]

Meanwhile, the League Council's procrastination in the matter of oil sanctions enabled Italy to accumulate quantities of that product. The Council's Committee of Experts finally submitted a report on February 12, 1936, stating that a general embargo on oil shipments to Italy would deplete her stores within three and a half months. While this could conceivably have checked the Italian advance in Ethiopia, the committee did not recommend the step. One of the points made in the report was that a general embargo on oil would be effective if the United States were to limit its exports to Italy to a normal peacetime basis. [67]

Il Progresso thereupon editorialized that, as it had foreseen, all that was needed to compel the League to drop the idea of a general oil embargo was for Washington to abandon its "pro-sanctionist policy." [68] The paper again referred to the subject on the occasion of the Council of Thirteen's urgent appeal to the belligerents to

[66] Deparment of State, *Press Releases*, XIV (March 7, 1936), 198. For a discussion of the legislation, see Shepardson and Scroggs, *op. cit.*, 142 ff.

[67] Arnold J. Toynbee, *Survey of International Affairs, 1935, Abyssinia and Italy* (London, 1936), II, 330–33. See also Feis, *op. cit.*, 270 and 305–6.

[68] February 16, 1936.

reopen peace negotiations on March 3 (which appeal was another expedient to delay oil sanctions). This "quasi-ultimatum," it said, could not scare Italy. Apart from the fact that Italy already had sufficient reserves of oil, the threat from Geneva was futile, for Italy could now rely on American supplies. Apparently London, Paris, and Geneva had overestimated the importance of President Roosevelt's extra-legal appeal against abnormal war trade when signing the extended Neutrality Act. [69]

During the course of the re-enactment of the law, the Italian-American press did not fail to note a positive correlation between the action of Congress and the activity of Italian Americans. *La Capitale* remarked that the extension of the act "coincided exactly" with the Italian-American attitude as expressed in the thousands of telegrams that "rained" on Washington. [70] After the Senate had passed the Neutrality Resolution, Pope informed his readers that he for one was not surprised, for he had returned from his interviews with the nation's leaders in Washington fully reassured as to the final outcome of their deliberations. "It is perhaps the first time that a movement of our community has assumed such political importance and has received such prompt and equitable satisfaction. And it is a precedent we must not forget." [71] The same idea was stressed in Detroit's *La Tribuna Italiana d'America*[72] and in the *Corriere del Connecticut*. The latter declared that if the Italian viewpoint was taken into account in Washington, it was owing to the hundreds of thousands of Italian-American votes. Therefore, Italians were exhorted to become American citizens. [73]

In sum, Italian-American opinion, inflamed by Fascist propaganda, came to view the neutrality law of August, 1935 primarily

[69] March 4, 1936.

[70] February 15, 1936.

[71] *Il Progresso*, February 20, 1936.

[72] February 21, 1936.

[73] *Corriere del Connecticut* (New Haven), February 21, 1936. It is interesting to note that isolationist Congressman Hamilton Fish was cited in Chicago as saying that voters of Italian descent owed Senator Borah a debt of gratitude for his work in favor of "the just Italian cause relative to neutrality," and that they could show their appreciation by remembering this at the polls. *L'Italia* (Chicago), April 2, 1936.

from the standpoint of Italy's best interest. Thus only can the following fluctuations of sentiment be reconciled: Americans of Italian origin approved the law before it was applied; attacked the administration for applying the law too soon (i.e., before either the League or the belligerents had declared a state of war); attacked the administration for going beyond the letter of the law when it warned Americans against trading with the belligerents except at their own risk; attacked the administration for exercising its, authority (specifically granted by the law) to prohibit Americans from traveling on belligerent ships except at their own risk; criticized the law as being in contravention of the American-Italian Treaty of Commerce and Navigation; and finally demanded the re-enactment of this same law when it was about to expire (February 29, 1936), in order to prevent the passage of a more objectionable one, thereby completing a full cycle of criticism.

Pro-Fascist propaganda, then, *noticeably* influenced the course of American neutrality. This study, however, could scarcely show exactly how decisive this influence actually was. Many national officials and legislators certainly yielded to Italian-American persuasion or pressure; but others must certainly have yielded to American, in contrast to Italian-American, sentiment. An opinion poll at the time revealed that although American sympathies lay with Ethiopia, seven out of ten voters said they were against supporting the League of Nations even in economic sanctions against Italy.[74]

At this point it is appropriate to append a brief epilogue. It is only fair to emphasize that, except for a number of die-hard editors[75] and a few other pro-Fascist leaders, Italian-American

[74] George Gallup, "What We, the People, Think about Europe," *The New York Times Magazine*, April 30, 1939, 2.

[75] Almost all the Italian-American press protested its loyalty to America when Italy attacked France, and formally abjured fascism after Pearl Harbor, but the conversions were in many cases questioned. A more definite stand against fascism began to result in the once pro-Fascist press from official American statements making a distinction between the Italian people and their Fascist Government. See Institute for Advanced Study, *A Survey of the Italian Language Press in the United States* (mimeographed, Princeton, September, 1942), 12–16; "The Foreign-Language Press," *Fortune*, XXII (November, 1940), 102; Alberto Cupelli, "The U. S. Italian Language Press Dances to the Nazi Tune," *Il Mondo*, VII (March, 1944), 3–9; and John Norman, "Repudiation of Fascism by the Italian-American Press," *Journalism Quarterly*, XXI (March, 1944), 1–6.

loyalty to America amply proved itself in the recent war with Italy. Of course, there always will be some filial devotion to the mother-country, as was demonstrated when Italian-American leaders again went to Washington, this time unsuccessfully, to try to induce the Senate Foreign Relations Committee to have the severe provisions of the Italian Peace Treaty revised and renegotiated.[76]   Senator Arthur Vandenberg, chairman of the committee, urged his Republican colleagues to resist "pressure" from constituents of Italian origin.[77]   Although the treaty was ratified without change, the disappointed constituents were later able to perform an important service for both the American and Italian governments by helping in some measure to defeat the Communists in the crucial Italian elections of April 18, 1948. With the open encouragement of high public officials, the Italian-American press and public sent thousands of letters to relatives and friends in the old country urging them to vote against communism.[78]   It is only elaborating on the obvious, therefore, to conclude that this press and public has been, is now, and will continue to be a noteworthy factor in American politics and foreign relations as regards Italy.

[76] U. S., Senate (80th Cong., 1st Sess.): *Treaties of Peace with Italy, Rumania, Bulgaria, and Hungary* (Hearings before the Committee on Foreign Relations. Washington, 1947), *passim.*

[77] *New York Herald Tribune*, May 30, 1947.

[78] *Il Progresso*, April 7, 1948; *New York Times*, April 2, 1948; *Time*, March 29, 1948; and *Christian Science Monitor*, March 1, 25, and 26, 1948.

The Nonapplication of Sanctions Against Japan, 1931–1932

By Ernest Ralph Perkins*

When the Japanese military forces struck in Manchuria on the evening of September 18, 1931, the course of aggression culminating in the world's most disastrous war began. To meet this crisis the strongest weapon forged by the peace-loving nations was the doctrine of nonrecognition of changes wrought by aggression, set forth by Secretary of State Stimson in identic notes to China and Japan on January 7, 1932,[1] and adopted after considerable delay on March 11 by the League of Nations.[2] That this moral and diplomatic sanction, if such it may be called, proved too weak a weapon either to check the course of Japanese expansion or to discourage similar military adventures by European dictatorships was proved by events.

It has been widely believed that the responsibility for failure to invoke the more powerful weapons of economic sanctions and, as a final resort, military sanctions rested with the United Kingdom, particularly with the Foreign Minister, Sir John Simon. The use of such sanctions is popularly presumed to have been advocated by the American Government, or at least by Secretary of State Stimson. More than 2,000 pages of documents on the far eastern crisis have been published by the Department of State in the volumes of *Foreign Relations of the United States* dealing with the years 1931 and 1932. In this maze of documentation and in Mr.

*Ernest Ralph Perkins is editor of *Foreign Relations of the United States*, Department of State, Washington.

[1] U. S., Department of State, *Foreign Relations of the United States, Japan 1931–1932* (Washington, 1943), I, 76 (hereafter cited as *Japan, 1931–1932*).

[2] *Ibid.*, 210.

Stimson's recent book, *On Active Service in Peace and War*, there may be found much new light on the official attitude of the American Government toward the possible invocation of economic or military sanctions and to a less extent on the part played by the leaders of some other governments. [3]

II

Lack of information and realization as to the true nature and extent of the crisis militated against decisive action by the American Government in the early stages of developments when a strong united front with the members of the League of Nations might perhaps have been effective. To be sure, Dr. John C. Ferguson, adviser to the Chinese Government, warned the American Minister in Peiping, Mr. Nelson T. Johnson, on September 11, 1931, that according to his information Japan would occupy Manchuria within three months. The Minister recorded this conversation in a memorandum, but in doing so he expressed the view that such action seemed "fantastic" and "improbable," [4] and he did not report the warning to the Department of State until September 21. The Japanese attack on the night of September 18 was, of course, reported on the 19th by American missions as well as by the press, but in Tokyo the American Embassy was assured that it was a minor local clash which the Japanese were determined to settle peacefully. In view of this, Ambassador Forbes felt that a cancellation of his projected trip home would be misconstrued, and so he sailed that afternoon. [5] In Washington, Secretary Stimson, pressed by correspondents, said that so far the Chinese and

---

[3] A good review of much of the evidence on this subject is given by Sara R. Smith in *The Manchurian Crisis, 1931–1932* (New York, 1948), which does not accept the theory of American support for proposed sanctions. The writer apparently did not, however, make use of the material in the State Department's *Foreign Relations* volume on the Far East for 1931. The 1932 *Foreign Relations* volumes, cited below, as well as Henry L. Stimson and McGeorge Bundy, *On Active Service in Peace and War* (New York, 1948) have been published more recently.

[4] U. S., Department of State, *Foreign Relations of the United States, 1931* (Washington, 1946), III, 3 (hereafter, *Foreign Relations, 1931*); and *Foreign Relations of the United States, Japan, 1931–1941* (Washington, 1943), I, 3 (hereafter, *Japan, 1931–1941*).

[5] *Foreign Relations, 1931*, III, 11.

Japanese Governments were not involved, and he authorized the statement for attribution that "there seems to be no ground for indicating any violation of the Kellogg Pact."[6]

Reports of the next few days, however, dispelled the illusion that the Manchurian affair was only a minor local incident, and on September 22 Minister Johnson telegraphed his conviction that the steps taken by Japan must fall within any definition of war, and that the signatories of the Kellogg Pact stood at the bar of the nations of the East to answer for their sincerity.[7] On the same day, before the receipt of this telegram, Secretary Stimson had telegraphed to Minister Hugh Wilson at Geneva to inform Sir Eric Drummond, Secretary-General of the League of Nations, that it was apparent that the Japanese military had initiated a widely extended and carefully prepared movement of aggression with a strategic goal in mind; that the military chiefs and the Foreign Office were evidently sharply at variance; and that consequently it would be advisable, in preparing to support the fulfillment of treaty obligations, that Japanese nationalistic feeling be not aroused against the Japanese Foreign Office and incited to support the Army.[8]

By September 21 reports of the reaction in League circles began to come from State Department representatives there: Minister Hugh Wilson, Consul General Prentiss Gilbert, and Mr. Norman Davis.[9] Wilson reported on September 22 that the Council was considering sending an investigating commission to Manchuria. He declared that the Council was profoundly impressed with the urgency and seriousness of the situation and that American co-operation was earnestly desired.[10] On the next day Gilbert telegraphed that he was receiving constant appeals on the part of representatives of the world powers that their governments

[6] *Ibid.*, III, 16.

[7] *Japan, 1931–1941*, I, 5.

[8] *Foreign Relations, 1931*, III, 26.

[9] *Ibid.*, III, 22 ff.

[10] *Ibid.*, III, 37.

looked to the United States for action as the chief hope in a situation, the gravity of which they considered could not be overstated.[11] Wilson followed this with a telegram declaring that the urgent desire for co-operation by the United States was steadily increasing and that Drummond had approached him with a tentative proposition that an American be invited to sit in the League Council or in a Council committee, preferably the former.[12] By trans-Atlantic telephone, on September 23, Norman Davis urged the participation of the United States in the League deliberations and in the investigating committee. Secretary Stimson strongly dissented with respect to the investigating committee which he believed would ally all the nationalistic elements in Japan against Foreign Minister Shidehara and in favor of the military elements. As to sitting on the Council or committee, he thought it best to express sympathy and approval and "to reserve technical co-operation to pull them out of trouble if they got into trouble."[13] On the next day, the Under Secretary of State, Mr. William R. Castle, told the British Chargé that we were very much opposed to any move which might inflame the nationalistic spirit of Japan and unite the people of that country behind the militaristic element rather than the civilian element.[14]

III

The possible use of sanctions began to figure in diplomatic correspondence on September 26 when Gilbert telegraphed from Geneva that it was felt there that "military pressure is out of the question and that there would be great reluctance to exert economic pressure which would further dislocate world trade."[15]

On September 30, the president of the League Council was able to announce that the Japanese Government had given assur-

[11] *Ibid.*, III, 38.
[12] *Ibid.*, III, 39.
[13] *Ibid.*, III, 43–47.
[14] *Ibid.*, III, 63.
[15] *Ibid.*, III, 71.

ance that it had no territorial designs in Manchuria and that Japanese troops would be withdrawn to the railway zone as rapidly as the safety of Japanese nationals and their property could be assured. With this breathing spell the Council adjourned until October 14.[16]

On October 5, Secretary Stimson cabled Gilbert at Geneva a statement of American policy for the information of Drummond. Asserting that it was most desirable that the League should in no way relax its vigilance nor fail to assert all the authority and pressure within its competence in order to regulate Chinese and Japanese action, Mr. Stimson declared that the American Government, acting independently through its representatives abroad, would endeavor to reinforce League action, and would make clear that it was not oblivious of the obligations assumed by the disputants to their fellow signatories in the Kellogg Pact and the Nine-Power Treaty.[17]

The above statement appears somewhat ambiguous. The pressure within the competence of the League would certainly seem to include sanctions, but the support promised by the United States was to be given through its representatives abroad, apparently only diplomatic action being contemplated. Such diplomatic influence upon both the Japanese and the Chinese had already been brought to bear by the American Government and was continued throughout the far eastern crisis whenever there seemed to be any useful opportunity.

As Japanese action belied Japanese promises of peaceful withdrawal, the crisis was no less acute when the time for reassembling the Council approached. Gilbert was authorized to sit with the Council as an observer and to take part in discussion when matters relating to the Kellogg Pact were under consideration.[18] In a trans-Atlantic telephone conversation on October 13, the Secretary of State stressed to Gilbert the importance of invoking the Kellogg

16 *Ibid.*, III, 96, 97.
17 *Ibid.*, III, 117.
18 *Ibid.*, III, 183–84.

Pact as a warning against a future act of war and not in such a way as to indicate that war had already taken place. Said the Secretary: "You see if those people say that an act of war has already taken place it would open the whole question of sanctions, with which we have nothing to do." Gilbert replied: "They are avoiding, of course, making any sanctions." [19]

Stimson cabled Gilbert on October 19 that if discussion of the application of the Kellogg Pact had been concluded, he saw no reason why Gilbert should continue to sit at Council meetings, especially as it was essential that he should not be present if action under Article 16 of the Covenant should be discussed. [20] This article was the one providing for the application of economic and military sanctions.

The Council adjourned on October 16 to meet again in Paris on November 16. Ambassador Dawes at London was ordered on November 10 to proceed to Paris to keep in touch with the League leaders but not to take part in meetings of the Council. [21] Dawes was instructed to feel his way cautiously, and added words of caution were given by Stimson in a trans-Atlantic telephone conversation the same day. "The difficulty has been that the League we think has gone off a little bit too rapidly," said Stimson, apparently referring to the setting of November 16 as a date for the withdrawal of Japanese troops. Dawes was told to keep his "hand on the shoulder or coat collar of Briand and not let him go too fast." [22]

On November 16, Johnson reported from Peiping that there was no evidence of any intention on the part of the Japanese to withdraw from the stand they had taken in Manchuria. [23] Also on the same day Ambassador Forbes cabled a warning against exercising pressure at Geneva upon Japan, giving what appeared

[19] *Ibid.*, III, 179.
[20] *Ibid.*, III, 248.
[21] *Japan, 1931–1941*, I, 41–44.
[22] *Foreign Relations, 1931*, III, 407–14.
[23] *Ibid.*, III, 451.

to be the collective wisdom of diplomats of all countries at Tokyo.[24]

By November 17 Stimson was thoroughly disgusted at Japanese recalcitrance, and also felt that Sir John Simon was too lenient in his apparent willingness to recognize some of Japan's claims to dubious treaty rights as a prior condition for negotiations between the two disputants. Stimson stood firmly for negotiations in the presence of neutral observers, declaring that if Japan refused it would be necessary to outlaw her and let her sizzle in a Chinese boycott and under condemnation by the moral pressure of the world. Though the Japanese army was "as hardboiled as an Easter egg," our (presumably the American Government's) views if publicly stated would be "sufficiently forcible to crack the egg."[25] This was to Dawes, and on the next day Stimson cabled that the outlook for a settlement which the United States could accept in the light of treaties was getting to be increasingly hopeless and that the only recourse left might be to make public "the whole damning case against Japan," and rest upon the reaction of public opinion.[26]

In the meantime the attitude of both the French and the British was also stiffening, with apparently a greater willingness to take strong measures. On November 18, in a meeting of the twelve members of the Council who were not parties to the dispute, Briand urged that the League exhaust every avenue of conciliation, and twice reiterated that if it failed, he was willing to go "absolutely to the limit."[27] Dawes reported, shortly after this meeting, a private conversation with Simon in which the latter favored action under Article 15, an investigating commission, and if that failed proceeding under Article 16, sanctions. Simon felt that the League should go to the limit of its powers, with the provision that the United States would independently assume the same attitude.[28]

[24] *Ibid.*, III, 452.
[25] *Ibid.*, III, 470–71.
[26] *Ibid.*, III, 477–78.
[27] *Ibid.*, III, 481.
[28] *Ibid.*, III, 484–85.

The next forenoon, November 19, there took place a very significant trans-Atlantic telephone conversation between Stimson and Dawes.[29] With League leaders considering action under various articles of the Covenant, Dawes reported he would be invited to attend the Council. Stimson warned: "That is just the time you ought not to be there because that means that they are going to take up the question of sanctions." He continued:

> I will tell you for your confidential guidance that in case the League should take up the proposal of an embargo by the League, I have no doubt that this Government would do its best not to interfere with that embargo but I don't want to have it announced beforehand. I don't want to have that announced until after the League has done its own action and I doubt whether it is advisable for the League to go on with an embargo, but in case they should—.[30]

Later in the same conversation Stimson told Dawes:

> This is confidential for you. We do not see how we can do anything more ourselves as a government than to announce our disapproval and to announce that we do not recognize any treaties which may be forced by Japan under the pressure of military occupation. We do not ourselves believe in the enforcement of any embargo by our own Government, although we would not probably in any way allow our Government to interfere through the fleet with any embargo by anyone else. We believe an embargo is a step to war and if an embargo is decided upon by the League, it would be very likely for that embargo to lead to war.[31]

Stimson agreed with Dawes that Sze, Chinese representative to the League, wanted to get all the nations of the world in war with Japan, and added: "We have no sympathy with that and we do not intend to get into war with Japan."[32]

Dawes declared that "Simon's position was that he wants to go the limit."[33]

[29] *Ibid.*, III, 488–98.

[30] *Ibid.*, III, 489. A break in conversation is indicated on the original memorandum of conversation. Apparently either the stenographer lost the rest of the sentence or Dawes interrupted.

[31] *Ibid.*, III, 496.

[32] *Ibid.*, III, 496–97.

[33] *Ibid.*, III, 497.

To this Stimson replied:

We do not want to discourage them from going ahead with that if they want to, but we do not want in any way to tie ourselves up to it because our principles are entirely different. That is the line which you must follow. We will not do anything to discourage their taking action under Articles 15 and 16 of the League if they want to. Confidentially, though you must not say this beforehand, I do not anticipate that this Government would allow its fleet to do anything to interfere with such an embargo if it was imposed. In other words, if that was done, we would stand aside and not interfere with it and I think very likely a good many of our people would sympathize with that embargo and it would reduce the trade of Japan with this country. That would be entirely unofficial—not an act of government. So far as this Government is concerned, the only act we see we could do would be to publish the papers and the correspondence, announce our disapproval of the action of Japan, possibly calling it a violation of these treaties and then announce as we did in 1915 that we would not recognize any treaties that were created under military force.[34]

Following this conversation, the Secretary conferred with President Hoover and then called Dawes again. He said that the President fully concurred with everything Stimson had told Dawes about our position.[35] He added that if the League went ahead, we would publish our notes immediately after such action. For two months, Stimson said, he had been keeping everything quiet in an effort to give the Japanese Government an opportunity to get control of the Army, and American public opinion had not been educated on it at all.[36] But Hoover and Stimson agreed that if the League went ahead and the American Government published its correspondence, "the support of American public opinion would be overwhelming."[37]

It will be noted that the information as to the position of the American Government given to Dawes in these conversations was confidential and for his information, not for transmittal to other governments. Just how much the League leaders knew

[34] *Ibid.*
[35] *Ibid.*, III, 499.
[36] *Ibid.*, III, 500.
[37] *Ibid.*, III, 502.

of the American position is not clear, but on November 21 Dawes reported that in a meeting of the twelve Council members exclusive of China and Japan, Briand had said that the members of the Council should not have too great expectations regarding the United States, that the American Government was not ready to go beyond the Pact of Paris and contemplated no sanctions. Briand said the Council must go slowly, for if it went too far it might disassociate itself from the United States.

The Council confined itself to serious consideration of the appointment of an investigating commission, which had previously been proposed and in which it was hoped the United States would take part.[38] From these discussions came the Lytton Commission. To General McCoy, the American member of this Commission, Dr. George H. Blakeslee served as adviser.

In reviewing developments up to the end of 1931, Mc George Bundy concedes, apparently with Mr. Stimson's approval, that in this period the American Government had somewhat of a restraining influence on discussions of collective action and did not step out boldly against aggression.[39]

IV

Stimson and Bundy give the occupation of Chinchow, January 2, 1932, as the turning point after which Stimson's attempts at conciliation by restraint were ended for good and an entirely new phase of American policy began.[40] The weapons of this new phase were, however, those of nonrecognition and publicity which in November had been decided upon as the strongest sanctions the American Government would use. Whether Stimson at any time while Secretary of State did urge within department or White House discussions the application of economic or military sanctions is not clear, though the absence of any record in the files of the Department of State or in *The Far Eastern Crisis* and *On Active*

[38] *Ibid.*, III, 523–26, especially 525.
[39] Stimson and Bundy, *On Active Service*, 232.
[40] *Ibid.*, 231.

Service in Peace and War that he did make such a recommendation would seem to indicate that he did not. In the latter book it is stated that on January 23 and 29, 1932 the situation in the Far East was discussed at length in the cabinet. The President believed that any policy of embargo or sanctions might lead to war and he was absolutely opposed to that. This effectively blocked any support by the American Government for economic sanctions.[41] It is stated that Stimson took a leading part in this discussion but what he advocated is not clearly recorded. In his diary, however, he wrote that the only difference he could see between his point of view and Hoover's was that he (Stimson) would rely on the unconscious effect of American military and economic strength, letting the Japanese fear this because they would not be told we would not use it against them.[42]

In the diplomatic correspondence published in *Foreign Relations of the United States* for 1932 references to the possible application of economic or military sanctions against Japan are few and scattered. There is no indication that such sanctions were at any time during the year under serious consideration by either the United States or the members of the League.

When Mr. Willys R. Peck, American consul general at Nanking, delivered Stimson's nonrecognition note of January 7 to Foreign Minister Eugene Chen, he was informed that the Chinese Government had decided to sever relations with Japan and to appeal to the League to invoke the economic sanctions provided for in Article 16 of the Covenant.[43] A few hours later, however, Chen summoned Peck and told him that the Chinese Government had decided to hold in abeyance the severing of relations and the appeal to the League in the hope that the American note might accomplish the same results.[44]

[41] *Ibid.*, 243–44.
[42] *Ibid.*, 245.
[43] Telegram No. 4, Nanking, January 8, 1932, 2 p.m., U. S., Department of State, *Foreign Relations of the United States, 1932* (Washington, 1948), III, 14–15 (hereafter, *Foreign Relations, 1932*).
[44] Telegram No. 5, Nanking, January, 1932, 5 p.m., *ibid.*, III, 16.

Minister Johnson at Peking was not at all optimistic about the effectiveness of the nonrecognition note. In two telegrams on January 13 he reported that among the Chinese there was slight expectation that Japan's aggressive policy would be checked by the note and he gave as his opinion that: "Nothing short of outside force or an economic collapse at home will persuade Japan to retire from her present position." [45]

Soon after this the Japanese were attacking at Shanghai. But this did not bring forth a demand from the Chinese Government for sanctions as might have been expected. Consul General Cunningham telegraphed on January 25 that Chen had resigned as foreign minister because Chang Kai-shek insisted on following a passive policy. Chen had intended to implement Article 16. [46]

From Geneva, Gilbert reported on January 27 that Yen, the Chinese delegate on the Council, said that he had been instructed to invoke Articles 15 and 16 but had refrained from doing so in the hope of receiving satisfaction through the existing League procedure. There was a feeling among some of the League committee to whom this statement was made that Yen felt himself on uncertain ground because of the resignation of Chen and the likelihood of a more moderate policy on the part of his successor. [47] On January 29 China did invoke Articles 10 and 15, but not Article 16. [48]

Stimson's instructions to Gilbert at Geneva on January 30 were to take no initiative in discussions but, if asked, to say in confidence that the United States would view with satisfaction a declaration by the Council or member states in support of the nonrecognition note of January 7. [49] In contrast with this rather negative attitude was a proposal made at the suggestion of President Hoover that the President and the British King make a direct appeal to the Japanese Emperor for cessation of hostilities and negotiations in

[45] *Ibid.*, III, 25–26; 26–27.
[46] *Ibid.*, III, 64.
[47] *Ibid.*, III, 72.
[48] *Ibid.*, III, 90.
[49] *Ibid.*, III, 121.

which neutrals would take part. This proposal was discussed in trans-Atlantic telephone conversations between Secretary Stimson and Prime Minister MacDonald on January 30 and 31. The participation of the King was ruled out by the British for constitutional reasons, but MacDonald offered to make the appeal himself if Hoover would. The plan was then set aside with the possibility of renewal. [50]

On February 6 in another trans-Atlantic conversation between Stimson and Simon, the former explained his suggestion that the governments in Washington and London should refrain a short time from representations, thus giving a chance for local efforts at Shanghai to bring about a truce. [51] During this discussion the question of sanctions was incidentally mentioned.

Sir John Simon commented: "What I like about your plan or your whole scheme is that it keeps us well away from this question about economic things and all of Article 16. I think it is wise to keep away from that."

Stimson replied: "We have to; we are outside the League."

Simon added: "I don't think that sort of thing is the way to do it."

To this Stimson answered: "What I think I can hardly breathe aloud. I am willing to keep Japan guessing as to what we are going to do but that I don't discuss, it is a little dangerous over the telephone even." [52]

In the above statement we have the nearest approach in the official record that Secretary Stimson may privately have favored more drastic measures than he officially proposed.

A trans-Atlantic conversation two days later between Stimson and Gibson reflects a similar mood on Stimson's part. He agreed with Simon that it would not be wise for the Council "to rock the boat" by taking vigorous action while negotiations were pending, but added that he would not be very troubled if they did, as he

[50] *Ibid.*, III, 124–28; 128–29; 136–40; 142–43; 147.
[51] *Ibid.*, III, 234–40.
[52] *Ibid.*, III, 240.

was "not in a very pacific frame of mind." [53]   Stimson felt that the British had "let us down" when they were unwilling to join the United States in an appeal under the Nine-Power Pact, preferring to content themselves with League action. "You can tell him [Simon] so," he said over the trans-Atlantic telephone to Atherton at the Embassy in London, February 16. [54]   The British also wanted to tone down the appeal by leaving out specific reference to Manchuria.

Reports of this refusal by Simon to go along with Stimson in a joint appeal may have been the basis for the supposition which arose that Stimson had proposed sanctions and Simon had turned them down.   Stimson acted alone by setting forth the American position in his letter of February 23 to Senator Borah, [55] while Simon did follow through with similar action in the League.

The French ambassador in a conversation on February 18 pointed out to Stimson that the difficulty was "that both Japan and China had made up their minds that neither we nor the nations of Europe would fight.   In the words of the Chinese proverb it was a case of straw guns and snow swords." [56]   On the day the letter to Borah was sent, Stimson had another conversation with the French Ambassador.   Stimson pointed out that it would be necessary for the League Assembly to decide as to the rights and wrongs in the case before they came to punishment and that it was premature to ask what the United States would do.   "Well," said the Ambassador, "if they go ahead and decide that, will you then do something?"   Stimson replied: "We will then discuss with them in the light of their decision." [57]

Secretary Stimson also told the British Ambassador, on February 25, that attempts being made to sound out the American position were premature, and added that this country was so far ahead of

[53] *Ibid.*, III, 251–52.
[54] *Ibid.*, III, 353.
[55] *Japan, 1931–1941*, I, 83.
[56] *Foreign Relations, 1932*, III, 374–75.
[57] *Ibid.*, III, 428–29.

the League that they could not complain that we were standing in their path. It was Stimson's view that the sanctions of Article 16 were only to be invoked in case, after an investigation and report under the authority of the League, a nation declared war against another nation which had complied with the report. He then added his opinion that the League could devise sanctions which were not, like an embargo, liable to lead to war but which would be very effective against Japan. He cited the sanction of his note of January 7 as an example and said he felt the League could devise many other sanctions which would be effective but not warlike.[58] The same day he discussed the far eastern crisis with the German Ambassador and told him that he did not intend to intimate that he was "in favor of any forcible measures or anything that would lead to more hostility than was already in existence."[59]

The next day, February 26, Secretary Stimson telegraphed Wilson at Geneva along much the same line as that taken in the conversation described above, stating specifically: "I see no advantage and much danger in a discussion now between this Government and the authorities of the League as to the possibility of a general embargo against Japan." He denied vigorously reports circulating in Geneva that the American Government was inclining toward the application of an economic boycott and said he had no reason to believe such a proposal would command any substantial support in Congress. He did think that lesser sanctions of public opinion would meet with general favor.[60] Over the trans-Atlantic telephone Stimson had already told Wilson that the question of an economic boycott had never been discussed in the Cabinet.[61]

Wilson discussed the Secretary's telegram with Drummond who felt that any proposal for economic sanctions would be rejected

[58] *Ibid.*, III, 441–42.
[59] *Ibid.*, III, 442–43.
[60] *Ibid.*, III, 452–53.
[61] *Ibid.*, III, 453, footnote 8. Compare statements in *On Active Service in Peace and War*, 243–44, previously cited at footnote 41, regarding cabinet meetings of January 23 and 29, 1932.

by the League, apparently chiefly for the reason that it was felt that Japan might meet such action by war.[62] The diplomats at Tokyo as usual were taking a dim view of any sanctions, Forbes reporting that his British and French colleagues believed the Borah letter had done much harm. The three ambassadors hoped that no further provocative statements would be coming from Washington, and Forbes declared that an economic boycott such as was urged by some responsible people in the United States would be looked upon in Japan as tantamount to war.[63]

The resolution adopted by the Assembly of the League on March 11 affirmed the nonrecognition doctrine and a continuation of conciliation and investigation but stopped short of economic sanctions.[64] Secretary Stimson expressed the gratification of the American Government with this resolution.[65]

On April 4, Mr. Atherton reported from London a conversation with Prime Minister MacDonald. The latter asked: "How far are you ready to take action beyond what you, with the League, have already taken"? He said the League could not invoke Article 16 without causing conflict. Atherton replied that he had no knowledge, personal or official, of his government's conception of policy in the Far East beyond the expressions already made.[66] On April 30, Secretary Stimson, on a visit to Geneva, reported conversations with British and other League leaders, but gave no intimation that sanctions were discussed.[67] From Tokyo, Ambassador Grew reported on June 13 that the Japanese realized "the practical impossibility at present of compelling Japan by force of arms to relinquish its grip on Manchuria" and that "the threat of an economic boycott does not frighten them." Grew considered that contrary to popular opinion abroad "the nation as a whole can view with confidence the possibility of complete

[62] *Ibid.*, III, 456–57.
[63] *Ibid.*, III, 457–58.
[64] *Japan, 1931–1932*, I, 210–12.
[65] *Ibid.*, I, 213.
[66] *Foreign Relations, 1932*, III, 664–66.
[67] *Ibid.*, III, 734–35.

suppression of intercourse with foreign countries other than the nearby Asiatic coast for a period of years." [68]

As the time for the presentation of the report of the Lytton Commission approached, Secretary Stimson's one concern seems to have been that there should be no weakening of the nonrecognition stand. He told Mr. Osborne, the British Chargé, on September 7 that the Assembly could hardly do less than adopt this policy. When the latter suggested that perhaps they would be called upon to go farther, Stimson replied he could make no suggestions on that point. [69] He gave strict instructions to Wilson at Geneva on September 23 that the United States was not to take the lead in formulating policy as to action by the League. Though he stated that it was altogether likely that the United States would co-operate if the League suggested "constructive steps," there is no mention of the possible attitude of the American Government as to sanctions in this instruction. [70]

V

After the defeat of President Hoover in the November election there was, of course, little likelihood of the outgoing administration initiating any such drastic change in foreign policy as the imposition of sanctions would have been. Stimson apparently believed that events had justified his policy with respect to the Far East. On November 17 he told the Irish minister that his action of January 7 had been endorsed by the Assembly on March 11 and his views as to facts had now been confirmed by the Lytton Report. He said he was "in the easy position of the man who had laid his cards face up on the table and had nothing more to say." [71] He reaffirmed this view in a telegram on November 19 to guide Wilson in his conversations at Geneva. Viewing the outcome of his policies with what proved in the event too great optimism, he

[68] *Ibid.*, IV, 76-78.
[69] *Ibid.*, IV, 228.
[70] *Ibid.*, IV, 271-72.
[71] *Ibid.*, IV, 347.

232 of State that

authorized Wilson to say on his own authority and without committing the Department of State that

in view of accumulating evidence of the increasing economic pressure which has been brought upon Japan by her Manchurian adventure, as exemplified in the fall of the yen, the doubling of the budget, the transgressing of her debt limit and the inconclusive result of her military operations, it should be only a matter of probably a short time when she will seek responsively to confer on the subject of Manchuria; . . .[72]

The record as presented in the official American correspondence, published in the *Foreign Relations* volumes reviewed above, shows clearly that at no time during the Manchurian crisis was the American Government willing to proceed with the use of either economic or military sanctions. Further revelations by participants in policy making of that period are needed to determine definitely the reason for this and how decisions of policy were arrived at. The part played by the members of the League, especially the United Kingdom, in this crisis is as yet far less well documented than is the American record. It is to be hoped that much light on that side of the story will be shed at an early date by the publication of British papers on the subject in *Documents on British Foreign Policy, 1919–1939*, the series now being edited by Professor Ernest L. Woodward.

[72] *Ibid.*, IV, 347–49.

The United States and Chinese Territorial Integrity, 1908

By Jessie Ashworth Miller[*]

It was August, 1908. The bits of news trickling in from China were thin and colorless. To the ill-informed American public this seemed a good omen. An editorial in the *Journal of the American Asiatic Association*, describing a banquet given for Sir Robert Hart, Inspector-General of the Chinese Customs Service, remarked that the speeches were somewhat lacking in interest due chiefly to the fact that there was "in the immediate future of the Chinese Empire no great international issue and no acute question of international politics." The great Chinese problem of five years before had "been settled if not for all time, at least for the next generation."[1]

Actually, behind the scenes, transactions of considerable moment were taking place. The years following the Russo-Japanese War had brought about a new, and to the Chinese, alarming re-alignment of the great powers. A series of agreements had, in effect, secretly divided the Chinese Empire into areas in which Japan, Russia, Britain, and France were each especially interested —an economic partition which, the Chinese feared, was but the prelude to a political division of the Empire.[2] The Chinese were particularly apprehensive concerning the pretentions of Japan in southern Manchuria and were looking abroad for financial aid and diplomatic support to enable them to strengthen their own

---

[*] Jessie Ashworth Miller is Lecturer in Sociology at Ursinus College.

[1] Editorial, *Journal of the American Asiatic Association*, VIII (August, 1908), 193.

[2] John G. Reid, *The Manchu Abdication and the Powers, 1908–1912* (Berkeley, Calif., 1935), 10–12; John V. A. MacMurray, comp. and ed., *Treaties and Agreements with and concerning China, 1894–1919* (New York, 1921), I, 674–78; Victor Yakhontoff, *Russia and the Soviet Union in the Far East* (New York, 1931), 374–76; Ernest B. Price, *The Russo-Japanese Treaties of 1907–1916 concerning Manchuria and Mongolia* (Baltimore, 1933), passim.

hold on the province. The previous year tentative overtures for a loan had been made to the American banker, Mr. E. H. Harriman, but the panic of 1907 had prevented consideration of the plan.[3] By August, 1908, however, Wall Street was again feeling confident and a number of financiers were looking toward Manchuria as a profitable field of investment. Among them was Mr. Harriman who had his eyes fixed on the South Manchuria Railway. He and his associate, Mr. Jacob Schiff, had requested the State Department to call Willard Straight, United States Consul General in Mukden, home for consultation.[4]

Straight himself had for almost two years been waging an energetic battle against Japanese aggression. He was convinced that in a China made strong by American financial aid lay the best hope for the maintenance of the Open Door. Before his departure for Washington he and T'ang Shao-yi, Governor of the Province of Fengtien, drafted an agreement providing for a loan to China of twenty million dollars to be used to establish a bank which in its turn would finance railway construction, mining, timber, and agricultural developments. The names of the bankers to be approached were not specified, but it was tacitly understood that Harriman would first be consulted.[5]

Governor T'ang, like Straight, was preparing to go to Washington. He had been appointed special envoy to the United States to express China's appreciation for the remission of the Boxer Indemnity. An equally important, though less publicized, part of his mission, was to continue the loan negotiations initiated by Straight and to conclude, if possible, a German-Chinese-American entente.[6] Kaiser Wilhelm II had been trying since 1906 to maneuver the United States into a joint declaration on the open door

[3] Herbert Croly, *Willard Straight* (New York, 1925), 242.

[4] George Kennan, *E. H. Harriman, A Biography* (New York, 1922), II, 26; A. Whitney Griswold, *The Far Eastern Policy of the United States* (New York, 1938), 139.

[5] Croly, *op. cit.*, 266.

[6] Rex to Schoen, August, 1908, *Die Grosse Politik der Europäische Kabinette, 1871–1914*, ed. J. Lepsins, A. Menelssohn Bartholdy, F. Thimme (Berlin, 1922–27), XXV, 96 (hereafter cited as *Grosse Politik*).

and integrity of China and believed that his plan was, at last, about to succeed.[7]   In many ways the moment did seem most auspicious for the German-Chinese and the Straight-T'ang moves.   Germany and the United States alone of the major powers were not included in the various secret treaties concerning China, and hence seemed to have the most to gain from the maintenance of China's territorial integrity; the German ambassador in Washington, Speck von Sternberg, had become a close personal friend of Roosevelt; but above all Chinese-American friendship had reached a new peak of cordiality.

The more courteous and just administration of American immigration laws, the reform of the American consular service in the Far East, the establishment of a United States Court for China, and the remission of the Boxer Indemnity had been climaxed by the visit of Secretary of War Taft to Shanghai.   Although in a public address Taft had cautioned that he did not know how far the United States would go in defense of Chinese territory, the extreme sincerity of his words, his reiteration of the traditional principles of the open door and integrity of China, his emphatic assertion that the United States must be regarded not alone as a country interested in the trade of China but as a power owning territory in China's immediate neighborhood, had encouraged the Chinese to think that they had indeed found an ally in their struggle against Japan.   The general tone of the American press, its enthusiasm for the Chinese reform movement, its endorsement of the principles of the open door and the territorial integrity of China, and its critical attitude toward Japanese policies were additional factors in strengthening the Chinese hope of American aid.   Willard Straight and T'ang seemed indeed to have adequate grounds for optimism over the future of their plans.[8]

[7] Tschirschky to Sternberg, September 23, 1906, *ibid.*, XXV, 71; Sternberg to Bülow, September 9, 1907, *ibid.*, XXV, 72–74; Bülow to Sternberg, October 17, 1907, *ibid.*, XXV, 74–75; Rex to Schoen, August, 1908, *ibid.*, XXV, 96.

[8] For a more detailed analysis of American press opinion at this time, see Jessie A. Miller, *China in American Policy and Opinion, 1906–1909* (Clark University, unpublished manuscript, 1940).

II

Hardly had Straight left Mukden for Washington, however, before the first note of discouragement was sounded. It appeared from an unexpected source—the American press. On August 11 the *New York Herald* suddenly launched a formal campaign in favor of an alliance with China. In a prominent front page article it reported an interview between its Paris correspondent and Li Sum-ting, editor of the *Hongkong-China Mail*. Japan, stated Li, was doing her best to close the open door to China, and was prevented from fighting the United States, the only country which stood in her way, solely by lack of money. Her position, moreover, was strengthened by her alliance with England. To counterbalance this, Li strongly advocated an alliance between the United States and China. The leading editorial of the day echoed and gave unqualified support to Li's words:

An American-Chinese Alliance—Why Not? . . . The boldness of such a suggestion should not make one discuss it as visionary. The political visions of today are the realities of tomorrow. . . . The swaddling clothes of tradition should not be allowed to prevent the free development of American interests, nor should measures considered by prudent and enlightened American statesmen as necessary for the protection of those interests be flouted or anathematized solely because they may be "contrary to the traditional policy of the country."
. . . Realization of the ambitious programme "Asia for the Japanese" would sound the death knell of American commercial development. An alliance between the United States and China would prevent the realization of that programme, would compel China to walk resolutely in the path of progress, would insure for the United States her share in the commerce of Asia and would guarantee peace in the Far East quite as much as the Triple Alliance and the Franco-Russian Alliance have guaranteed the peace of Europe.
Such results are not to be despised.[9]

On August 16 the *New York Times* replied to the *Herald* in a long editorial on the Far Eastern question. It concluded that "any treaty we could now make with China would make the situation worse, not better."[10]

[9] *New York Herald*, August 11, 1908.
[10] *New York Times*, August 16, 1908.

However, having initiated its campaign the *Herald* proceeded to carry it through with dramatic thoroughness. From the middle of August until the end of November the question of the "alliance" was seldom absent from the front page headlines. Comment from other newspapers was reprinted in detail; businessmen, educators, state and national officials were interviewed and their opinions reported at length. Frequently from four to six pages were devoted to an analysis of opinion.

Whether or not they were greatly interested in the alliance, other newspapers could hardly ignore the vigorous campaign being conducted by the *Herald*. A few southern and Pacific coast papers supported its stand.[11] Others, although they did not specifically endorse the alliance, believed that the door to China "must be kept open if we have to take it off its hinges," and hence were seized upon by the *Herald* as tacit supporters of the project.[12] Also, throughout the cotton regions of the South the *Herald* staff was able to find individuals of local though not of national reputation who agreed that "Asia for the Japanese would sound the death knell of America's commercial development," and that if the South hoped to find an outlet for her cotton goods closer political relations must be established with China.[13]

For the most part, however, the *Herald*'s campaign was regarded with contempt. It was variously characterized as "the most impossible of many crazy things that have been suggested by New York newspapers,"[14] "midsummer madness,"[15] "chatter . . . [and] pure moonshine,"[16] and "as preposterous a proposal

[11] *Mobile Star*, quoted by *New York Herald*, August 15, 1908; Portland *Morning Oregonian*, quoted by *Herald*, August 12, 1908; see *ibid.*, August 14, 15, and 29 for quotations from the Louisville *Courier-Journal*, *Tacoma News*, and *American Lumberman*.

[12] See the *Herald*, August 13, 15, 22, and 23 for quotations from the *Chicago Evening Post*, *Baltimore Sun*, *New Haven Journal-Courier*, *Denver Republican*. See also Columbus *Ohio State Journal*, August 29, 1908; *Duluth* (Minnesota) *News Tribune*, August 23, 1908.

[13] The *New York Herald* for August 12, 13, and 14 carried long lists of mayors, local Chamber of Commerce officials, businessmen, educators, etc., who favored an agreement with China.

[14] New York *Morning Telegraph*, quoted by *New York Herald*, August 23, 1908.

[15] New York *Sun*, quoted by *Herald*, August 22, 1908.

[16] New York *Evening Sun*, quoted by *Herald*, August 22, 1908.

as has ever been broached."[17]   When taken seriously it was
described as "mischievous, . . . fraught with danger,"[18] the
"devil's business and mean at that."[19]   The *Hartford Times* pointed
out that since the Middle Kingdom had "neither an army nor a
navy, nor much prospect of either such an alliance would really
mean a United States protectorate over China with an obligation
of fighting the battles of China with both Russia and Japan."[20]
For such a task we were totally unprepared.   To undertake it
"would involve the maintenance of a sea power in the Far East
which would make our present Pacific fleet look like a toy squadron."[21]   However easily this might fit into place in our "progressive
imperialism," it was "repugnant to our best traditions and should
be strongly resisted."[22]   "We are not," vehemently protested the
Philadelphia Inquirer, "going into the business of benevolent assimilation in China.   We will help her all we can in every way. . . .
We will help Japan and the Marquesas Islands in the same way.
. . . We want as close relations with China as possible, but we
are not going to fight her battles nor take over her diplomacy."[23]
"No administration at Washington would dare to make a treaty
of alliance between this country and any European state, and much
less would Americans permit themselves to be yoked to the sluggish
and dangerous weight of China's interests."[24]   In brief, only an
alliance with one of the Balkan states had in it greater possibilities
in the way of embarrassing complications.[25]

Only two periodicals of importance, the *Journal of the American*

[17] *Boston Herald*, August 18, 1908.

[18] *Richmond News-Leader*, quoted by *Herald*, August 22, 1908.

[19] *Buffalo Commercial*, quoted by *Herald*, August 23, 1908.

[20] Quoted by *Herald*, September 5, 1908.

[21] *Burlington Free Press*, quoted by *Herald*, August 15, 1908.

[22] *Detroit Times*, quoted by *Herald*, August 14, 1908.

[23] *Philadelphia Inquirer*, August 22, 1908.

[24] *Pittsburgh Press*, quoted by *Herald*, August 22, 1908.

[25] *Detroit Free Press*, quoted by *Herald*, August 15, 1908.   Other papers which
expressed their objections to an alliance with China included the *Chicago Record-Herald*,
*Pittsburgh Dispatch, Omaha Bee, Camden Post-Telegraph, Albany Evening Journal, Houston
Chronicle,* and *Boston Herald*.

Asiatic Association and the *Forum*, considered the proposal worthy of mention. The former commented that "the hectic effort of a great New York newspaper to bring about an alliance between the United States and China has excited more amusement than interest among people who are capable of discerning the absurdity of the project."[26] The latter likewise dismissed the suggestion as one that need not be taken seriously, and, in addition, warned its readers that according to many reports Germany was trying to bring about friction between Japan and the United States. Continued friction, it stated, breaks out into flame, and once the fire is started

Japan might have to call on her ally for assistance which might place England in an extremely embarrassing position. It is hardly conceivable that England could be found fighting against the United States, and yet by the terms of her alliance she might be forced into that position, and it would be a triumph of German diplomacy, worthy of the best traditions of the Bismarkian era, if she could bring that about . . . .[27]

Most individuals in government circles refused to commit themselves regarding the alliance. Two, however, Representative George E. Foss, Chairman of the House Committee on Naval Affairs, and Mr. Charles Denby, United States Consul General at Shanghai, came out flatly against it.[28]

At this point Li Sum-ting, himself, reached the United States. His arrival was made the occasion by the *Herald* for an outburst of enthusiasm. In an elaborate day-to-day account it described in terms of the greatest exaggeration his welcome to New York, his trip to Washington (where, according to the *Herald*, his appointment with President Roosevelt was canceled because of Japanese pressure),[29] and his tour of the South. The latter was, indeed, something of a triumph for the New York paper. Li visited a

[26] Editorial, *Journal of the American Asiatic Association*, VIII (September, 1908), 225.
[27] *The Forum*, XL (October, 1908), 307.
[28] *New York Herald*, August 21, 1908. Congressman A. J. Saboth of Illinois, President H. P. Judson of the University of Chicago, and Dean Walter C. Clarkson of Florida Law School "doubted the wisdom of an alliance with China." *Ibid.*, August 12 and August 14, 1908.
[29] *Ibid.*, November 24, 1908.

number of Southern cities where he was lavishly entertained by city officials, newspaper editors, and local Chambers of Commerce. In Savannah, Georgia, the Cotton Exchange suspended trade in his honor; everywhere it was predicted that he would succeed in bringing China into closer commercial relations with the United States.[30]

Li's tour closed at the end of November, and with it ended the *Herald*'s campaign for an alliance with China. Why it was initiated remains a matter of conjecture. It may have been merely a bit of sensationalism designed to increase the circulation of the paper. At the time it was generally regarded as an attempt to embroil the United States in trouble with Japan,[31] a determined effort to parallel the achievement of the *New York Journal* which ten years earlier claimed to have forced the war with Spain.[32] It may have been a sincere effort to promote closer ties with China. During the previous spring J. R. Ohl, the *Herald*'s Far Eastern correspondent had worked closely with Willard Straight's publicity program for building up United States sympathy for China. Ohl may have instigated the *Herald*'s campaign with the idea of aiding Governor T'ang in his projected mission. In any case the actual effect of the episode was to indicate how thoroughly opposed the American people were to an alliance with either Germany or China. The press of the country, which during the past two years had been almost unanimous in its expressions of sympathy for China, was now almost equally unanimous in its determination not to be drawn into her quarrels. Had the United States Government contemplated making a political agreement with China, it hardly could have gone ahead with its plans after such a forceful expression of opinion. This both Peking and Berlin must have realized.

[30] See, for example, the Washington *Evening Star*, September 28, 1908; Richmond *Times-Dispatch*, November 1, 1908 and November 3, 1908; Charleston *News and Courrier*, November 2, 3, and 4, 1908; *New York Herald*, November 7, 1908.

[31] *Philadelphia Record*, August 22, 1908.

[32] *Washington Times*, August 25, 1908.

III

In the meantime events in connection with the visit of the American fleet to the Orient cast further doubt on the probable success of T'ang's mission. On October 18, 1908, the American squadron, upon reaching Yokohama, was accorded an "overwhelming reception"—an ovation later characterized by Roosevelt as the "most noteworthy incident of the cruise."[33]   It was reported that:

Officers, men, and correspondents were unanimous in describing the welcome of the Japanese as the warmest and most enthusiastic encountered on the entire voyage; and Ambassador O'Brien was assured that it outdid in magnificence even that accorded Admiral Togo when he returned from his brilliant victory over the Russian Fleet.[34]

In striking contrast was the visit to Amoy. For some time Washington had felt concern lest a stop at a Chinese port be interpreted as support of Peking against Tokyo.[35]   Hence it was decided that after leaving Yokohama the fleet should be divided, part sent to Manila for maneuvers and only part dispatched to Amoy. This rather obvious discrimination, the lack of concern for Chinese susceptibilities, plus the fact that the port selected for the call did not rival Shanghai in commercial importance and was, moreover, hundreds of miles distant from the capital city, not unnaturally dampened the enthusiasm of the Chinese. None the less, the Imperial Government appropriated 400,000 taels for entertainment, and telegrams of felicitation from all parts of China poured in upon the American consul at Amoy.[36]   Despite these expressions of friendship the Chinese reception after that in Japan was at best but an anticlimax.[37]   The American press, with a few exceptions, either overlooked the occasion entirely or, ignoring the

[33] Theodore Roosevelt, *Autobiography* (New York, 1913), 553.

[34] Thomas A. Bailey, *Roosevelt and the Japanese American Crisis* (Stanford, 1934), 286.

[35] *Ibid.*, 290–91.

[36] Two of these were from newspapers that three years before had taken a leading part in the anti-American boycott. See Thomas Bailey, "The World Cruise of the American Battleship Fleet, 1907–1909," *Pacific Historical Review*, I (December, 1932), 415.

[37] *Ibid.*

natural Chinese chagrin and often not mentioning that the fleet
had been divided, commented unfavorably upon the Chinese
apathy and lack of interest. "Evidently," said the *New York Times*,
"China is not Japan." [38]   Peking was keenly disappointed over the
visit and over the American reaction.

From this point it seemed that even the stars in their courses
fought against Governor T'ang and the success of his mission.   On
November 15 news was received of the deaths (within a few hours
of each other) of the Empress Dowager and the Young Emperor
Kuang Hsü.   A two-year-old child, Pu-yi, now ascended the
Dragon Throne; his father Prince Ch'un was chosen Regent; and
his aunt, Kuang Hsü's widow, became the new Empress Dowager. [39]
Whether the new regime would be progressive or reactionary was
unknown, but it was thought that a crisis, perhaps internal revolution and the end of the dynasty, was at hand.   In America, however, the tendency was to regard the situation with optimism. [40]
It was not realized that Yuan's participation in the *coup d'état* of
1898, Kuang Hsü's last wish for Yuan's execution, and Yuan's
opposition to the selection of Pu-yi as successor to the throne all
combined to draw upon the Viceroy the anger and resentment
of the late emperor's widow and brother. [41]   They were anxious
for an excuse to break him and only T'ang's success in securing
American aid sufficient to counteract Japanese aggression could
strengthen his position and prevent his dismissal from office. [42]   Yet
that part of T'ang's mission had failed almost before it had begun.

[38] November 2, 1908.   See also, *New York Herald*, October 31, 1908; *Albany Evening
Journal*, October 30, 1908; New York *Evening Post*, October 30, 1908; Charleston
News and Courier, November 8, 1908; *New York Tribune*, November 12, 1908.   In most
papers the visit of the fleet to China received no editorial comment.

[39] *Papers Relating to the Foreign Relations of the United States, 1908* (Washington, 1912),
116.

[40] *Montgomery Advertiser*, November 18, 1908; also, *Seattle Daily Times*, November 16,
1908; *Detroit Journal*, November 17, 1908; Washington *Evening Star*, November 15, 1908;
Wheeling Register, November 17, 1908; Des Moines *Register and Leader*, November 22,
1908; *Leavenworth Times*, November 18, 1908.

[41] J. O. P. Bland and E. Backhouse, *China Under the Empress Dowager* (London, 1910),
458–60; Croly, *op. cit.*, 276; Reid, *op. cit.*, 17.

[42] Croly, *op. cit.*, 276; Reid, *op. cit.*, 17.

The Roosevelt administration was already on the point of signing an agreement relating to China—signing it not with Peking but with Tokyo.

IV

In the fall of 1907 Mr. Aoki, the Japanese Ambassador in Washington, had proposed to Roosevelt a Japanese-American agreement similar to that recently reached by Japan and France. Roosevelt had responded cordially but the Japanese Government had declined to accept the proposal. In early October, 1908, however, Mr. Takahira, the new Japanese Ambassador was instructed to ascertain whether Roosevelt was willing to enter into an understanding similar to that suggested in the previous year by Mr. Aoki. The Japanese Cabinet had changed and the new ministry, headed by Count Katsura, regretted that the proposal had not been adopted.[43] Why had the Japanese position shifted? Roosevelt's conciliatory policy in the California school question and the voyage of the battleship fleet may have been in part responsible. Probably of greater importance was the desire of the European Entente Powers to check any understanding between the United States and Germany, and Japan's determination to prevent the successful culmination of Straight's and T'ang's projects.

Roosevelt apparently received Takahira's overtures in the same hearty manner he had shown toward Aoki, for on October 26, 1908, the Japanese Ambassador handed to the President the draft form for a joint declaration, as approved by his government. On November 7 the same proposals were submitted to Secretary Root.[44]

Willard Straight, who as a member of the State Department[45] was consulted regarding the negotiations, was seriously concerned

[43] Philip C. Jessup, *Elihu Root* (New York, 1938), II, 35.

[44] Jessup states that "Whether or not the matter was first discussed informally by Root and Takahira, who were on terms of very friendly intimacy, does not appear . . ." *ibid.*, 35–36.

[45] Straight had been assigned temporarily to the Division of Far Eastern Affairs in the Department of State.

for the future of his own and of T'ang's negotiations, and questioned the advisability of making a joint declaration of this nature. He wrote:

The effect of such an exchange of views upon our relations with other powers might . . . be unfortunate. . . . Our present position in the Far East is particularly satisfactory. We have the confidence of China. Germany is anxious to co-operate with us, and other powers respect our beneficent influence in Far Eastern affairs.[46]

Straight went on to explain that Germany, as the only power which would then have no understanding with Tokyo, might be offended by such a move. Moreover, Japanese agreements with England, France, and Russia "instead of guaranteeing the open door and the integrity of China more firmly" had constituted "a recognition of special spheres of influence which [had] been acquired at China's expense." Doubtlessly an understanding between Japan and the United States would be regarded by Peking as similarly hostile to its interests. Particularly would this be true in view of the inclusion in the proposed declaration of an agreement to maintain the existing status quo—a phrase which might later be interpreted in favor of the Japanese position at the expense of China and the United States. Also, as Straight was quick to note, the Japanese draft made no mention of the territorial integrity of China. The United States, he warned Secretary Root,

is so far definitely committed . . . to the support of the *territorial integrity and administrative entity* of China that subscription to a declaration which did not confirm its former expression would be a severe blow to American prestige in the Orient, a prestige attained largely by adherence to this very principle, and our consent to the omission thereof would be interpreted as a sign of weakness and surrender on the part of the Government.[47]

Although Root was unwilling to accept Straight's general thesis, that nothing was to be gained and much to be lost by joining Japan in a statement of policy, he did suggest to Takahira that to the

[46] Jessup, *op. cit.*, II, 37, quoting from the Archives of the Department of State.
[47] *Ibid.*

Japanese draft there be added the phrase "and to exercise their influence to maintain the territorial integrity and administrative entity of China, in accordance with the policy frequently declared by both of them." "I am," he wrote, "inclined to think that without some such clause both countries might be regarded as having abandoned that position, which, of course, neither of us wishes to do."[48] Takahira replied that the situation had so changed that the inclusion of the suggested clause "was unnecessary and might affect the susceptibilities of the Chinese." However, after further conversations and an exchange of notes, it was agreed that the final text should state a determination "to preserve the common interests of all powers in China by supporting by all pacific means at their disposal the independence and integrity of China and the principle of equal opportunity for commerce and industry of all nations in that Empire."[49] It will be noted that the word "territorial" was omitted.

By November 21, complete agreement had been reached concerning the phraseology of the declaration. On that day Root sent the text to Minister Rockhill and instructed him to show it confidentially to the Peking Ministry. He continued:

The Imperial Chinese Government will appreciate the fact that this action of the United States is the logical fruit of our traditional and frequently enunciated policy of friendly interest in and concern regarding the welfare of the Chinese Empire and has been prompted by our desire to reaffirm that policy by gaining a renewed definite and particular assurance of adherence thereto.

The Department feels that such a declaration should be peculiarly satisfactory to the Imperial Chinese Government at this time and I rely upon you to insure its most beneficial effects.[50]

Rockhill reported that when he showed the text of the agreement to Yuan Shih-k'ai he was "surprised" to be met "with considerable

[48] *Ibid.*

[49] *Ibid.*, II, 37–38; United States, Senate (61st Cong., 2nd Sess., Document No. 357), *Treaties, Conventions, International Acts, Protocols,* and *Agreements between the United States and Other Powers, 1776–1909,* compiled by William M. Malloy (Washington, 1910), I, 1045–47.

[50] Jessup, *op. cit.,* II, 38–39, quoting from the Archives of the Department of State.

disappointment and some irritation." The Chinese Viceroy asked whether the notes would be exchanged if the Chinese Government objected, and when informed that they undoubtedly would be, complained that "the United States' desire to strengthen the status quo in China could have been more effectually accomplished" if Washington had awaited the arrival of the special Chinese Ambassador. The Japanese, thought Yuan, had rushed through the agreement in order to checkmate T'ang's mission.[51] The following day, however, the Viceroy reported that after a careful re-examination of the proposed declaration the Chinese were "entirely satisfied," and their first misapprehensions dissipated.[52]

Secretary Root decided, perhaps as a result of the Chinese reaction, to delay the signature of the agreement until after T'ang's arrival.[53] However, since the Japanese already had made public announcement of the conclusion of the agreement,[54] this was no more than a gesture with little real significance. When the Chinese envoy reached Washington on November 30, he was shown the notes at noon of the same day. The formal signature took place at four o'clock that afternoon.[55] T'ang, "an impressionable and easily disconcerted man, was much depressed,"[56] but by the time he interviewed Secretary Root on December 9, he, like Yuan, had decided to put the best face possible on the matter. The Chinese translation of the notes, he remarked, was "not accurate." He had sent a "new and careful" one to Peking and was "confident" that his government "would be very much pleased by the transaction."[57]

The polite phrases of the Envoy and of his superiors in Peking did little to conceal their suspicion and keen disappointment.

[51] Rockhill to Root, December 3, 1908, *ibid.*, II, 39–40. For similar views concerning the Chinese reaction, see Croly, *op. cit.*, 275; and Rex to von Bülow, Peking, December 15, 1908, *Grosse Politik*, XXV, 99.

[52] Jessup, *op. cit.*, II, 40.

[53] *Ibid.*

[54] *New York Herald*, November 26, 1908; *Century*, LIX (February, 1911), 625.

[55] Jessup, *op. cit.*, II, 40.

[56] Croly, *op. cit.*, 276.

[57] Memorandum of Interview between T'ang and Root, December 9, 1908, Roosevelt Papers, Library of Congress (hereafter, L.C.).

Although Rockhill told his colleagues the Chinese were overjoyed, "this," reported the German minister, "is decidedly not the case. The Chinese have a great distrust of it." Na-t'ung, an important Manchu official, was said to have remarked pointedly to Rockhill that since several agreements about China had already been arranged, one more would not matter. In brief, the whole affair, as Count von Rex put it, "touched the Chinese most painfully."[58]

Was Peking's distrust of the Root-Takahira agreement and of the American policy embodied therein justified? On this there are two schools of thought. Professor Griswold maintains that in recognizing the "existing *status quo*" the United States had endorsed the many special privileges which Japan had, or claimed to have obtained, in Manchuria; that recognition of and acquiescence in the leaseholds, railway, mining and other rights transferred from Russia to Japan by the Treaty of Portsmouth, the spheres of influence recognized by Japan's treaties with Russia, England and France, and above all the principle, so firmly established by the Anglo-Japanese Alliance of 1905, that propinquity itself creates special interests, were now a part of the American Far Eastern policy; that instead of supporting China against Japan the United States had bound itself to a policy of friendly noninterference in Japan's Manchurian ventures. "With Japan inflamed over the immigration crisis and confronted by new exclusion laws," he suggests, "it would be fantastic to suppose that she would have handed over to the United States two such munificent concessions as a pledge to keep hands off the Philippines and to respect the open door and the territorial integrity of China. She had given the first concession. What had she received in return?"[59] Was it not recognition of her predominant position in Manchuria, just as the Taft-Katsura agreement of 1905, in exchange for a similar assurance, had given her a free hand in Korea? Several pieces of evidence do suggest that this was both the Japanese and the American understanding.

[58] Rex to von Bülow, Peking, December 15, 1908, *Grosse Politik*, XXV, 96–98.
[59] Griswold, *op. cit.*, 124–30.

On October 21, 1908, Count Komura, Minister of Foreign Affairs, in an interview with J. C. O'Laughlin was asked whether Japan still upheld the principles of the open door and the integrity of China. "Those have been, and continue to be, our principles," replied Komura.

"Do you include Manchuria and Mongolia for the purposes of that declaration within China?" queried O'Laughlin.

"No," was the blunt rejoinder. Komura went on to say:

In Mongolia we have very slight interests. But in Manchuria we have a condition that may be described as anomalous. Southern Manchuria constitutes our outer line of defense. We feel sure the present Russian Government will not renew the war against us. We are not so sure about a future Russian Government. Therefore we must see to it that our interests are not disturbed and that we are in a position to protect ourselves.

However, he continued, "Japan has no intention, either in Manchuria or in any part of China" of violating "the principle of the Open Door." [60]

O'Laughlin was not permitted to take stenographic notes of the interview, but immediately thereafter he wrote out a memorandum of the conversation and forwarded it to Roosevelt. That document now bears the stamp, "Department of State, December 2, 1908," and the notation, "Read by Root and Bacon." Whether or not it reached Roosevelt before the signing of the Root-Takahira agreement cannot be ascertained. It is significant, however, that Komura, in a conversation with an American known to be close to Roosevelt, [61] definitely excluded Manchuria from the scope of a statement relating to the integrity of China, and did so while negotiations looking toward a joint declaration of policy were in progress. There is no evidence to suggest that the Foreign Minister later modified the stand he had taken. Indeed, later events indicate that Japan adhered firmly to this position.

The nearest approach to an authoritative explanation of the

---

[60] For the whole conversation, see the memorandum of October 21, 1908, Roosevelt Papers, L.C.

[61] O'Laughlin is characterized as one of Roosevelt's "intimate correspondents" by Jessup, *op. cit.*, II, 343. He served for a few months at the close of Roosevelt's administration as Assistant Secretary of State.

American interpretation is to be found in a number of statements made at a later date by Theodore Roosevelt. In December, 1910, he wrote to President Taft:

> Our vital interest is to keep the Japanese out of our country and at the same time to preserve the good will of Japan. The vital interest of the Japanese, on the other hand, is in Manchuria and Korea. It is, therefore, peculiarly our interest not to take any steps as regards Manchuria which will give the Japs cause to feel, with or without reason, that we are hostile to them, or a menace—in however slight a degree—to their interests. . . . I utterly disbelieve in the policy of bluff. . . . I do not believe in our taking a policy anywhere unless we can make good; and as regards Manchuria, if the Japanese choose to follow a course of conduct to which we are adverse, we cannot stop it unless we are prepared to go to war, and a successful war about Manchuria would require a fleet as good as that of England, plus an army as good as that of Germany. The Open Door policy in China was an excellent thing, and I hope it will be a good thing in the future, so far as it can be maintained by a general diplomatic agreement; but, as has been proved by the whole history of Manchuria, while under Russia and under Japan, the "Open Door" policy, as a matter of fact, completely disappears as soon as a powerful nation determines to disregard it, and is willing to run the risk of war rather than forego its intentions.[62]

Similar statements made to Secretary Knox[63] suggest that Roosevelt's China policy was determined by what he considered a more urgent matter. In order to maintain peace with Japan and at the same time to protect the American position in the Philippines it is not improbable that he did agree tacitly not to interfere with Japanese ambitions in Manchuria.

On the other hand, it may be argued that if the State Department had no official knowledge of the qualifications placed by Komura on the phrase "the integrity of China" (and there is no evidence that it had),[64] it could not be considered to have given its consent thereto. From this point of view the joint declaration hid no "bargain" detrimental to China but should be accepted at its face value and interpreted according to the exact legal and

[62] Roosevelt to Taft, December 22, 1910, Roosevelt Papers, L.C.

[63] Knox to Taft, December 19, 1910, Knox Papers, L.C.

[64] Statements made by Bailey and by Jessup suggest that both the State Department Archives and the Root papers are silent on this point.

technical meaning of its words. Japan had perhaps reversed her policy of the previous year (when she turned down the Aoki proposal) not because she received new concessions, but because she feared the results of T'ang's visit and wished to prevent its success.[65] Finally, it is suggested, the United States, if not Japan, was motivated by a desire to ease the tension which existed between the two countries, and to restore cordial relations between them; hence the agreement merely reaffirmed but in no way altered the American position. Secretary Root himself wrote, many years after the event:

My arrangements . . . negatived the special interests of Japan in China. My idea was that both the United States and Japan had rights and interests in China—there was more interest and more occasion for exercise of rights on the part of Japan, but they were the same rights as ours though vastly more important for them than for us.[66]

Whichever interpretation is accepted, it is difficult to believe that the American Secretary of State really expected, as he wrote to Rockhill, that the agreement would be "peculiarly satisfactory" to China. Both Straight and the American Ambassador in Tokyo, Mr. O'Brien, had warned of the probability of a hostile reaction. Nor can Rockhill's "surprise" at Yuan's objections be accepted as genuine, unless it is assumed that the American diplomat was singularly blind and insensitive to Peking's suspicions of Japan.

---

[65] Sir Claude MacDonald, the British Ambassador to Japan, informed London that the Tokyo government recently had "ascertained that the German Emperor is awaiting the arrival of Tong Shao Yi for the purpose, if possible, of sowing dissension between China and Japan." Although they did not think he would succeed, the Japanese Minister for Foreign Affairs took the precaution of warning the Chinese Envoy. See *British Documents on the Origins of the World War, 1898–1914*, ed. G. P. Gooch and Harold Temperley (London, 1926–30), VIII, 461. T'ang was told that "Japan was China's best friend" and that an alliance between his government and "any other power, would be regarded by Japan as meaning suspicion of her." Memorandum of interview between Root and T'ang Shao-yi, December 9, 1908, Roosevelt Papers, L.C. Clearly Tokyo did not intend that the T'ang mission, at least in its entirety, should succeed.

[66] Jessup, *op. cit.*, II, 40–41, quoting a letter from Root to Jessup, September 13, 1932. For further analysis of the Root-Takahira agreement see Thomas A. Bailey, *A Diplomatic History of the American People* (New York, 1940), 574–75; Griswold, *op. cit.*, 129; A. Gerard, *Ma Mission au Japon, 1907–1914* (Paris, 1919), 99–100; Reid, *op. cit.*, 18–19; Ernest B. Price, *The Russo-Japanese Treaties of 1907–1916 Concerning Manchuria and Mongolia* (Baltimore, 1933), 42; Tyler Dennett, *Roosevelt and the Russo-Japanese War* (New York, 1925), 314–15.

Certainly, in view of the Chinese aspirations toward an understanding with the United States—aspirations well known in diplomatic circles—the conclusion of a joint declaration with Japan at this particular time hardly could be regarded as less than a direct rebuff. So it was understood in Peking. [67]

The Chinese perhaps would have been touched even more painfully (to use Rex's phrase) had they glimpsed Roosevelt's correspondence with Rockhill and Ambassador James Bryce. In 1908 the Dalai Lama, who in 1904 had fled from his capital because of a British invasion, was preparing to return to Lhasa and was understood to be taking with him new plans for opposing British influence in Tibet. [68] While the Dalai Lama was in Peking Rockhill, himself a Tibetan scholar of distinction, had a long talk with him and forwarded a report of the conversation to Roosevelt. The account of this "extraordinary interview" struck the President as so important that he gave it to Bryce who, in turn, sent it to the English Government. "If we can do a good turn to England in this matter," Roosevelt then wrote to Rockhill, "I shall be glad; and if you find out anything as to what passes between the Lama and the Chinese at Peking, pray let me know about it in full." [69] On the same day he informed Bryce:

I have sent your letter to Rockhill calling his especial attention to Morley's statement as to how useful it would be to know anything that passes between the Lama and the Chinese at Peking, and have asked Rockhill to let me know if he can find out anything on the subject. If he does I shall forward it to you. [70]

Apparently Rockhill was successful in the task assigned him, for on December 17 Roosevelt thanked him for his communication about the Dalai Lama: "It was just what I wanted." [71] One wonders whether the favor to England was likewise a kindness to America's good friend China.

[67] *Century*, LIX (February, 1911), 625.
[68] Reid, *op. cit.*, 66 and 338.
[69] Roosevelt to Rockhill, September 7, 1908, Roosevelt Papers, L.C.
[70] Roosevelt to James Bryce, September 7, 1908, Roosevelt Papers, L.C.
[71] Roosevelt to Rockhill, December 17, 1908, Roosevelt Papers, L.C.

V

The special Chinese Envoy to the United States remained in Washington for some weeks after the signature of the Root-Takahira agreement.[72] During that time any lingering hope he may have had of securing American political aid against Japan was dissipated fully by his conversations with Roosevelt. The United States, the President pointed out, had been unable to consider a guarantee of China's integrity in conjunction with China and Germany because it feared that such action might encourage the Peking Government to adopt a policy hostile to Japan. Should this have resulted in war, China would have been totally unarmed, and neither Germany nor the United States could have come to her defense—Germany because she was not in a position to send her fleet into the Pacific, and the United States because her public opinion would not have permitted it. "If there had to be an American-Japanese war, it could only be for purely American interests."[73] Roosevelt could hardly add, though he frequently expressed the view in private correspondence, that both the Chinese and the German Kaiser were so "jumpy" and unreliable that one could have only the most cautious dealings with them.[74]

For the moment T'ang's efforts to secure financial aid seemed to have a better chance of success than the political aspects of his program and throughout December negotiations proceeded smoothly. The partial failure of his mission, however, had had violent repercussions in Peking. Yuan Shih-k'ai, regarded by westerners as the strongest and most progressive of the Chinese statesmen, was dismissed from office; T'ang was recalled abruptly from America; and the loan negotiations were brought to an end. There were "suspicions in Washington of Japanese activity in high quarters at Peking."[75] Tokyo, it was thought, had used the Root-

---

[72] Croly, *op. cit.*, 276–80.

[73] Roosevelt also told Bernstorff that he had explained his views "quite frankly" to the Chinese Ambassador, "Tong Shao-yi," and added: "Lies had short legs. One is always found out." See Bernstorff to the Foreign Office, January 2, 1909, *Grosse Politik*, XXV, 97.

[74] Roosevelt to Arthur Lee, October 17, 1908, Roosevelt Papers, L.C.

[75] January 9, 1909. Griswold, *op. cit.*, 140 n. 1, quoting from the Rockhill Papers.

Takahira agreement to convince the Prince Regent of the hopelessness of securing American support. Yuan's position, already insecure, thus had been undermined further and his fall from office made inevitable.[76] The move took the State Department by surprise. Apparently neither it nor the British Foreign Office had foreseen this as a possible consequence of the recent Japanese-American accord.[77] It was something, Straight thought, that the Japanese had been planning for years—yet it came so unexpectedly that he could but laugh at "the ridiculous figure he and all concerned were cutting."[78]

The American press, for its part, was not only surprised, but failed almost completely to grasp the significance of the chain of events which had begun with the conclusion of the Root-Takahira agreement and ended with the dismissal of Yuan. News items from Peking had reported that the entry of the United States into the circle of nations with dual agreements concerning China had caused both surprise and apprehension. The terms, it was remarked, were "definite with regard to American interests," but "vague with reference to China." Like similar arrangements it would not, it was feared, "prevent the development of Japan's forward policy in Manchuria."[79] None the less, in the newspapers in the United States the declaration was welcomed almost unanimously, and was acclaimed as a great victory for American diplomacy, an assurance of peace in the Pacific, and a renewed guarantee for the open door and the integrity of China. The agreement, it was thought, "should be in no respect unwelcome to China," but rather should be hailed "as calculated greatly to contribute to her

[76] Croly, *op. cit.*, 276; Reid, *op. cit.*, 16–17; *Springfield Republican*, January 7, 1909. Some writers present the view that Yuan was dismissed simply because the new Peking Government strongly disliked him. This is implied, for example, by H. B. Morse and H. F. MacNair, *Far Eastern International Relations* (New York, 1931), 536.

[77] MacDonald, the British Ambassador at Tokyo, complained indignantly at Yuan's dismissal. Komura explained that Yuan received only what he deserved, according to Gerard, *op. cit.*, 103. See also, Reid, *op. cit.*, 21.

[78] Archibald Butt, *Taft and Roosevelt: the Intimate Letters of Archie Butt* (New York, 1930), 273–74.

[79] *New York Tribune*, December 3, 1908; *Nation*, LXXXVII (December 10, 1908), 564–65.

welfare and to guarantee her security."[80]   It should be particularly welcome at the beginning of a new and untried regency when a complete transformation of the governmental system was in progress, when China, if ever, had need of honest and disinterested moral support.   The agreement between the United States and Japan "should be worth immeasurably more to the Middle Kingdom than any 'alliance'" concerning which there had been "so much visionary vaporing."   That there was some dissatisfaction in Peking was not at all surprising, since all Chinese could not be expected to be fully acquainted with the fixed principles of American foreign policy.   They would soon come to realize, however, that the declaration was far more effective and potent than they had supposed.[81]   It indicated clearly that the United States and Japan were China's natural friends and allies.   Their joint declaration would "suffice to warn off other nations which might . . . be tempted once more to renew their maneuvers against the territorial integrity of China."[82]   Any further encroachments would now lead to serious international complications.[83]   Under the new arrangement not only was China's territorial integrity guaranteed, but the exchange of notes between the United States and Japan gave definite assurance that China's progress along the best lines, industrial and political, would be promoted.[84]   Its importance could "not be overestimated in respect of its effect to maintain peace between the two nations, the peace of the Pacific, the territorial integrity of China, and the open door. . . . "[85]   To whomever the credit belonged, "whether to Mr. Roosevelt or Mr. Root or the Japanese statesmen" it could not be given too freely or too generously for it was "a patriotic service of the highest order."[86]

[80] *Boston Herald*, December 1, 1908; Louisville *Courier-Journal*, November 30, 1908.
[81] *New York Tribune*, December 3, 1908 and December 4, 1908.
[82] *Commercial and Financial Chronicle*, LXXXVII (December, 1908), 1451.
[83] *Salt Lake Tribune*, December 29, 1908; Portland *Morning Oregonian*, December 3, 1908.
[84] Philadelphia *Public Ledger*, November 30, 1909; *Commercial and Financial Chronicle*, LXXXVII (December, 1908), 1456.
[85] *Albany Evening Journal*, December 1, 1908.
[86] New York *Evening Post*, December 1, 1908.

Even the *New York Herald*, but recently so vociferously anti-Japanese, welcomed the joint declaration, and announced:

Every purpose which the *Herald* had in view has been achieved. America's material interest in Asia and her territorial possessions in the Pacific are effectively safeguarded now that Japan has been forced, thanks to the *Herald*'s campaign, to renounce a policy that threatened the independence, political and commercial, of China.[87]

Only a few newspapers questioned the value of the agreement. One, the *Detroit Journal*, asked, "Is Japan tying Uncle Sam's hands?" It would be much easier it continued, to be enthusiastic if the agreement were with any other nation, for "it would be so like Japan to see the wisdom of such a treaty, and give no serious thought to the matter of observing the terms . . . should occasion arise to do something specifically provided against in the compact.[88] The New York *Press* also doubted the wisdom of "tying up" with an Asiatic power.[89] The editor of the *Springfield Republican*, whose comments during the entire period showed greater insight than did the editorials of any other paper, remarked on the skill of Japanese diplomacy and saw in the Root-Takahira agreement the reason for Yuan's fall from office.[90] These and a few other dissenting voices were, however, lost amidst the sounds of rejoicing—rejoicing over the new guarantees of the open door and integrity of China!

In conclusion it may be pointed out that, although the response of the press to the *Herald*'s campaign for an alliance with China had indicated clearly an unwillingness on the part of the American

---

[87] *New York Herald*, December 4, 1908. Other papers which voiced their strong approval of the Root-Takahira agreement included: *San Francisco Chronicle*, December 10, 1908; *Wheeling Register*, November 20, 1908; *Houston Post*, November 30, 1908; *Christian Science Monitor*, December 3, 1908; *Topeka State Journal*, December 2, 1908; *Milwaukee Journal*, December 3, 1908; *Indianapolis News*, November 30, 1908; *Cleveland Plain Dealer*, November 29, 1908; *Ohio State Journal*, December 3, 1908; *Charleston News and Courier*, December 1, 1908; *Richmond Times Dispatch*, November 30, 1908; New York *Sun*, December 5, 1908; Washington *Evening Star*, November 30, 1908; *Literary Digest*, XXXVII (December 12, 1908), 883; *World Today*, XVI (January, 1909), 9; *Nation*, LXXXVII (December 10, 1908), 564–65; *American Journal of International Law*, III (January, 1909), 168; *Review of Reviews*, XXXIX (January, 1909), 3.

[88] *Detroit Journal*, November 28, 1908.

[89] New York *Press*, quoted in the *Literary Digest*, XXXVII (December 5, 1908), 832.

[90] *Springfield Republican*, January 7, 1909.

people to *fight* for the integrity of China, the press had not indicated any lessening of *concern* for Chinese integrity. The maintenance of China as a political entity had come to be regarded as essential for the preservation of the Open Door, and that in turn was considered a matter of vital importance to the United States. The majority of the American newspapers, without regard to sectional or party lines, clearly favored the continued diplomatic and moral support of those policies. Theodore Roosevelt's belief that Japan's advance into Manchuria was inevitable and should not be blocked was not, insofar as can be judged by a study of the press, shared by his fellow countrymen. Had they understood the Japanese interpretation of the Root-Takahira agreement they would, in all probability, have agreed with Willard Straight that, like the Korean withdrawal, "it was a terrible diplomatic blunder to be laid at the door of T. R." [91]

[91] Croly, *op. cit.*, 276.

England and the United States, 1897–1899

By Nelson M. Blake*

Events of the last several years have given fresh proof of the gravitational pull which draws England and the United States together during periods of international crisis. As most students realize, this force in world politics first became clearly operative during the Spanish-American War. Not so generally understood, however, are certain antecedent and accompanying circumstances. The factors in the situation to which this study will give particular attention are these: the emergence of a movement for Anglo-American collaboration before 1898, the relation of this to the situation in the Far East, the mixed response of the British government and people to the actual outbreak of war in April, 1898, the seriousness with which an Anglo-American alliance was discussed during 1898, and the important role played by mobilized public opinion both in promoting this proposal and in making it politically impossible.

I. Development of Anglo-American Cordiality

As early as 1877 a British writer asserted that the Anglo-Saxons were inevitable conquerors who would within fifty years be in exclusive possession of the continents of North America, Africa, and Australia—thus achieving a monopoly of the undeveloped resources of the globe. He looked forward with approval to "a great commercial and political Anglo-Saxon league—an offensive and defensive alliance to maintain Anglo-Saxon civilization against the world."[1] This conviction that the Anglo-Saxons were a

*Nelson M. Blake is Associate Professor of History, Syracuse University.

[1] J. E. Chamberlain, "A Dream of Anglo-Saxondom," *The Galaxy*, XXIV (1877), 790.

chosen people uniquely endowed with a genius for government was a characteristic and widely-shared nineteenth century myth. All that was needed for the "race" to secure its imperial destiny was for its member nations to unite. An earnest evangelist for this gospel was the English journalist, W. T. Stead, editor first of the *Pall Mall Gazette* and then of the English *Review of Reviews*. One of Stead's admirers was Cecil Rhodes, who suggested that men of wealth and vision ought to contribute their fortunes to the endowing of a secret society on the pattern of the Jesuits to work for Anglo-Saxon union and the domination of the world.[2] Another rich builder of empires in the air, Andrew Carnegie, advocated the reunion of the United States and England as an Anglo-Saxon federal republic.[3]

But the enthusiasts for Anglo-American unity were sowing their seed on hard soil. The instinct of most Americans was still to regard England as their country's hereditary enemy. Such was the tendency of the national history taught in the schools; such was the prejudice of a generation which well remembered the unfriendliness of the English upper classes during the Civil War. The American Irish—most of them only one or two generations removed from their ancestral sod—hated Britain bitterly and their hatred was a potent factor in national affairs since their vote possessed crucial value in the closely contested elections of the eighties and nineties. American agrarian radicals were strongly Anglophobe because in their simple analysis the grievances of the Western farmer all stemmed from the gold standard imposed at the dictation of the British money power. Scarcely less hostile were such American expansionists as Theodore Roosevelt, Senator Henry

[2] W. T. Stead, ed., *The Last Will and Testament of Cecil John Rhodes with Elucidatory Notes* (London, 1902), 64–76.

[3] Andrew Carnegie, "A Look Ahead," *North American Review*, CLVI (June, 1893), 685–710. Interest in Carnegie's proposal was apparently keen because the *North American Review* published several other articles on the subject: Goldwin Smith, "Anglo-Saxon Union: A Response to Mr. Carnegie," CLVII (August, 1893), 170–85; Major Sir G. S. Clarke, "A Naval Union with Great Britain," CLVIII (March, 1894), 353–65; Arthur Silva White, "An Anglo-American Alliance," CLVIII (April, 1894), 484–93; Lord Charles Beresford and Capt. A. T. Mahan, "Possibilities of an Anglo-American Reunion," CLIX (November, 1894), 551–73.

Cabot Lodge of Massachusetts, and Senator John T. Morgan of Alabama. They were agitating for a great navy, an isthmian canal, strategic bases in the Caribbean and the Pacific, and—in their more exhilarated moments—the acquisition of Canada. They assumed that the rise of the United States to world power must inevitably be resented and resisted by the British and they were not dismayed at the possibility of an Anglo-American conflict. Appeals for Anglo-Saxon unity based on sentimental theories of race met little response.

Events, however, were moving in a direction which made many men turn to the idea of an Anglo-American understanding on the practical basis of common interest. The conclusion of the Franco-Russian alliance in 1894 was a disquieting development to many Englishmen. It emphasized the isolation of Great Britain and opened up the possibility that a combination of some or all of the European powers might fall upon the Empire and destroy it. If this danger seemed as yet somewhat remote, a more immediate problem concerned the Far East where Russian pressure was increasing and where developments which might close the ports of China to British commerce were threatened.

Amidst such threats of impending trouble, a growing number in Britain saw the great advantage of attempting to transform the traditional hostility of the United States into friendship. American travellers commented on the increasing cordiality of their British hosts.[4] Early in 1895 the great London *Times* recognized the new trend by engaging George W. Smalley, one of the most prominent American journalists, to write a daily dispatch from New York.[5] For ten years Smalley was to be a powerful influence in improving Anglo-American relations.

It was natural that English publicists should be quicker than American to point out that the United States had much to lose in the event of Britain's defeat in a great world war. As early as

[4] New York *Sun*, May 5, 1895; *Boston Evening Transcript*, November 2, 1895.

[5] New York *World*, May 12, 1895; Bayard to Cleveland, May 24, 1895, Cleveland Papers. These and other private papers used in this study are all located in the Library of Congress.

1896, however, Professor George Burton Adams of Yale took his stand as a strong advocate of Anglo-American solidarity in the new stern age of world politics. "As for ourselves," he wrote, "in the narrow sense, it is no doubt true that, in any possible future, our position is far more secure than that of England, and yet it is certain that our own best and highest interests, and those of all men everywhere, demand the unity and common action of the Anglo-Saxon race."[6]

Though the Venezuelan boundary dispute was a temporary setback to the movement for closer relations, its eventual result was to promote them. Those who wanted to draw the countries together were impelled to work harder because of the war scare, while the American jingoes were mollified by Britain's final change of policy. In a year when the Kruger telegram incident had dramatized the unfriendliness of Germany the British government decided that it could ill afford to arouse further hostility in America. Not only was the boundary dispute settled but a general arbitration treaty would have been consummated except for the Senate's refusal to consent to ratification.

However disappointed the English may have been at the Senate's rough handling of this proposal, they had no reason to doubt the friendly intentions of the new McKinley administration. The President was cordial in his relations with Sir Julian Pauncefote, the British Ambassador, and made a particularly flattering reference to Anglo-American ideals in one of his early speeches.[7] More than satisfactory also was McKinley's appointment of the urbane and eloquent John Hay to the London Embassy. The administration's relations with England displayed their honeymoon spirit to the full on the occasion of Queen Victoria's Diamond Jubilee in June, 1897. Whitelaw Reid, the politically ambitious publisher of the *New York Tribune*, prevailed upon McKinley to send him as Ambassador Extraordinary to England where he

[6] *Why Americans Dislike England* (Philadelphia, 1896), 31.

[7] London *Times*, March 12, 1897; Bertha Ann Reuter, *Anglo-American Relations during the Spanish-American War* (New York, 1924), 59.

paraded, banqueted, and consorted with royalty to his heart's content—and Hay's amusement.[8]

The course of Anglo-American amity did not long run smooth. Within two weeks of the Queen's Jubilee the English and the Americans were exchanging insults as of old—the occasion being a leak to the press of a strongly-worded American note on the perennial issue of the seals in Behring Sea.[9] Likewise disappointing was the failure of the British government to offer more than fair words to the Wolcott Commission, which in fulfillment of a Republican campaign pledge visited England and the continent in 1897 seeking the remonetization of silver on an international basis.[10]

II. Great Britain and the Open Door Policy

But issues more important than either seals or silver were arising to draw England and the United States together again.   In December, 1897, the American public suddenly awakened to the seriousness of the Far Eastern situation.   A gigantic partition of the Chinese empire seemed to be in progress.   This development, which threatened to destroy the predominance of Great Britain in the China trade, had serious implications also for the United States.   Our material stake in the Far East was still small, but our ambition for the future was great.

In emphasizing the English origins of John Hay's Open Door note of 1899, scholars have failed to give proper weight to the fact that United States policy was also much influenced by two years of discussion of the question in the American press.   When the McKinley administration at first appeared to have no other policy than watchful waiting, New York businessmen were critical. "The non-committal attitude of the administration toward the

[8] Royal Cortissoz, *The Life of Whitelaw Reid* (New York, 1921), II, 215–18; William Roscoe Thayer, *The Life and Letters of John Hay* (Boston and New York, 1915), II, 160–61.   Cf. Reuter, *Anglo-American Relations*, 56–58.

[9] *New York Tribune*, July 16, 1897; Hay to Roosevelt, September 29, 1897, Theodore Roosevelt Papers.

[10] Cf. Allan Nevins, *Henry White: Thirty Years of American Diplomacy* (New York and London, 1930), 128; Jeannette P. Nichols, "Silver Diplomacy," *Political Science Quarterly*, XLVIII (December, 1933), 586.

present situation in China," asserted the New York *Journal of Commerce*, "is not at all satisfactory to the representatives of large mercantile interests in this city who are familiar with the possibilities of American trade in the far east."[11]   In January, 1898, Standard Oil, Westinghouse, Bethlehem Iron, Carnegie Steel, the China and Japan Trading Company and other firms joined in a move to urge upon the government the importance of resisting the establishment of exclusive trading rights in China by the partitioning powers.[12]

It was easier to point with alarm to the Far Eastern situation than to suggest an effective course of action.   Few Americans believed that the disintegration of China could be halted.   Some newspapers advocated that we share in the partition; others that we merely insist upon the preservation of our treaty rights despite any change of sovereignty.   Most of them advocated independent American action, but a few called for joint action with Great Britain and perhaps with Japan as well.[13]   Although not many Americans were ready for actual alliance, there was a growing belief that we shared common interests with the British.   In the words of George W. Smalley:

> There is a strong support here for England in China—partly interested because we mean to develop our Chinese trade and want open ports— partly anti-German Emperor—partly kinship, which, after all, does count as between England and other powers much as we may growl with her on our own account.[14]

Joseph Chamberlain and Arthur Balfour, two of the most influential members of the Salisbury government, urged that American sympathy for the Open Door be translated into official action. Since Ambassador Hay was sight-seeing with Henry Adams in

[11] Quoted in *Public Opinion*, XXIV (January 6, 1898), 6. See also *Outlook*, LVIII (January 1, 1898), 1; New York *Sun*, January 28, 1898; Charles Denby, Jr., "America's Opportunity in Asia," *North American Review*, CLXVI (January, 1898), 32–39.

[12] New York *Sun*, January 31, 1898.

[13] An alliance of those three nations, claimed the Memphis *Scimitar*, would be the "most direct and effective means of preventing a monopoly of Chinese markets by the European powers." *Public Opinion*, XXIV (January 6, 1898), 5–6. Cf. New York *Sun*, January 6, 1898, and *Outlook*, LVIII (January 8, 1898), 103.

[14] Letter to White, January 19, 1898, Henry White Papers.

Egypt, approaches were made to Henry White of the London
Embassy. The latter was too well posted on the conservative
spirit dominating the State Department to offer much encouragement, but he did read to the two ministers an interesting extract
from a letter written by Senator Lodge. If he had his way, said
Lodge, he would be glad to have the United States say to England
"that we would stand by her in her declaration that the ports of
China must be opened to all nations equally or to none." [15] The
result was a direct, though unofficial approach to President McKinley. In a memorandum dated March 8, 1898, Sir Julian Pauncefote inquired whether the British government could count on the
co-operation of the United States in opposing action by foreign
powers which might restrict freedom of commerce in China. The
American reply was a polite refusal on the grounds that we had
no information indicating that trade would be restricted through
foreign occupation of the Chinese ports. [16]

III. FRIENDSHIP IN THE SPANISH-AMERICAN WAR

But the American rebuff was not severe enough to discourage
Balfour and Chamberlain from the hope that sometime in the near
future the United States might take a more pronounced stand. It
was this consideration which dominated English policy toward
the Spanish-American War soon to break out. The close connection between the Cuban and Chinese crises was recognized at the
time. Early in March Sir George William Des Voeux, a distinguished British colonial administrator, publicly urged that
England should seize the opportunity of expressing cordial sympathy with the United States in her Cuban policy and should
pledge the support of the British fleet against any attack on the
American coasts. This would prevent war with Spain, make

[15] Nevins, *White*, 16. See also White to Hay, February 21, 1898, White Papers;
White to Lodge, March, 1898, White Letter Book.

[16] Alfred L. P. Dennis, *Adventures in American Diplomacy, 1896–1906* (New York,
1928), 170–71. The American decision must have been largely based on the administration's preoccupation with the Cuban crisis. Reports from Charles Denby, Sr.,
our Minister to China, gave little grounds for complacency. *Ibid.*, 180–81, 202–207.

general American sympathy with the English, and materially
assist in the solution of the China question. [17]

The British government's decision to support the United States
in its difficulties with Spain had been made almost two years before
and can be dated with rough accuracy. In May, 1896, Lord
Salisbury was advising Spain to reject President Cleveland's offer
of mediation in the Cuban situation, whereas in August, 1896, the
British Ambassador in Spain, reflecting a change in his government's policy, helped his American colleague thwart the effort
of the Spanish government to line up the European powers in a
common front opposed to American intervention. [18] Thereafter,
the British Foreign Office declined to lend support to any European
combination to protect the Spanish Empire against the United
States—an idea which the Austrian government supported with
consistency and which had some support from Germany and
France. [19]

As the Cuban crisis developed during the early months of 1898,
prevailing English opinion became increasingly sympathetic. For
one thing, the British were more inclined than other Europeans
to give the United States credit for humanitarian motives. But,
apart from this, England's isolation was arousing real concern and
America's good-will was ardently desired. Cause and effect became entangled. Approval in the United States for England's
policy in China led to English sympathy for us in our troubles with
Spain, while Americans reading of British support for the United
States discovered an unsuspected affection for England.

Appreciation for British friendship grew as trans-Atlantic reports

[17] New York *Sun*, March 9, 1898.

[18] Salisbury to the Queen, May 25, 1896, *Letters of Queen Victoria*, 3rd series, ed.
G. E. Buckle (London, 1930–32), III, 45; Taylor to Olney, August 18, 1896, Richard
Olney Papers; Orestes Ferrara, *The Last Spanish War: Revealed in "Diplomacy"* (New
York, 1937), 50–62.

[19] But subsequent British claims that England's opposition alone had saved the
United States from European intervention were misleading. Russia too opposed any
step vigorous enough to jeopardize her old reputation for friendship with America,
while elsewhere Spain encountered more sympathy than readiness for action. See
Ferrara, *Last Spanish War*, 79–111; and *Die Grosse Politik der Europäischen Kabinette,
1871–1914* (Berlin, 1922–27), XV, 3–19.

—frequently emanating from London—warned of the possibility that the continental governments might side with Spain in the event of war. The idea of an Anglo-Saxon alliance for mutual support in China and Cuba was soberly discussed. Ambassador Pauncefote's call on President McKinley in connection with the British Open Door proposal occasioned wild speculation. The suggestion that the British fleet might be available for the protection of our coasts was made in the English press and was even the subject of a question in the House of Commons.[20]

American diplomats found English sympathy very useful. Through the British Ambassador at Madrid we were kept well informed of what was going on in Spanish official circles, while in London Henry White was enabled to secure for the American navy two cruisers that had been built in England for Brazil. His daring proposal that the British government sell us destroyers from its own navy made a powerful appeal to Balfour and Chamberlain, but the step was not taken because of the objections of more cautious ministers.[21]

Despite all this, the English very much hoped that war between the United States and Spain could be prevented.[22] Much of McKinley's popularity in Britain arose from the belief that he was attempting to withstand the stampede of the jingoes. It was hoped that a demonstration of English sympathy with America would strengthen the President's hand and contribute to peace by inducing Spain to make concessions. When in April it appeared that the Spanish government was yielding to this pressure, British opinion, both official and unofficial, was earnest in its hope that war might now be avoided.

It was this hope that impelled England to participate in a bit of pageantry on April 7, 1898. The representatives of the six major

[20] London *Times*, March 9 and 11, 1898; Henry White to General Porter, March 12, 1898, White Letter Books.

[21] White to Hay, March 12, 1898, White Papers.

[22] Because of the need for England and America standing firm in the Far East, declared the London *Times* (March 29, 1898), it would particularly dislike to see the United States become involved in hostilities over Cuba.

European powers called in a body on President McKinley and presented a mild note expressing the hope that further negotiations between the United States and Spain would lead to an agreement which would both secure peace and afford guarantees for the re-establishment of order in Cuba. The President's formal reply acknowledged the disinterested character of this communication, but expressed confidence that equal appreciation would be shown for the unselfish endeavors of the United States to fulfill a duty to humanity by ending an insufferable situation. All sting was removed from the collective action by the fact that Pauncefote had not only made certain that the American government would not object to the presentation of the note, but had even submitted the text in advance to the State Department.[23]

A week later, however, steps were taken which were less innocuous and which might have abruptly terminated the infant *rapprochement*. English sympathy for America was subjected to severe strain by McKinley's war message of April 11 and the hysterical demonstrations of the next several days. Said the London *Times*:

In the eyes of the civilized world the case of the United States cannot but be seriously prejudiced by the manner in which it is now presented. Even those who most readily admit all that can be said about Spanish misgovernment in Cuba find themselves driven to ask whether Congress is a body that can fitly be intrusted with the task of punishment and reconstruction.[24]

These developments were a shock to the diplomatic colony. Sir Julian Pauncefote and his French colleague, Jules Cambon, had advised the Spanish Minister in the preparation of his memorandum of April 10 informing the United States of the Spanish decision to declare an armistice in Cuba.[25] Naturally they were distressed to see that document completely ignored. On April 14 the Washington representatives of the six powers met to see what

[23] Ferrara, *Last Spanish War*, 129–30; London *Times*, January 24, 1902.

[24] April 14, 1898.

[25] Polo to Gullon, April 12, 1898, *Spanish Diplomatic Correspondence and Documents, 1896–1900, Presented to the Cortes by the Minister of State* (Translation published by U. S. Department of State. Washington, 1905), 120.

further step might be taken. Invitations went out over the signature of Pauncefote and the meeting was held at the British Embassy. Both of these circumstances may be explained by the fact that the British Ambassador was *doyen* of the diplomatic corps. What was more remarkable was that Pauncefote had prepared the draft of a note which, it was proposed, each of the representatives should send to his home government suggesting collective action to urge upon the United States a favorable consideration of the Spanish note of April 10 "as offering a reasonable basis for an amicable solution, and as removing any grounds for hostile intervention which may have previously existed." [26] After extended discussion the ambassadors agreed to send identic dispatches to their home governments following the general lines of Pauncefote's draft but with some rather significant alterations—some of them made by Cambon in the process of translating the document into French. The strictures on the latest American steps were rendered more severe and it was proposed that the great powers should state categorically that intervention by the United States in Cuba would "not be justified." [27]

Serious misunderstanding was caused by the impression which prevailed—at least in German circles—that this step was proposed by the British government and perhaps represented the wish of Queen Victoria herself. This was not so. Pauncefote's role was a personal one and he was probably responding to the importunities of the Austrian Ambassador when he called the meeting and drafted the note. The vigor of the final document was intensified by Cambon and he, in turn, was influenced to press for strong measures through his intimacy with Archbishop Ireland, who was in Washington at the Pope's request working for peace. [28]

[26] Text made public by the German government. See *New York Tribune*, February 13, 1902.

[27] Bülow to the Emperor, April 15, 1898, *Die Grosse Politik*, XV, 22–24.

[28] Cf. London *Times*, February 12, 13, 15, 1902; New York *Sun*, February 13, 1902; George W. Smalley, *Anglo-American Memories*, 2nd Series (New York and London, 1912), 178–85; Ferrara, *Last Spanish War*, 139–51; Genevieve Tabouis, *Jules Cambon: par l'un des siens* (Paris, 1938), 90–91.

News of what had been going on came to the London government as an unpleasant surprise. To Balfour, who was in charge of the Foreign Office in the absence of Lord Salisbury, what was proposed seemed nothing less than reading the United States a lesson in international morality. Pauncefote was informed that the British government would cooperate to the extent of expressing the hope that the Cuban armistice might afford an opportunity for peaceful settlement, but it objected to committing itself to a judgment adverse to the United States.[29] Two days later a new instruction was sent to the ambassador stating that the government had resolved to take no action.[30] Joseph Chamberlain probably influenced the final decision. Much disturbed by the proposal from Washington, he protested that joint action would forfeit for Great Britain the American gratitude which she had won up to then by her sympathy.[31] Pauncefote's part in a proposed condemnation of the United States was a skeleton which for the time being remained safely hidden in the diplomatic closet. Thanks to Balfour and Chamberlain, the British government was saved from taking a step which would have aroused serious American resentment.

But American conduct during the final crisis did not entirely escape British criticism. On April 21 Queen Victoria wrote in her diary: "War seems hopelessly declared, and the respective Spanish and United States Ministers have left their posts! It is

[29] Blanche Dugdale, *Arthur James Balfour, First Earl of Balfour* (London, 1936), I, 262.

[30] *Parliamentary Debates*, 4th Series, CIII (February 14, 1902), 39.

[31] J. L. Garvin, *The Life of Joseph Chamberlain* (London, 1932), III, 299. It was not only the British government which regarded the proposal as futile and dangerous. The Russian Foreign Office disapproved; so also did the French and German; in the end the Austrian alone supported the idea. England was hardly justified in claiming later that she alone had frustrated a European combination against the United States. Nevertheless, her course had been such as to displease the Kaiser who appended to one of the German diplomatic documents some acid comments on the pharisaical conduct of a government which suggested measures to be taken by all the powers, apparently participated until they compromised themselves with the belligerents, then drew back, declared it had no part and secretly joined with the strongest of the combatants and incited it against the continental powers. *Die Grosse Politik*, XV, 28–29. Cf. Ferrara, *Last Spanish War*, 148–49; and L. B. Shippee, "Germany and the Spanish-American War," *American Historical Review*, XXX (July, 1925), 761.

monstrous of America." [32] The high Tory *Saturday Review* pronounced our action to be a "crime against humanity" [33] and
declared:

Whatever may be thought in Washington, in England we have not
forgotten what happened during the Venezuelan affair, nor more recently
the conduct of the United States with regard to the Behring seal fishery
question. The sudden effusion of friendliness toward England during
the past fortnight, so far from being grateful to us, fills us rather with a
sense of indecent humbug. . . . Whatever hysterical hypocrisy may
declare, there is no real friendliness as yet in England . . . toward the
Union. [34]

So strong indeed was English criticism at the end of April that
McKinley expressed disappointment to Smalley. Taking editorial
note of the President's perplexity, the London *Times* explained
that on the whole the English sided with the United States in
believing that Spanish misgovernment in Cuba justified American
intervention. On the matter of form English opinion was not so
clear and unanimous. Many believed that with a little more
patience everything could have been squeezed out of Spain without
the general inconvenience caused by war. [35]

But British criticism of the final steps which plunged America
into war was only a passing phenomenon. Except among the
extreme conservatives, opinion soon shifted back to its pro-American leaning. This contrasted with the hostile tone of most continental newspapers—a point which the British took pains to see
that we did not miss. French, German, and Austrian journals
were culled for anti-American sentiments which were quoted by
the British press and then requoted in the American.

[32] *Letters of Queen Victoria*, 3rd Series, III, 244.

[33] LXXXV (April 16, 1898), 513.

[34] LXXXV (April 30, 1898), 582. Similar sentiments were expressed in some of
the Canadian papers. In the Toronto *Mail and Express*, the following appeared:

No doubt if we knew what exactly is true
You're anxious for Cuba, not Cuba for you.
I'm sure that you wish it, would think it quite grand
To have the whole continent at your command.

Quoted in New York *Sun*, March 22, 1898.

[35] London *Times*, April 29, 1898.

The American response to these evidences of English friendship was such as to delight Henry White when he visited America in April. It was the old crowd of jingoes—Lodge, Morgan, Frye, and Foraker—who were now most anxious to stroke the lion's mane. [36] Gratitude was expressed in practical terms. Proposed new tonnage dues that might have injured British shipping were killed; appropriations to pay the damages assessed against the United States in the Behring Sea arbitration were quietly passed; negotiations for the regulation of sealing were taken out of the hands of John W. Foster whom the Canadians disliked; and plans were set in motion for a Joint High Commission to settle all outstanding difficulties between Canada and the United States. [37] To both Henry White and G. W. Smalley, President McKinley asserted that it was his great desire to bring about a friendly understanding with England during his term of office. [38]

IV. Discussion of an Anglo-American Alliance, 1898–99

In many quarters the friendly understanding was taken for granted and discussion revolved around the possibility of an alliance. To the *Outlook*, it seemed that the war's most important result might be "the creation of a good understanding between England and the United States, leading eventually to a real and definite alliance between them in the interest of the world's civilization." [39] Times had changed and Richard Olney might be cited as evidence. The champion of a stern anti-British policy in 1895 had by the end of 1897 become an outspoken advocate of Anglo-American co-operation. This was the subject of an address by the former Secretary of State at a New England dinner in New York

[36] Thayer, *John Hay*, II, 165–66; Nevins, *White*, 133–34. Cf. Lionel M. Gelber, *The Rise of Anglo-American Friendship: A Study in World Politics, 1898–1906* (London, 1938), 21–23.

[37] *Congressional Record*, XXXI (1898), 4007, 5853; London *Times*, April 29–30, 1898; Nevins, *White*, 134–35.

[38] White to Hay, April 30, 1898, White Papers; London *Times*, April 23, 29, 30, 1898.

[39] LVIII (April 30, 1898), 1060.

in December, 1897, and of another at Harvard University the following March.[40] There was, said Olney, a patriotism of race as well as of country—and the Anglo-American was as little likely to be indifferent to the one as to the other. So popular was the theme of race patriotism that during 1898 and 1899 no fewer than six books and fifty-six magazine articles dealing with the subject were published in the United States, Great Britain, and Canada.[41] Among the authors were Olney, Joseph Chamberlain, James Bryce, Sir Richard Temple, Lord Charles Beresford, Sir Charles Dilke, Carl Schurz, and Lyman Abbott, as well as a host of lesser luminaries. Not all of these advocated an Anglo-American alliance, but all dealt with the matter as a vital issue of the day.

The form that such an understanding might take was disputed. The anti-imperialists of both countries were still talking largely in terms of a general arbitration treaty despite the recent manhandling of the Olney-Pauncefote pact.[42] But the expansionists dreamed of bolder projects. "Shoulder to shoulder," Joseph Chamberlain told John Hay, "we could command peace the world over. . . . I should rejoice in an occasion in which we could fight side by side. The good effect of it would last for generations." Hay assured the President that he had given no encouragement to what seemed an "impracticable" suggestion; yet he thought that the new attitude of the British was most valuable to America and might be still more so in the near future.[43] Within a month the Ambassador gave public testimony to his own conviction that the United States should join with England in shouldering the white man's burden. For his most important speech abroad, at the Lord Mayor's banquet on April 21, Hay chose as his subject "A Partnership in Beneficence."[44]

[40] Cf. Olney to Henry White, March 14, 1898, White Papers. The second address attracted much interest when published as a magazine article: "International Isolation of the United States," *Atlantic Monthly*, LXXXI (May, 1898), 577–88.

[41] Based on a study of: Library of Congress, *Select List of References on Anglo-Saxon Interests* (2nd issue with additions, Washington, 1906).

[42] London *Times*, April 22, 1898; May 3, 1898.

[43] Hay to McKinley, April 4, 1898, Charles S. Olcott, *The Life of William McKinley* (Boston and New York, 1916), II, 130.

[44] *Addresses of John Hay* (New York, 1907), 78–79.

English politicians began to compete in pledges of friendship for the United States. Sir William Harcourt, the Liberal leader, asserted that the fixed and unalterable basis of Liberal policy was peace and friendship with America.[45] When Hay expressed to Chamberlain the hope that he would not allow the opposition party to have a monopoly on expressions of good-will, the Colonial Secretary was encouraged—if encouragement was necessary—to outdo Harcourt on the hands-across-the-sea theme.[46] In a speech at Birmingham on May 13, Chamberlain drew a gloomy picture of world politics. He dealt with the threat of Russia and Britain's perilous isolation. The first duty of England was to draw closer together the British Empire. As for the second:

It is to establish and maintain bonds of amity with our kinsmen across the Atlantic. . . . I do not know what the future has in store for us, I do not know what arrangements may be possible with the United States, but this I know and feel—that the closer, the more cordial, the fuller and the more definite, these arrangements are with the consent of both people, the better it will be for both and for the world. . . . And I even go so far as to say that, terrible as war may be, even war itself would be cheaply purchased if in a great and noble cause the Stars and Stripes and the Union Jack should wave together (*loud and prolonged cheers*) over an Anglo-Saxon alliance.[47]

The speech was an international sensation. In Madrid it was considered anti-Spanish and resentment against England was intensified.[48] Chamberlain's hostility to Russia had been as patent as his pro-Americanism and the speech was denounced in St. Petersburg and also in Paris, the other terminal of the Franco-Russian alliance.[49] In Berlin the Kaiser warned the British Ambassador that an Anglo-American alliance was unlikely; the United States was anxious to secure Britain's good-will during

[45] London *Times*, May 9, 1898.

[46] Hay to H. C. Lodge, May 25, 1898, Tyler Dennett, *John Hay: From Poetry to Politics* (New York, 1933), 220.

[47] Garvin, *Chamberlain*, III, 301–302.

[48] Drummond Wolff to Salisbury, May 15, 1898, *British Documents on the Origins of the War*, ed. G. P. Gooch and Harold Temperley (London, 1926–38), II, 253.

[49] *New York Herald*, May 15, 1898. Cf. *Public Opinion*, XXIV (May 19, 1898), 616.

the war, but when peace came she would revert to isolation.[50] But Chamberlain professed not to "care a hang" what they said about his speech on the continent. It was the English and American reaction that he was watching. In his own country the impenitently anti-American *Saturday Review* pronounced the proposal to be the "most delusive of dreams,"[51] but in most other quarters the response was enthusiastic. The *Daily Chronicle*, usually critical of Chamberlain, called his speech a "brave and historic plea," while the London *Times* thought it a foregone conclusion that events should take the direction the Colonial Secretary had suggested.[52]

In the United States the English statesman's words were well received. "Mr. Chamberlain may have been dreaming," asserted the *New York Herald*, "but it would be the consummation of the most momentous event since the Christian era if the dream came true."[53] The New York *Evening Post*, usually friendly to England, supported Chamberlain's idea; so also did the *New York Tribune*, often hostile. Even among the politicians, where kind words for Britain had always been considered dangerous, there was friendly comment. Senators Cullom of Illinois, Foraker of Ohio, Platt and Depew of New York all expressed public approval of the Chamberlain speech.[54]

Details of an actual treaty of alliance supposed to be under discussion in Washington were published in the London *Daily Telegraph*.[55] Despite a denial that such negotiations were in progress, interest in the idea mounted. Five hundred distinguished guests attended an Anglo-American dinner in London on June 3 and the next month the Yankeephils organized an Anglo-American

[50] Lascelles to Salisbury, May 26, 1898, *British Documents on the Origins of the War*, I, 34–35.

[51] LXXXV (May 21, 1898), 669.

[52] Quoted in *New York Herald*, May 14, 1898. The *Admiralty and Horse Guards Gazette* called for an immediate alliance with both the United States and Japan. Arthur J. Marder, *The Anatomy of British Sea Power* (New York, 1941), 312.

[53] May 16, 1898.

[54] London *Times*, May 17, 1898; *New York Herald*, May 16, 1898.

[55] *Outlook*, LIX (June 4, 1898), 253.

League. Supporting the movement was a brilliant array of gentle-
men—the Duke of Sutherland, Earl Grey, the Earl of Jersey,
Baron Farrer, Baron Brassey, Baron Tennyson, Baron Monkswell,
Lord Charles Beresford, Sir John Lubbock, and James Bryce.[56]

Meanwhile Dewey's brilliant victory at Manila Bay had focused
attention on the Philippines. The new situation advanced Anglo-
American friendship in several ways. During the subsequent
blockade Dewey's cordial relations with the British ships sent to
the scene appeared in striking contrast to the friction that developed
between the American and German fleets.[57]   Moreover, the
English at once made plain their hope that the United States
would permanently establish itself in the islands. Early in May—
long before American opinion on the issue had had time to crys-
tallize—the London *Times* asserted that it would welcome American
annexation "as the best solution of the problem for all parties
concerned."[58] If the United States became one of the dominant
naval powers in the Pacific, the policy of open trade would be
enormously strengthened. The *Times* was particularly anxious
that Germany, France, or Russia should not be given an opportunity to get the islands:

In future America will play a part in the general affairs of the world
such as she has never played before. When the American people realize
this . . . they will not do things by halves. They will not cripple
their future action in the Far East by permitting the establishment of a
Power or Powers having antagonistic interests in a strong position which
their own efforts have given them the best claim to hold.[59]

English interest in the future of the Philippines mounted during
the summer. Ambassador Hay telegraphed Secretary of State

[56] *New York Herald*, July 14, 1898. So touched with this demonstration of blue-
blooded friendship were Whitelaw Reid, Richard Watson Gilder, and Lyman Abbott
that they drew up an expression of American gratitude and expended great labor in
securing an impressive list of signatures from statesmen, authors, professional people,
and businessmen. *An American Response to Expressions of English Sympathy* (New York,
1899). Cf. *Letters of Richard Watson Gilder*, ed. Rosamond Gilder (Boston and New
York, 1916), 303.

[57] Thomas A. Bailey, "Dewey and the Germans at Manila Bay," *American Historical
Review*, XLV (October, 1939), 59–81.

[58] May 9, 1898.

[59] May 12, 1898.

Day at the end of July that the British government would prefer to see the United States keep the islands.[60] Similar advice came to the administration through other channels. In September Joseph Chamberlain urged the advantages of annexation upon the eager Senator Lodge.[61] A month later Balfour gave Henry White his opinion that German ambition could be circumvented only by the United States keeping the whole group; if we gave up any part of them, Germany would do her best to establish a footing there.[62] When our decision to keep the entire archipelago was finally announced, Lord Salisbury assured White that he believed we had made a wise decision.[63]

And so 1898, which had opened with a crisis in China and an English appeal for American support, ended with the United States a Far Eastern power itself. American imperialists had discovered—to their surprise—that, far from trying to thwart our expansion, Britain welcomed us to the arena of world politics with open arms. Our predisposition to line up with England in the Far East had now been strengthened by a realization that England's support would be useful to us in holding our Pacific possessions; as a colonial power ourselves, moreover, we felt a new sympathy for the British imperial mission.

Joseph Chamberlain continued his ardent wooing. On January 29, 1899, in his Birmingham stronghold the Colonial Secretary declared that Providence intended Great Britain to be a great governing power, but she would no longer be alone since the United States was entering the lists and sharing the task. The first business of the Salisbury government was "to draw closer the bonds which unite us to the other members of the English-speaking race and to promote their co-operation in the great work of civilization which appears to be the mission of the Anglo-Saxon race."[64]

[60] Lester B. Shippee and Royal B. Way, "William Rufus Day," *The American Secretaries of State and Their Diplomacy*, ed. Samuel Flagg Bemis (New York, 1927–1929), IX, 100–101.

[61] Lodge to Henry White, September 23, 1898, White Papers.

[62] White to Hay, October 29, 1898, White Letter Book.

[63] White to Hay, November 2, 1898, *ibid.*

[64] London *Times*, January 30, 1899. Arthur Balfour spoke in a similar vein to his constituents at Manchester. *Ibid.*, January 31, 1899. Cf. earlier views, *supra*, footnote.

Every personal factor indeed seemed to favor close relations. This was the ambition of Sir Julian Pauncefote, who had been at the Washington Embassy since 1889 and who enjoyed unusual respect and trust. On the American side, President McKinley was thoroughly grateful for British friendship during the war and he gave firm support to John Hay, his new Secretary of State, who made the maintenance of Anglo-American solidarity the corner-stone of his policy. Succeeding Hay as Ambassador to Great Britain was Joseph H. Choate of New York, one of the most famous and successful lawyers of the day and an outspoken Anglophile. Whatever could be done toward giving permanent form to the new Anglo-American friendship, these men would attempt.

V. Opponents of Anglo-American Collaboration

But often in politics, as in physics, action brings equal and opposite reaction. Avid discussion of the idea of an Anglo-Saxon alliance inevitably aroused suspicion both in England and America. Some Englishmen, for example, could not forget the quarrels of the recent past; they suspected the Yankees of hypocrisy in these belated affirmations of affection. When a visitor to Queen Victoria commented on the *rapprochement*, she responded tartly that she could see none.[65] To men like the historian, Goldwin Smith, who considered the United States to have been the aggressor in the war with Spain, Britain's support of our imperialism appeared dangerous folly:

It is doubtful whether you will have gained anything which will pay you for having incurred the enmity of Spain, helped, as I fear you have, to develop on this continent a great power of violence and rapine, and incurred the taint of moral complicity with the set of men at Washington who for their political ends have trampled on international right and disturbed the peace of the world.[66]

The very fact that Joseph Chamberlain was the leading advocate of an Anglo-American alliance was enough to create grave mis-

[65] John Buchan, *Lord Minto: A Memoir* (London, 1924), 117.

[66] To Lord Goschen, May 23, 1899, *A Selection from Goldwin Smith's Correspondence*, collected by Arnold Haultain (London, n.d.), 327–28.

givings among the anti-imperialists of both countries. John Morley asserted that he would be very glad to see a union between the two countries for their mutual good and the good of civilization, but that an alliance of the jingo elements in England and America would be a menace to the world and a curse upon the peace of both nations.[67] On the American side, Carl Schurz wrote:

I distrust that kind of British friendship which would hurry us into an imperialistic policy and then make us dependent upon British aid, obliging us in turn to give American aid in promotion of British policies. . . . [68]

Another cause for misgiving was the fact that the appeal for an alliance was still so largely based on racial arguments. The latter were effectively analyzed by Professor Charles Waldstein of Cambridge University. The word "Anglo-Saxon," he said was not descriptive of the actual populations of the United States and Great Britain; its use was, moreover, a dangerous step toward the curse of what he aptly called "ethnological chauvinism." He urged instead an English-speaking Brotherhood, based on common ideals.[69] •

But it was the Irish who most disliked the idea of an Anglo-Saxon alliance. Even the possibility of a new general arbitration treaty had put them on guard early in 1898; an Anti-British Alliance Association had been promptly organized in New York City.[70] It was Chamberlain's famous speech, however, that had really put the Anglophobes into the trenches. Expressions of protest were speedily organized. Marchers paraded through the streets of Philadelphia carrying slogans which read: "England Sent Small-Pox Infested Rags to New York in 1862," "George Washington Would Never Trust England," "Andrew Jackson Hated and Fought England," and "Has McKinley Forgotten

[67] Sir William Harcourt, Lord Kimberley, and Sir Charles Dilke gave similar warnings. London *Times*, June 10, 1898; *Outlook*, LIX (June 18, 1898), 408.

[68] To Richard Watson Gilder, August 8, 1898, *Speeches, Correspondence and Political Papers of Carl Schurz*, ed. Frederic Bancroft (New York, 1913), V, 477. See also Schurz, "Anglo-American Friendship," *Atlantic Monthly*, LXXXII (October, 1898), 433–40.

[69] Charles Waldstein, *The Expansion of Western Ideals and the World's Peace* (New York and London, 1899), 113–94.

[70] *Irish World*, January 22, 1898; February 5, 1898.

the Alabama Affair?" [71]   At an Irish-American rally in Chicago
a speaker declared that to the last drop of their blood the Irish
would be loyal to America, but not a shot would they fire to advance the interests of England. "Judas" Chamberlain could put
that in his pipe—or in his eye-glass, if it suited him better—and
smoke it! [72]

The reference to "Judas" Chamberlain was a reminder that the
proposal of an Anglo-American alliance, which would have been
unpopular with the Irish in any case, was doubly so in its present
association with the Colonial Secretary. The Irish remembered
vividly the most spectacular act of Chamberlain's political career,
his desertion of Gladstone in 1885 and consequent assassination
of the first Home Rule bill. In a letter to the London *Times*,
Michael Davitt of the Irish Parliamentary Party boasted that the
Irish could now pay him back with compound interest by making
an alliance of any kind between England and the United States
impossible. [73]

On the issue of imperialism the Irish position was stated bluntly.
It was not the Philippines, but Canada that we should annex. All
"Anglomen" were in favor of our taking the islands, because they
thought that their possession would render us dependent on English friendship. [74] The politics of the moment made strange bed-
fellows; in their resistance to colonial expansion the Irish were
allied with the blue bloods of the Anti-Imperialist League—men
like Moorfield Storey, Charles Francis Adams, and Senator Hoar.

The Irish found more vigorous comrades-in-arms among the
German-Americans, who disliked all talk of an Anglo-Saxon
Alliance and organized mass meetings to protest against Cham-

[71] *Ibid.*, May 28, 1898.

[72] *Ibid.*, June 4, 1898.

[73] London *Times*, May 18, 1898. Father George McDermot wrote of Chamberlain:
"It is the duty of Irish Americans to make his influence a mockery in their country, to
oppose with unsleeping vigilance any power or authority that favors him, so that,
disappointed and disgraced by failure, he may retire from the sphere of an influence
only exercised to gratify his vanity, his ambition, his resentment." "The Anglo-
American Alliance and the Irish Americans," *Catholic World*, LXVIII (October,
1898), 82.

[74] *Irish World*, November 5, 1898.

berlain's proposal.[75] They resented also the anti-German tone of the American press in 1898, particularly the frequent quotation of unfriendly comments from German newspapers. They became convinced that an unholy alliance involving British bankers and the two great news services, Reuters and the Associated Press, was attempting to create bad feeling between Germany and the United States.[76] In May, 1899, publishers of the most important German-American newspapers met at Chicago to protest against the Germanophobia of the Associated Press and to organize an association to protect their mutual interests.[77]

This German-American protest movement was very welcome to the German government, which was seriously concerned over its unsatisfactory relations with the United States. Since attempts to influence the American press through European methods had failed,[78] the main reliance of German diplomacy had to be placed upon the German-Americans. Their vote was believed to be of such importance to the Republicans that the McKinley administration would be compelled to avoid all contact with the Anglo-Saxon alliance idea. Well remembering the fate of Lord Sackville-West, Ambassador Holleben was careful not to become too deeply involved, but even without much direction from the Embassy, German-American protest against the alliance was vociferous throughout 1899.[79]

In reality, however, the Anglo-American alliance was a less imminent peril than it seemed to the Irish and the Germans. The diplomats were finding even the prosaic business of settling the outstanding controversies between the two countries almost too

[75] *Ibid.*, May 28; July 2, 1898.

[76] Richard Bartholdt, *From Steerage to Congress: Reminiscences and Reflections* (Philadelphia, 1930), 180–81.

[77] Emil Witte, *Revelations of a German Attaché: Ten Years of German-American Diplomacy* (Translated from the German. New York, 1916), 116–17.

[78] *Ibid.*, 1–47; Alfred Vagts, *Deutschland und die Vereinigten Staaten in der Weltpolitik* (New York, 1935), I, 583–85.

[79] *Ibid.*, I, 587–89. Resentment against Anglo-Saxon alliance talk had much to do with the organization of both the National German-American Alliance and the American Irish Historical Society.

much for them. Progress made on other issues was rendered barren by the Joint High Commission's failure to deal successfully with the Alaskan boundary—a problem pushed abruptly to the fore by the Klondike gold rush. Since the Canadians refused to assent to any agreement until the Alaskan question had been disposed of, the High Commission was compelled to suspend its labors at the end of February, 1899.

Hay's disappointment was great, since the *impasse* handicapped the project which was now his greatest concern—to prepare the ground diplomatically for the building of a Central American canal. Just before the adjournment of the High Commission, Lord Salisbury had promised that, if the Commission succeeded in settling all the questions submitted to it, the British government would at once assent to Hay's canal proposals; he added confidentially that it would do so in any case, but, if the Commission failed, it must adhere to diplomatic form and allow a certain time to elapse before giving way.[80] With this prize to work for, Hay struggled throughout the summer to discover a formula for disposing of the Alaskan issue. But the sensible suggestion that we should lease Canada a port in the disputed area brought warnings from the powerful Whitelaw Reid and from Senator Cushman K. Davis, chairman of the Foreign Relations Committee,[81] while the Democrats were believed to be sharpening their knives for just such an issue. Although McKinley was willing to go ahead, Hay drew back; he was unwilling to risk "the unspeakable disgrace of making such a creature as Bryan President."[82]

To John Hay the turn of events during 1899 seemed most unfair. He complained to our Ambassador at Berlin: "It is one of the ironies of fate that while we have been bickering with England all year and doing everything that Germany asks of us, we should be threatened by a German rush for Free Silver because we are supposed to be too friendly with England. Such is the logic of

[80] White to Hay, February 17, 1899, White Letter Books.
[81] Davis to Hay, July 31, 1899, Joseph H. Choate Papers.
[82] Hay to Choate, August 18, 1899, *ibid.* Cf. Hay to White, September 9, 1899, White Papers.

politics."[83] This was the Secretary of State's reaction to finding himself under attack for having consummated a "secret alliance" with England.

The situation in Ohio was particularly alarming. A governor was to be elected in 1899 and the Democrats were exerting every effort to carry the President's home state as a blow to the prestige of the national administration. Since over one-fifth of the population of the state was of immediate German and Irish stock,[84] denunciations of "the secret and vicious alliance now in evidence between England and the Republican Administration" were likely to be very effective.[85] In an attempt to kill the bogy, Hay wrote a trenchant open letter to Colonel Charles Dick, chairman of the Ohio Republican State Committee:

There is no alliance with England or with any Power under heaven, except those known and published to the world—the treaties of ordinary international friendship for purposes of business and commerce. No treaty other than these exists; none has been suggested on either side; none is in contemplation. It has nevered entered into the mind of the President or of any member of the government to forsake, under any inducement, the wise precept and example of the fathers which forbade entangling alliances with European powers.[86]

A million copies of Hay's letter were distributed as campaign literature.[87] In the November election, the Republicans won a smashing victory; but not the Anglo-American alliance. John Hay confided to Henry White:

The fact is a treaty of alliance is impossible. It would never get through the Senate. As long as I stay here no action shall be taken contrary to my conviction that the one indispensable feature of our foreign policy should be a friendly understanding with England. But an alliance must remain in the present state of things an unattainable dream.[88]

Just at this inopportune moment when the administration was carefully exorcising the specter of foreign entanglements, Joseph

---

[83] September 21, 1899, Vagts, *Deutschland und die Vereinigten Staaten*, I, 594.

[84] *Twelfth Census of the United States: 1900*, I, xx, cxcv.

[85] New York *World*, August 31, 1899; *Irish World*, September 9, 1899.

[86] London *Times*, September 14, 1899; *New York Herald*, December 2, 1899.

[87] Hay to White, November 20, 1899, White Papers.

[88] September 24, 1899, Dennett, *John Hay*, 221.

Chamberlain made a speech which seemed to assume that the Anglo-American alliance was a fact. "The union," he asserted, "the alliance, if you please—the understanding between the two great nations is indeed a guarantee for the peace of the world." He invited Germany to join in a triple alliance with England and the United States.[89] This time there were no friendly echoes from America. The *New York Herald* commented with scant politeness that Chamberlain was talking through his hat, while the State Department issued a hasty denial that any alliance existed or was contemplated.[90] The rebuff was made more pointed by the President's annual message to Congress. Although McKinley made a distinct gesture of friendship toward Germany, his reference to England lacked the warmth of other occasions. The German ambassador attributed this to the excesses of Chamberlain, to considerations for the Irish vote, to England's aspirations for a harbor in the disputed Alaskan territory, and to the unsatisfactory condition of the Nicaraguan canal question. The time was ripe, he advised his Foreign Office, for Germany to improve its relations with the United States.[91]

By the end of 1899, the first wave of Anglo-American affection born of the events of 1898 had spent itself. The United States was still grateful; England still friendly. But talk of an Anglo-Saxon alliance became less frequent; to maintain the good understanding seemed problem enough.

VI. Significance of Anglo-American Friendship, 1898–99

The good understanding was itself of course a revolution in world politics. In 1895 there had been serious talk of war between England and the United States; by 1898 war between the two

[89] Garvin, *Chamberlain*, III, 506–508.

[90] *New York Herald*, December 2, 1899.

[91] Vagts, *Deutschland*, I, 592–93. Chamberlain's proposal had a curt response from Germany also—much to his indignation since his gesture had followed certain informal discussions between himself and Count Bülow the preceding month. Cf. Baron von Eckardstein, *Ten Years at the Court of St. James, 1895–1905*, tr. and ed. George Young (London, 1921), 130.

seemed impossible. The transition had begun with Britain's realization of the dangers of "splendid isolation." The Empire needed friends—especially as the Far Eastern situation became serious. For the principle of the Open Door England found much support in American public opinion as early as December, 1897. The McKinley administration was cautious, but its attitude was sufficiently sympathetic to encourage the Salisbury administration. This was the situation when the Cuban crisis led the United States into war in the spring of 1898. The British government's policy during the conflict was consistently pro-American, despite the feeling that American conduct in April, 1898, had been unnecessarily bellicose—a feeling which led Pauncefote into a serious error, certain to have antagonized the McKinley administration had not Balfour and Chamberlain saved the situation. During the next several months Anglo-American friendship was so close as to make an alliance the subject of constant discussion. Despite all this talk no alliance resulted, in part because of the sudden eruption of the Alaskan boundary dispute, but more especially because the Irish, the Germans, the anti-imperialists, and Democratic political strategists raised such a clamor that the McKinley administration had to disassociate itself completely from the alliance idea. But Anglo-American friendship had many opportunities to express itself in less vulnerable forms like the Open Door policy, friendly American neutrality during the Boer War, the Hay-Pauncefote treaties, and the new British naval policy which quietly adapted itself to American supremacy in the Caribbean area.

The Civil War Blockade Reconsidered

By Edwin B. Coddington [*]

The war between the North and the South has always attracted the interest of a large band of devoted students, and yet a thorough examination of one of the more colorful and important features of that struggle has been neglected. When on April 19, 1861, President Lincoln proclaimed the intention of the United States to institute a blockade of Southern ports,[1] he created a policy which immediately affected the nature of the conflict, as well as American foreign relations. Since a blockade is an act of war in which "the two parties in the contest must become belligerents," the Federal Government thus adopted a plan which invalidated its theory of the struggle as a purely domestic one in which the Southern "insurgents" would not be accorded the rights of belligerency.[2]

A logical but impractical application of this concept would have been the establishment of a domestic embargo, whereby Southern ports would have been closed to foreign trade by act of Congress. Under this arrangement the North could not have claimed the belligerent right to seize vessels on the "high seas bound for a blockaded port," an act which is comparable to the "right of search."[3] When the British Government learned that a domestic embargo was being considered, it became concerned and warned that such a method of excluding foreign commerce from Southern ports would have the characteristics of a paper blockade and

[*]Edwin B. Coddington is Professor of History, Lafayette College.

[1] A second proclamation on April 27 extended the blockade to ports in Virginia and North Carolina. James D. Richardson, ed., *A Compilation of the Messages and Papers of the Presidents* (1896–99), VIII, 3215–16.

[2] James Russell Soley, *The Blockade and the Cruisers* (New York, 1883), 28; and James G. Randall, *Constitutional Problems under Lincoln* (New York, 1926), 59–65.

[3] Soley, *The Blockade*, 28–30.

would incur its opposition. Whether this attitude affected the decision of Northern leaders to abandon the idea of an embargo is questionable. Certainly the legal advantages of a blockade, maintained in conformity with international law, and other considerations, such as a desire to avoid the bloody excesses of civil strife and fear of reprisal, forced the United States to concede belligerent rights to the Confederacy without formal recognition.[4]

I. BRITISH REACTION TO THE BLOCKADE

A review of the blockade must revolve around the central question of its effectiveness, which includes an inquiry into Great Britain's attitude. By virtue of her position as the foremost maritime power, her reaction to the blockade assumed vital importance to its success. Should she have insisted, before recognizing its legality, upon standards of efficiency that would have permitted of virtually no violations, the Northern Government in all likelihood would have failed in this phase of its grand strategy. Fortunately for the United States this development did not occur. As relations between the North and the South became more strained after the formation of the Confederacy in February, 1861, British officials worried about the effects of a possible war on English commerce.[5] Yet when the blockade was declared "in pursuance . . . of the Law of Nations"[6] no objections were raised, for it was felt that American precedent would require it to be effective.[7] The Law of Nations in this case meant to Great Britain the definition contained in the Declaration of Paris, 1856, that: "Blockades, in order to be binding, must be effective; that is to say, maintained by a force sufficient really to prevent access to the coast of the enemy."[8] Although the United States had refused

---

[4] Ephraim Douglass Adams, *Great Britain and the American Civil War* (New York: Longmans, Green, 1925), I, 244–52; and Randall, *Constitutional Problems*, 65–69.

[5] Adams, *Great Britain and the American Civil War*, I, 57–75.

[6] Richardson, *Messages and Papers*, VIII, 3215.

[7] Adams, *Great Britain and the American Civil War*, I, 244, 246.

[8] Text as given in John Bassett Moore, *Digest of International Law* (Washington, 1906), VII, 562. For a slightly different wording of the text see *Official Records of the Union and Confederate Navies in the War of the Rebellion* (Washington, 1922), 2nd series, III, 299; hereafter cited as *O. R. N.*

to sign the agreement, partly because the Declaration had likewise abolished privateering, its precarious diplomatic position after the outbreak of hostilities and its traditional policies guaranteed acceptance of the definition.[9]

For several months after "early and easy acquiescence" in the blockade, the British Government gave the matter little consideration. The thinking of such men as Lord Russell, the Foreign Secretary, was affected by assumptions that the war would be of such short duration as not to cut off next year's supply of cotton, and that guarding approximately 3,500 miles of coast line would impose an impossible task on the Federal navy. Furthermore a "*regular* blockade'" could not possibly prevent trade with the South.[10] The geographical factor unduly impressed the British, and the Confederates constantly tried to increase their exaggeration of its significance as part of an effort to induce the European powers to repudiate the blockade.[11]

The length of the coast line and the peculiar formation of the shore seemingly presented the blockading fleet with insuperable difficulties. A large proportion of the coast from "North Carolina to Florida on the Atlantic side and from West Florida to Galveston, Texas, was a double line, with interior channels, making it possible to travel much of the distance between the ports without frequent exposure to the open sea. . . ."[12] This advantage to the South was offset to a large extent by the arrangement of the Southern railroads, which served at all adequately only the seven largest seaports. It was to these ports (Norfolk, Wilmington,

[9] According to Jay Monaghan, *Diplomat in Carpet Slippers: Abraham Lincoln Deals with Foreign Affairs* (New York, 1945), 81–83, Secretary Seward had induced Lincoln to proclaim a blockade "in pursuance . . . of the law of nations" before the full implications of such a move were thoroughly investigated. As a result Lincoln's efforts to outlaw Southern privateering were thwarted and European recognition of Confederate belligerency, which he had ardently hoped to avoid, became inevitable. This judgment of Seward seems harsh, for it is difficult to see what other feasible course the North could have followed to prohibit commerce between the South and the rest of the world.

[10] Adams, *Great Britain and the American Civil War*, I, 246, 252.

[11] *O. R. N.*, 2nd series, III, 357, 483, 497, 622.

[12] Frank Lawrence Owsley, *King Cotton Diplomacy: Foreign Relations of the Confederate States of America* (Chicago, 1931), 250.

Charleston, Savannah, Mobile, New Orleans, and Galveston) that important blockade-runners directed their ships to carry on what became the bulk of Southern foreign trade during the war. It should be added that much of the total coast line was contained in the state of Florida, but that the whole area lacked rail connections with the rest of the South. The same condition existed in respect to Texas. In terms of railroads, industrial resources, agricultural development, and population, which means military potential, the vital area of the Confederacy lay between the Mississippi River and the Atlantic Ocean, bounded on the south by the Florida-Georgia line and the Gulf of Mexico, and on the north by the border states of Kentucky and Maryland.[13]

Assuming that its effects would prove immaterial to the British, Lord Russell did not show any active interest in the blockade until late November, 1861. He heard then that Americans planned to sink vessels filled with stones across the entrance bar of Charleston harbor. This proposal seemed to indicate the necessity of employing " 'uncivilized,' if not illegal methods" to bolster the ineffectual efforts of blockading squadrons.[14] Reports of their ineffectiveness had been coming to him since the summer from British consuls resident in the South and from representatives of a Confederate diplomatic mission to Europe.[15] The "Stone Boat Fleet" affair served to confirm previous impressions of the blockade, but it likewise moved Russell to obtain an opinion from Lord Lyons, British minister to the United States. Lyons wrote:

I am a good deal puzzled as to how I ought to answer your question whether I consider the Blockade effective. It is certainly by no means strict or vigorous along the immense extent of coast to which it is supposed to apply. I suppose the ships which run it successfully both in and out are more numerous than those which are intercepted. On the other hand it is very far from being a mere Paper Blockade. A great many vessels

[13] *Dinsmore's New Railroad Map of the United States and the Canadas, Showing All the Railroads Completed and in Progress* . . . (New York, 1860); Soley, *The Blockade*, 36; Edwin B. Coddington, *A Social and Economic History of the Seaboard States of the Southern Confederacy* (Ph.D. Dissertation, MS., Clark University, 1939), chap. 5; Jefferson Davis Bragg, *Louisiana in the Confederacy* (Baton Rouge, 1941), 76, 84–87.

[14] Adams, *Great Britain and the American Civil War*, I, 253.

[15] *O. R. N.*, 2nd series, III, 231, 246; Owsley, *King Cotton Diplomacy*, 253–56.

are captured; it is a most serious interruption to Trade; and if it were as ineffective as Mr. Jefferson Davis says in his Message, he would not be so very anxious to get rid of it.[16]

This statement presents in excellent fashion the dilemma which faced the neutral person of that day and the historian of later times in trying to estimate the effectiveness of the blockade. Those people interested in denouncing it on the grounds that it failed to meet the standards of the Declaration of Paris would find comfort in Lyons' opinion. The same satisfaction would be obtained by those who might wish to uphold the blockade. Confederate authorities and their sympathizers in England and France belittled the evidence on captured vessels and stressed the number of violations to prove the ineffectiveness and consequently the illegality of the blockade.[17] This approach to the question has been ably developed in recent years by Professor Owsley, who has gone so far as to say: "Old Abe sold America's birthright [traditional insistence upon neutral rights] for a mess of pottage."[18]

The British Government came to regard the blockade in a different light. A conditioning factor in determining its attitude was England's position as the leading naval power. Foreseeing a future war in which her situation might be reversed from that of neutrality to belligerency, leaders there decided to observe Northern efforts with indulgence.[19] Lord Palmerston, the Prime Minister, admitted that such was the case in a conversation on March 14, 1865, with Mr. J. M. Mason, head of the Confederate mission to England.[20] Sir Alexander Milne, who was in command of the North American and West Indies naval station from 1860 to March 15, 1864, refrained, in his protection of British commerce against illegal acts of the belligerents, from establishing precedents

[16] Lord Lyons to Lord John Russell, November 29, 1861, Russell Papers, as quoted in Adams, *Great Britain and the American Civil War*, I, 254.

[17] *O. R. N.*, 2nd series, III, 246, 263, 293, 299, 373, 379-84, 411-13, 483, 495-98, 882-89.

[18] Owsley, *King Cotton Diplomacy*, 291. See also chapter 8 entitled: "The Ineffectiveness of the Blockade."

[19] Adams, *Great Britain and the American Civil War*, I, 263.

[20] *O. R. N.*, 2nd series, III, 1273-74.

which might hamper England's use of sea power in a future conflict.[21] The government likewise refused to be carried away by
an imposing array of statistics on violations, for, as contended in
a Parliamentary debate on the blockade in March, 1862, "nearly
all the alleged blockade runners were in reality merely small
coasting steamers, which, by use of shallow inner channels, could
creep along the shore and then make a dash for the West Indies."
As a clinching argument the discrepancy of 100 per cent between
the price of cotton in the South and in England was cited.[22] Actually this point proved nothing in respect to the blockade, because
of the unofficial embargo on the exportation of cotton maintained
by Southerners during the first year of the war. The British felt
then that the normal course of trade had been seriously interrupted
and that much neutral commerce had disappeared with the advent
of danger.[23] Under these circumstances a liberal interpretation
of the Paris definition by Lord Russell was not surprising when he
wrote Lyons on February 15 that:

> Her Majesty's Government . . . are of opinion that, assuming that
> the blockade was duly notified, and also that a number of ships is stationed
> and remains at the entrance of a port, sufficient really to prevent access
> to it or; to create an evident danger of entering or leaving it; and that
> these ships do not voluntarily permit ingress or egress, the fact that various
> ships may have successfully escaped through it (as in the particular in-
> stance here referred to) will not, of itself, prevent the blockade from being
> an effectual one, by international law.[24]

The Confederates fussed and fumed over this statement, especially the phrase "sufficient . . . to create an evident danger,"
for to them it completely destroyed the purpose of the Paris definition. There is justification in their complaint that the British
had granted the Union navy generous latitude in executing a
difficult assignment with what were at first woefully inadequate

---

[21] James P. Baxter, 3rd, "The British Government and Neutral Rights," *American Historical Review*, XXXIV (October, 1928), 11.

[22] Adams, *Great Britain and the American Civil War*, I, 270.

[23] *O. R. N.*, 2nd series, III, 340; Adams, *Great Britain and the American Civil War*, I, 245–46.

[24] *O. R. N.*, 2nd series, III, 495–96.

forces.[25] They remained unhappy when Russell almost a year later in a communication to Mason restated the British position in more explicit language:

It appears to her Majesty's Government to be sufficiently clear that the declaration of Paris could not have been intended to mean that a port must be so blockaded as really to prevent access in all winds, and independently of whether the communication might be carried on of a dark night or by means of small low steamers or coasting craft creeping along the shore; in short, that it was necessary that communication with a port under blockade should be utterly and absolutely impossible under any circumstances.

He ended by saying that to the British Government the Paris definition meant that "a blockade in order to be respected by neutrals must be *practically* effective."[26]

This interpretation at the time it was written constituted a fair estimate of the blockade, for by 1863 the Federal Government had established a tight enough cordon around the Southern coast to require extraordinary efforts and an unusual outlay of capital on the part of those who risked sending vessels through it. During the previous two years the navy was being built up to necessary strength. Writers on the Civil War all agree that at the time of the two presidential proclamations no more than a few vessels were at the immediate disposal of the Federal Government. Outside of Chesapeake Bay no blockade of any sort existed until late in May, 1861, and Northern efforts at that early date proved totally inadequate and remained so for at least two months more. By no stretch of the imagination of any serious student has the blockade been considered effective by any reasonable standards until the end of 1861.[27] Some writers have declared it ineffective

---

[25] Soley, *The Blockade*, 12–18.

[26] *O. R. N.*, 2nd series, III, 688. Italics by the writer.

[27] Soley, *The Blockade*, 35, 43, 84–85, 89–90, 121. See also James G. Randall, *The Civil War and Reconstruction* (New York, 1937), 573–74; Adams, *Great Britain and the American Civil War*, I, 245–46; Carl Russell Fish, *The American Civil War: An Interpretation* (New York, 1937), 208–9, 217; J. T. Scharf, *History of the Confederate States Navy from Its Organization to the Surrender of Its Last Vessel* (New York, 1887), 433–34; Owsley, *King Cotton Diplomacy*, 250–51, 290.

until two years after the beginning of hostilities, while a few of the Owsley-Scharf school of thought have refused to admit that it ever measured up to the rules established by the Declaration of Paris.[28]

Despite these conflicting opinions it would be safe to say that until the summer of 1862 the North had perpetrated a bluff which was aided and abetted unwittingly by the South and was accepted at face value by the British. Ironically, while the Confederates made futile attempts to have Great Britain denounce the blockade they pursued a policy that undermined the force of their arguments. Had it not been for a fatuous belief in the efficacy of "King Cotton" as a diplomatic weapon to force foreign recognition of their new government, the Southerners might have achieved their aims by employing their main source of wealth more realistically. There is this to be said, however: assuming that they had not been blinded by a belief in "King Cotton Diplomacy," the nature of their political thinking would probably have prevented efficient use of cotton for prosecution of their cause. The exigencies of war required a unifying control by the central government over all exports of that commodity, a development partially achieved toward the end, but inconceivable to political leaders at the outset.[29]

II. Southern Embargo on Cotton

In obedience to a misguided notion of the best way to utilize the economic power of cotton, the Southern people and not the Confederate Government imposed an embargo on the export of their main cash crop. Shipment of cotton even from the plantations was prevented as a result of public sentiment inspired and backed by newspapers, the influence of important business groups, and the policies of "state and local officials and public safety com-

---

[28] Fish, *The American Civil War*, 217; Owsley, *King Cotton Diplomacy*, 253, 284; Scharf, *Confederate States Navy*, 488–90; Samuel Bernard Thompson, *Confederate Purchasing Operations Abroad* (Chapel Hill, 1935), 6, 43–47.

[29] Thompson, *Confederate Purchasing*, 5, 72–73, 84–99; Owsley, *King Cotton Diplomacy*, 34–35.

mittees."[30] During the summer of 1861 cotton factors, together with "insurance and warehousemen" in the various seaports, urged planters not to send that article to market. An indication of the success of the nonexportation campaign is found in the figures given for the amount of cotton which arrived at the five most important ports, Memphis, New Orleans, Savannah, Mobile, and Charleston, from September, 1861 to January, 1862. A little less than 10,000 bales were sent to these ports in comparison to approximately 1,500,000 bales in the same months of the previous year.[31] It might be assumed that by its failure to act the Confederate Government was unsympathetic to the embargo; actually the opposite was true. The Southern people largely through voluntary methods had accomplished all that the administration could desire in creating economic pressure abroad without incurring the dangers of diplomatic repercussions from the passage of a Confederate statute for that purpose. Talk favorable to the embargo occurred in the Confederate Congress, and bills or resolutions were introduced to enforce the unofficial policy; yet nothing came of these moves.[32]

Since the embargo had not received official sanction, Judah P. Benjamin, the Secretary of State, in the spring of 1862 had the temerity to place the blame for the greatly reduced shipments of cotton abroad on those foreign nations which had recognized an illegal blockade and had refused to send vessels through it to get Southern goods. He did admit that "as a measure of self-defense" the South had a "policy of refusing to accumulate cotton" at the various ports. He tried to shift the responsibility, however, by claiming: "The truth is that cotton was not withheld from the ports until long after the European powers had indicated their intention to respect Mr. Lincoln's interdiction of their commerce with the South." As for a policy of forcing foreign recognition of the Confederacy, he expressed indignant surprise that "the

---

[30] Owsley, *King Cotton Diplomacy*, 51.

[31] *Ibid.*, 30, 43.

[32] *Ibid.*, 32–34.

suggestion so artfully insinuated by Northern agents that cotton is kept back for the purpose of coercing foreign powers into any particular line of policy can scarcely find credence with the enlightened cabinet of St. James." [33] Secretary Benjamin wrote an excellent lawyer's brief, but bad history.

The agitation for an embargo started early in the summer of 1861 and was designed to force recognition of the Confederacy and abandonment of the blockade by means of foreign intervention. The newspapers hoped for an effectual blockade, "the stricter the better," for then the South's best customers would move more quickly in her behalf. But as long as a "sham blockade" was permitted "'no foreigner can get any of our cotton.'" [34] Such expressions received the attention of the foreign press, and the impression grew abroad that it was useless to send ships through the blockade to get cotton. Reports of British consuls resident in the South served to strengthen this idea. In an effort to discourage blockade-running the United States Government through its representatives in Europe was not averse to confirming the belief that the Confederate Government was responsible for the cotton famine. [35]

The embargo was but one of three phases in a program to use cotton as a diplomatic weapon. When it appeared that non-exportation had failed to obtain the desired reaction from England and France, the South resorted to more drastic action in the form of curtailment of production and destruction of existing supplies. In presenting to Europe its plea against the blockade, the government could claim innocence of complicity in the embargo, but such was not the case in the effort to restrict the planting of cotton and to promote its burning. Congress approved by joint resolution in March of 1862 the idea already accepted in the newspapers, farmers' conventions, and state legislatures that the forthcoming crop be curtailed. Likewise in the same month it passed a law

[33] *O. R. N.*, 2nd series, III, 382–83.
[34] Owsley, *King Cotton Diplomacy*, 26.
[35] See *ibid.*, 29, 39–42.

providing for the destruction of such crops as cotton and tobacco whenever there appeared to be danger of their seizure by Federal forces. Ostensibly passed as a military measure, the statute was motivated in part by a desire to increase diplomatic pressure on England and France.[36]

Although faith in "King Cotton Diplomacy" explains much of the agitation to reduce cotton and tobacco production, other factors should be mentioned. The South struggled not only for political independence but also freedom forever from Northern economic domination by better utilization of its own resources.[37] Achievement of this goal meant among other things a fundamental change in agriculture from an emphasis on the growth of cash crops to greater production of foodstuffs. Military necessity and fear of the blockade demanded that the shift take place immediately.[38] Beginning in the summer of 1861 government officials, state legislatures, patriotic Southerners, and especially the public press exhorted farmers and planters to substitute the raising of food crops for cotton.[39] Typical of such pleas was a long editorial in the Columbus, Georgia, *Sun* which started in this fashion: "Plant Corn and be Free, or Plant Cotton and be Whipped." The paper went on to say that cotton was "still king, but like all other kings it must be fed."[40] Legislative fiat, both state and Confederate, and a public sentiment materially reduced the amount of

[36] *Ibid.*, 45–47.

[37] Coddington, *Seaboard States*, 110–11, 186–88.

[38] E. Merton Coulter, "The Movement for Agricultural Reorganization in the Cotton South during the Civil War," *North Carolina Historical Review*, IV (January, 1927), 24.

[39] See *Savannah Republican*, July 4, 15, 1861, January 15, 1862, March 12, April 7, 1863, October 13, 1864; *Charleston Mercury*, August 27, 1861, October 8, 1863; *Charleston Courier* (Tri-weekly edition), March 27, April 1, 10, 1862, June 2, 1863; *Richmond Whig*, December 9, 1861; *Hillsborough Recorder*, April 16, 1862; Atlanta *Southern Confederacy*, November 30, 1861; *Southern Cultivator*, XX (January, 1862), 12; *ibid.* (March and April, 1862), 85; *ibid.* (May and June, 1862), 112; *ibid.*, XXI (January and February, 1863), 22; Georgia, *Acts of the General Assembly*, Reg. Sess., 1861, Resolutions, No. 12, passed December 14, 1861. See also John Christopher Schwab, *The Confederate States of America, 1861–1865: A Financial and Industrial History of the South during the Civil War* (New York and London, 1901), 277–78.

[40] Reprinted in the *Savannah Republican*, March 21, 1862.

cotton raised and stored during the war.[41]   In contrast to a yield
of 4,500,000 bales in 1861, the crop of 1862 came to only 1,500,000
bales.[42]   Those of the next two years were approximately 500,000
and 300,000 bales respectively, while, according to one estimate,
at least 2,500,000 bales were burned by the Confederate Government because its armies were forced to retreat.[43]

For various reasons, among them hatred of the blockade, the
South had embarked on a program which either rendered useless
at a vital period or destroyed a large proportion of its liquid capital.
Mr. G. B. Lamar, banker, cotton trader, and later blockade-
runner, who probably reflected the opinion of other businessmen, questioned the wisdom of the embargo as early as September,
1861, when he wrote: "The *U States* has laid us under Blockade, to
render our products valueless and Unavailable to us—It is a
question of policy how far we may facilitate their intentions of
harming us, by withholding our produce—."[44]   Gradually this
point of view became accepted, and after the spring of 1862 the
embargo was slowly lifted.

III. Blockade-Running After 1862

As the embargo was abandoned, Southern and foreign merchants
began to engage more actively in blockade-running, which at
first was of an improvised character.[45]   Not until 1863 did it

[41] See Georgia, *Acts of the General Assembly*, Reg. Sess., 1862, No. 1; South Carolina,
Acts of the General Assembly, Sess., 1862–63, Nos. 4619, 4620; *Richmond Dispatch*, April
10, May 4, 1863; *Charleston Courier* (Tri-weekly edition), May 6, 8, 31, 1862, April 11,
June 2, 1863; *Savannah Republican*, April 20, 21, 1863; *Savannah Morning News*, October
31, 1862.

[42] *Charleston Courier* (Tri-weekly edition), December 20, 1862.

[43] Owsley, *King Cotton Diplomacy*, 51.

[44] G. B. Lamar to C. G. Memminger, September 2, 1861, Personal Press Copy
Books of G. B. Lamar, the National Archives, Division of Treasury Department
Archives, Civil War Records of the Fifth Special Treasury Agency, 28F, hereafter
cited as G. B. Lamar Copy Books. See Edwin B. Coddington, "The Activities and
Attitudes of a Confederate Business Man: Gazaway B. Lamar," *The Journal of Southern
History*, IX (February, 1943), 3, 14.

[45] See *The War of the Rebellion: A Compilation of the Official Records of the Union and
Confederate Armies* (Washington, 1880–1900), 4th series, II, 562, hereafter cited as *O. R.*;
James Ford Rhodes, *History of the United States from the Compromise of 1850 to the End of
the Roosevelt Administration* (New York and London, 1928), V, 396; Francis B. C.
Bradlee, *Blockade Running during the Civil War; and the Effect of Land and Water Trans-
portation on the Confederacy* (Salem, 1925), 21, 29–30; *O. R. N.*, 2nd series, III, 371;
Thompson, *Confederate Purchasing*, 43; *Richmond Dispatch*, December 2, 1863.

assume the aspects of a well-established business which would
attract the more cautious investor.[46] Practically all of the larger
concerns in the seaboard states were incorporated or started operations sometime during that year,[47] for economic conditions had
become ideal for this type of venture. Cotton could be bought
in the South for about half its price in England, while conversely
the large variety of goods demanded in the Confederacy sold for
more than twice what they were worth abroad.[48] By this time,
however, the increased efficiency of the Union navy resulting
from acquisition of fast cruisers, many of which were converted
blockade-runners, required of the companies a very heavy financial
outlay. No longer were slow seagoing vessels profitable; only
expensive steamers of low, long, narrow, and swift lines and with
special equipment were possible. Competition between private
concerns and government contractors in England depressed the
price of cotton in the South and increased the prices of the desired
ships.[49] Cargo-carrying capacity having been sacrificed to speed
and shallow draught, various schemes were employed for effective
use of such boats. For example, steam presses reduced the cotton

[46] *Charleston Mercury*, November 11, 1863.

[47] South Carolina, *Acts of the General Assembly*, Sess., 1862–63, Nos. 4650, 4651;
ibid., Sess., 1863, Nos. 4681, 4689, 4690, 4694; Virginia, *Acts of the General Assembly*,
Adj. Sess., 1863, chap. 68; *ibid.*, Called Sess., 1863, chap. 48; Lamar to Memminger,
May 6, 1863, G. B. Lamar Copy Books, 28E; *id.* to Messrs. Newman and Strasburger,
May 19, 1863, and *id.* to Messrs. J. J. Hartstein [Hartstene] and C. A. L. Lamar, June
16, 1863, *ibid.*; *Savannah Republican*, June 17, 30, July 9, 1863.

[48] Schwab, *Confederate States of America*, 30; Rhodes, *History of the United States*, V,
396; George Gary Eggleston, *A Rebel's Recollections* (New York, 1905), 88. The goods
demanded in "enormous quantities" were wool, cotton, silk, and flax textiles; iron
and steel goods in a raw, semi-finished or finished condition; leather and articles
manufactured from it such as shoes, boots, saddlery, harness, etc.; clothing of all
kinds; liquors and wines; preserved goods and sweets; salt; drugs and chemicals;
paper, manufactures of brass, lead, pewter, tin, "together with an innumerable variety
of other articles of less importance." *O. R. N.*, 2nd series, III, 620.

[49] Soley, *The Blockade*, 156–57; Bradlee, *Blockade Running*, 79–80; Rhodes, *History
of the United States*, V, 397, 401; C. A. L. Lamar [son] to G. B. Lamar, August 8,
September 16, October 18, 1863, Personal Press Copy Book of C. A. L. Lamar, 28C,
the National Archives, Division of Treasury Department Archives, Civil War Records
of the Fifth Special Treasury Agency. C. A. L. Lamar claimed in the October 18
letter to his father that the inflated demand for ships created a situation where "boats
that were contracted for 4 months ago & near being finished at a cost of 13000£ are
Selling like hot cakes at from 20–25000£. . . ."

to the smallest possible bulk, so that from 500 to 1,200 bales could be carried at one time.[50]   A regular shuttle service developed between Confederate ports and the islands of Bermuda, Nassau, and Cuba, approximately 500 to 850 miles off the coast, to deposit Southern products at these places and pick up foreign goods which had been brought across the Atlantic in heavy freighters of "great capacity and stoutly built."[51]   To insure successful evasion of the United States fleet, highly paid and skillful crews were hired to man blockade-runners; competent pilots were especially desired.[52] By adopting such methods these private companies imported immense quantities of goods but too often of the wrong type.   The military requirements of the government and essential needs of civilians were of secondary importance.   Instead the factors of market conditions, value per weight or size, and convenience in handling determined the articles to be brought in.   As a result luxury goods such as wines and liquors, fine cloths and clothes, jewelry, and other items similar in character but useless for purposes of war became unduly prevalent in the Southern ports.[53] The army and navy frequently paid exorbitant prices for supplies.[54]

The flamboyant nature of the trade, sometimes tainted by corruption, attracted to it many unsavory characters whose speculative activities and free spending created a false sense of values

[50] Rhodes, *History of the United States*, V, 397; Thompson, *Confederate Purchasing*, 91.

[51] Soley, *The Blockade*, 39.   See Thompson, *Confederate Purchasing*, 8, who says that it was "discovered almost at the beginning, that the most successful method of getting supplies through the blockade was to ship them to the Sea Islands [Bermuda and Nassau] . . . , where they were reloaded into small fast steamers for running the blockade."

[52] Thompson, *Confederate Purchasing*, 43; Rhodes, *History of the United States*, V, 401. When blockade-runners were captured their pilots were never exchanged but held as prisoners of war; "and the demand for those available for service, increasing in proportion to their diminished number, there was much competition between rival blockade running companies, to the great detriment of the public service." Bradlee, *Blockade Running*, 79–80.

[53] G. B. Lamar to C. B. Baylies, November 8, 1862, G. B. Lamar Copy Books, 28E; Scharf, *Confederate States Navy*, 474.   See also advertisements of sales of imported goods in Southern newspapers such as *Charleston Courier* (Tri-weekly edition), April 10, 1862, February 14, 1863; *Richmond Whig*, July 23, November 11, 1862; *Richmond Dispatch*, March 5, 1863; *Charleston Mercury*, July 23, October 31, 1863, August 17, 1864; *Savannah Republican*, September 20, 1864.

[54] Scharf, *Confederate States Navy*, 474; Thompson, *Confederate Purchasing*, 76–84.

and tended to undermine the morale of civilians and the men in the armed services.[55] These conditions disturbed all thoughtful and patriotic Southerners. They suggested drastic measures to abolish abuses which drained the Confederacy of its resources without adequate compensation in the form of military supplies.[56] Furthermore, the government was guilty of using inefficient methods in its purchasing operations abroad. Frequent rivalry existing between agents of the various departments or bureaus and in turn between them and representatives from the states revealed the need for "co-ordination and centralization."[57]

By means of executive orders and legislative acts beginning in September, 1863, and ending in April, 1864, the Confederate Government placed blockade-running on an efficient basis by centralizing all purchases for the trade in the hands of two officials, one stationed at home and the other in Europe. It obtained more ships, sold immense quantities of cotton on its own account, and strictly regulated the activities of private companies by forcing them to allot 50 per cent of their cargo space for government exports and imports.[58] The "new plan" was not perfect in execution, owing in large part to the frenzied opposition of the shipping interests which connived with state officials to evade the stricter controls.[59] It did increase the flow of materials for the armed services at lower costs, although luxury articles in defiance of the

[55] *Savannah Republican*, June 30, 1863; Eggleston, *A Rebel's Recollections*, 89; *O. R.*, 4th series, III, 553–54; *ibid.*, 1st series, XXVII, pt. 3, 870; Bradlee, *Blockade Running*, 80; G. B. Lamar to De Rosset [t] and Brown, June 8, 1864, G. B. Lamar Copy Books, 28G.

[56] *Charleston Mercury*, June 1, 1864; Thompson, *Confederate Purchasing*, 83 87; *O. R. N.*, 2nd series, III, 896–97.

[57] Thompson, *Confederate Purchasing*, 22, 76–77.

[58] See *ibid.*, 84–89; Confederate States of America, *Public Laws*, First Cong., Sess. 4, chap. 23; *O. R.*, 4th series, III, 80–81, 552–55.

[59] See Frank Lawrence Owsley, *State Rights in the Confederacy* (Chicago, 1925), 130–32, 136–49; Coddington, "Confederate Business Man," *loc. cit.*, 30–33. Previously the War Department had ordered private companies to reserve one-third of their tonnage for government use. *O. R.*, 4th series, III, 954. The "new plan" supplanted a loosely knit organization which had taken a year and a half to evolve. See Thompson, *Confederate Purchasing*, 23.

law still appeared at the seaports.[60] Before the full benefit of this arrangement was felt the war was over.[61]

In demonstrating Confederate successes in breaking through the blockade, figures have been given on the amount of military supplies imported, the quantity of cotton bales exported, the profits made by the blockade-running companies,[62] and the number of violations. These estimates have been cited as proof of the ineffectiveness of Northern efforts to deprive the South of military essentials. Such analyses are unconvincing because they tend to divorce a study of the blockade and its effects from a consideration of Southern wartime economy in its entirety. It is hard to imagine a conquest of the South without the establishment of a blockade, defective as it may have been. Without the blockade, overseas trade, upon which sound currency largely rested, could have been restored to normal after relaxation of the embargo. In that case the problem of Confederate finances, which appeared so insoluble until the very last, need not have assumed such immense proportions. As it was, decreasing confidence in the currency deprived the government and civilians of supplies produced in the South. To overcome this difficulty officials resorted to the impressment of goods and the tax in kind, which resulted in a tendency among farmers to reduce their production of marketable foodstuffs and thus created new obstacles.[63] Inflation disrupted the ordinary

---

[60] Thompson, *Confederate Purchasing*, 97–99; Owsley, *King Cotton Diplomacy*, 287. For luxury items, see *Charleston Mercury*, August 17, 1864; *Savannah Republican*, September 20, 1864; T. C. De Leon, *Four Years in Rebel Capitals: An Inside View of Life in the Southern Confederacy, from Birth to Death* (Mobile, 1890), 281; Rhodes, *History of the United States*, V, 407; Schwab, *The Confederate States*, 244.

[61] Thompson, *Confederate Purchasing*, 126–27.

[62] *Ibid.*, 16–19, 43–45, 97–99; Owsley, *King Cotton Diplomacy*, 284–91, 574.

[63] *Richmond Dispatch*, November 6, 1863; *Southern Churchman*, March 29, 1865; *O. R.*, 4th series, II, 969; *ibid.*, III, 294–97, 595–96, 932; *ibid.*, 1st series, XLVI, pt. 2, 1289, 1297–99; *ibid.*, 1st series, XXXIII, 1128; Schwab, *The Confederate States*, 202–8; *Charleston Courier* (Tri-weekly edition), January 5, October 22, 1864; *ibid.* (Daily edition), January 1, 1864; *Richmond Dispatch*, March 12, August 20, 1863, October 28, 1864; *Richmond Whig*, November 3, 1863; Confederate States of America, *Public Laws*, First Cong., Sess. 3, chap. 38; *Raleigh Standard* (Weekly edition), January 20, 1864; *Augusta Chronicle and Sentinel*, November 15, 1864; *Southern Cultivator*, XXIII (February, 1865), 19–20; Broadus Mitchell, *William Gregg, Factory Master of the Old South* (Chapel Hill, 1928), 219–21.

channels of trade, causing speculation which in turn accentuated the scarcity of goods and lowered morale.[64]

IV. THE EFFECTIVENESS OF THE BLOCKADE

Blockade-running met perhaps the immediate but not the basic requirements of Southern war economy. The greatest need was for all types of capital goods, which included machinery for industry, equipment for railroads, and heavy tools for agriculture. An inadequate transportation system in large measure explains the South's military failures and the loss of a will to fight. Ill-adapted by arrangement and condition for a prolonged struggle, the railroads required significant changes to improve their efficiency. Some success was obtained in connecting lines in such large cities as Charleston and Savannah, and several new roads were built to expedite the movement of supplies, but these efforts were insufficient. Wear and tear at an extraordinary rate soon reduced many of them to a crippled condition. The government acted to prevent the collapse of the more important roads by establishing strict controls over their use and by seizing rails and equipment from abandoned lines.[65] Such steps were but palliatives and

[64] *Savannah Republican*, January 1, 1862; De Leon, *Four Years in Rebel Capitals*, 236–37; *Richmond Dispatch*, March 20, April 17, 1862, March 12, 23, April 3, 1863; *Richmond Whig*, December 9, 1862; *Charleston Courier* (Tri-weekly edition), April 5, 26, July 1, 1862, February 12, 1863; Schwab, *The Confederate States*, 135, 235–36; J. G. de Roulhac Hamilton, ed., *The Correspondence of Jonathan Worth* (Raleigh, 1909), I, 260; J. G. de Roulhac Hamilton, ed., *The Papers of Thomas Ruffin* (Raleigh, 1918–20), III, 296–97; Eggleston, *A Rebel's Recollections*, 83; *Savannah Republican*, September 20, 1862, March 20, June 4, 1863; *Charleston Mercury*, September 3, 1863; *O. R.*, 1st series, XXXIII, 1098; G. B. Lamar to Mrs. Dr. Ries, May 29, 1862; *id.* to *id.*, June 11, 1862; *id.* to James M. Ball, October 6, 1862; *id.* to George W. Lamar, Jr. [nephew], June 29, 1863; *id.* to I. Thiveat, May 9, 1863, G. B. Lamar Copy Books, 28E.

[65] Charles W. Ramsdell, "The Confederate Government and the Railroads," *American Historical Review*, XXII (July, 1917), 795–808; U. B. Phillips, *History of Transportation in the Eastern Cotton Belt to 1860* (New York, 1908), 383, 386; Carl R. Fish, "The Northern Railroads, April, 1861," *American Historical Review*, XXII (July, 1917), 786, 788–89; *O. R.*, 1st series, XXXVI, pt. 3, 279; *ibid.*, 4th series, I, 394, 405–6, 485–86, 617; II, 271, 348, 365–66, 393, 655; III, 392–93; *Charleston Courier* (Tri-weekly edition), November 19, 1861; *Savannah Republican*, September 27, 1861, June 20, 1862. The city of Petersburg, Virginia, at the beginning of the war was the terminal for four roads coming in from the north, east, south, and west. It soon became the big bottleneck for supplies and men sent to the Army of Northern Virginia, whose main task was to defend Richmond. Because of local opposition and fumbling moves of Confederate officials, all transportation continued to be broken at this point throughout the conflict. See Ramsdell, "The Confederate Government and the Railroads," *loc. cit.*, 796–98; *O. R.*, 4th series, I, 394, 405–6, 485–86.

failed to remedy what became a hopeless situation.

Cut off from Northern suppliers and unable to place orders with Southern heavy industries which were engaged to capacity in the manufacture of munitions, the railroad companies could only place their hopes on Europe, but the blockade intervened. General Lawton wrote Lee in March, 1864, that "not a bar of railroad iron nor a single locomotive has been brought into the Confederacy." [66] Scarcity of rails delayed construction on the Piedmont road between Danville, Virginia, and Greensboro', North Carolina, which became the life line for the Army of Northern Virginia after General Grant had cut connections south of Petersburg in 1864. [67] For the repair of locomotives need existed for copper, pig-tin, steam gauges, cast steel, files, and other small but vital items. Only a small supply of these materials came through the blockade. [68] The financial statements of various railroads, while creating the illusion of prosperity, furnish further evidence of rapid deterioration of physical assets. The accumulation of huge surpluses at first puzzled contemporary observers, but the reasons were soon revealed by the companies themselves. In 1863 the directors of the East Tennessee and Georgia Railroad Company, acknowledging the impossibility of procuring engineers, cars, iron, and materials to make repairs, decided to distribute among stockholders funds annually reserved for such purchases. Another company admitted an improved financial status, but the directors wanted to build up a rehabilitation fund to be spent after the war and thus refused to declare an unusually large dividend. [69] In its desperation for supplies, by 1864 one of the principal corporations of Virginia allowed the fare for passen-

[66] *O. R.*, 1st series, XXXIII, 1237. Not a single bar of railroad iron was rolled in the Confederacy. See *ibid.*, 4th series, III, 1092.

[67] *Ibid.*, 4th series, III, 227.

[68] *Ibid.*, 1092.

[69] *Charleston Courier* (Tri-weekly edition), December 4, 1862, April 7, 1863; *Augusta Chronicle and Sentinel*, March 21, 1863. For other annual reports see *Richmond Dispatch*, March 20, October 26, 1863, December 21, 1864; Virginia, *Documents*, 1863–64, *passim; Savannah Republican*, March 12, 1863; Atlanta *Southern Confederacy*, May 17, August 24, 1863; South Carolina General Assembly, *Reports and Resolutions*, Annual Sess., 1863, 52–65; *Charleston Courier* (Tri-weekly edition), May 2, 1863.

gers to be paid in tallow or its equivalent in some other product.[70] Although other reasons explain the decline of the railroads, such as lack of man power, continued use of the facilities to capacity, and destructive raids of the enemy,[71] the blockade remained the primary cause. The effects of this situation on the economy are almost too obvious to mention. Military efficiency was impaired, and maldistribution of goods and foodstuffs resulted in more suffering among city dwellers than among those in the country.[72]

Similar conditions affected manufacturing concerns to the detriment of the war effort. As in the case of the railroads, many companies were seemingly more prosperous than ever, if dividends were considered as the sole criterion. Many complaints were voiced against the high prices charged by manufacturers for their goods and the huge financial surpluses accumulated by them. It was little realized at first that the inability to replace worn-out machinery largely accounted for illusory profits. The experience of the Battersea Company, a textile concern in Petersburg, Virginia, typifies affairs elsewhere. It reported that "the expenditure of a large amount [of money] will be necessary in order to place the mill and machinery in a condition to meet the competition that will arise on the resumption of trade with the world on the reopening of the ports; but no part of the profits of the company has been set apart for this purpose."[73]

Textile manufacturers not only suffered from deterioration of machinery but lacked sufficient quantities of oils and other items used in production. More important, the scarcity of raw wool increased after 1862, for several reasons. The Texas crop of that

[70] *Richmond Dispatch*, December 21, 1864.

[71] *Ibid.*, April 7, 1863; *Charleston Mercury*, August 31, 1864; *O. R.*, 1st series, XXXVIII, pt. 2, 929; *ibid.*, pt. 5, 584; *ibid.*, XLIV, 792; *ibid.*, 4th series, II, 485; *ibid.*, III, 1093.

[72] Coddington, *The Seaboard States*, 181, 184; Charles W. Ramsdell, *Behind the Lines in the Southern Confederacy* (Baton Rouge, 1944), 96.

[73] Virginia, *Documents*, 1862–63, No. 27, p. 4. For protests against high prices for manufactured articles and financial conditions of concerns, see also *Richmond Whig*, March 12, December 13, 1862; *Hillsborough Recorder*, May 7, 1862; *Charleston Courier* (Tri-weekly edition), April 26, May 1, 10, 15, November 8, 15, 25, 29, December 13, 1862; *Charleston Mercury*, June 1, 1864; Virginia, *Documents*, 1862–63, No. 22, pp. 3–4, 6, 27; *ibid.*, No. 28; Mitchell, *William Gregg*, 208, 211, 219–21, 232–35.

year was poor, and that of 1863 failed to reach the Mississippi before communications were severed by the capture of Vicksburg and Port Hudson. Little wool was obtained throughout the rest of the South or by importations from England.[74]

Since Southern industry could not meet the demands of civilians and the government for cotton and woolen goods, people resorted to homespuns. This development in turn created a need for hand looms, spinning wheels, and cards. The market was never sufficiently supplied with the last item, an instrument used to comb raw cotton or wool, because machines to make hand cards were run through the blockade with great difficulty. It then became the practice of many individuals to send wool or cotton to a factory where special machines did the work. Again the blockade limited the amount of such equipment available.[75] Inadequate manufacturing facilities and the blockade deprived the South of many other commodities which, if considered separately, were rather unimportant but assumed significance when studied in relation to all factors involved in a sound economy. The production of foodstuffs depended upon proper maintenance of farm tools and machinery. The plantation blacksmith usually had little difficulty in keeping plows and hoes in order, but the repair of reapers and threshers was a different matter, for new parts were unobtainable.

[74] *Charleston Mercury*, June 1, 1864; Charles W. Ramsdell, "The Control of Manufacturing by the Confederate Government," *Mississippi Valley Historical Review*, VIII (December, 1921), 239–40; *Southern Cultivator*, XX, 24, 210; *ibid.*, XXI, 81.

[75] Bell Irvin Wiley, *Southern Negroes, 1861–1865* (New Haven, 1938), 59; *Southern Cultivator*, XXI (March and April, 1863), 64; *Richmond Whig*, November 12, 1862; Atlanta *Southern Confederacy*, November 16, December 10, 1862; *Charleston Courier* (Tri-weekly edition), October 28, 1862, April 14, 1863; Raleigh *Standard* (Weekly edition), April 22, 1863, advertisement; *Hillsborough Recorder*, June 4, 1862, advertisement. The shortage of hand cards was a subject of great concern to the state governments, always conscious of civilian needs. The production of homespuns depended upon the availability of cards, which were made of scarce materials—leather and wires. For an example of some of the primary sources examined, see Georgia, *Acts of the General Assembly*, Reg. Sess., 1862, Resolutions, No. 8, November 21, 1862; *ibid.*, No. 3; *ibid.*, Reg. Sess., 1863, No. 1; Allen D. Chandler, ed., *Confederate Records of the State of Georgia* (Atlanta, 1909), II, 360–63, 395, 666–67; South Carolina General Assembly, *Reports and Resolutions*, Annual Sess., 1863, First Annual Report of the Auditor of South Carolina, November 12, 1863, 151; North Carolina, *Public Laws*, Adj. Sess., 1862–63, Resolutions, January 26, 1863; Virginia, *Senate Journal and Documents*, 1863–64, No. 14.

With no usable threshing machines available, some farmers resorted to crude methods of beating the heads of wheat on barrels and then letting the wind blow away the chaff. One writer blames the lack of good harvesting, threshing, and grinding facilities for much of the flour shortage.[76] In an age of poor refrigeration, the preservation of meats, butter, and eggs depended upon salt; manufacturers also used it to preserve green hides and to set the color of cloth dyes. Faced with a serious deficiency, state governments took steps to encourage its production. The principal Southern source of salt, the immense wells of Saltville, Virginia, could not be developed as expected largely because of inadequate transportation facilities.[77] Last but not least of the scarce articles which affected economic life in countless ways, barrels and nails may be mentioned.[78]

V. The Blockade: Defective but Important

The dislocation of Southern economy by the blockade could have been more complete. The suspicion grows that the Northern Government did not choose to make it airtight. An examination of Union policies in respect to the land blockade established by law and presidential proclamation, July 13 and August 16, 1861, respectively, reveals among various factors in a complicated situation a strong desire to obtain Southern products, even if it meant in the end the restoration of almost unrestricted commercial intercourse.[79] It has been estimated that nearly 450,000 bales of cotton came from "the blockaded South by way of Nassau, Bermuda, Tampico, Vera Cruz, Matamoras, and Belize."[80] It may be that

[76] Wiley, *Southern Negroes*, 52–53.

[77] Ella Lonn, *Salt as a Factor in the Confederacy* (New York, 1933), 17–18, 20, 35, 78–79, 85–87, 90, 96–104, 107–9, 139–59, 211–14, 223, 229.

[78] G. B. Lamar to W. J. Anderson Company, December 31, 1862, G. B. Lamar Copy Books, 28E.

[79] E. Merton Coulter, "Commercial Intercourse with the Confederacy in the Mississippi Valley, 1861–1865," *Mississippi Valley Historical Review*, V (March, 1919), 378–93.

[80] Owsley, *King Cotton Diplomacy*, 289.

"powerful private industries" in the North which pressed for the resumption of trade with the enemy in the Mississippi Valley[81] were allowed also to obtain cotton shipped through the blockade. There is the suggestion that in its anxiety to prevent recognition of the Confederacy and the building of a Southern navy in British shipyards the Northern Government refrained from greater efforts against blockade-running as a sop to English commercial interests.[82] The policy of permitting licensed trade within areas occupied by Union forces along the Atlantic and Gulf coasts opened the way to illicit traffic with the enemy and operated against the purposes of the blockade.[83]

A knowledge of these loopholes in the execution of the program to isolate the South from the rest of the world serves to increase uncertainty in the minds of many students about the effectiveness and thus the legality of the effort. Further study may confirm these doubts, but on the basis of present evidence it would seem that even an imperfect blockade was an important element in weakening Southern economy under the stress of war. The complete story of the blockade in all its ramifications has yet to be told.

[81] Coulter, "Commercial Intercourse with the Confederacy," *loc. cit.*, 393.

[82] Monaghan, *Diplomat in Carpet Slippers*, 195, 306–8, 371–72.

[83] Richard S. West, Jr., *Gideon Welles: Lincoln's Navy Department* (New York, 1943), 243–44; Scharf, *Confederate States Navy*, 445–46.

The Fall of Protection in Britain

By Albert H. Imlah*

Early in 1842, in the depths of a world-wide commercial depression, Sir Robert Peel introduced, and Parliament passed, Britain's first distinctively free trade budget. The outcome is well known. The bold but calculated experiment was a huge success almost from the outset. Under it Britain found a policy eminently suited to her national needs and interests and entered a period of unexampled prosperity and social peace. Moreover, the fact that the markets of this giant among trading nations were open freely to the products of other lands promoted commercial development throughout the world and eased international tensions.

Less well known are certain underlying causes for this sharp change in British policy. As a result the significance of the last years of British protectionist history is blurred and distorted. It is commonly supposed that the system of high tariffs abandoned by Britain at this time was, with the exception of the Corn Law policy added in 1815, essentially the same system under which, towards the end of the eighteenth century, she gained her head start in the industrial age. From this it followed that protection was the life-giving impulse for her factories, and that Britain threw it aside only when her infant industries were firmly established. In the words Bismarck used in 1879 when he sought to exploit for his own protectionist purposes the influence Britain's astounding prosperity under free trade exerted over men's minds, "the mighty athlete" stepped into the open market only after hardening her sinews under high tariffs.

The true sequence was rather different. British protectionism,

*Albert H. Imlah is Professor of History, Tufts College and The Fletcher School of Law and Diplomacy.

like many other subjects of reform, was at its worst in its last years. It was so much more severe in its effects after the Napoleonic Wars than in the preceding infant period of British industrialism that it constituted virtually a new system. In this vigorous form it clearly hindered rather than helped the realization of Britain's economic opportunities. It aggravated her postwar problems, throwing her international economy out of balance, intensifying domestic distress and social unrest in each successive business depression. The British abandoned protectionism more because of an acute sense of its economic and social inadequacy than from any feeling that they had acquired fitness for free competition under it.

II

The system of "official" trade valuations used by Britain in this period is chiefly responsible for obscuring and distorting the facts connected with British foreign commerce prior to 1854 when a sound method of recording values was established. The word "official" is always used, without quotation marks, in government reports on the value of British foreign trade from 1697 to 1853. It inspires confidence, but it had a special meaning, rarely explained, which should evoke great caution in using the figures. It refers to values based on tables of prices drawn up in 1696.[1] Thereafter the same tables were used, practically unchanged, for a century and a half. By the nineteenth century they had long since ceased to represent the market values of the goods of trade. Their only usefulness was to show, in the aggregate, changes in quantity from year to year by means of a kind of common measure expressed in pounds sterling.

When one tests the *ad valorem* effect of British customs duties by these essentially fictitious figures on the value of British imports, one indeed concludes that Britain employed very high protectionist practice in the early years of her industrial development. To judge by these "official" records, net customs duties averaged

[1] G. N. Clark, *Guide to English Commercial Statistics, 1696–1782* (London, 1938), 8–12, 40–41.

about 43 per cent of the value of net imports in 1798, the first year for which net import values can be calculated from the printed records on a United Kingdom basis, that is, with the data for Ireland assimilated according to the method followed after the Act of Union of 1801. With higher war-time levies the average rate rose to a high of 103.5 per cent of the "official" value of net imports in 1814. After the war they tapered off slowly, but still averaged 50.7 per cent for the decade 1832–41. Meanwhile, by the same deceptive trade valuations, exports showed a phenomenal rate of growth, rising from 19.1 millions sterling in 1798 to 102.2 millions in 1841,[2] and showing a handsome surplus over imports throughout the period. Bismarck's argument seems amply validated.

It is not necessary to rely on these fictitious valuations in the period from 1798 on. Beginning in that year, when a convoy tax was imposed, exporters of British produce and manufactures were required to declare the value of their goods. Continued after the war, this series supplies reasonably authentic values on exports. That these have not been more generally used is perhaps to be explained, apart from the lure of that word "official" attached to the 1696 valuations, by the lack of a comparable series on imports and re-exports to balance the account. Happily British imports and re-exports were both chiefly composed of unprocessed goods. Their real, or current market value can therefore be calculated quite accurately from 1798 on by means of price indices.[3] Using these series on real values we can appraise the last half century of British protectionist history more nearly as it actually was.

Tested by real values, British customs duties at the end of the eighteenth century were very moderate. In 1798, the first year for which real values of imports and re-exports can be calculated

<hr/>

[2] Import values before 1801 from *Parliamentary Papers*, 1831–32, XXXIV, H.C. 315, "Official and Declared Values," 2–4; after 1800, from *Parliamentary Papers*, 1898, LXXXV, Cmd. 8706, "Customs Tariffs of the United Kingdom from 1800 to 1897," 48–49. Net customs rates are computed from data on customs revenue (drawbacks and overpayments deducted) after 1800, *ibid.*, 45; before 1800, from data in the annual statements on "Ordinary Revenue and Extraordinary Expenditure."

[3] See Albert H. Imlah, "Real Values in British Foreign Trade, 1798–1853," *The Journal of Economic History*, VIII (November, 1948), 133–52.

with some precision, net customs collections averaged only 16.4 per cent on the real value of net imports. This, it will be noted, is less than two-fifths of the rate shown by the "official" values. The average rate was probably somewhat higher in 1790, probably about 20 per cent, since prices had increased more rapidly than tariff schedules in the first years of the war. At this time Britain was the least protectionist in practice of any of the European countries.

Conditions changed rapidly during the twenty-two years of Britain's participation in the Revolutionary and Napoleonic Wars. The compelling problem was revenue. Where less than 20 millions sterling had covered all the costs of government in 1792, the last year of peace, 50 millions did not suffice in 1798, and expenditure ran over 92 millions in 1815. Interest charges alone in 1816 were more than 60 per cent larger than the whole cost of government in 1792. Additional revenue had to be found, and the search for it prompted increases in all kinds of taxes.[4] Even an income tax was imposed in 1799 and, after being prematurely dropped at the Peace of Amiens, was re-imposed in 1803.

Yet customs duties bore the brunt of the burden. In 1792 they had contributed about 25 per cent of the total revenue. In 1815 they supplied about 30 per cent of a total revenue almost four times that of the prewar years. Then, rejecting the recommendation of the Cabinet that the income tax be retained, Parliament decreed the total repeal of the "hated impost," even requiring that the records be destroyed.[5] Under these circumstances it was scarcely

[4] As Sydney Smith wrote in 1820 when the country was still groaning under the load, the consequences of the war were "TAXES upon every article which enters into the mouth, or covers the back, or is placed under the foot; taxes upon everything which is pleasant to see, hear, feel, smell, or taste; taxes upon warmth, light, and locomotion; taxes on everything on the earth, and the waters under the earth, on everything that comes from abroad or is grown at home; taxes on the raw material, taxes on every fresh value that is added to it by the industry of man; taxes on the sauce which pampers man's appetite, and the drug which restores him to health, on the ermine which decorates the judge, and the rope which hangs the criminal; on the poor man's salt, and the rich man's spice, on the brass nails of the coffin, and the ribband of the bride; at bed or board, couchant or levant, we must pay." Quoted by Sidney Buxton, *Finance and Politics* (London, 1888), II, 19–20.

[5] E. Halévy, *A History of the English People, 1815–1830* (New York, n.d.), 6–8; A. Hope-Jones, *The Income Tax in the Napoleonic Wars* (Cambridge [England], 1939), 1–4, 110–25.

possible to make any large reductions in the customs duties and their share of total revenue rose above the prewar level and continued to mount as other taxes were reduced and as the volume of imports grew. By 1830 they contributed 38 per cent of government income. In 1840 they supplied 45 per cent,[6] almost twice the prewar proportion.

High prices and high tariffs soon evoked a strongly protectionist spirit. On farm and in factory new vested interests were called into existence and, amid the economic difficulties of the postwar years, new and old alike manifested a strong sense of dependence on the tariff to keep them afloat. As early as 1817 the President of the Board of Trade admitted that many of the burdens on foreign imports operated to hurt British exports by depriving foreigners of the means of paying for British goods. But he felt he could do nothing. Whenever he proposed to reduce restrictions he had half the manufacturers in the country in arms against him. Each claimed it would ruin him.[7]

The protective force of these war-built customs duties increased very substantially in the peace years. Not that the imposts themselves were generally raised after the war. On the contrary, the Tories in the twenties succeeded in making some reductions even in the duties on grain, and the Whigs effected a few further cuts in the thirties. But British customs schedules consisted mainly of specific duties—so much on each pound of wool or gallon of wine—and the reduction of specific duties did not begin to keep pace with the sharp fall in prices which followed the war. Silberling's wholesale price index of thirty-five commodities, all but coal being articles of import, was 155 in 1798 and reached a high of 198 in 1814 (1790 = 100). After the war, prices fell off quickly, reaching new lows in each succeeding depression. By 1842 the index was

[6] In 1860, when the free trade program was almost complete, customs duties still supplied 38 per cent of the total revenue, but this was collected mainly from luxuries and on a much larger volume of imports. The average rate on net imports, both taxed and free, was 12.8 per cent—computed from data in *Parliamentary Papers*, 1865, LV, Cmd. 3513, "Statistical Abstract of the United Kingdom," 4, 7, 12–13.

[7] Hansard, *Parliamentary Debates*, XXXV (March 13, 1817), 1046–51.

down to 94.[8] While prices were at war levels, the new duties were not very onerous, measured *ad valorem*. As stated above, net customs duties averaged 16.4 per cent on the market value of net imports in 1798. In 1814, with much higher duties, they averaged 26.6 per cent. But when prices declined much faster than the reductions made from time to time in the schedule of specific duties, the average customs rate rose correspondingly. It reached a peak of 45.2 per cent in 1826. In 1841 it was 31.8, and in 1842, 33.2 per cent, about double the average rate in 1798.[9] In short, it was not merely that the share of revenue derived from import duties was much higher than before the war, but also that the toll taken on market values was substantially heavier and tending to grow, since prices fell faster than duties were reduced. Imports bore the brunt of Britain's postwar revenue burdens, then, and the consequences, throwing her economy out of balance and darkening the promise of the nineteenth century, go far to justify the accusative fingers pointed at the protectionist system in the depressed years after 1837.

III

Foreign trade was vital to the economic welfare of Great Britain, in the early nineteenth century as later, and supplies the best index we have to her prosperity. More than any other large state, the United Kingdom was dependent for well-being on exchange of goods and services with other lands.[10] Only by importing a variety of goods could she maintain tolerable standards of living for her population of nearly 27 millions (1841) in a total area scarcely larger than New York and New England. Only by ex-

[8] Norman J. Silberling, "British Prices and Business Cycles, 1779–1850," *Review of Economic Statistics*, V (1923), 219–62.

[9] Fluctuations in the importation of commodities with high duties meant some variation in the average rate from year to year, with a strong tendency for the articles with the higher duties to be driven out of trade.

[10] Even then she was the giant among the trading nations of the world, the total of her exports and imports constituting, in 1840, fully 26 per cent of the total value of world trade. In calculating these percentages the total real value of British imports and exports is taken as $713,000,000 in 1841, from Imlah, "Real Values," *loc. cit.* The total value of world trade is taken as $2,700,000,000 in 1841, from Clive Day, *A History of Commerce* (New York, 1923), 271.

porting the products of her specialized skills and resources, and by supplementing these exports with the earnings of her merchant marine, of her commercial and technical experts working abroad, and of her foreign investments, could she pay for her imports. It is equally true that only by taking these imports on favorable conditions could she sell on satisfactory terms the goods and services her rapidly growing population was prepared to produce.

In some respects the first half of the nineteenth century should have been bonanza times for the British export trade. The great technical efficiency of her newly mechanized textile industries, the demand for her coal and her new machinery, legally exportable after 1825, created an opportunity with few parallels in economic history. But opportunity is not realization. Machine methods are mass production methods and require large and steady markets for successful operation. The quantity of British exports did expand phenomenally. The "official" values, a convenient measure of aggregate quantity change, show them to have doubled between 1798 and 1820, then nearly trebled by 1841. But again market values tell a different story, and furnish a clue to what lay behind the unrest of the masses and the disillusionment of manufacturers and traders in the prolonged depression which began in 1837. The declared values of exports for the five years 1838–42 were less than 17 per cent greater than in the years 1815–19. In the good year 1836 exports were worth only 3 per cent more than in 1815. In the poor years 1841 and 1842 they were, respectively, only 24 and 14 per cent more than in the bad year 1816, although population increased by approximately 40 per cent in this interval.

For the other side of the trade picture, re-exports and imports, we must turn to the estimated real values. According to these, the re-export trade actually fell off in value. Foreign and colonial goods exported were worth 21 per cent less in 1841 than in 1816. Meanwhile, in spite of the heavy tariff burden, imports rose a little more rapidly than population and much more rapidly than the real value of exports. They were worth 48 per cent more in the five years 1838–42 than in 1815–19. Quite contrary to the false witness of the "official" tables, Britain was, in terms of market values, an importing country throughout this period, and her unfavorable balance of visible trade grew steadily after the war.[11] That the growth in the real value of imports was much more rapid than for exports can not be attributed to increase in population, suggestively comparable though the rates of change were, but to two quite different phenomena. One was the tremendously expanding requirements of British export industries, like the textiles which were dependent on the rest of the world for almost the whole of their supplies of raw materials.[12] The growth in imports was more largely in rawstuffs for the export industries than in goods for home consumption. The other factor is to be found in the appreciably different rates at which prices for British export and import goods declined.

The prices of British export goods fell off much more rapidly than the prices of the raw materials and foodstuffs imported. Silberling's index is a reliable guide to the prices of import goods. It shows a decline of 38 per cent from 1815 to 1841 and 43 per cent by 1842. In contrast, prices of British exports, as a group, fell 59 per cent by 1841 and 61 per cent by 1842.[13] Cheaper machine processes undoubtedly account for some, but hardly for the whole of this difference between the rate of decline in the prices of raw materials and of British export goods.[14] There is a strong probability that, as the tariff reformers claimed, lack of foreign purchasing power, limited by British customs duties and trade restrictions,

---

[11] From 1798 there were only four years—1802, 1816, 1821, and 1822—which show a favorable balance of visible trade. In 1798–1802 the average annual negative balance was £10.3 millions; in 1818–22, £7.4 millions; and in 1838–42, £24.6 millions. See Imlah, "Real Values," *loc. cit.*

[12] In 1841 five times as many pounds of raw cotton were imported as in 1816. Exports of manufactured cotton about quadrupled, measured by the "official" values. Imports of the raw materials, and dyestuffs, for other textiles, and the exports of their finished goods, show only less remarkable expansion in quantities.

[13] This figure is reached by comparing the ratios of declared to "official" values for these years, the result constituting a kind of weighted export price index with its base 1696. A similar index for imports, using the estimated real values with the "official" values, shows a price decline of 39 per cent by 1841 and 49 per cent for 1842.

[14] Had machine methods been capable of cutting costs so much there should have been some improvement in factory wages, though, to be sure, there were no effective trade unions to improve the bargaining power of labor.

was a factor in pushing British export prices down. But, however this may be, it is unmistakably clear that the terms of trade were moving against the United Kingdom.

What explains these various facts and circumstances of Britain's trading position? It is clear that her die was cast as an importing country long before 1842. Her industrial system and the size of her population made dependence on imports of raw materials and foodstuffs inescapable, except, perhaps, at a prohibitive price in transfer of population and a rebuilding of economy. International payment for her imports could be made, in the long run, only if there were favorable markets abroad for her goods and services. In other words foreign purchasing power must be good. As the free traders rightly pointed out, this is what her import duties, quite apart from the retaliatory legislation they inspired in other states, tended to check.[15] Even when they did not actually exclude foreign goods they introduced another and large element of cost to the British consumer. In this way they restricted the British market for foreign commodities, thereby limiting foreign purchasing power for British goods and services. In consequence, British manufacturers were under special pressure to cut their prices in order to find markets for the goods which their machines must produce in quantity or not at all. They found compensation by pushing down all controllable expenses, such as wages, and by increasing production to reduce unit costs. But in depressing wages they further reduced domestic purchasing power for their own goods as well as for protected foodstuffs. Hence British manufacturers and labor alike failed to enjoy the fruits of superior machine methods. At the same time the earning power of the

[15] W. E. Gladstone, who, as vice-president of the Board of Trade, found that every day spent in the office "beat like a battering ram on the unsure fabric of my official protectionism" (John Morley, *The Life of William Ewart Gladstone* [New York, 1903], I, 250), put this matter quite simply in the House of Commons: "Suppose that 50,000 head of cattle were to be annually imported, such importation would produce but a small effect upon the prices of meat, but it would create an import trade to the amount of half a million of money, a trade which, in its nature, would lead by a smooth, certain course of operation to an export trade in return, of equal amount; which would contribute—he did not say in a moment, but in the course of years—to an increased demand for employment and labour." Hansard, *Parliamentary Debates*, LXIII (May 23, 1842), 645.

merchant marine was limited.[16] Payment of interest charges on British foreign investments was made more difficult and the capital itself was seriously imperilled in depression years.[17] Thus the ability of these two chief sources of invisible income to fill the growing margin between visible imports and exports was curtailed by the same self-inflicted forces which limited British export opportunities. In short, Britain's fiscal system threw her international economy out of balance and her domestic distress was, in part, the result. She was a potential athlete, capable of remarkable commercial achievement when the restrictive tariff bindings were removed. Had they remained, she stood in danger of becoming misshapen and weak, progressively more unfit for the contest, perhaps soon to join the list of ephemeral empires of the past in commercial decadence.

IV

Even before the depression of 1837 developed, accumulating experience under the postwar tariffs attracted some attention and comment. Perhaps the most noteworthy instance was the publication in 1830 by Sir Henry Parnell of his concisely reasoned and factually solid little volume, *On Financial Reform*. In it he concentrated his heaviest fire on the import duties on raw materials, foodstuffs and manufactured goods. He proposed reforms in all essentials similar to those Peel began to carry out in 1842, including an income tax if necessary to make up the revenue lost by reducing duties. Lord Althorp, when Chancellor of the Exchequer in 1831, gave the volume a particular "puff" by announcing that his "general view of finance" would be based on its principles. Unfortunately, he grasped the nettle very inexpertly and his accomplishments fell far short of his intentions.[18] Constitutional

[16] Though merchant tonnage increased by 12 per cent from 1815 to 1840 this growth did not begin to keep pace with the growth in the quantity of British exports and imports; and, though handsomely protected by the Navigation Acts, no interest complained more of foreign competition and distress. See G. R. Porter, *The Progress of the Nation* (London, 1838), II, 164.

[17] Very heavy capital losses were suffered in this depression of 1837, as shown by L. H. Jenks, *The Migration of British Capital to 1875* (New York, 1938), 103-4.

[18] E. Halévy, *History of the English People, 1830–1841* (New York, n.d.), 89-93.

reform soon became the order of the day and not until the next recession came did the tariff reformers capture the attention of the public.

After business activity began to decline in 1837 events crowded thick and fast. In 1838 the Anti-Corn Law League was organized and, with poor harvests, high food prices and widespread unemployment to reinforce its arguments, began its telling attack on the whole system of protectionism. In the same year the Chartists published their demand for manhood suffrage and annual elections. The noise they made for this large and premature dose of political change as a preliminary to social reform highlighted the unrest in the country and made tariff reform seem moderate and practical by contrast. Beginning in the same year also, a series of budget deficits put a stop to the small, and inadequate, tax reductions which had been made from year to year when revenue permitted. Indeed in 1840 customs and excise duties were boosted 5 per cent, and the assessed taxes 10 per cent, but failed to bring revenue into balance with expenditure.

In 1840 the House of Commons agreed to the appointment of a Select Committee to study the import duties. At its hearings the free traders made an impressive showing, and the report of the committee, supported by a large volume of data and opinion from a wide variety of sources, was a succinct and straightforward charter for free trade. It pointed out the incongruous and often incompatible aims of the existing tariff:

The duties are sometimes meant to be both productive of revenue and for protective objects, which are frequently inconsistent with each other; hence they sometimes operate to the complete exclusion of foreign produce, and in so far no revenue can of course be received; and sometimes, when the duty is inordinately high, the amount of revenue becomes in consequence trifling. . . . [The] attempt to protect a great variety of particular interests [is] at the expense of revenue, and of the commercial intercourse with other countries.[19]

Out of 1150 articles subject to duty some 741 actually entered in

[19] *Parliamentary Papers*, 1840, V, H.C. 601, "Report from the Select Committee on Import Duties," iii.

1839 and yielded a revenue of £22,962,610. Seventeen articles supplied 94.5 per cent of this amount. At the other end of the scale, 531 articles yielded only £80,000, in many cases because the duties were so high as to be almost prohibitory.

The effect of prohibitory duties, while they are of course wholly unproductive to the revenue, is to impose an indirect tax on the consumer, often equal to the whole difference of price between the British article and the foreign article which the prohibition excludes. . . . On articles of food alone . . . according to the testimony laid before the Committee, the amount taken from the consumer exceeds the amount of all other taxes which are levied by the Government. . . . [with] injurious effects upon wages and capital.[20]

The Committee found opinion among manufacturers swinging away from protection. Some of those "supposed to be the most interested in retaining these duties, are quite willing that they should be abolished, for the purpose of introducing a more liberal system into our commercial policy."[21] The *Spectator* brought out a special supplement summarizing the report and sold 30,000 copies.[22]

In the spring of 1841 the Melbourne Cabinet, already tottering, sprang a surprise in presenting its budget. Having failed to meet the deficit by increasing taxes, it now proposed to try the experiment of reducing the duties on sugar and timber to promote a larger flow for larger receipts, but without proposing any new tax to cover the interval before the full revenue expectations could be realized. With suspicion strong that it was a pre-election manoeuvre hastily devised to catch the free trade vote, it was defeated by 371 votes to 281. In the general election which followed, the Conservatives, under the leadership of Sir Robert

[20] *Ibid.*, v. The case of wheat seems to bear out this contention. While the average price in England in 1840 was 66s 4d a quarter, for example, in Prussia it averaged 37s 6d—*Parliamentary Papers*, 1850, LII, H.C. 460, "Return on the Prices of Wheat," 2, 23. Transportation costs were but a fraction of the differences. When the English market was thrown open to foreign grain after 1846, world prices rose towards English levels. The improvement for the English people lay in steadier supply and in improved foreign purchasing power for British export goods, hence better conditions of employment and of living.

[21] *Parliamentary Papers*, 1840, V, HC 601, "Report from the Select Committee on Import Duties," v.

[22] Halévy, *History of the English People, 1830–1841*, 351.

Peel, won a clear majority of 76 seats, carrying nearly half the urban constituencies and most of the financial centers with free trade leanings. Peel himself had studied Parnell's book, though, curiously, he had not read the "Report of the Committee on Import Duties."[23] In his election speeches, as in the debate in the Commons, he had been careful not to commit himself against free trade principles. It was the Whigs who were defeated, not free trade, and Peel became Prime Minister explicitly claiming "the liberty of proposing to Parliament those measures which I believe to be conducive to the public weal. . . . Free as the wind, I tell every man in the country that he has imposed no personal obligations upon me by having placed me in this office."[24]

Peel's bent was statesmanship and he had a job to do. Aware, as he wrote his friend Croker a little later, that England's "lot is cast" as an industrial country and that "something effectual must be done to revive, and to revive permanently, the languishing commerce and languishing industry,"[25] he tackled the task of bringing the fiscal system into harmony with the national needs and interests with courage and comprehension. Halévy has suggested that he was confronted by a choice "between the demagogies of Chartism and of the League."[26] But Peel did not need to choose demagogy at all. If there was an alternative it was that set forth in a long, carefully analytical leading article published in the independent radical *Spectator* shortly after the election. "Active evil we are not likely to get from Sir Robert Peel," it admitted. "Are we likely to get any good? Yes, if he understands his own position. . . . He is compelled to action through two circumstances—the distress of the country and the deficiency of the revenue." His choice was between grappling "thoroughly and fairly with the great question of the import duties" or of relapsing into discredited Tory methods of repression. If he chose the former he could establish a strong government in the best sense

[23] Morley, *Gladstone*, I, 251.
[24] Hansard, *Parliamentary Debates*, LIX (September 17, 1841), 555.
[25] L. J. Jennings, ed., *The Croker Papers* (New York, 1884), II, 175.
[26] "Peel in 1841," *Revue d'Historique Moderne*, XIII (March, 1938), 107.

of the term; if the latter he would soon have a weak government, deserted by the moderates and reviled by the country.[27]

There was no real choice for an honest and intelligent statesman to make. Peel certainly could not revert to strong arm methods of dealing with social unrest without estranging the support of moderate men everywhere and nullifying the clear implications of the constitutional decisions of the thirties which he had pledged himself and his party to maintain. The shape of the past, the condition of the country, the bent of his own mind,[28] all pointed the way to economic liberalism, the path of plenty and of social peace through a measure of economic internationalism. Two, at least, of his colleagues in the Cabinet were as sure of this as Peel's own actions soon proved him to be. The Duke of Wellington saw the editorial and drew Sir James Graham's attention to it. Cautiously conservative though he was, the Duke put tariff reform literally at the very top of the "must" list. They "must be the first things to do," he wrote, adding that they were in accord with Tory traditions. Graham, a constant and admiring reader of the *Spectator*[29] for some years and Peel's closest colleague, had already seen the leader and had called Peel's particular attention to it. The only objection he himself had to offer to the analysis was that an income or property tax must accompany tariff reductions, not be held in abeyance for future use should the larger volume of trade expected at the lower rates not produce enough revenue.[30] In other words the reforms must be put on a sound basis with an eye to permanence through a balanced budget, not left to the hazards of future revenue requirements.

Free trade and an income tax was the formula adopted. Care-

[27] *The Spectator*, XIV (July 31, 1841), 731.

[28] As early as 1829, before the publication of Parnell's book, when he was Home Secretary in Wellington's Cabinet, Peel had urged the need for imposing an income or property tax in order to reduce the burden of indirect taxation on the poor. "He wished to reach such men as Baring, his [Peel's] father, Rothschild, and others, as well as absentees and Ireland. . . . to reconcile the lower with the higher classes, and to diminish the burthen on the poor man." Lord Colchester, ed., *A Political Diary by Lord Ellenborough* (London, 1881), II, 213.

[29] It was under the brilliant direction of Robert Stephen Rantoul from 1828 to 1858.

[30] Sir Charles S. Parker, *Sir James Graham* (London, 1907), I, 307–8.

fully applied, they braced and strengthened and integrated the structure of Britain's institutional, as well as economic, life. Like British machines and representative government, they, too, were available for export; and the evident and abundant prosperity which Britain enjoyed under them induced some rather hesitant acceptance of free trade principles by other states—but not for long. Towards the end of the century, power considerations, reinforced by the "infant industries" argument and a misconception of the real course of Britain's development, turned the world back towards a new era of tariff walls and restrictive regulations. The twentieth century inherited and extended this reversal of trend, and already has made a strong bid to rival the eighteenth century in the intensity of competitive mercantilism, as well as in the frequency of general wars.

BIBLIOGRAPHY OF THE WORKS OF
GEORGE HUBBARD BLAKESLEE

By Marion Henderson, *Reference Librarian, Clark University*

I

BOOKS AND PAMPHLETS: AUTHOR

Conflicts of Policy in the Far East ("World Affairs Pamphlets," No. 6). New York: Foreign Policy Association, 1934.

With Harold Scott Quigley, *The Far East*. Boston: World Peace Foundation, 1938.

With Nathaniel Peffer, *The Lytton Report* ("Foreign Policy Association Pamphlets," No. 86). New York: Foreign Policy Association, 1932.

With James G. MacDonald, *Oriental Affairs in the Light of the Kyoto Conference* ("Foreign Policy Association Pamphlets," No. 62). New York: Foreign Policy Association, 1930.

The Pacific Area. Boston: World Peace Foundation, 1929.

Recent Foreign Policy of the United States. New York: Abingdon Press, 1925.

II

BOOKS AND JOURNALS: EDITOR

China and the Far East ("Clark University Lectures"). New York: Crowell, 1910.

Japan and Japanese American Relations ("Clark University Addresses"). New York: Stechert, 1912.

Journal of International Relations. Worcester: Clark University, 1919–1922. Vol. 10–12.

With G. Stanley Hall, *Journal of Race Development*. Worcester: Clark University, 1910–1919. Vol. 1–9.

Latin America ("Clark University Addresses"). New York: Stechert, 1914.

Mexico and the Caribbean ("Clark University Addresses"). New York: Stechert, 1920.

Problems and Lessons of the War ("Clark University Addresses"). New York: Putnam, 1916.

Recent Developments in China ("Clark University Addresses"). New York: Stechert, 1913.

III

ARTICLES IN BOOKS AND PERIODICALS

"Address at Presentation of Fidac Medal to Clark University, November 30, 1931," *Clark News*, VI (December 2, 1931), 3.

"American History," *American Yearbook, 1911* (New York: Appleton, 1912), 44–79.

"Assessing the Blame for the World War," *Current History*, XX (June, 1924), 458–59.

"Alfred Lewis Pinneo Dennis," *Journal of Modern History*, III (March, 1931), 62–63.

"America's Philippine Policy in the Light of Recent Developments in the Far East," Lake Mohonk Conference of the Friends of the Indians and other Dependent Peoples, *27th annual meeting* (October 20–22, 1909), 122–32.

"The Attack Upon the Established Church in South America," *Outlook*, CV (October 18, 1913), 377–79.

"Business Relations with South America," *Current Affairs*, June 22, 1914.

"The Chinese Situation," *Oriental Review*, September, 1912, 658–59.

"The Family of Nations," *The Advocate of Peace*, December, 1910, 263–65.

"The Far East," *Clark News*, VIII (March 21, 1934), 5.

"The Far East Conference," *Worcester Magazine*, XII (November, 1909), 317–18.

"The First Philippine Assembly," *Outlook*, LXXXVIII (January 25, 1908), 175–79.

"The Foreign Policy of the United States," *Interpretations of American Foreign Policy*, ("Harris Foundation Lectures," ed. Quincy Wright. Chicago: University of Chicago Press, 1930), 3–35.

"The Foreign Stake in China," *Foreign Affairs*, X (October, 1931), 81–91.

"The Future of American Samoa," *Foreign Affairs*, VII (October, 1928), 139–43.

"The Gentlemen from Manila," *Harper's Weekly*, LII (January 18, 1908), 14.

"The Government of Korea," American Political Science Association, *Proceedings*, VI (1909), 155–62.

"Hawaii, Racial Problem and Naval Base," *Foreign Affairs*, XVII (October, 1938), 90–99.

"The International Situation in the Pacific," *Public Opinion and World Peace*, ed. George H. Turner (Chicago: International Lyceum and Chautauqua Association, 1923), 93–100.

"Islands of the Pacific," *Survey of American Foreign Relations*, ed. Charles P. Howland (New Haven: Yale University, 1930), 274–314.

"The Japanese Monroe Doctrine," *Foreign Affairs*, XI (July, 1933), 671–81.

"Japan's Mandated Islands," *Department of State Bulletin*, XI (December 17, 1944), 764–68.

"Japan's New Island Possessions in the Pacific: History and Present Status," *Journal of International Relations*, XII (October, 1921), 173–91.

"Korea and Japan," *Outlook*, LXXXVII (November 2, 1907), 503–4.

"The Kyoto Conference of the Nations of the Pacific," *Current History*, XXXI (January, 1930), 723–28.

"The Mandates of the Pacific," *Foreign Affairs*, I (September 15, 1922), 98–115.

"The Meaning of the War," Clark University Library, *Publications*, IX (June, 1942), 13–21.

"The Missionary Opportunity in Korea," *Outlook*, LXXXVII (November, 1907), 703–04.

"Monroe Doctrine and the Proposed Constitution of the League of Nations," *Journal of Race Development*, IX (April, 1919), 420–28.

"Morality in Diplomacy," *Foundation Library*, ed. G. Stanley Hall and others, IX (Chicago: Educational Society, 1911), 511–21.

"The Necessity of International Legislation Agencies for the Settlement of Non-Justiciable Issues," American Society for Judicial Settlement of International Disputes, *Proceedings* (1913), 261–74.

"A New Basis Needed for the Monroe Doctrine," *North American Review*, CXCVIII (December, 1913), 779–89.

"Oceanica," *A Guide to Historical Literature*, ed. William H. Allison and others (New York: Macmillan, 1931), 944–68.

"Our Relations with South America and How to Improve Them," *International Conciliation*, No. 76 (March, 1914), 3–12.

"Outstanding Facts in the Present Situation in China," American Academy of Political and Social Science, *Annals*, CXXXVIII (July, 1928), 49–53.

"Pan American Cooperation; Its Possibilities and Limitations," Lake Mohonk Conference on International Arbitration, *21st Report* (1915), 25–30.

"Pan American Relations," Cornell University Conference on International Relations, *Proceedings* (Ithaca, June 15–30, 1915), 25–61.

"Panama and the Conquest of the Tropics," *Outlook*, CXI (September 22, 1915), 193–201.

"Panama Canal: South America and the Far East," *Outlook*, CXI (November 24, 1915), 717.

"The Panama Canal in Time of War," *Outlook*, CX (August 25, 1915), 967–76.

"Poland's Pitiable Condition," *Outlook*, LXXXIV (December 15, 1906), 921–25.

"Postwar Pacific Diplomacy," *Survey of American Foreign Relations*, ed. Charles P. Howland (New Haven: Yale University, 1930), 112–200.

"The Problem of the Far East in the Light of Historical Parallelisms and Precedents," *Chinese Social and Political Science Review*, XII (January, 1928), 130–35.

"Results of Honolulu Conference on Problems of the Pacific," *Current History*, XXVII (October, 1927), 69–73.

"Results of the Panama Canal on World Trade," *Outlook*, CXI (October 27, 1915), 490.

"A Selected List of Books on the Present War," *Journal of Race Development*, VIII (July, 1917), 44–78.

"Should the Monroe Doctrine Continue to Be a Policy of the U. S.?" American Society of International Law, *Proceedings*, 8th (April 22–25, 1914), 217–29.

"Significance of Japan's Claim to an Asiatic Monroe Doctrine," *China Weekly Review*, LXV (August 5, 1933), 407–9.

"Trend of History," Lake Mohonk Conference on International Arbitration, *22nd Report* (1916), 89–90.

"True Pan-Americanism: a Policy of Cooperation with the Other American Republics," *Journal of Race Development*, VII (January, 1917), 342–60.

"War Problem and the Obligations of the College," *Clark College Record*, XI (April, 1916), 124–43.

"Will Democracy Alone Make the World Safe?" *Journal of Race Development*, VIII (April, 1918), 491–505.

"Woman Suffrage in Finland," *Outlook*, LXXXVII (September 7, 1907), 35–39.

IV
ARTICLES IN NEWSPAPERS

"Bogoras on Russia: The Noted Revolutionist's Views of the Future," *Boston Evening Transcript*, September 12, 1906.

"Experts Want Monroe Doctrine Pan-Americanized," *New York Times*, May 31, 1914.

"Feud from Coveting a Desert," *Boston Evening Transcript*, August 9, 1913.

"Filipinos Going Slow," *Boston Evening Transcript*, January 11, 1908.

"Finland's New Freedom," *Boston Evening Transcript*, August 3, 1907.

"The First Congress of the Philippine People," *Boston Evening Transcript*, November 23, 1907.

"Germany's Defiance of the Law; What the U. S. Should Do," *Worcester Evening Gazette*, February 1, 1917.

"Getting South American Trade," *Boston Evening Transcript*, July 26, 1913.

"Hands Across the Great Canal," *Boston Evening Transcript*, August 20, 1913.

"High Prices Below the Tropics," *Boston Evening Transcript*, August 2, 1913.

"Institute of Politics of Exceptional Importance This Summer," *Worcester Sunday Telegram*, August 30, 1931.

"Japan-Hating Manchuria," *Boston Evening Transcript*, October 5, 1907.

"The Japanese in Korea," *Boston Evening Transcript*, November 16, 1907.

"Pacific Parley Leads to Lower Cable Charges," *Christian Science Monitor*, December 2, 1929.

"Rapid Progress of the Filipinos," *Worcester Telegram*, May 31, 1908.

"Siberia Full of Promise," *Boston Evening Transcript*, October 12, 1907.

"Want Monroe Doctrine Pan-Americanized," *Boston Sunday Herald*, May 31, 1914.

"What South America Thinks of Us," *Boston Evening Transcript*, July 23, 1913.